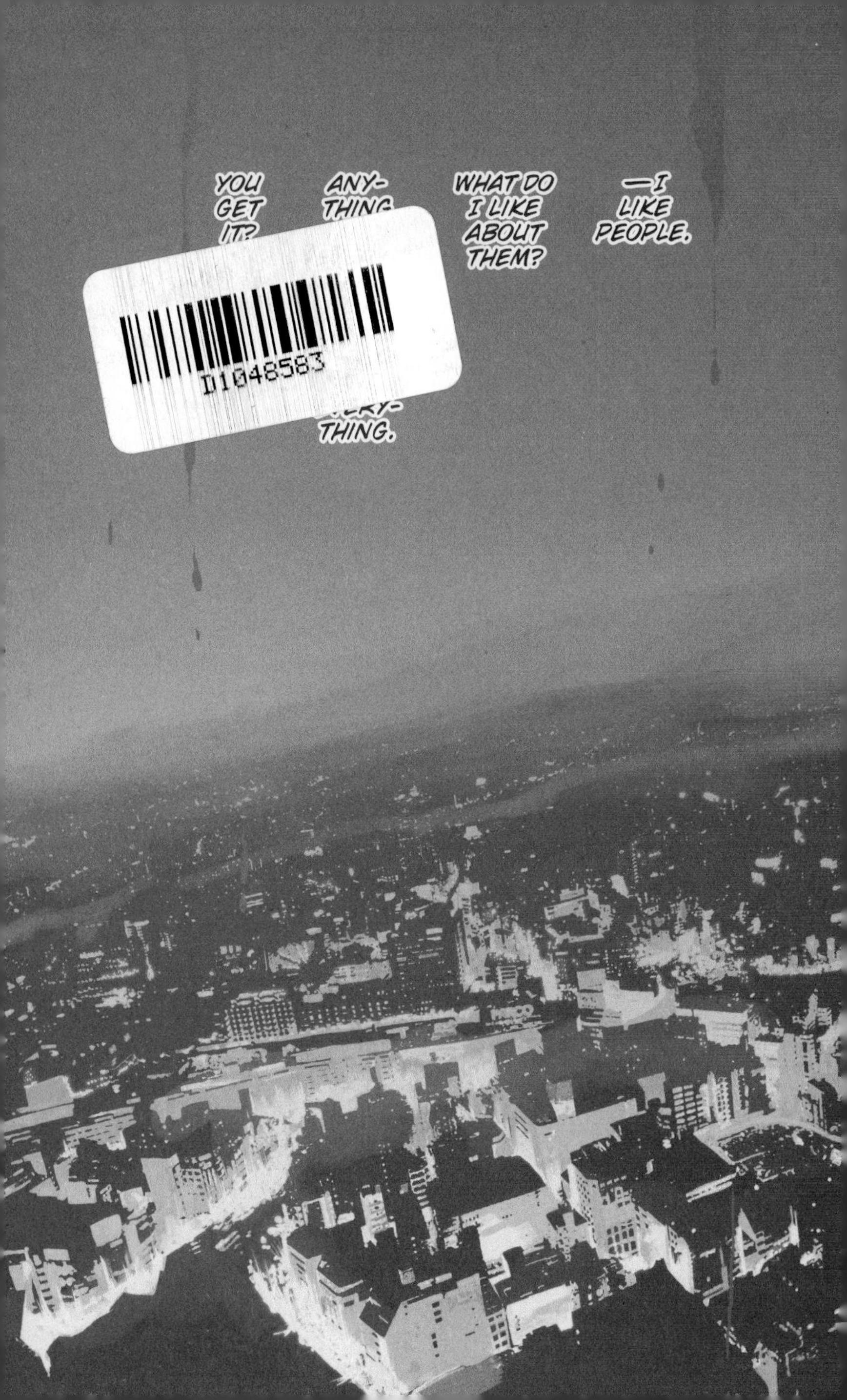
—I LIKE PEOPLE.
WHAT DO I LIKE ABOUT THEM?
ANY- THING
THING.
YOU GET IT?

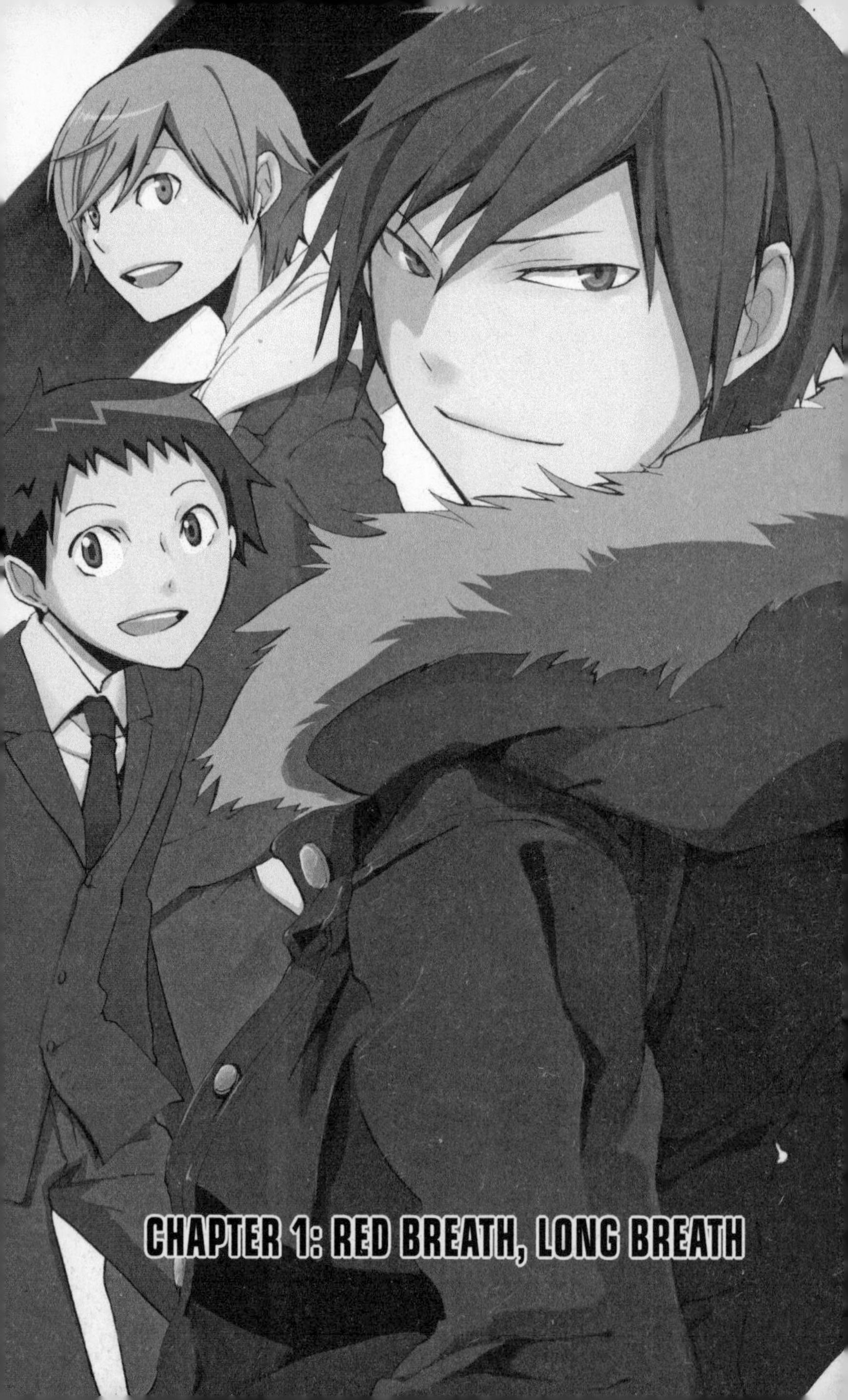

CHAPTER 1: RED BREATH, LONG BREATH

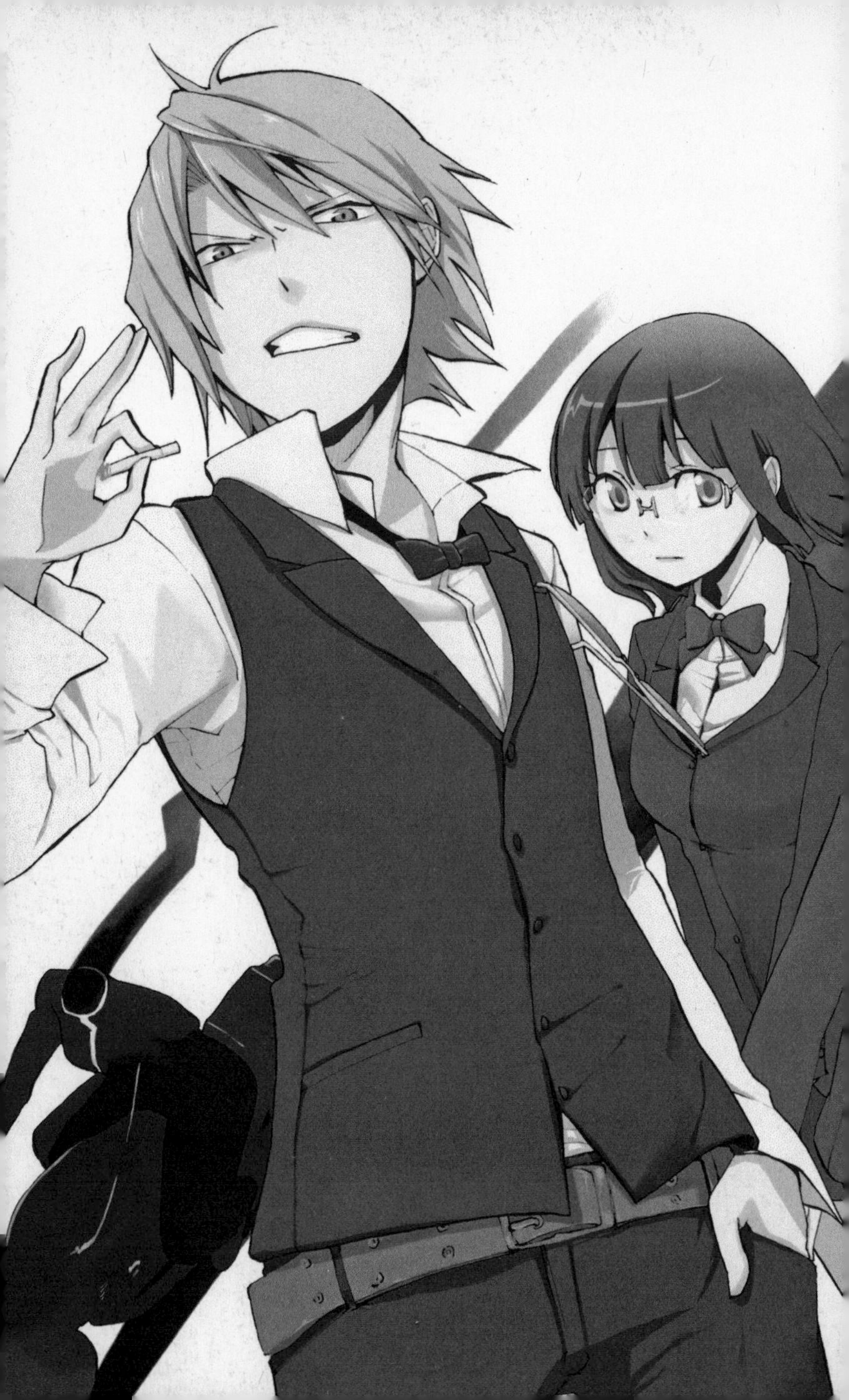

DRRR!!

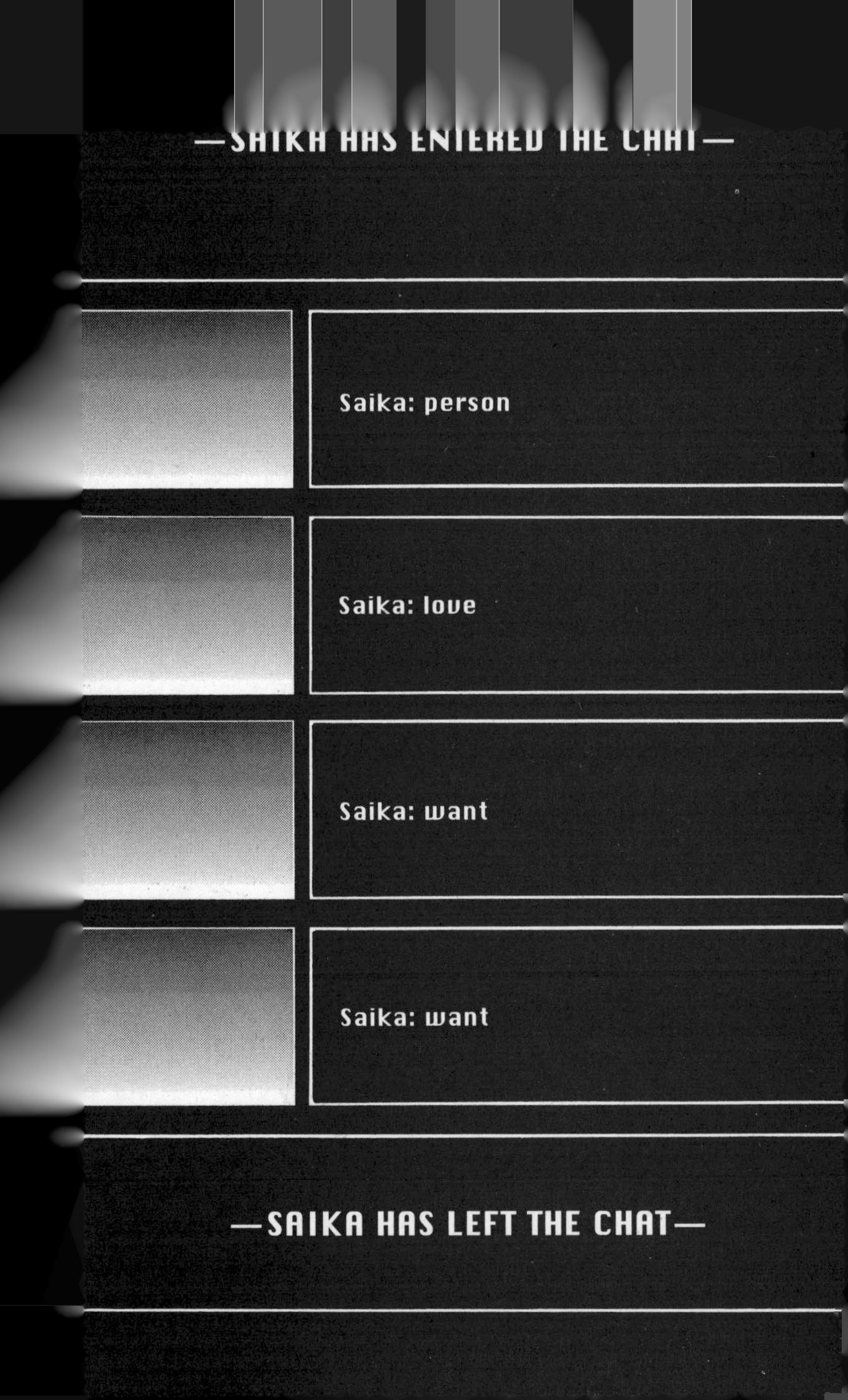
—SAIKA HAS ENTERED THE CHAT—
Saika: person
Saika: love
Saika: want
Saika: want
—SAIKA HAS LEFT THE CHAT—

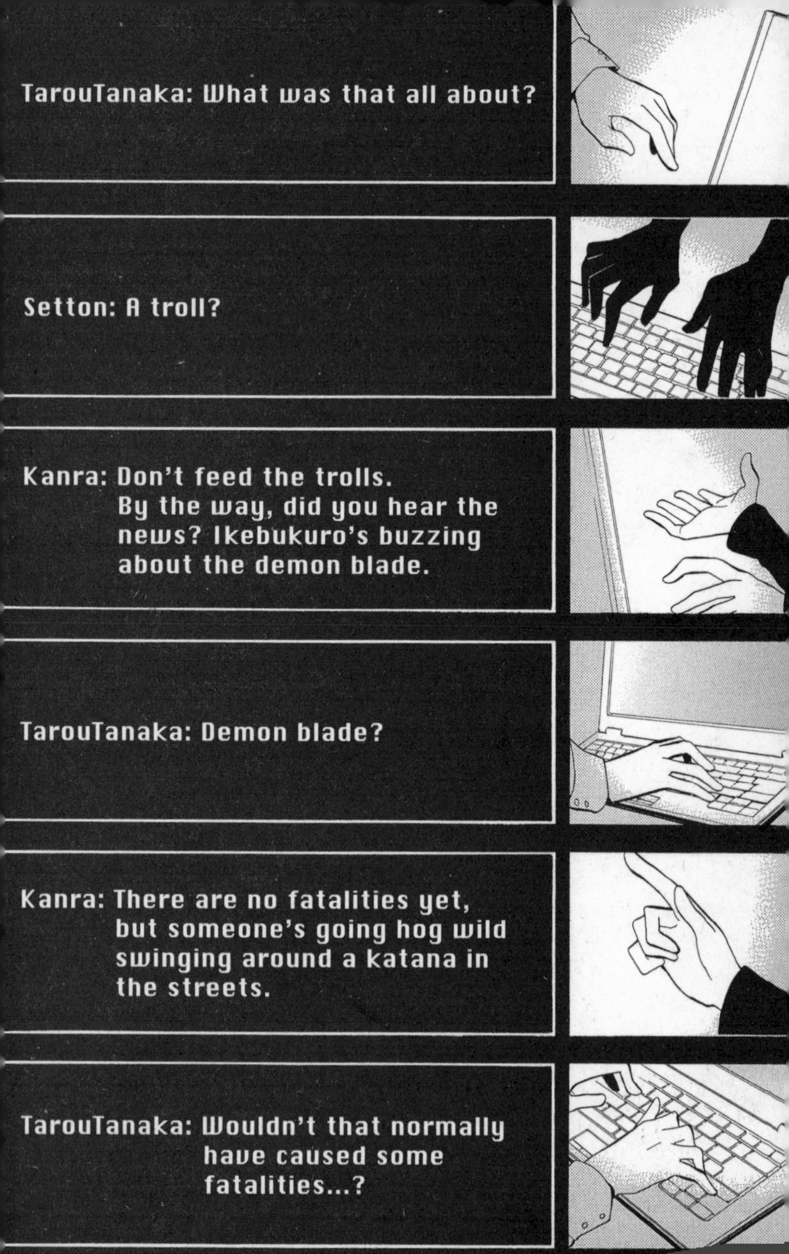
TarouTanaka: What was that all about?
Setton: A troll?
Kanra: Don't feed the trolls. By the way, did you hear the news? Ikebukuro's buzzing about the demon blade.
TarouTanaka: Demon blade?
Kanra: There are no fatalities yet, but someone's going hog wild swinging around a katana in the streets.
TarouTanaka: Wouldn't that normally have caused some fatalities...?

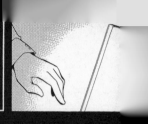

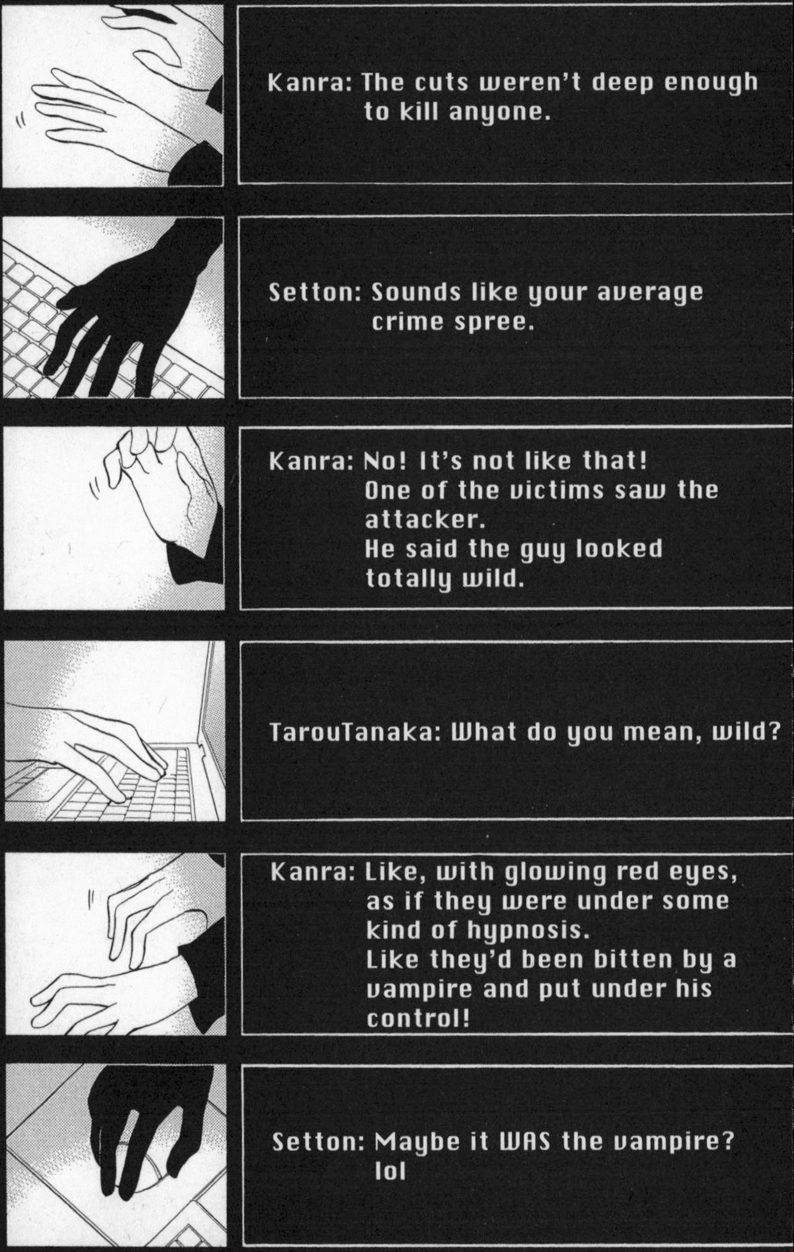
Kanra: The cuts weren't deep enough to kill anyone.
Setton: Sounds like your average crime spree.
Kanra: No! It's not like that! One of the victims saw the attacker. He said the guy looked totally wild.
TarouTanaka: What do you mean, wild?
Kanra: Like, with glowing red eyes, as if they were under some kind of hypnosis. Like they'd been bitten by a vampire and put under his control!
Setton: Maybe it WAS the vampire? lol

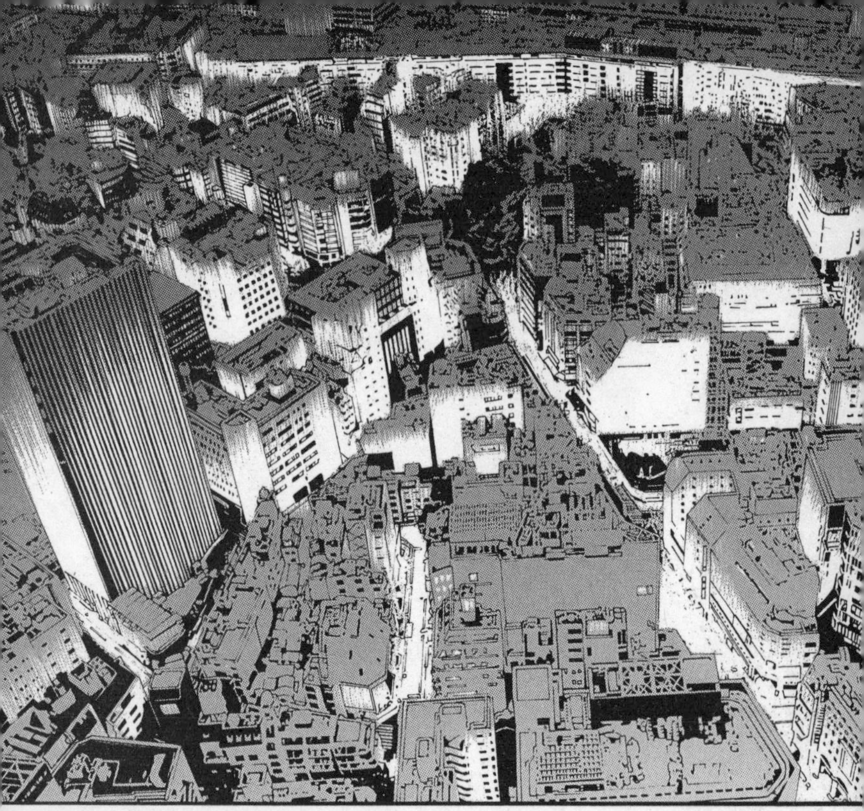

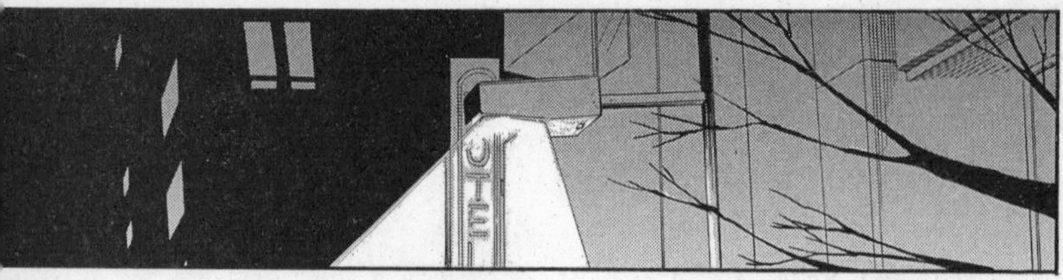

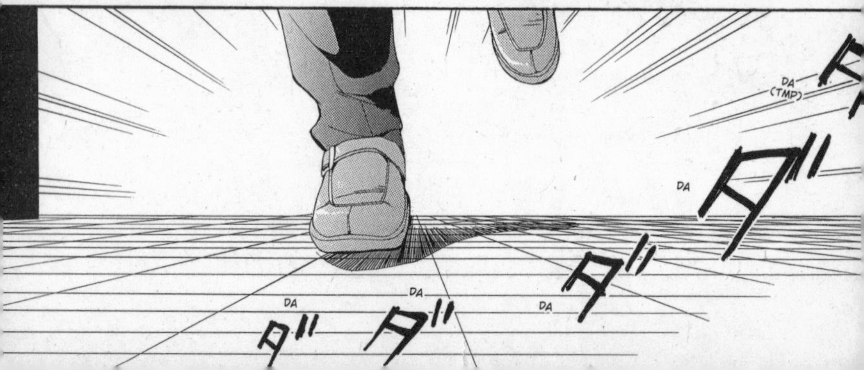
DA (TMP)
DA
DA
DA
DA

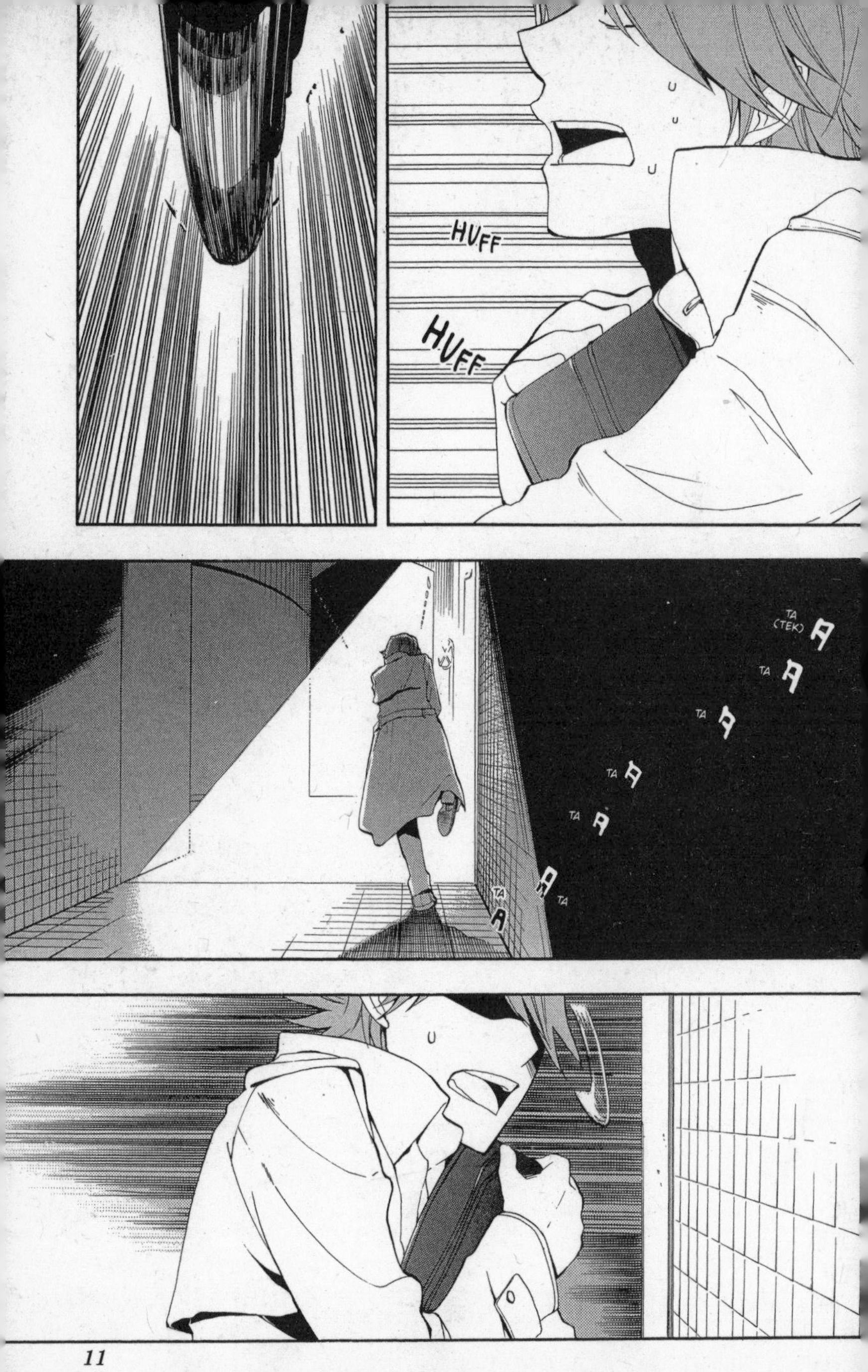
HUFF
HUFF
TA
(TEK)
TA
TA
TA
TA
TA
TA

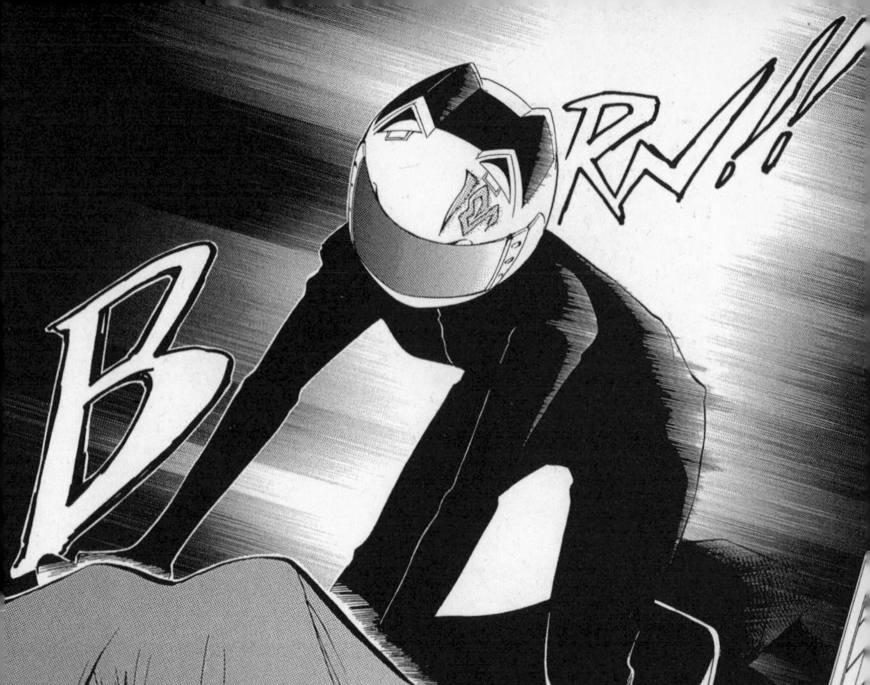
BRN!!
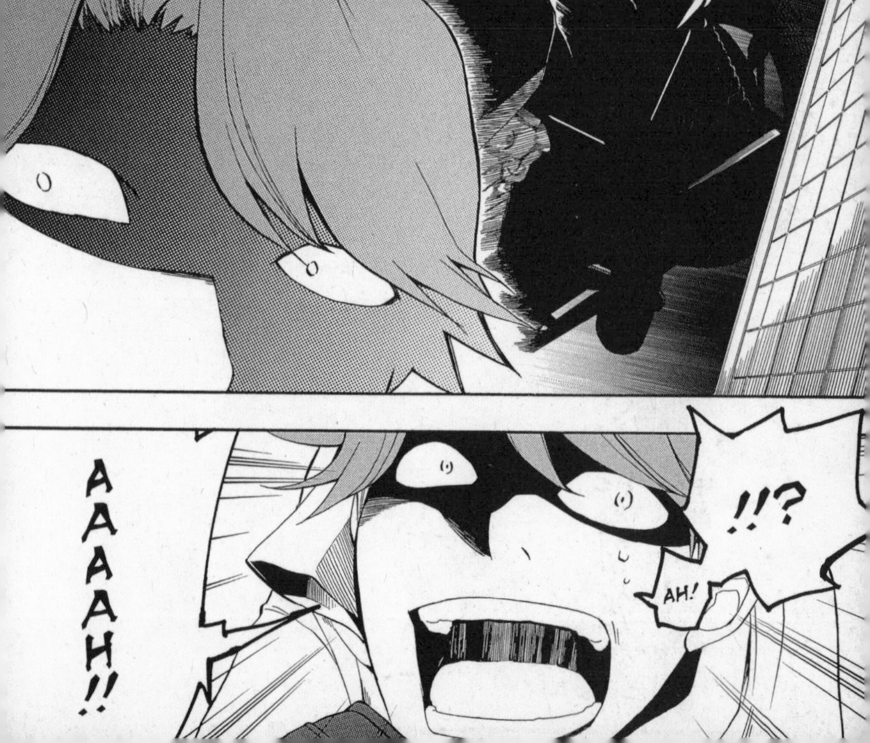
!!?
AH!
AAAAH!!

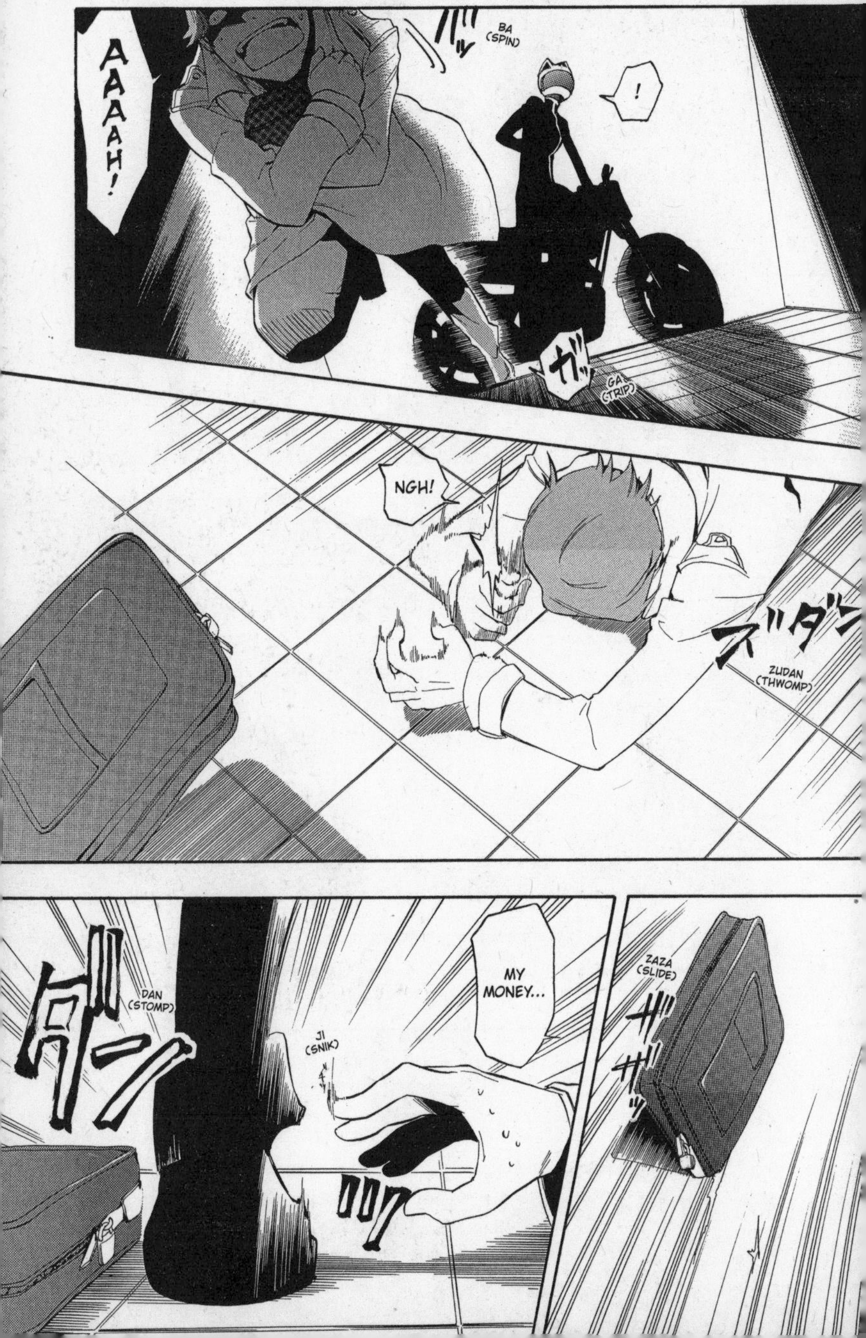
BA
(SPIN)
!
AAAAAH!
GA
(TRIP)
ZUDAN
(THWOMP)
NGH!
ZAZA
(SLIDE)
MY MONEY...
JI
(SNIK)
DAN
(STOMP)

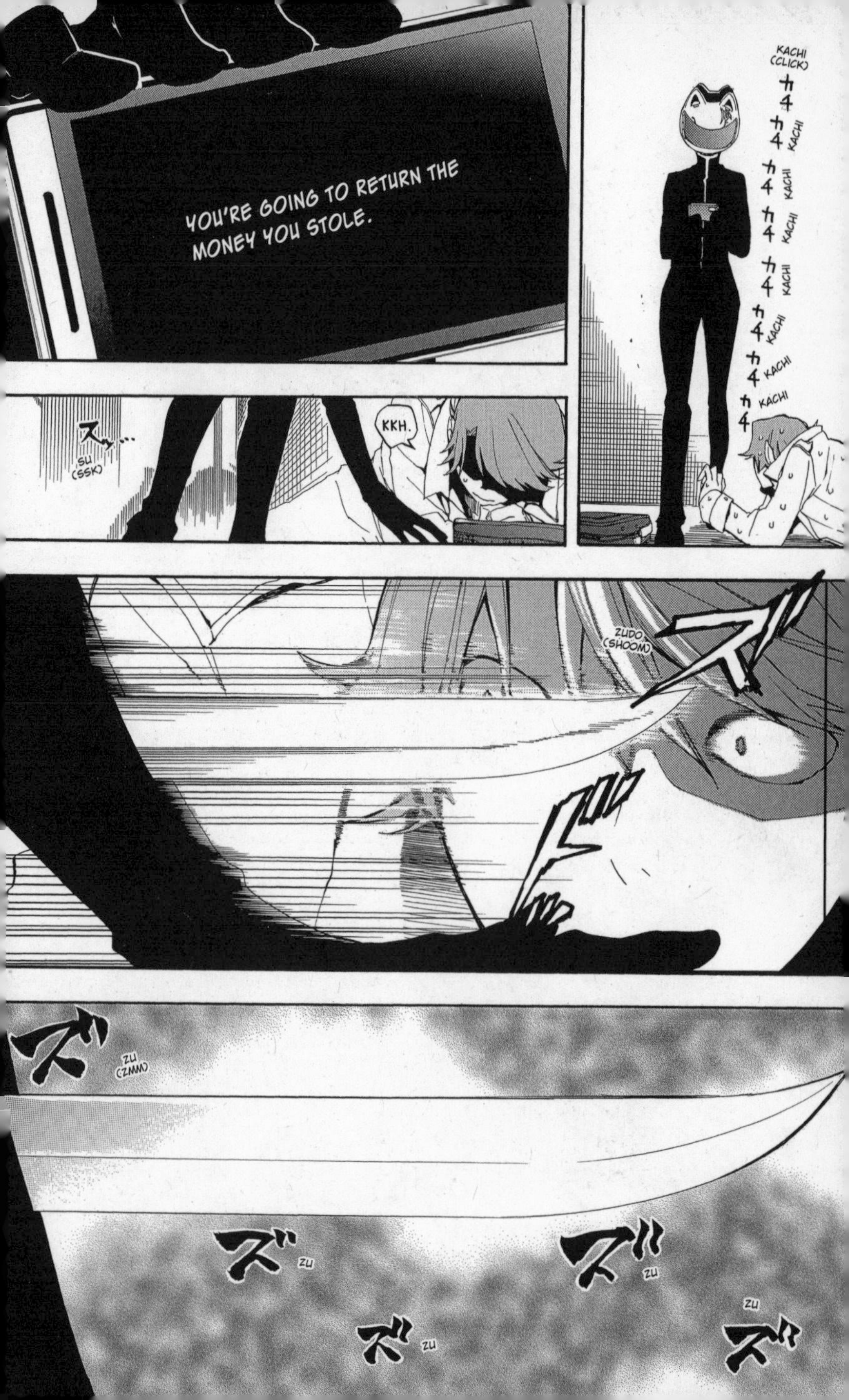
KACHI (CLICK)
カチ
カチ KACHI
カチ KACHI
カチ KACHI
カチ KACHI
カチ KACHI
カチ KACHI
カチ KACHI
YOU'RE GOING TO RETURN THE MONEY YOU STOLE.
KKH.
ス… SU (SSK)
ズド ZUDO (SHOOM)
ズ ZU (ZMM)
ズ ZU
ズ ZU
ズ ZU
ズ ZU

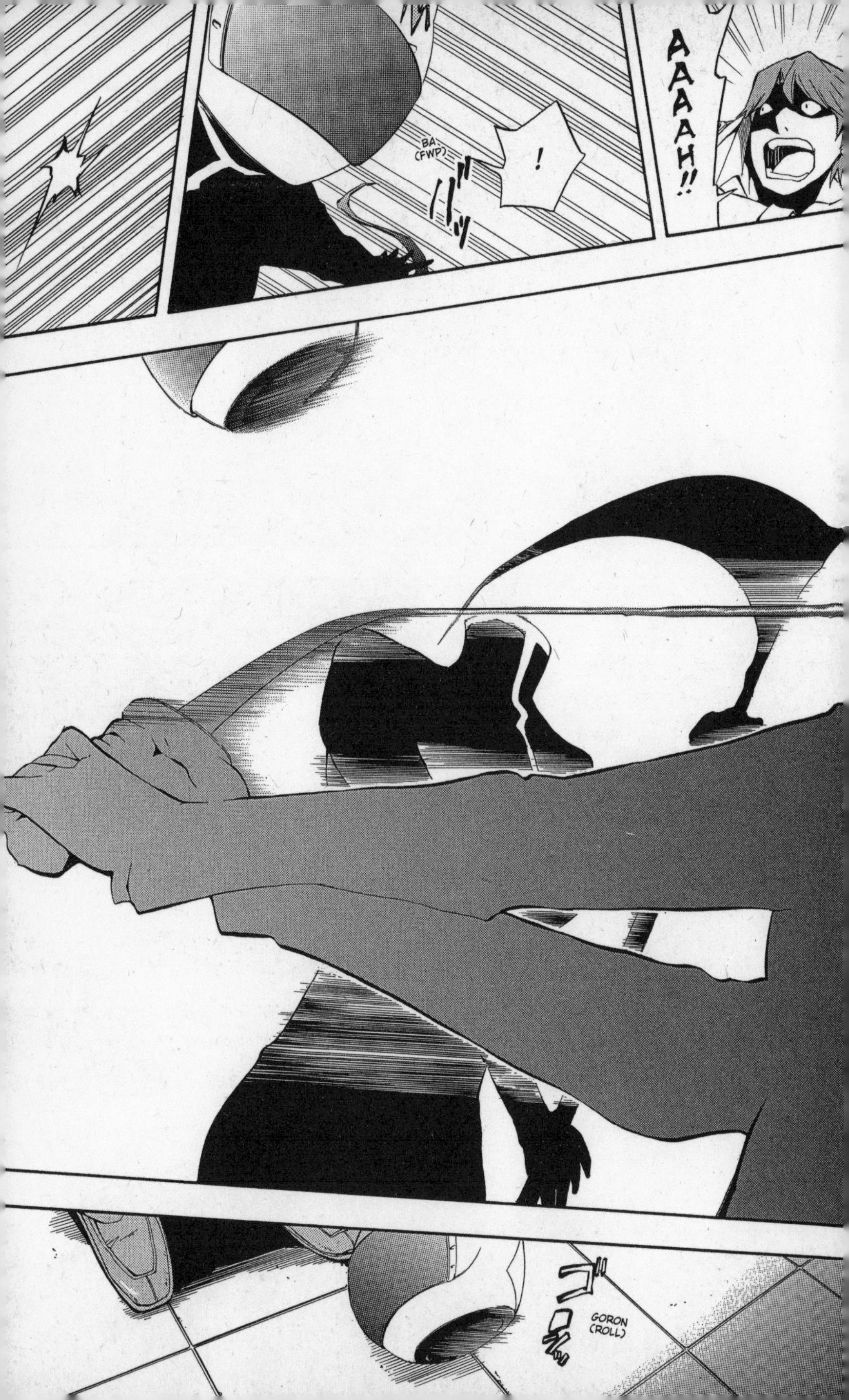
AAAAH!!
!
BA (FWP)
GORON (ROLL)

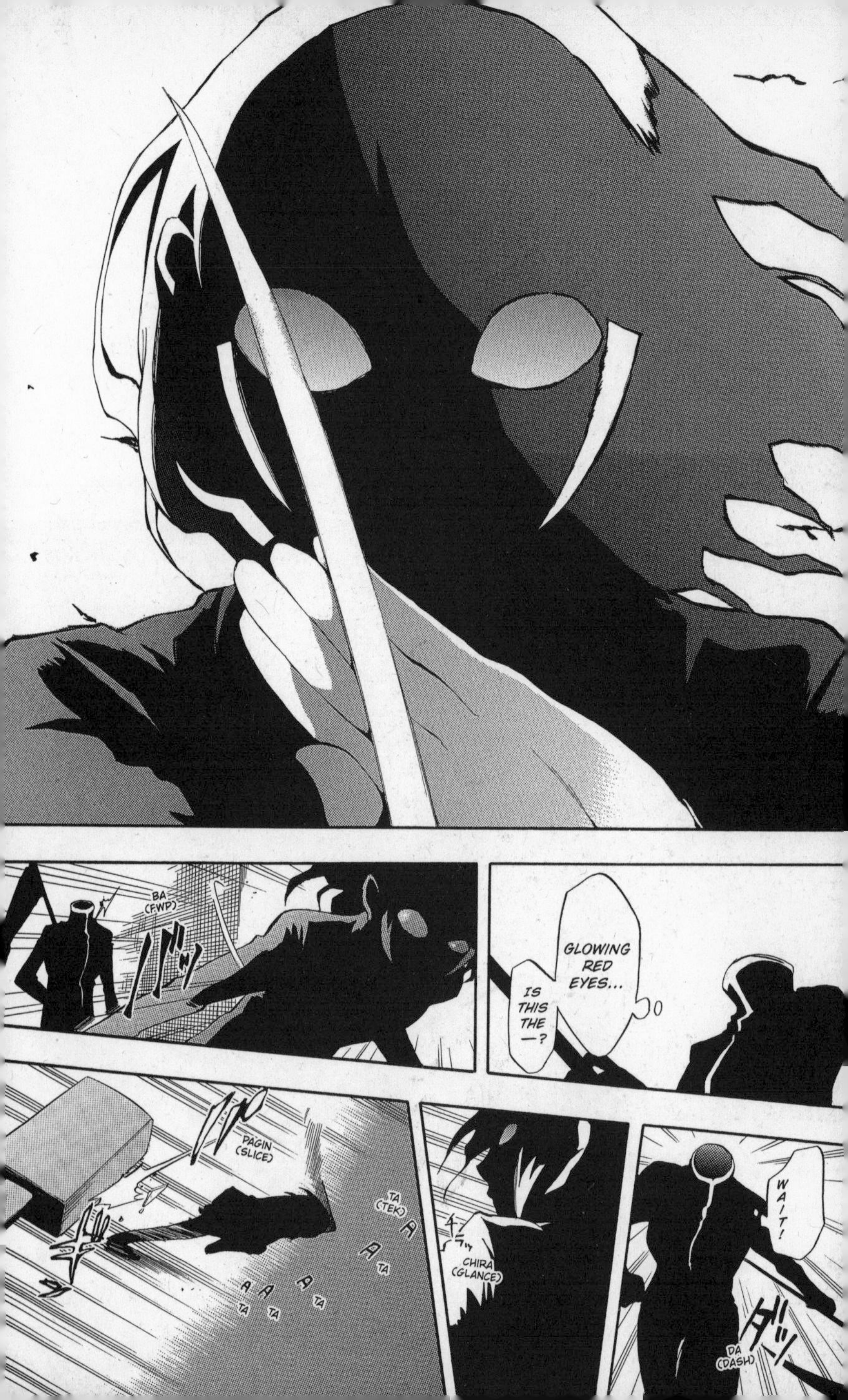
GLOWING RED EYES...
IS THIS THE—?
BA (FWP)
WAIT!
DA (DASH)
CHIRA (GLANCE)
PAGIN (SLICE)
TA (TEK)
TA TA TA TA

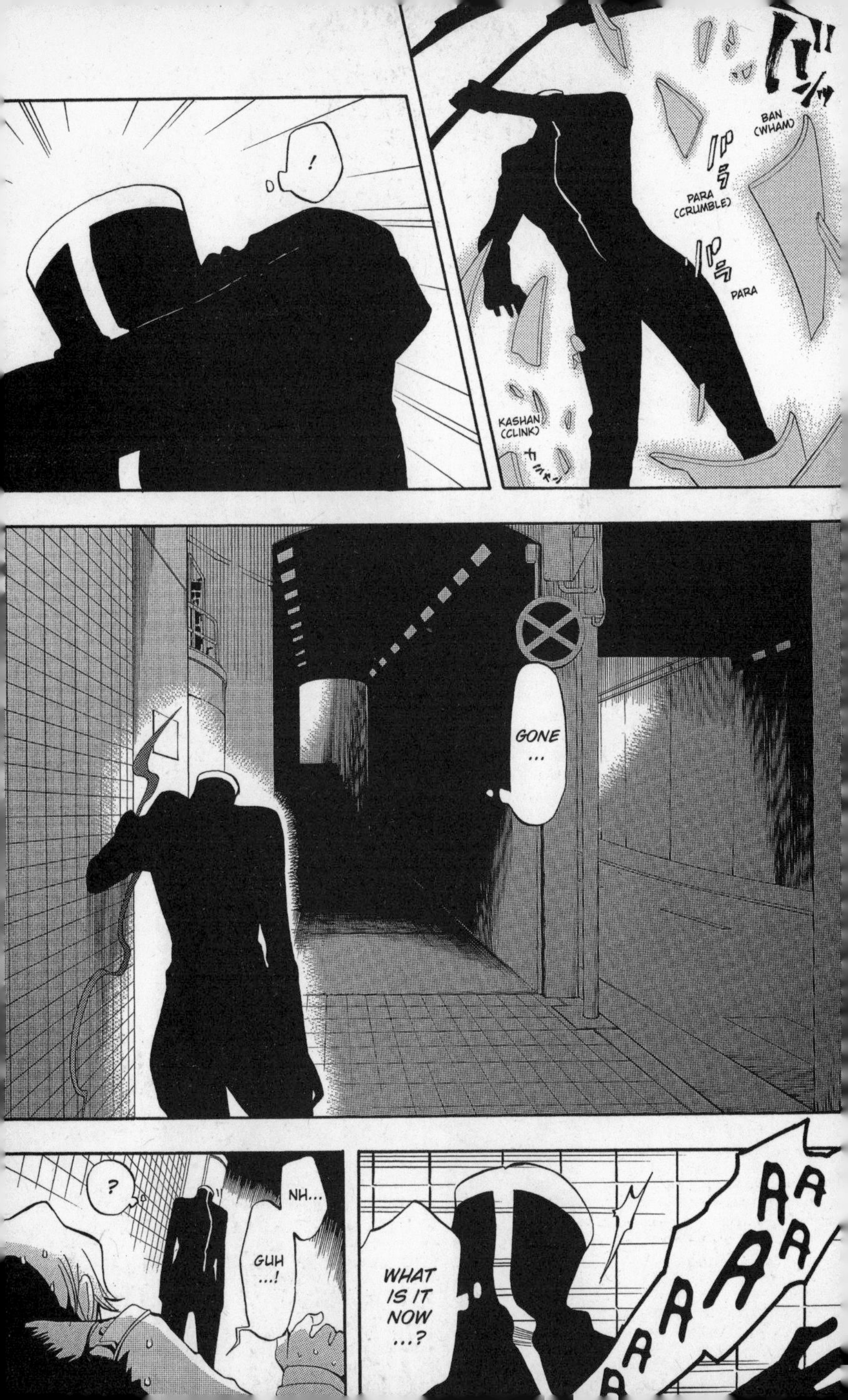
BAN (WHAM)
PARA (CRUMBLE)
PARA
KASHAN (CLINK)
!
GONE ...
AAAAAAAAAAA
WHAT IS IT NOW ...?
NH...
?
GUH ...!

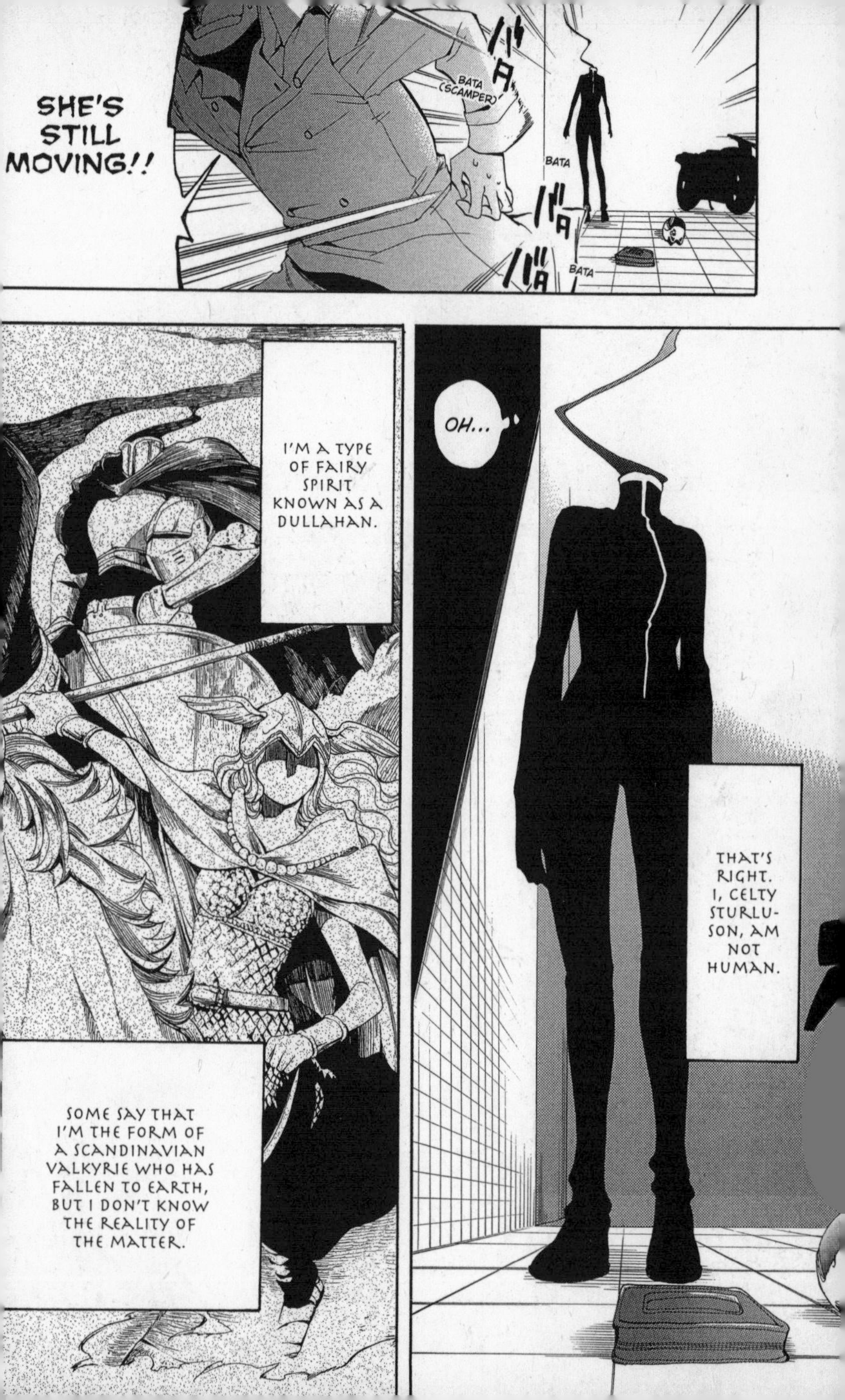
BATA (SCAMPER)
BATA
BATA
SHE'S STILL MOVING!!
OH...
THAT'S RIGHT. I, CELTY STURLUSON, AM NOT HUMAN.
I'M A TYPE OF FAIRY SPIRIT KNOWN AS A DULLAHAN.
SOME SAY THAT I'M THE FORM OF A SCANDINAVIAN VALKYRIE WHO HAS FALLEN TO EARTH, BUT I DON'T KNOW THE REALITY OF THE MATTER.

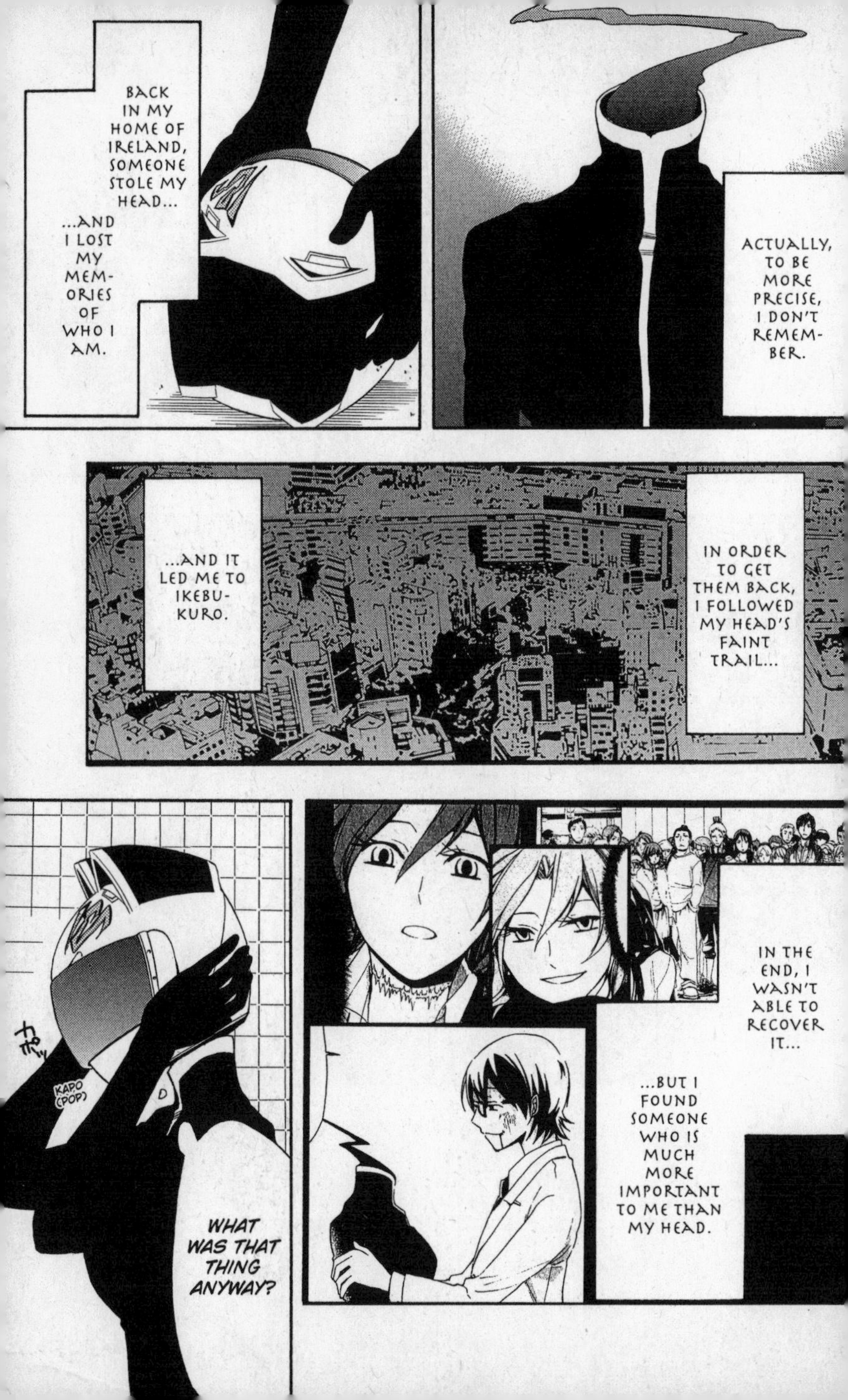
ACTUALLY, TO BE MORE PRECISE, I DON'T REMEMBER.
BACK IN MY HOME OF IRELAND, SOMEONE STOLE MY HEAD...
...AND I LOST MY MEMORIES OF WHO I AM.
IN ORDER TO GET THEM BACK, I FOLLOWED MY HEAD'S FAINT TRAIL...
...AND IT LED ME TO IKEBUKURO.
IN THE END, I WASN'T ABLE TO RECOVER IT...
...BUT I FOUND SOMEONE WHO IS MUCH MORE IMPORTANT TO ME THAN MY HEAD.
KAPO (POP)
WHAT WAS THAT THING ANYWAY?

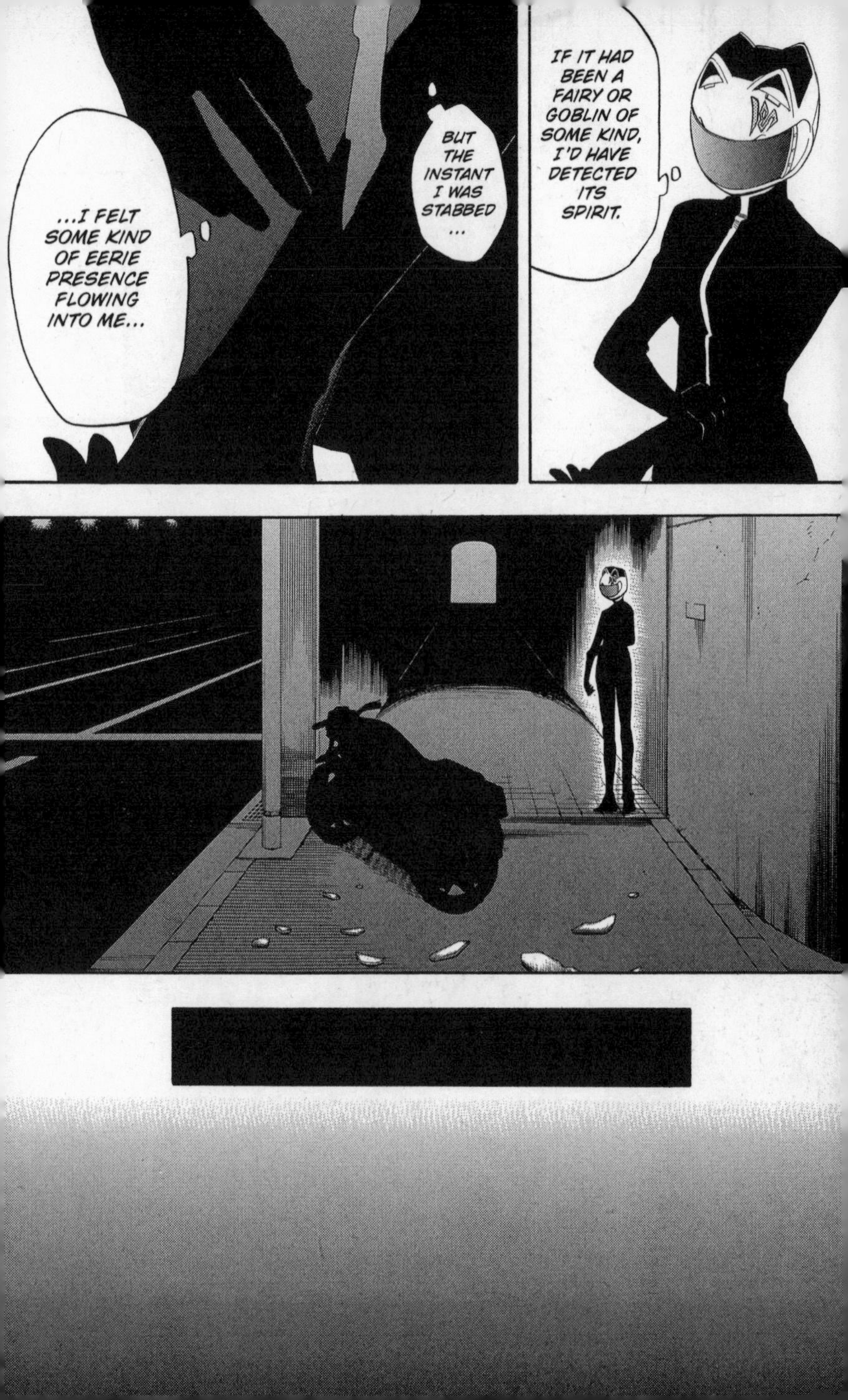
IF IT HAD BEEN A FAIRY OR GOBLIN OF SOME KIND, I'D HAVE DETECTED ITS SPIRIT.
BUT THE INSTANT I WAS STABBED...
...I FELT SOME KIND OF EERIE PRESENCE FLOWING INTO ME...

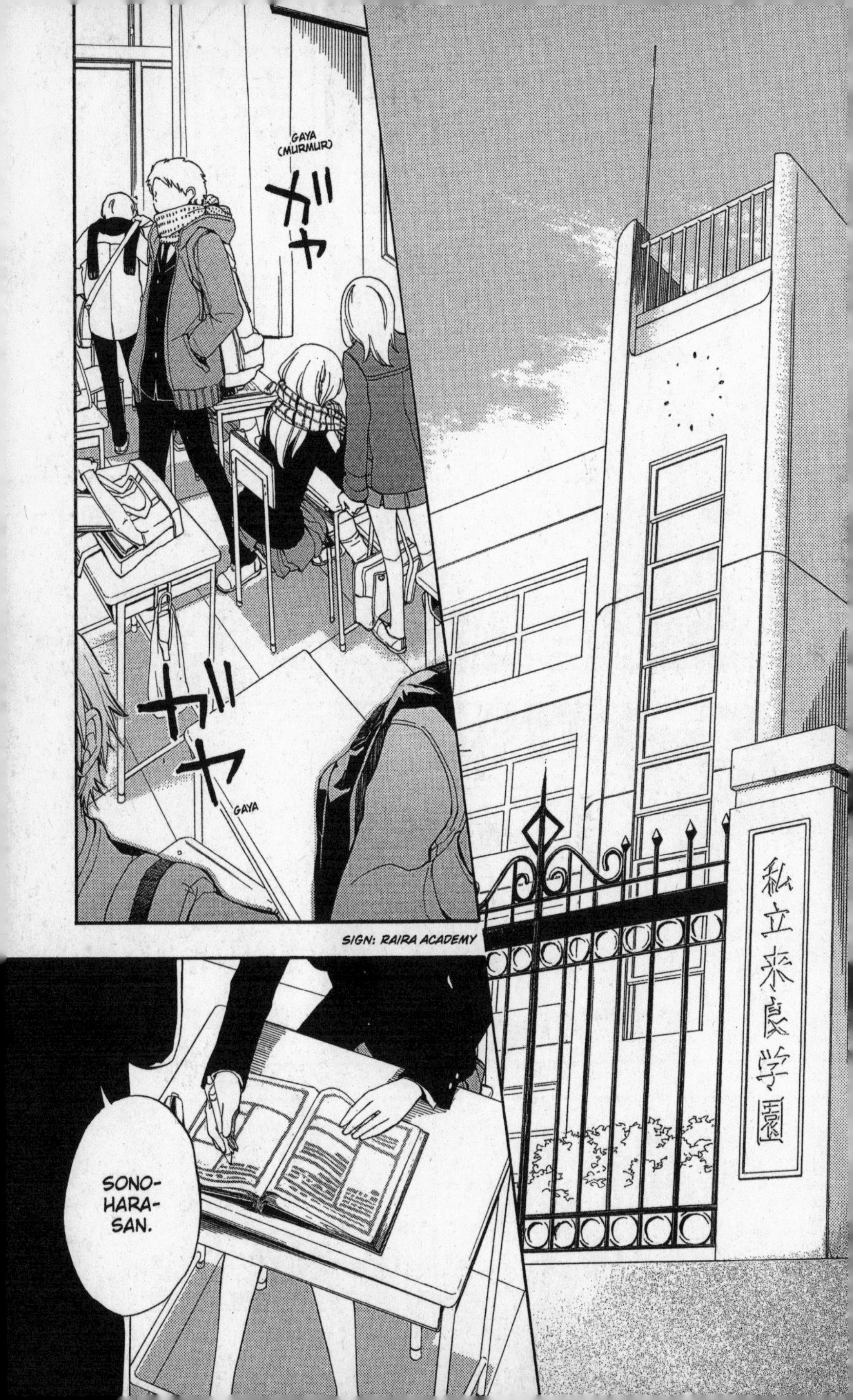
私立来良学園
SIGN: RAIRA ACADEMY
ガヤ
GAYA (MURMUR)
ガヤ
GAYA
SONO-HARA-SAN.

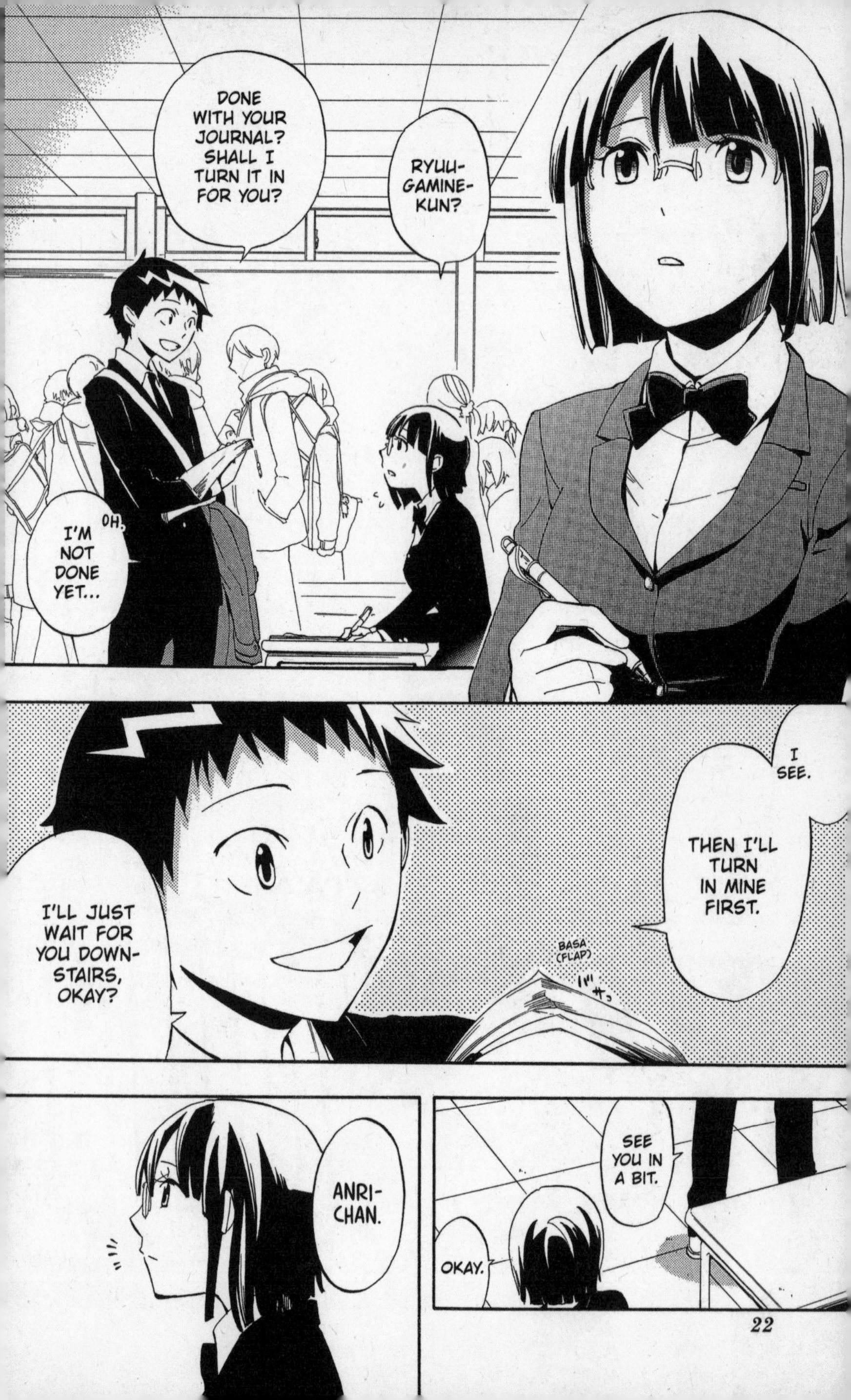
RYUU-GAMINE-KUN?
DONE WITH YOUR JOURNAL? SHALL I TURN IT IN FOR YOU?
OH.
I'M NOT DONE YET...
I SEE.
THEN I'LL TURN IN MINE FIRST.
BASA (FLAP)
I'LL JUST WAIT FOR YOU DOWN-STAIRS, OKAY?
SEE YOU IN A BIT.
OKAY.
ANRI-CHAN.

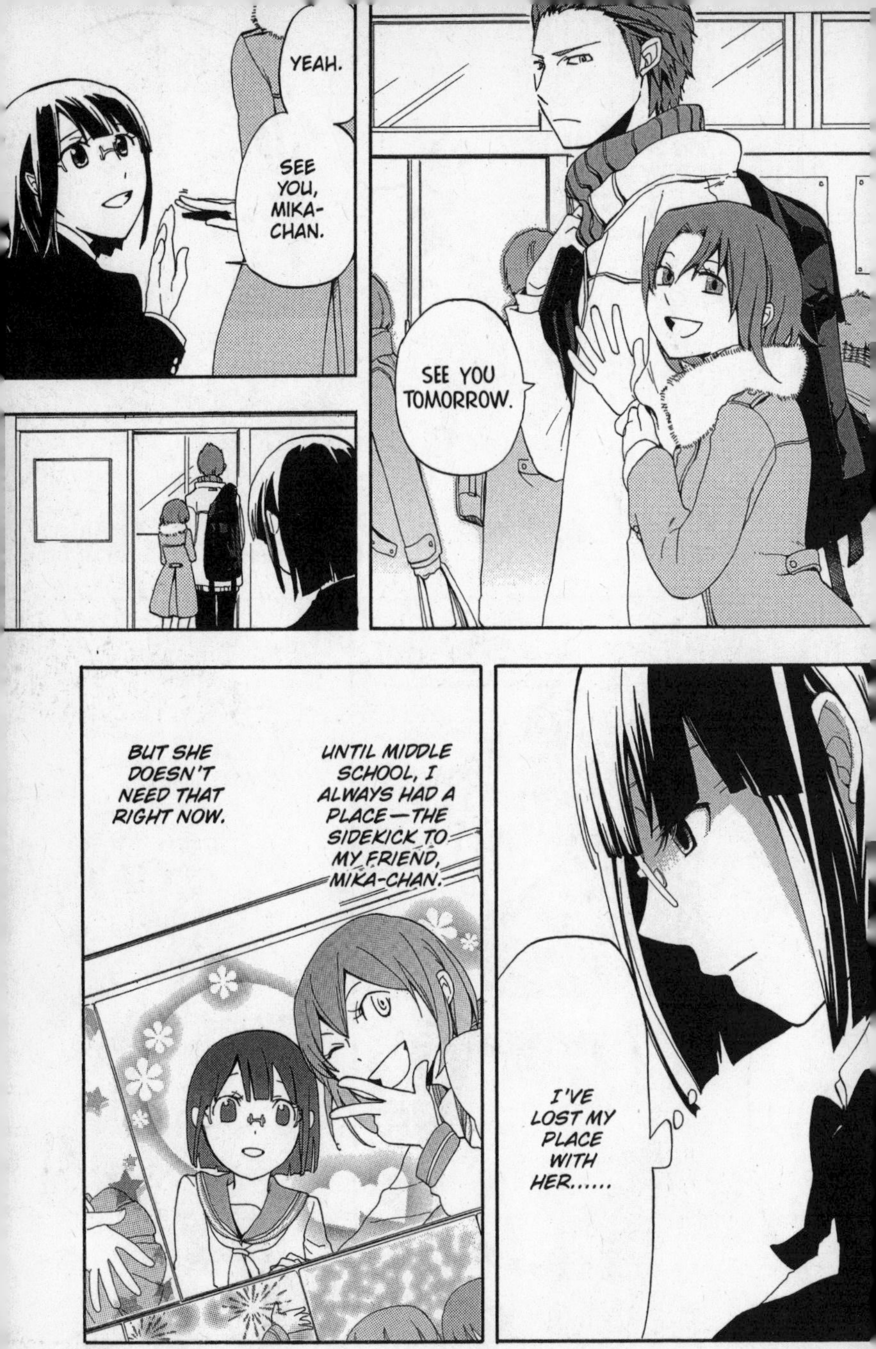
SEE YOU TOMORROW.
YEAH.
SEE YOU, MIKA-CHAN.
I'VE LOST MY PLACE WITH HER......
UNTIL MIDDLE SCHOOL, I ALWAYS HAD A PLACE—THE SIDEKICK TO MY FRIEND, MIKA-CHAN.
BUT SHE DOESN'T NEED THAT RIGHT NOW.

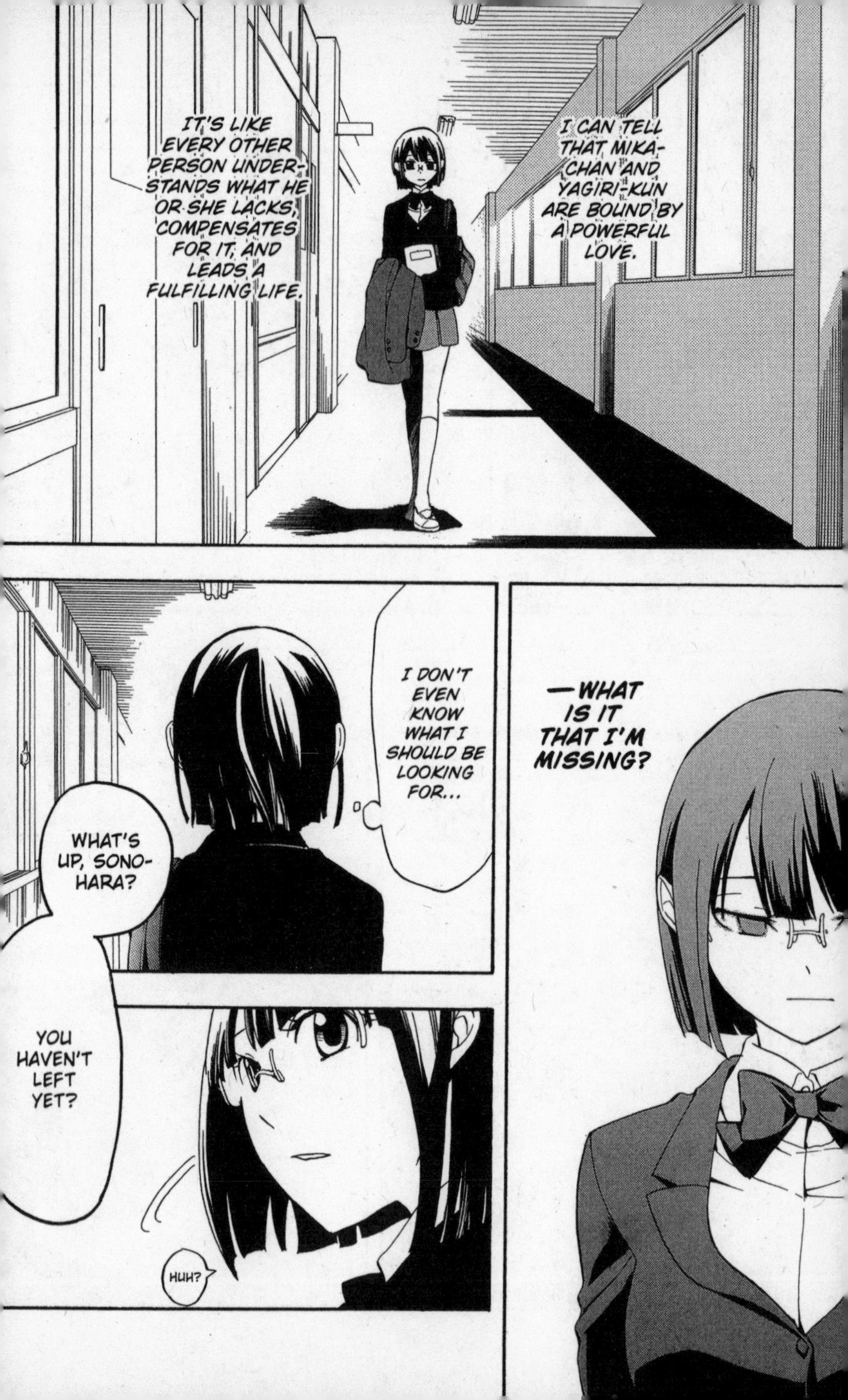
I CAN TELL THAT MIKA-CHAN AND YAGIRI-KUN ARE BOUND BY A POWERFUL LOVE.
IT'S LIKE EVERY OTHER PERSON UNDER-STANDS WHAT HE OR SHE LACKS, COMPENSATES FOR IT, AND LEADS A FULFILLING LIFE.
—WHAT IS IT THAT I'M MISSING?
I DON'T EVEN KNOW WHAT I SHOULD BE LOOKING FOR...
WHAT'S UP, SONO-HARA?
YOU HAVEN'T LEFT YET?
HUH?

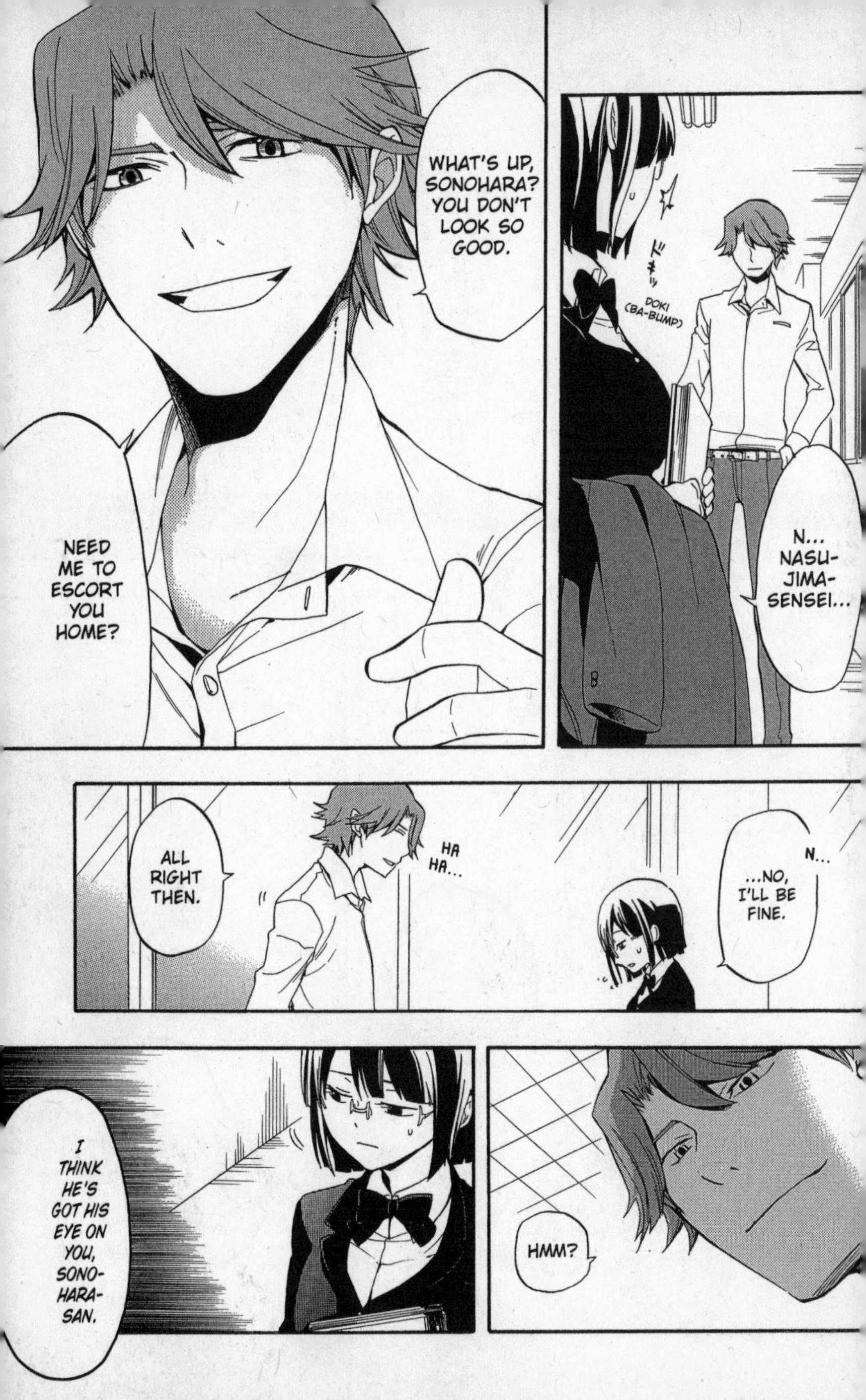
ドキッ
DOKI (BA-BUMP)
N... NASU-JIMA-SENSEI...
WHAT'S UP, SONOHARA? YOU DON'T LOOK SO GOOD.
NEED ME TO ESCORT YOU HOME?
N...
...NO, I'LL BE FINE.
HA HA...
ALL RIGHT THEN.
HMM?
I THINK HE'S GOT HIS EYE ON YOU, SONO-HARA-SAN.

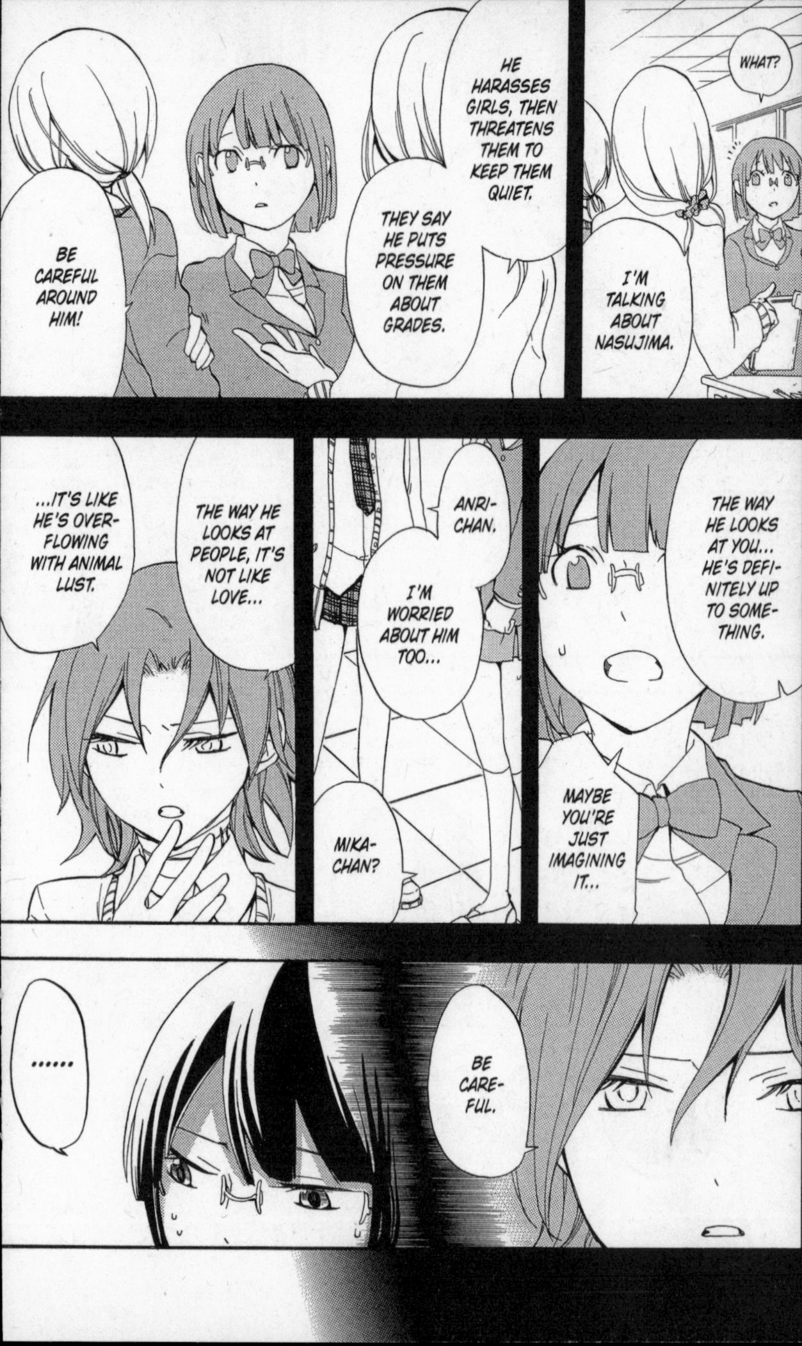
WHAT?
I'M TALKING ABOUT NASUJIMA.
HE HARASSES GIRLS, THEN THREATENS THEM TO KEEP THEM QUIET.
THEY SAY HE PUTS PRESSURE ON THEM ABOUT GRADES.
BE CAREFUL AROUND HIM!
THE WAY HE LOOKS AT YOU... HE'S DEFINITELY UP TO SOMETHING.
MAYBE YOU'RE JUST IMAGINING IT...
ANRI-CHAN.
I'M WORRIED ABOUT HIM TOO...
MIKA-CHAN?
THE WAY HE LOOKS AT PEOPLE, IT'S NOT LIKE LOVE...
...IT'S LIKE HE'S OVERFLOWING WITH ANIMAL LUST.
BE CAREFUL.
......

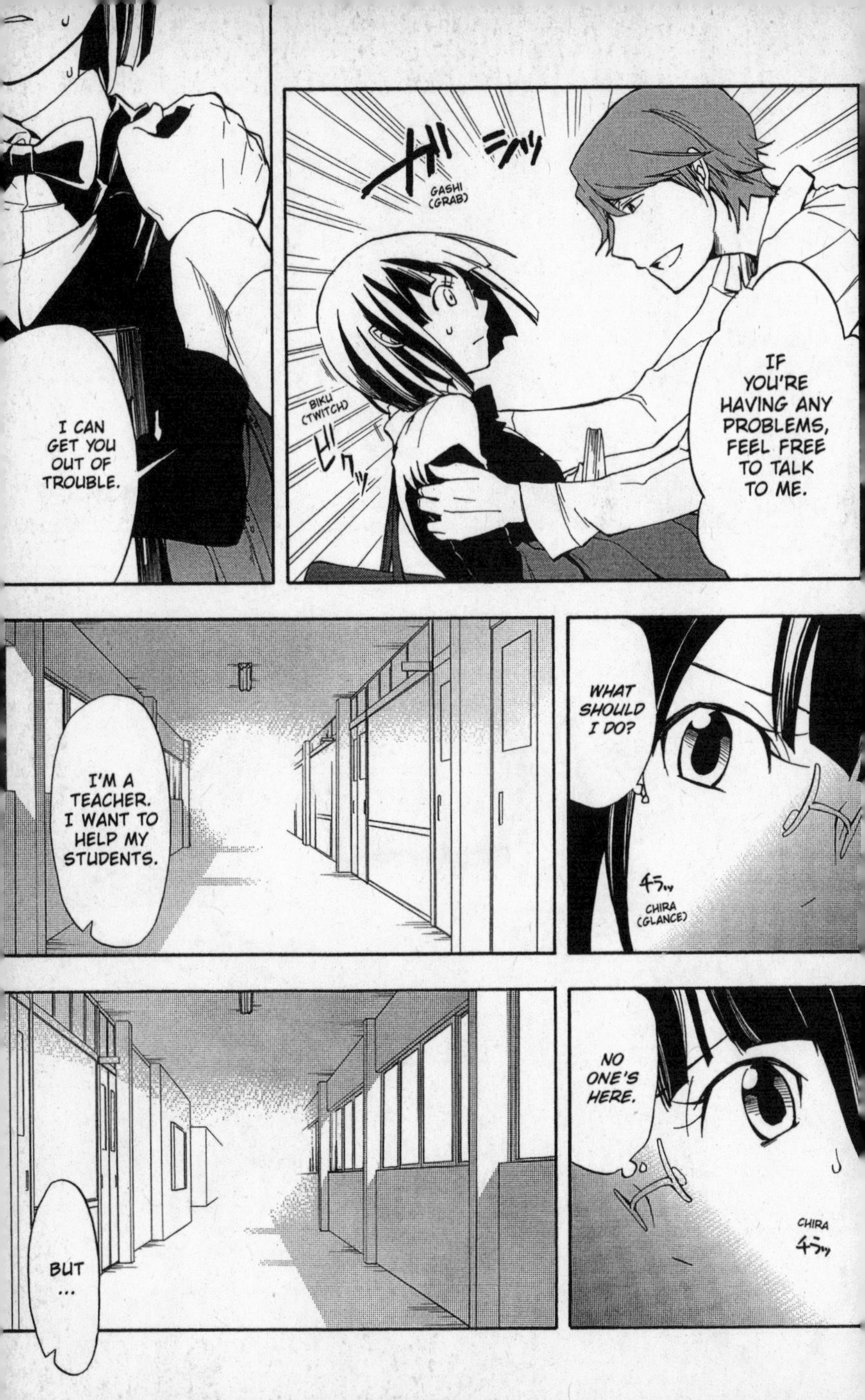
GASHI (GRAB)
BIKU (TWITCH)
IF YOU'RE HAVING ANY PROBLEMS, FEEL FREE TO TALK TO ME.
I CAN GET YOU OUT OF TROUBLE.
WHAT SHOULD I DO?
CHIRA (GLANCE)
I'M A TEACHER. I WANT TO HELP MY STUDENTS.
NO ONE'S HERE.
CHIRA
BUT ...

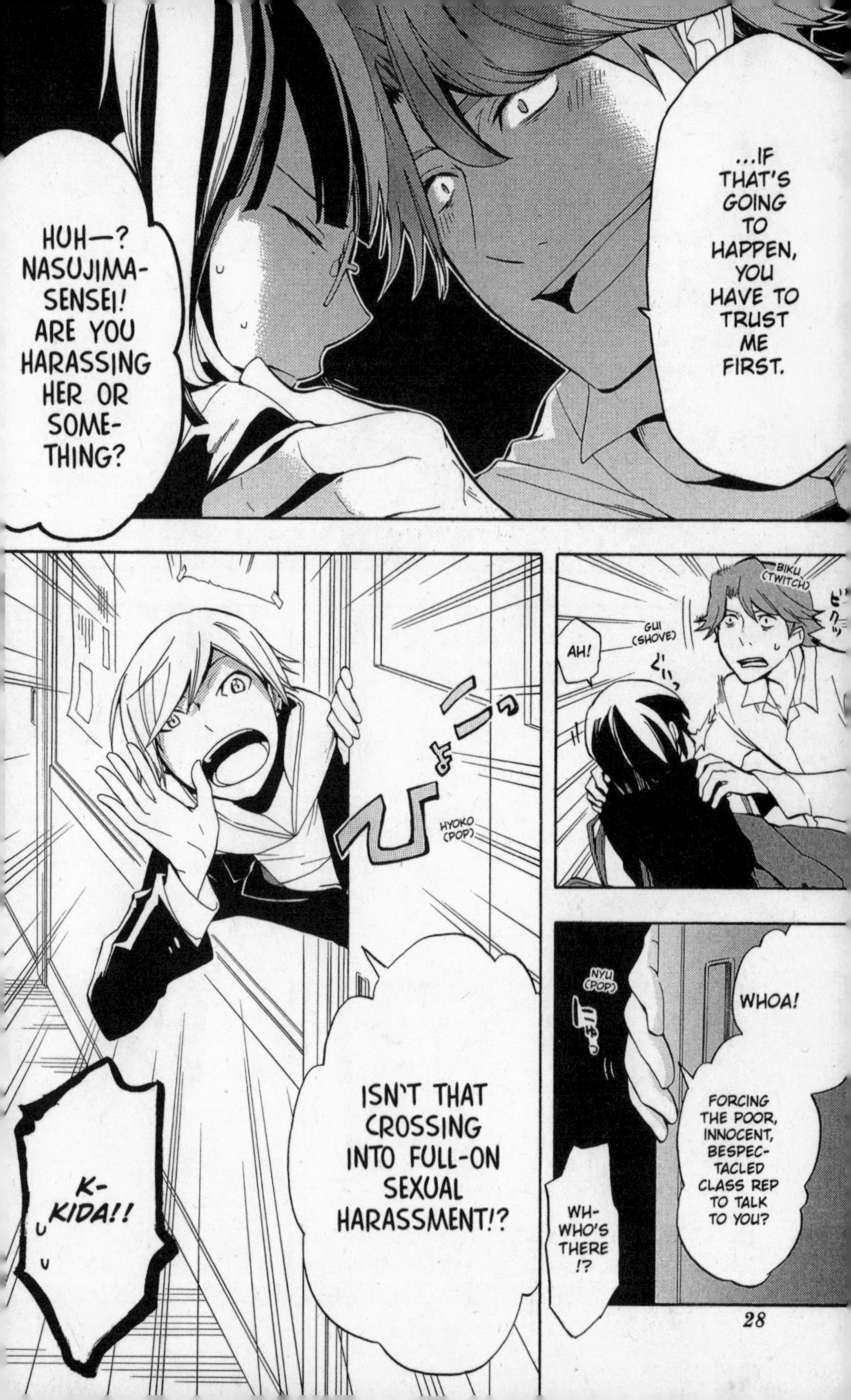
...IF THAT'S GOING TO HAPPEN, YOU HAVE TO TRUST ME FIRST.
HUH—? NASUJIMA-SENSEI! ARE YOU HARASSING HER OR SOMETHING?
BIKU (TWITCH)
GUI (SHOVE)
AH!
WHOA!
NYU (POP)
FORCING THE POOR, INNOCENT, BESPECTACLED CLASS REP TO TALK TO YOU?
WH-WHO'S THERE !?
HYOKO (POP)
ISN'T THAT CROSSING INTO FULL-ON SEXUAL HARASSMENT!?
K-KIDA!!

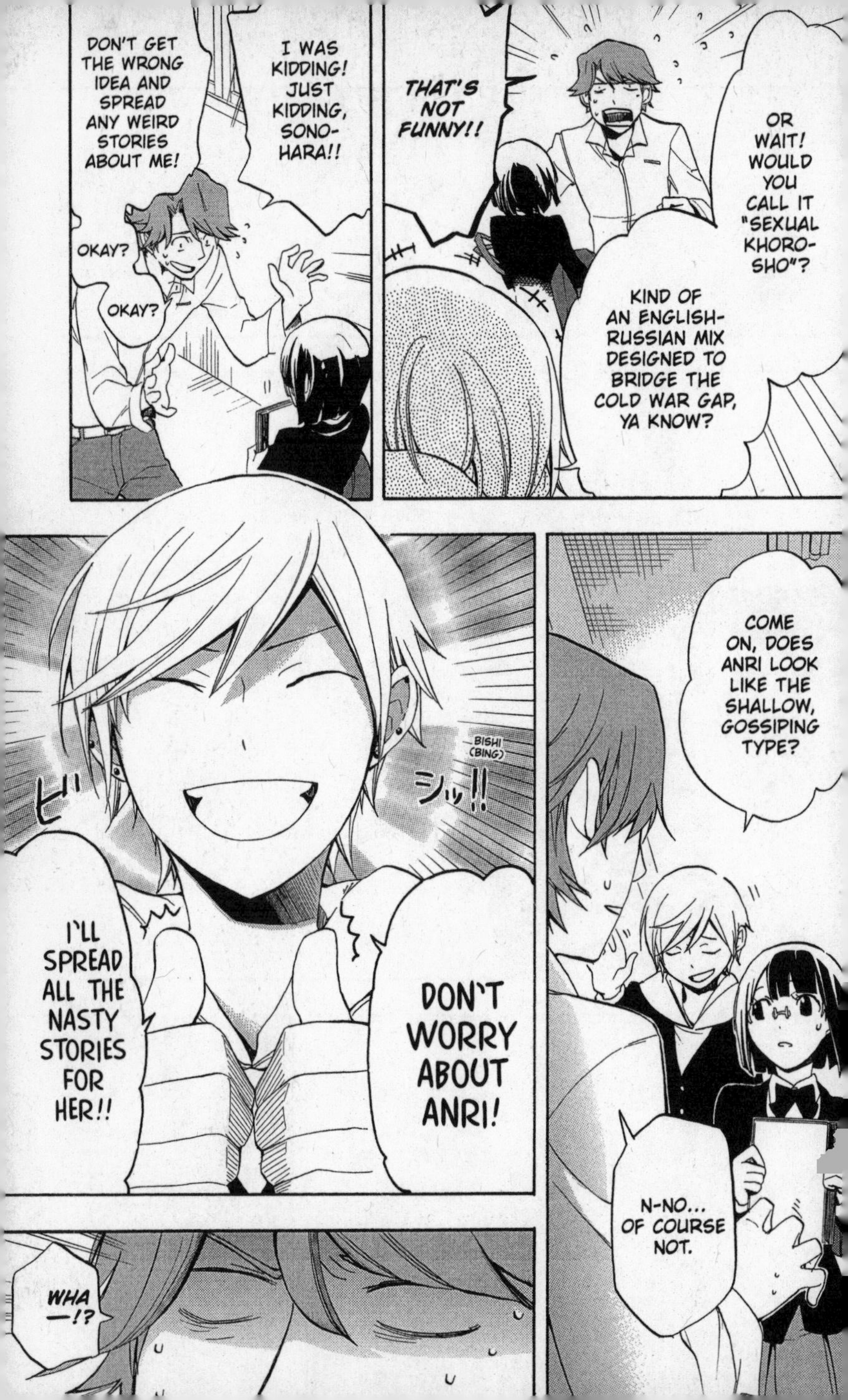
OR WAIT! WOULD YOU CALL IT "SEXUAL KHORO-SHO"?
KIND OF AN ENGLISH-RUSSIAN MIX DESIGNED TO BRIDGE THE COLD WAR GAP, YA KNOW?
THAT'S NOT FUNNY!!
I WAS KIDDING! JUST KIDDING, SONO-HARA!!
DON'T GET THE WRONG IDEA AND SPREAD ANY WEIRD STORIES ABOUT ME!
OKAY?
OKAY?
COME ON, DOES ANRI LOOK LIKE THE SHALLOW, GOSSIPING TYPE?
N-NO... OF COURSE NOT.
DON'T WORRY ABOUT ANRI!
BISHI (BING)
ビシッ!!
I'LL SPREAD ALL THE NASTY STORIES FOR HER!!
WHA—!?

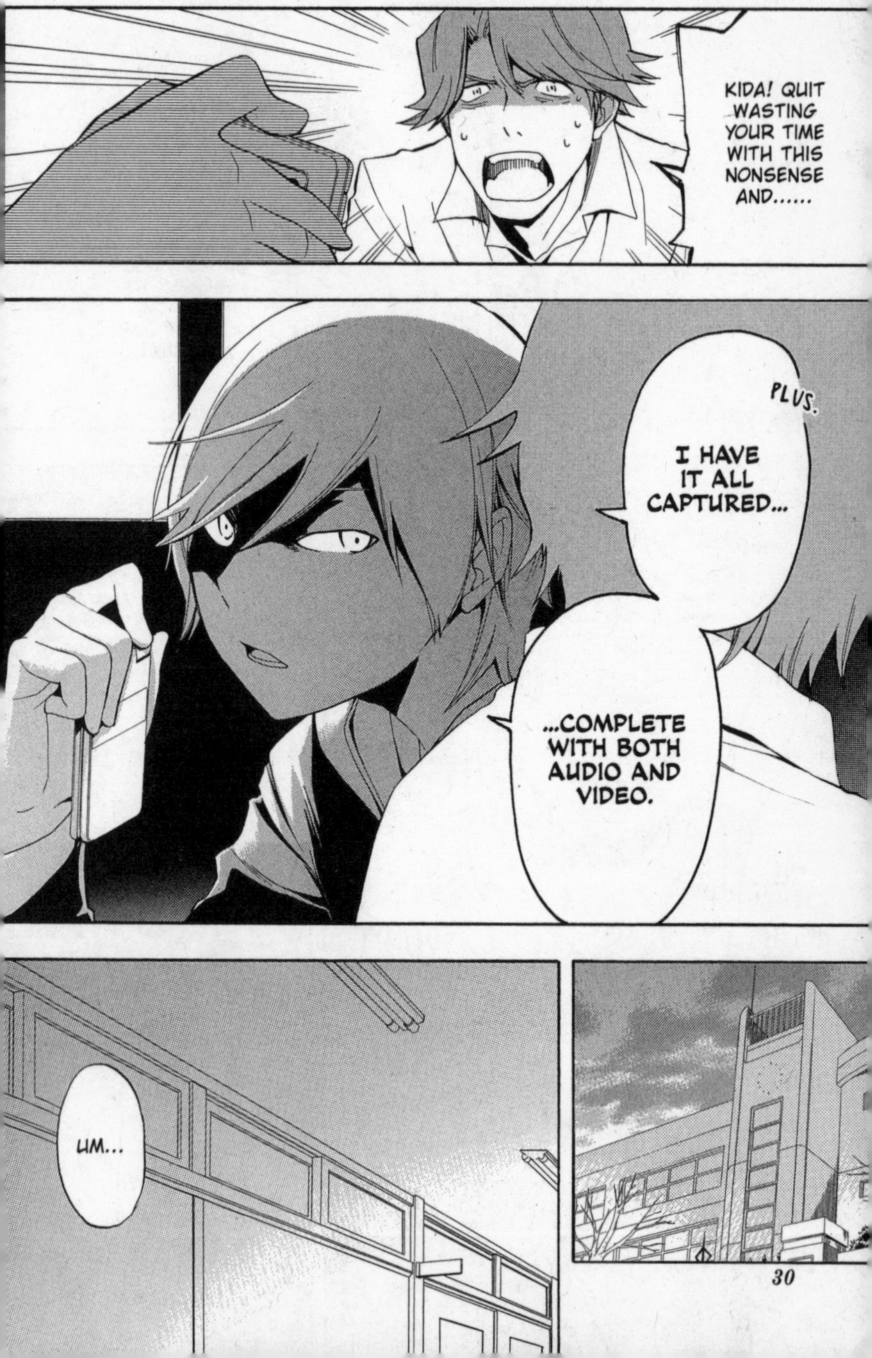
KIDA! QUIT WASTING YOUR TIME WITH THIS NONSENSE AND......
PLUS.
I HAVE IT ALL CAPTURED...
...COMPLETE WITH BOTH AUDIO AND VIDEO.
UM...

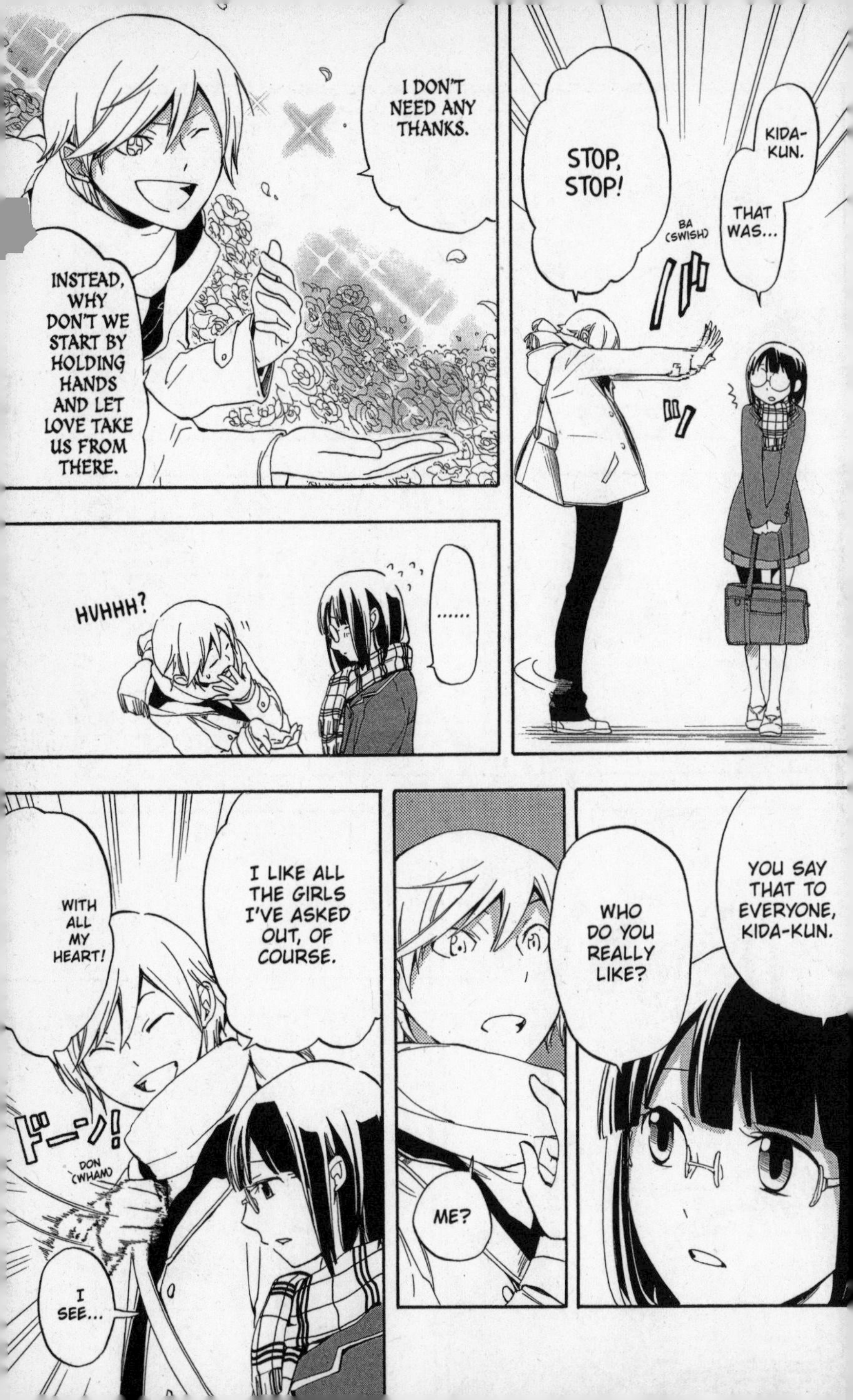
KIDA-KUN.
THAT WAS...
STOP, STOP!
BA (SWISH)
I DON'T NEED ANY THANKS.
INSTEAD, WHY DON'T WE START BY HOLDING HANDS AND LET LOVE TAKE US FROM THERE.
......
HUHHH?
YOU SAY THAT TO EVERYONE, KIDA-KUN.
WHO DO YOU REALLY LIKE?
ME?
I LIKE ALL THE GIRLS I'VE ASKED OUT, OF COURSE.
WITH ALL MY HEART!
DON (WHAM)
I SEE...

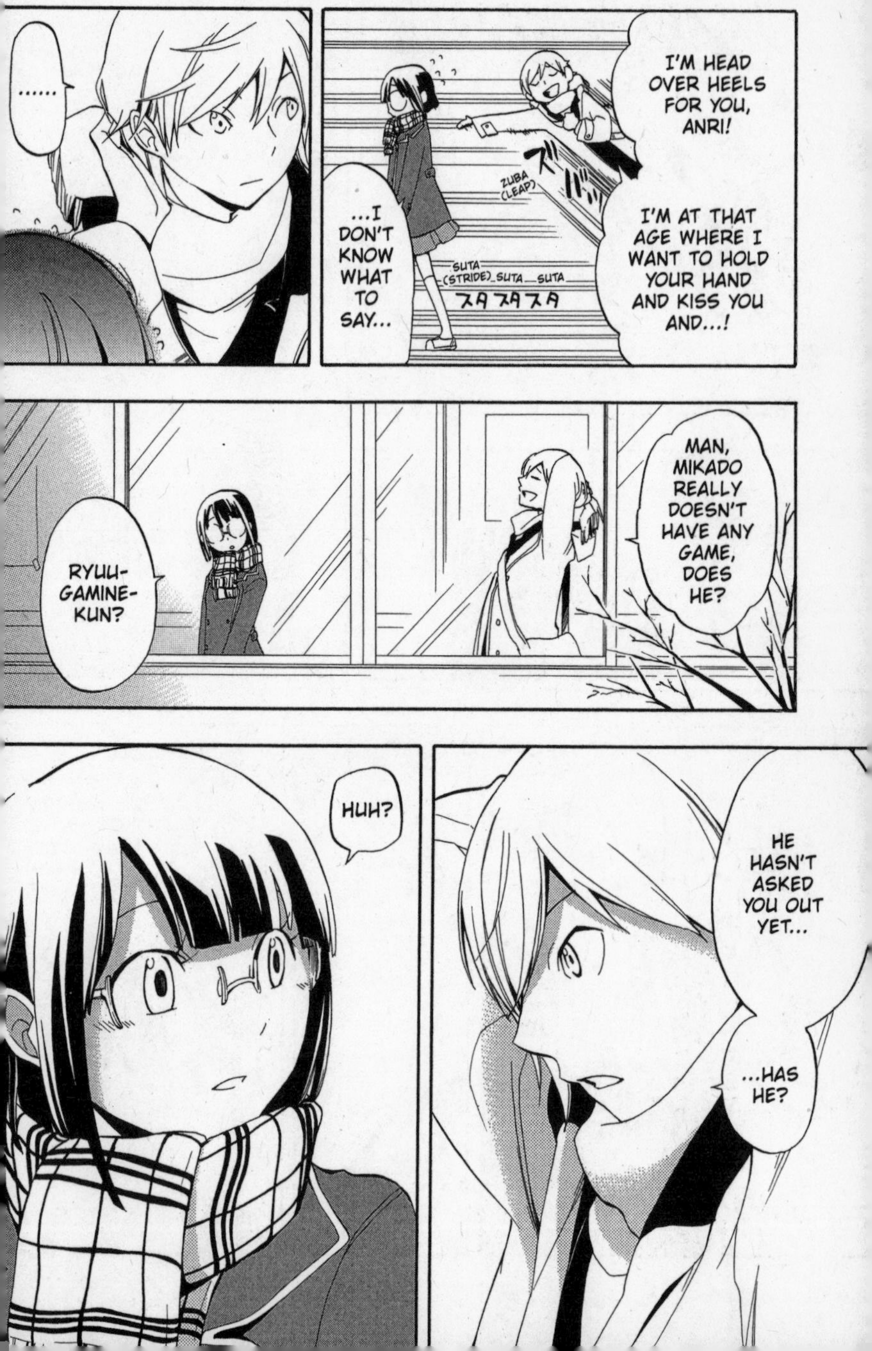
I'M HEAD OVER HEELS FOR YOU, ANRI!
ZUBA (LEAP)
ズバッ
I'M AT THAT AGE WHERE I WANT TO HOLD YOUR HAND AND KISS YOU AND...!
SUTA (STRIDE) SUTA SUTA
スタスタスタ
...I DON'T KNOW WHAT TO SAY...
......
MAN, MIKADO REALLY DOESN'T HAVE ANY GAME, DOES HE?
RYUU-GAMINE-KUN?
HE HASN'T ASKED YOU OUT YET...
...HAS HE?
HUH?

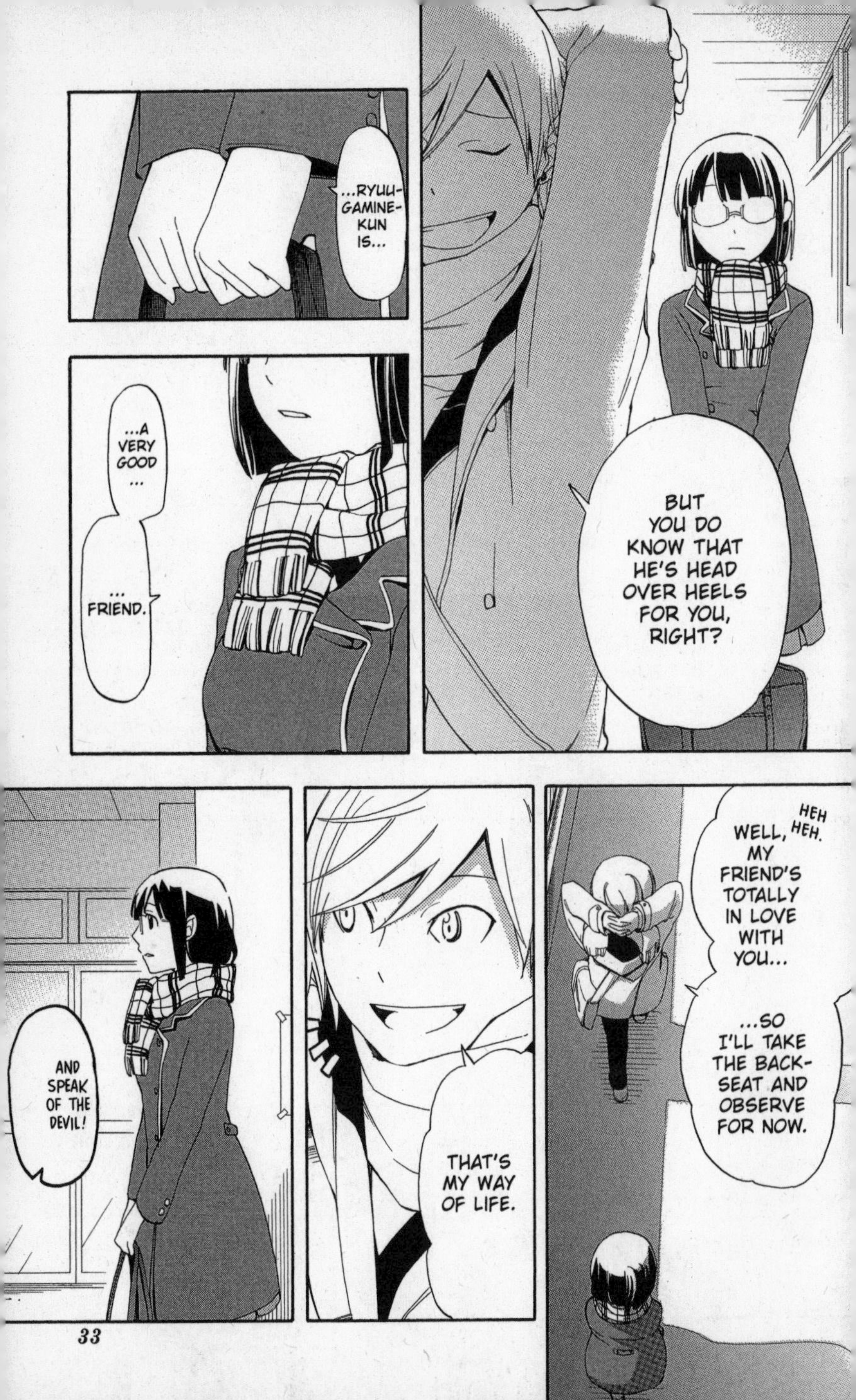
BUT YOU DO KNOW THAT HE'S HEAD OVER HEELS FOR YOU, RIGHT?
...RYUU-GAMINE-KUN IS...
...A VERY GOOD ...
... FRIEND.
HEH HEH.
WELL, MY FRIEND'S TOTALLY IN LOVE WITH YOU...
...SO I'LL TAKE THE BACK-SEAT AND OBSERVE FOR NOW.
THAT'S MY WAY OF LIFE.
AND SPEAK OF THE DEVIL!

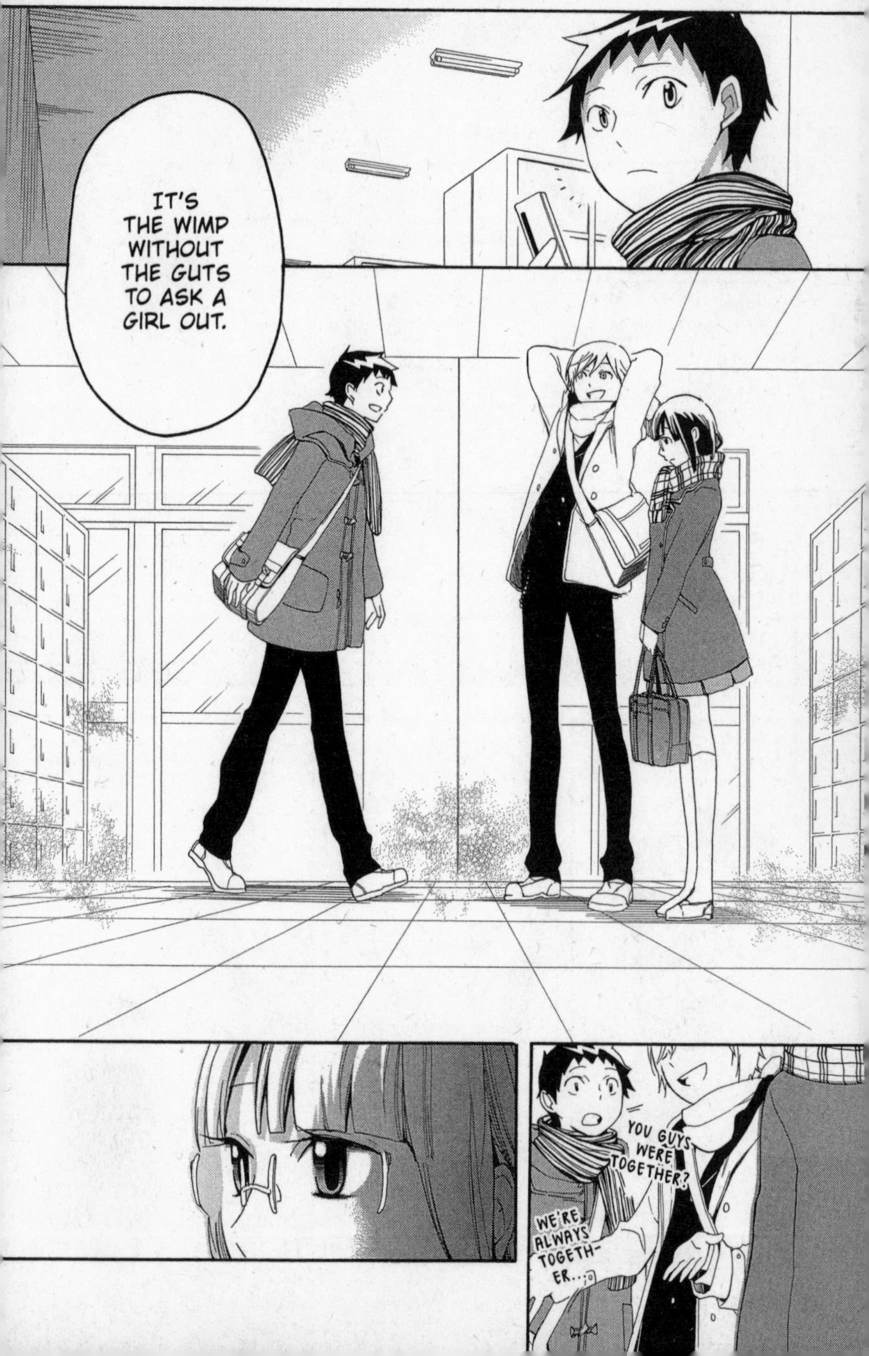
IT'S THE WIMP WITHOUT THE GUTS TO ASK A GIRL OUT.
YOU GUYS WERE TOGETHER?
WE'RE ALWAYS TOGETHER...

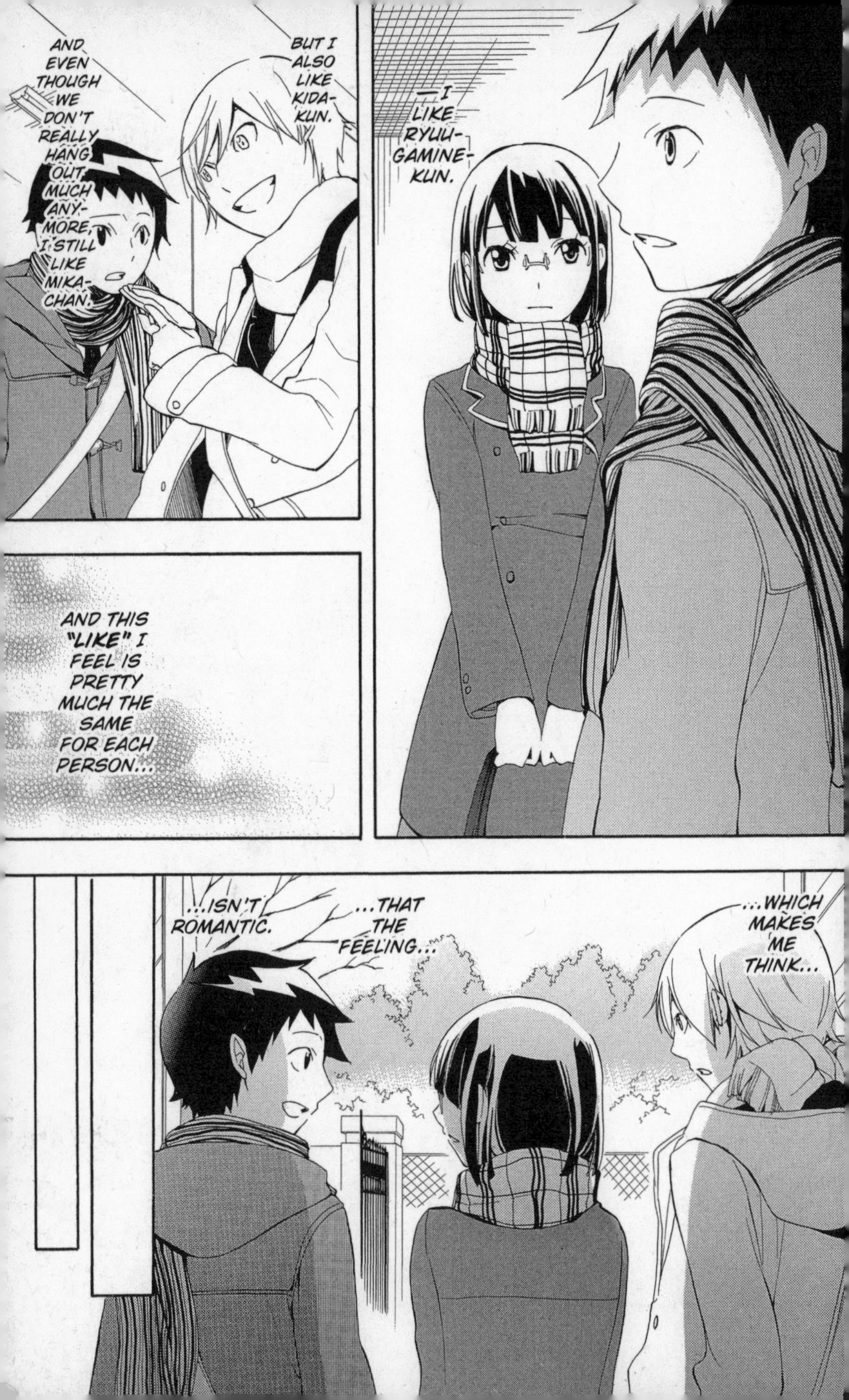
—I LIKE RYUUGAMINE-KUN.
BUT I ALSO LIKE KIDA-KUN.
AND EVEN THOUGH WE DON'T REALLY HANG OUT MUCH ANYMORE, I STILL LIKE MIKA-CHAN.
AND THIS "LIKE" I FEEL IS PRETTY MUCH THE SAME FOR EACH PERSON...
...WHICH MAKES ME THINK...
...THAT THE FEELING...
...ISN'T ROMANTIC.

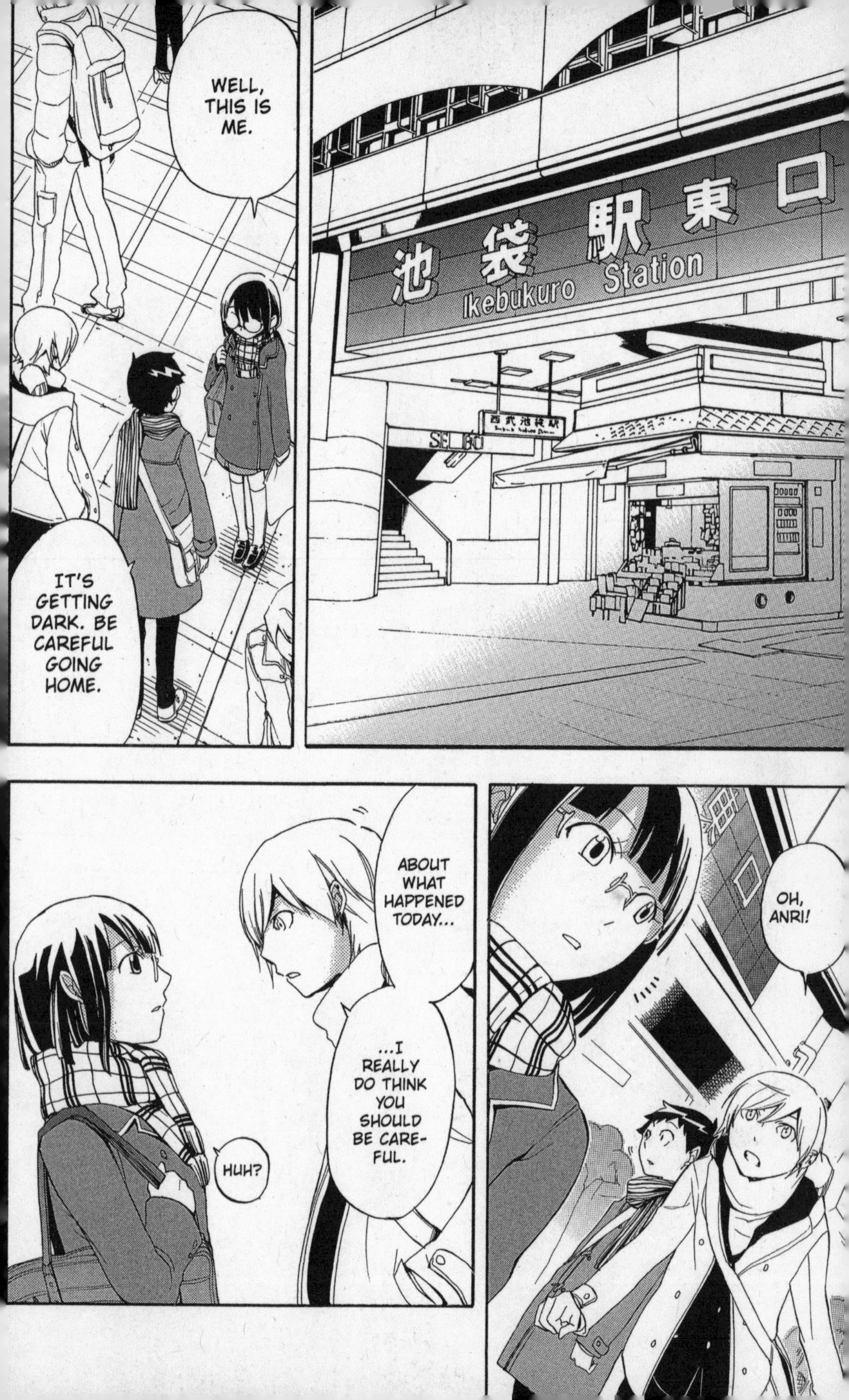
池袋駅東口
Ikebukuro Station
西武池袋駅
WELL, THIS IS ME.
IT'S GETTING DARK. BE CAREFUL GOING HOME.
OH, ANRI!
ABOUT WHAT HAPPENED TODAY...
...I REALLY DO THINK YOU SHOULD BE CARE-FUL.
HUH?

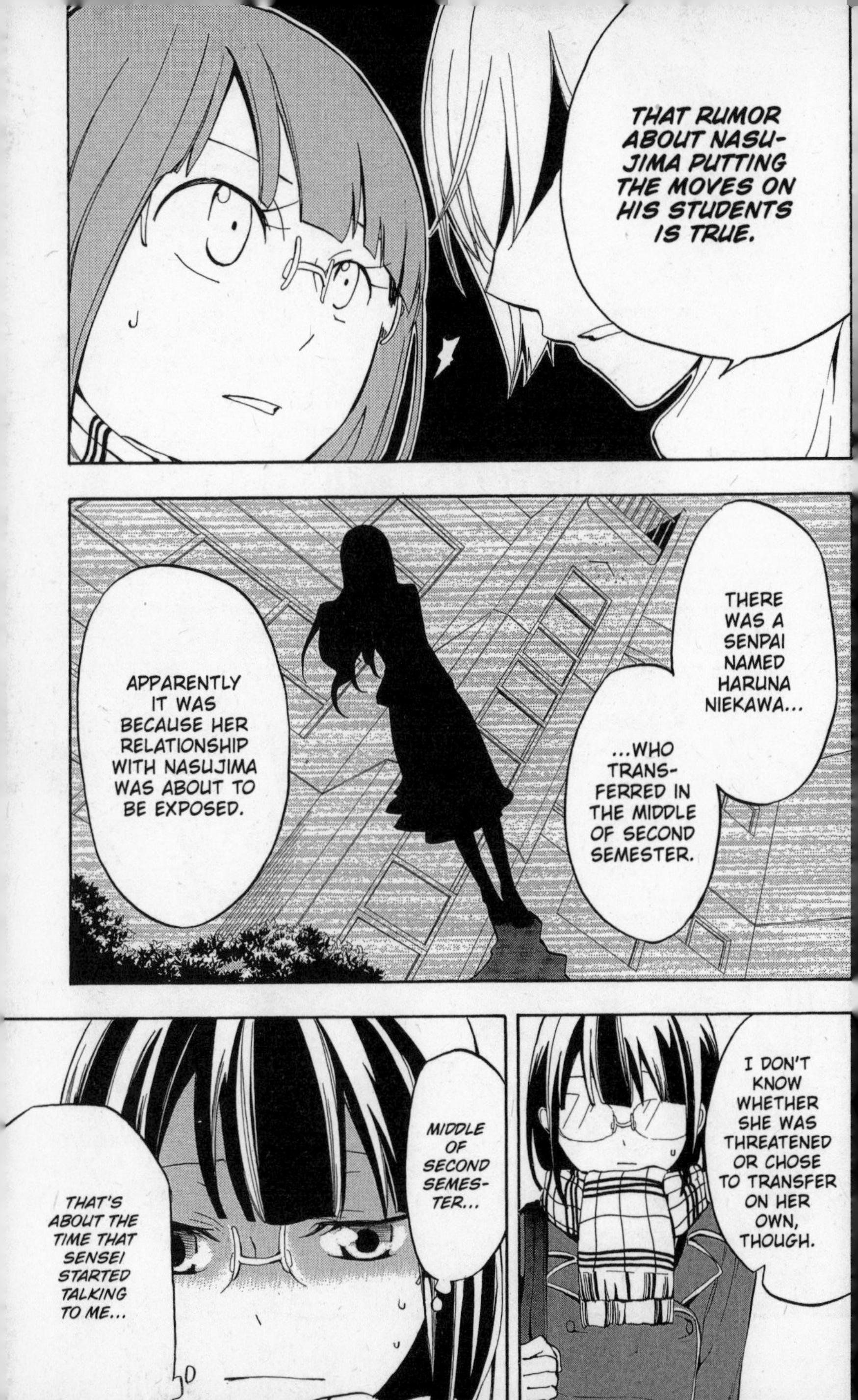
THAT RUMOR ABOUT NASUJIMA PUTTING THE MOVES ON HIS STUDENTS IS TRUE.
THERE WAS A SENPAI NAMED HARUNA NIEKAWA...
...WHO TRANSFERRED IN THE MIDDLE OF SECOND SEMESTER.
APPARENTLY IT WAS BECAUSE HER RELATIONSHIP WITH NASUJIMA WAS ABOUT TO BE EXPOSED.
I DON'T KNOW WHETHER SHE WAS THREATENED OR CHOSE TO TRANSFER ON HER OWN, THOUGH.
MIDDLE OF SECOND SEMESTER...
THAT'S ABOUT THE TIME THAT SENSEI STARTED TALKING TO ME...

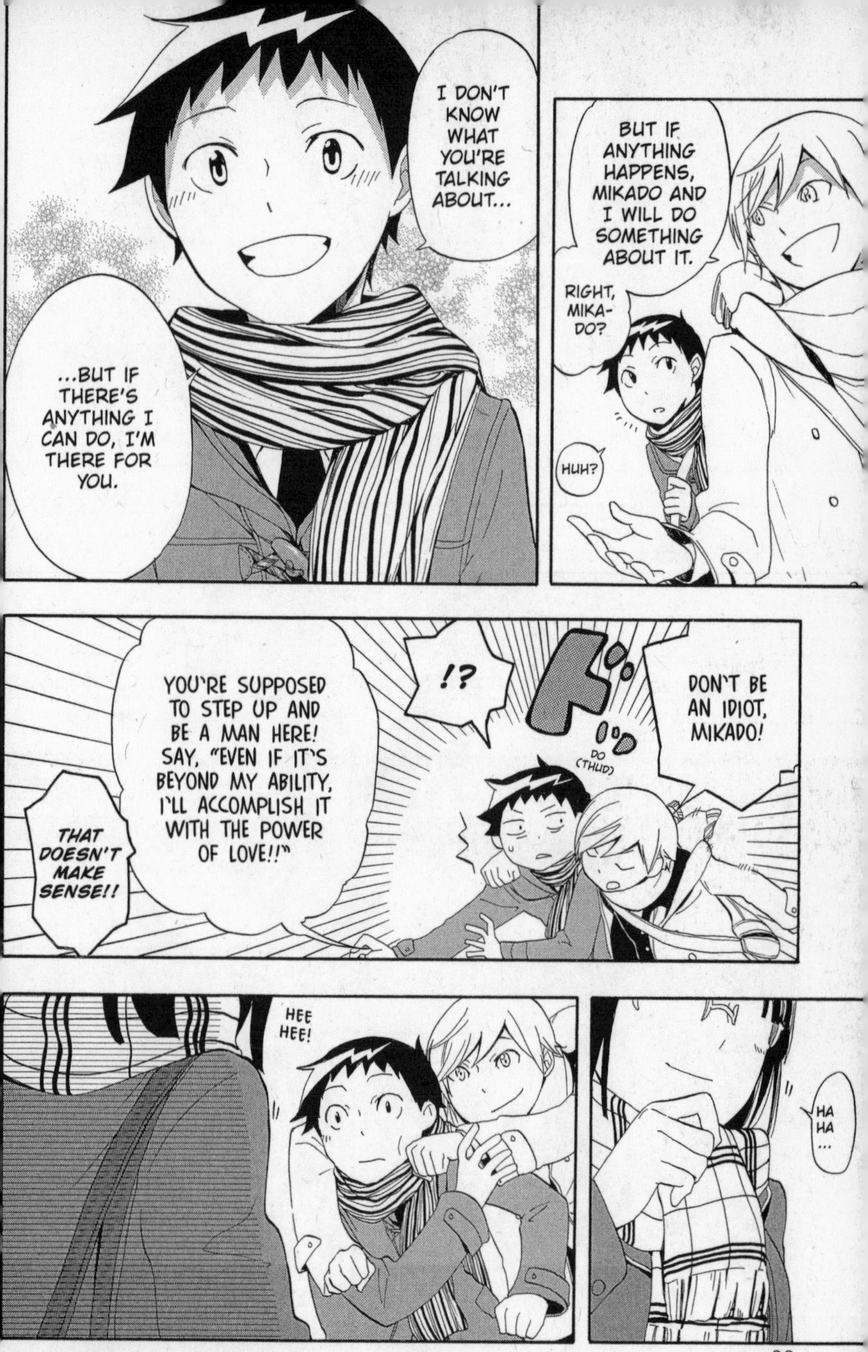
BUT IF ANYTHING HAPPENS, MIKADO AND I WILL DO SOMETHING ABOUT IT.
RIGHT, MIKA-DO?
HUH?
I DON'T KNOW WHAT YOU'RE TALKING ABOUT...
...BUT IF THERE'S ANYTHING I CAN DO, I'M THERE FOR YOU.
DON'T BE AN IDIOT, MIKADO!
DO (THUD)
!?
YOU'RE SUPPOSED TO STEP UP AND BE A MAN HERE! SAY, "EVEN IF IT'S BEYOND MY ABILITY, I'LL ACCOMPLISH IT WITH THE POWER OF LOVE!!"
THAT DOESN'T MAKE SENSE!!
HA HA ...
HEE HEE!

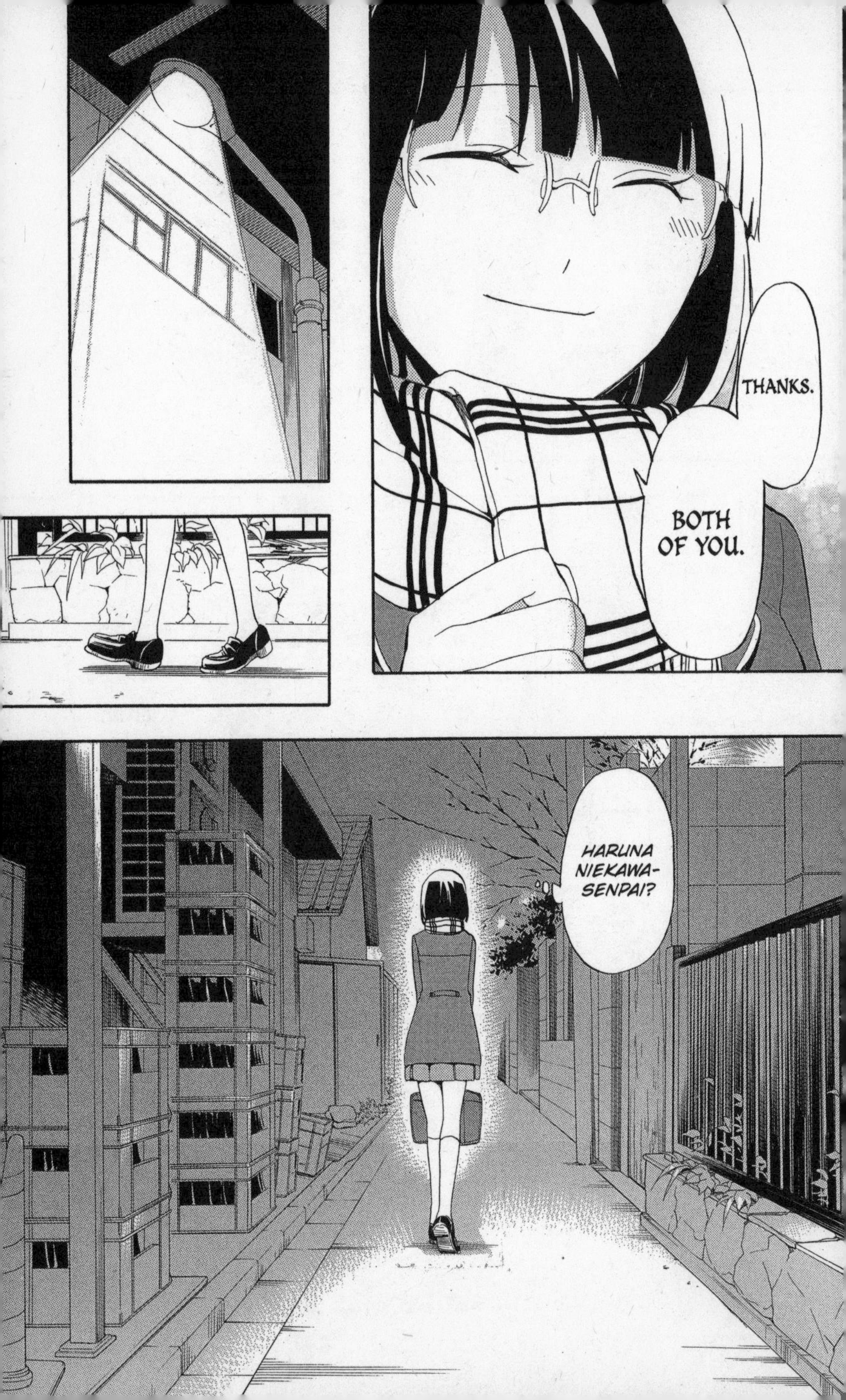
THANKS.
BOTH OF YOU.
HARUNA NIEKAWA-SENPAI?

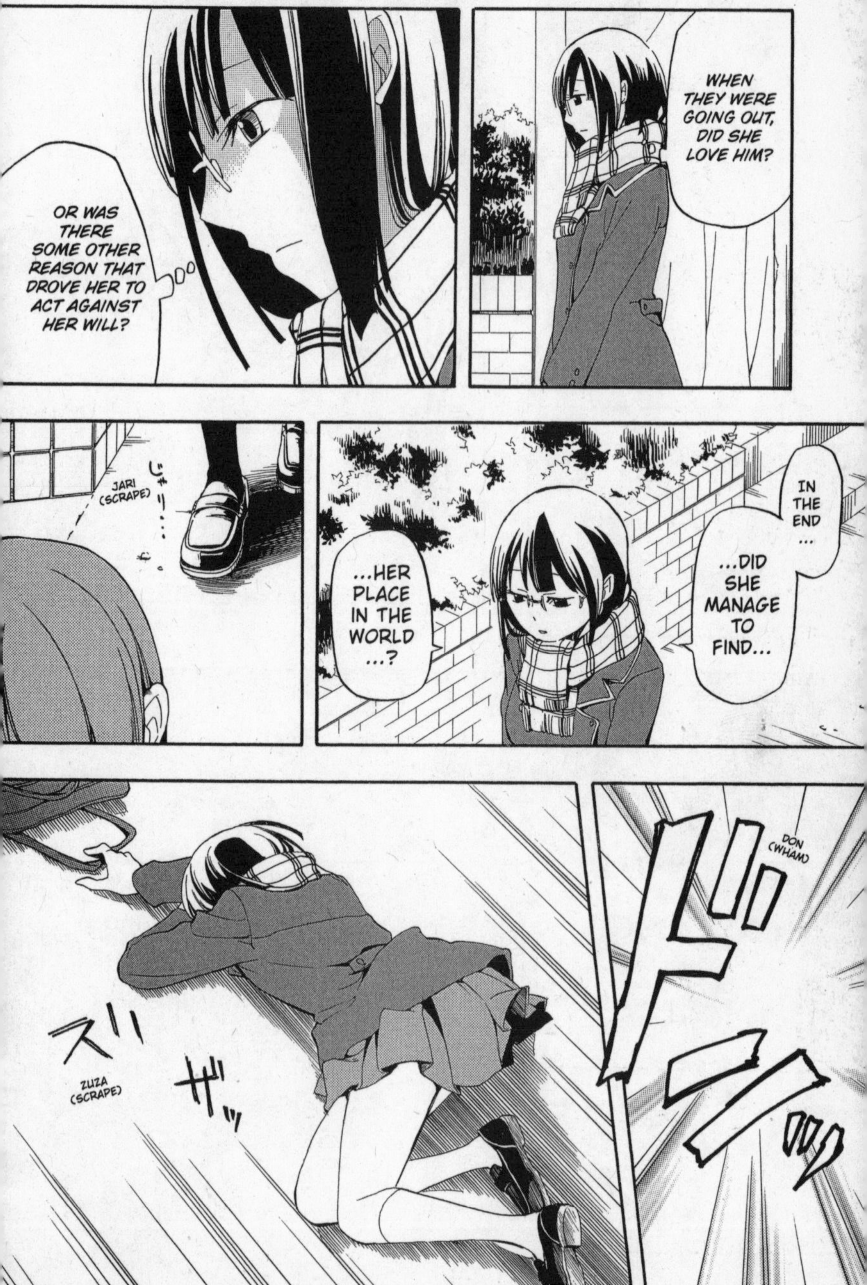
WHEN THEY WERE GOING OUT, DID SHE LOVE HIM?
OR WAS THERE SOME OTHER REASON THAT DROVE HER TO ACT AGAINST HER WILL?
IN THE END...
...DID SHE MANAGE TO FIND...
...HER PLACE IN THE WORLD...?
じゃり…
JARI (SCRAPE)
ドン
DON (WHAM)
ズザッ
ZUZA (SCRAPE)

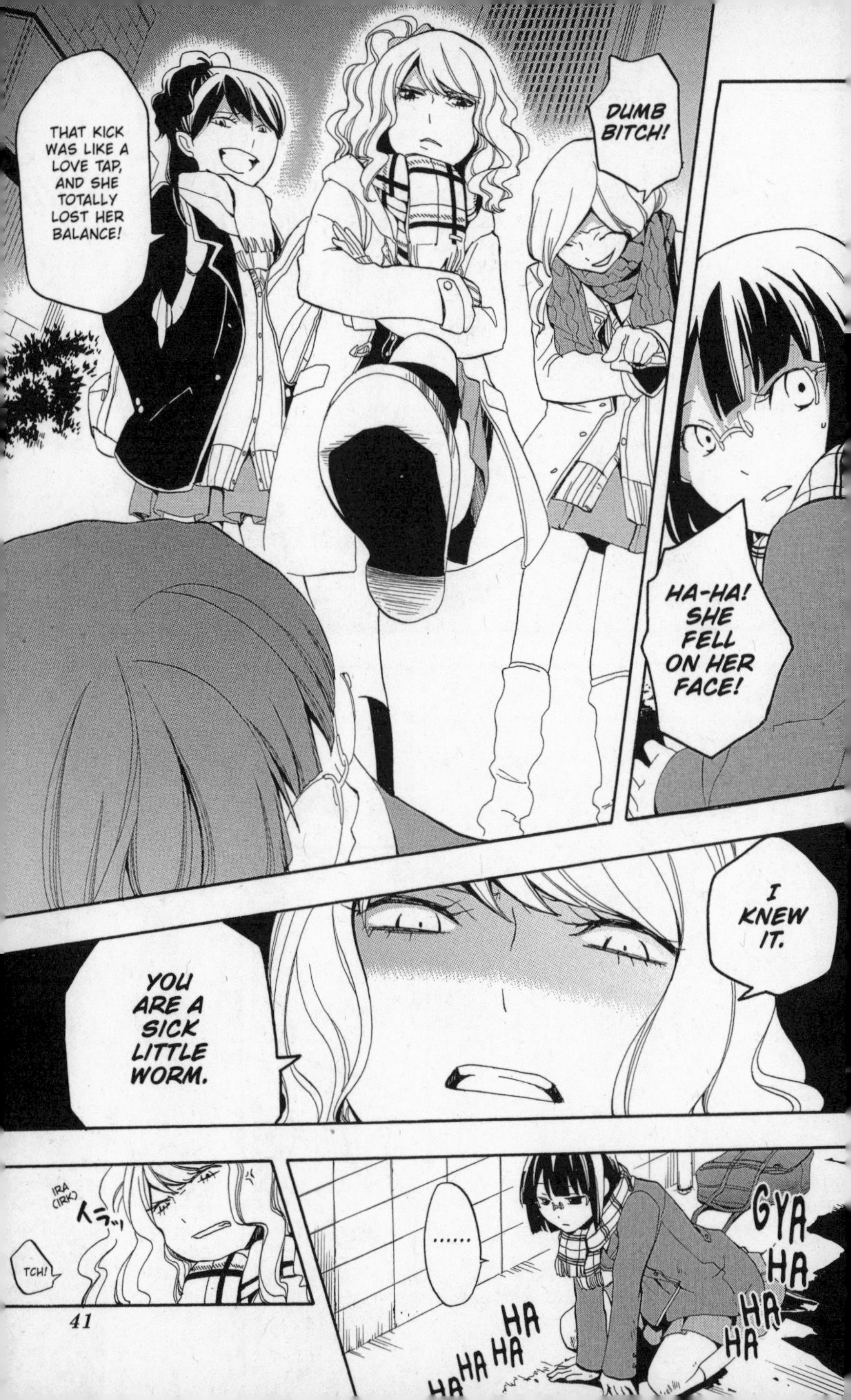
DUMB BITCH!
THAT KICK WAS LIKE A LOVE TAP, AND SHE TOTALLY LOST HER BALANCE!
HA-HA! SHE FELL ON HER FACE!
I KNEW IT.
YOU ARE A SICK LITTLE WORM.
GYA HA HA HA HA
HA HA HA HA HA
......
IRA (IRK)
TCH!

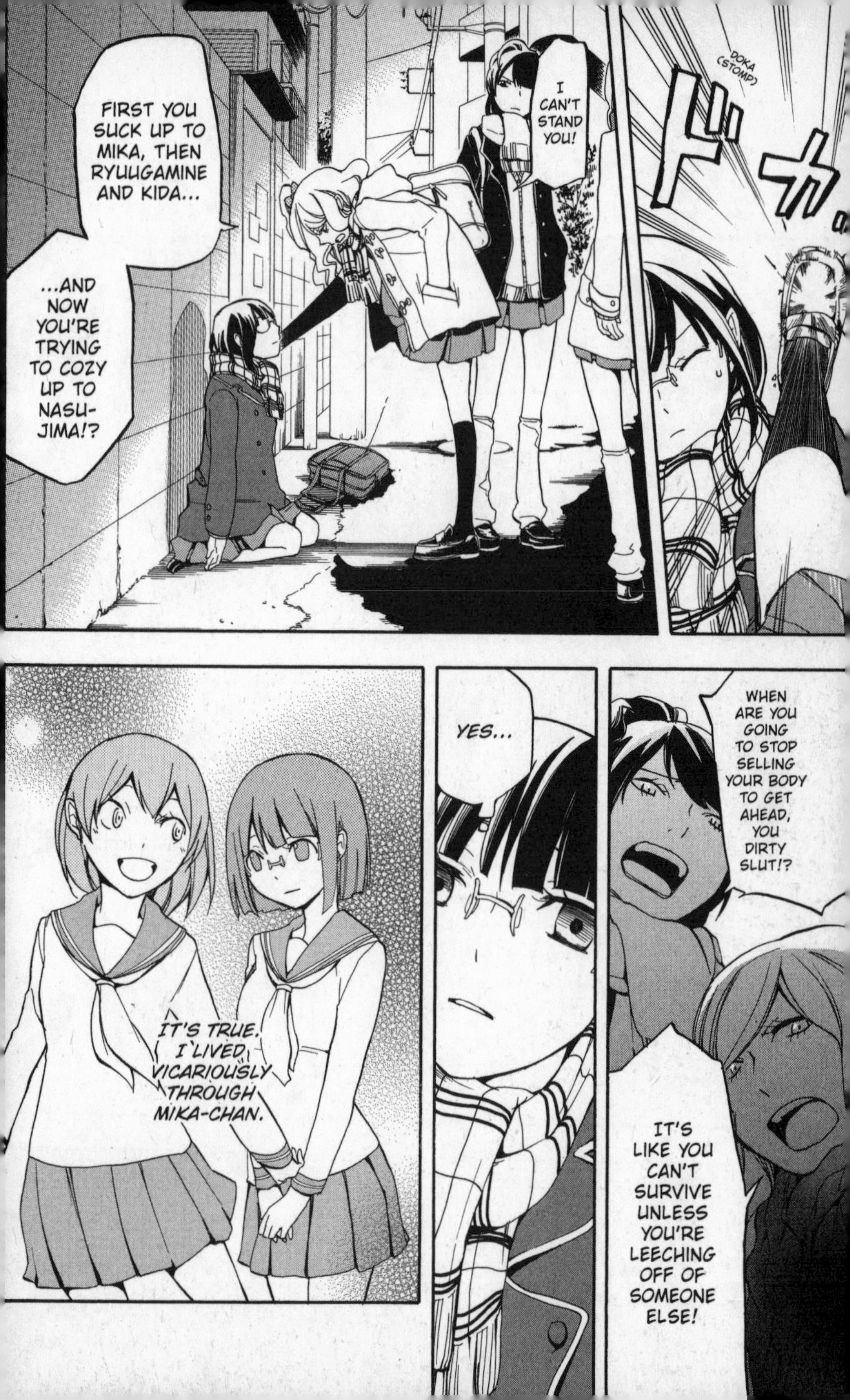
DOKA (STOMP)
I CAN'T STAND YOU!
FIRST YOU SUCK UP TO MIKA, THEN RYUUGAMINE AND KIDA...
...AND NOW YOU'RE TRYING TO COZY UP TO NASUJIMA!?
WHEN ARE YOU GOING TO STOP SELLING YOUR BODY TO GET AHEAD, YOU DIRTY SLUT!?
IT'S LIKE YOU CAN'T SURVIVE UNLESS YOU'RE LEECHING OFF OF SOMEONE ELSE!
YES...
IT'S TRUE. I LIVED VICARIOUSLY THROUGH MIKA-CHAN.

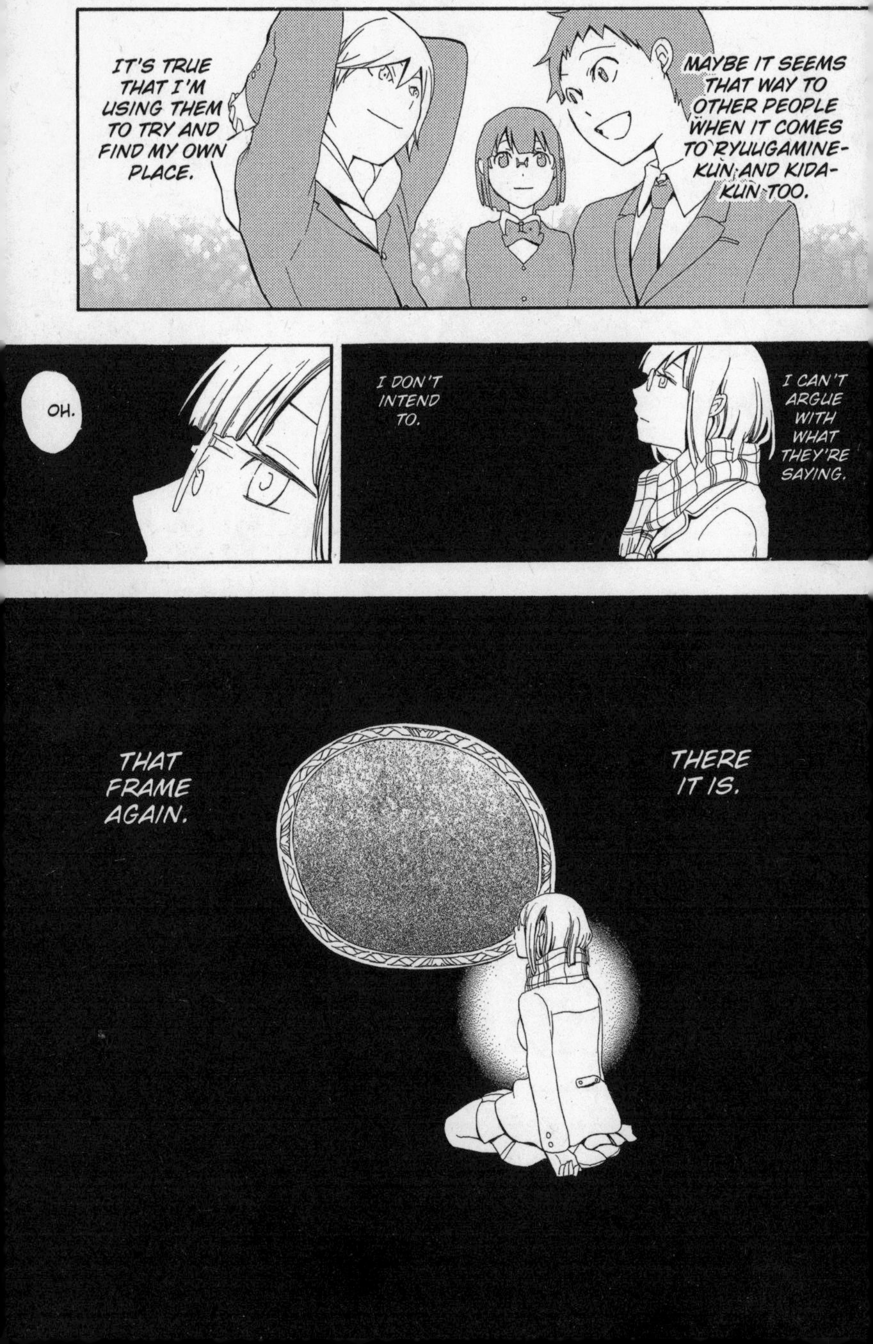
MAYBE IT SEEMS THAT WAY TO OTHER PEOPLE WHEN IT COMES TO RYUUGAMINE-KUN AND KIDA-KUN TOO.
IT'S TRUE THAT I'M USING THEM TO TRY AND FIND MY OWN PLACE.
I CAN'T ARGUE WITH WHAT THEY'RE SAYING.
I DON'T INTEND TO.
OH.
THERE IT IS.
THAT FRAME AGAIN.

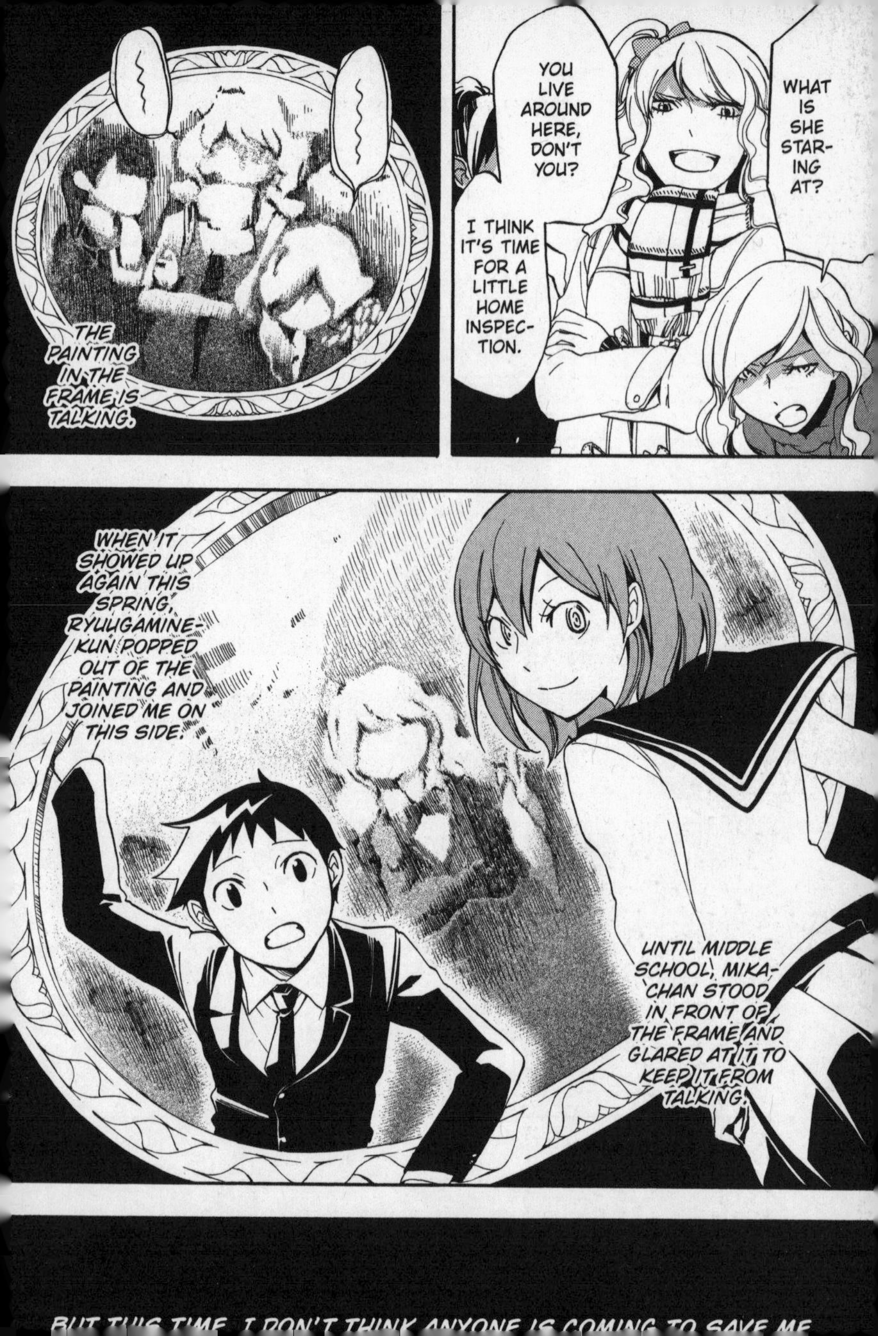
WHAT IS SHE STARING AT?
YOU LIVE AROUND HERE, DON'T YOU?
I THINK IT'S TIME FOR A LITTLE HOME INSPECTION.
THE PAINTING IN THE FRAME IS TALKING.
UNTIL MIDDLE SCHOOL, MIKA-CHAN STOOD IN FRONT OF THE FRAME AND GLARED AT IT TO KEEP IT FROM TALKING.
WHEN IT SHOWED UP AGAIN THIS SPRING, RYUUGAMINE-KUN POPPED OUT OF THE PAINTING AND JOINED ME ON THIS SIDE.
BUT THIS TIME, I DON'T THINK ANYONE IS COMING TO SAVE ME.

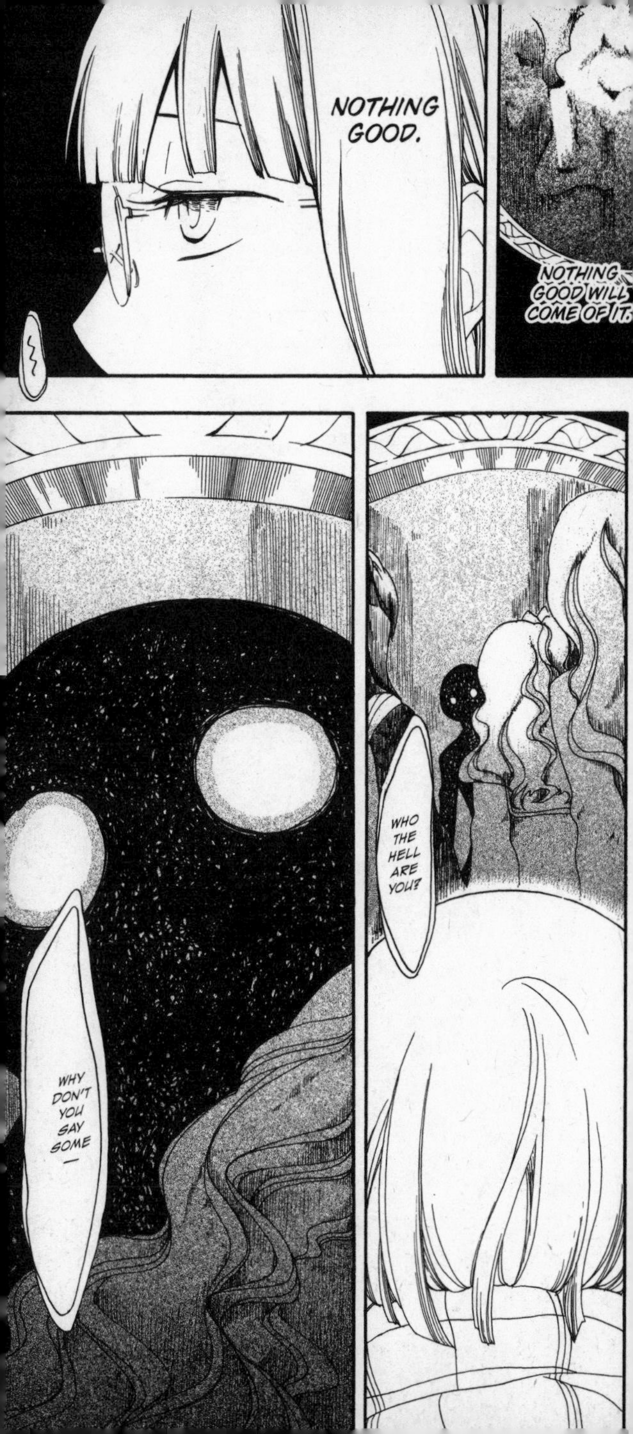
NOTHING GOOD WILL COME OF IT.
NOTHING GOOD.
WHO THE HELL ARE YOU?
WHY DON'T YOU SAY SOME—

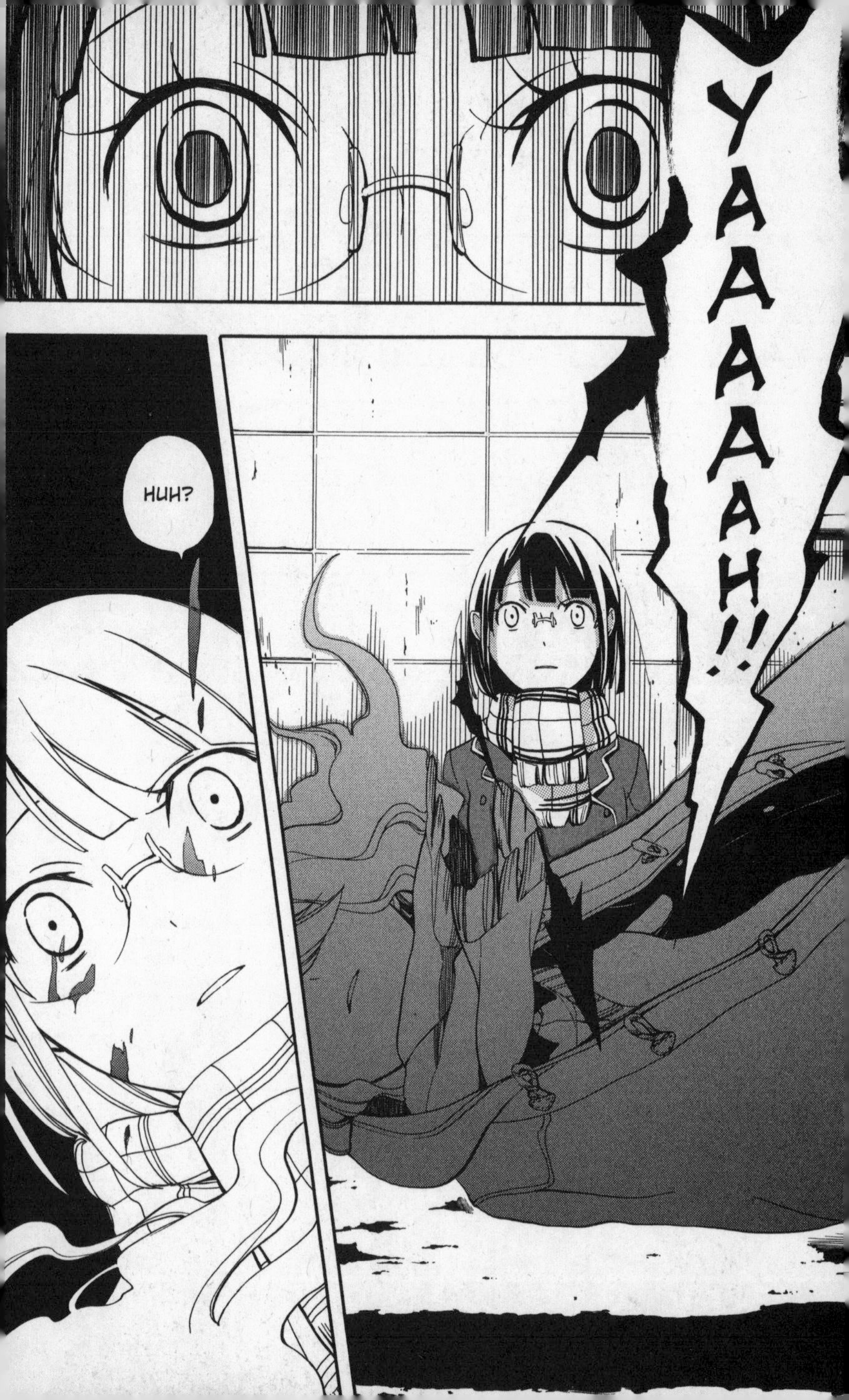
YAAAAAH!!!
HUH?

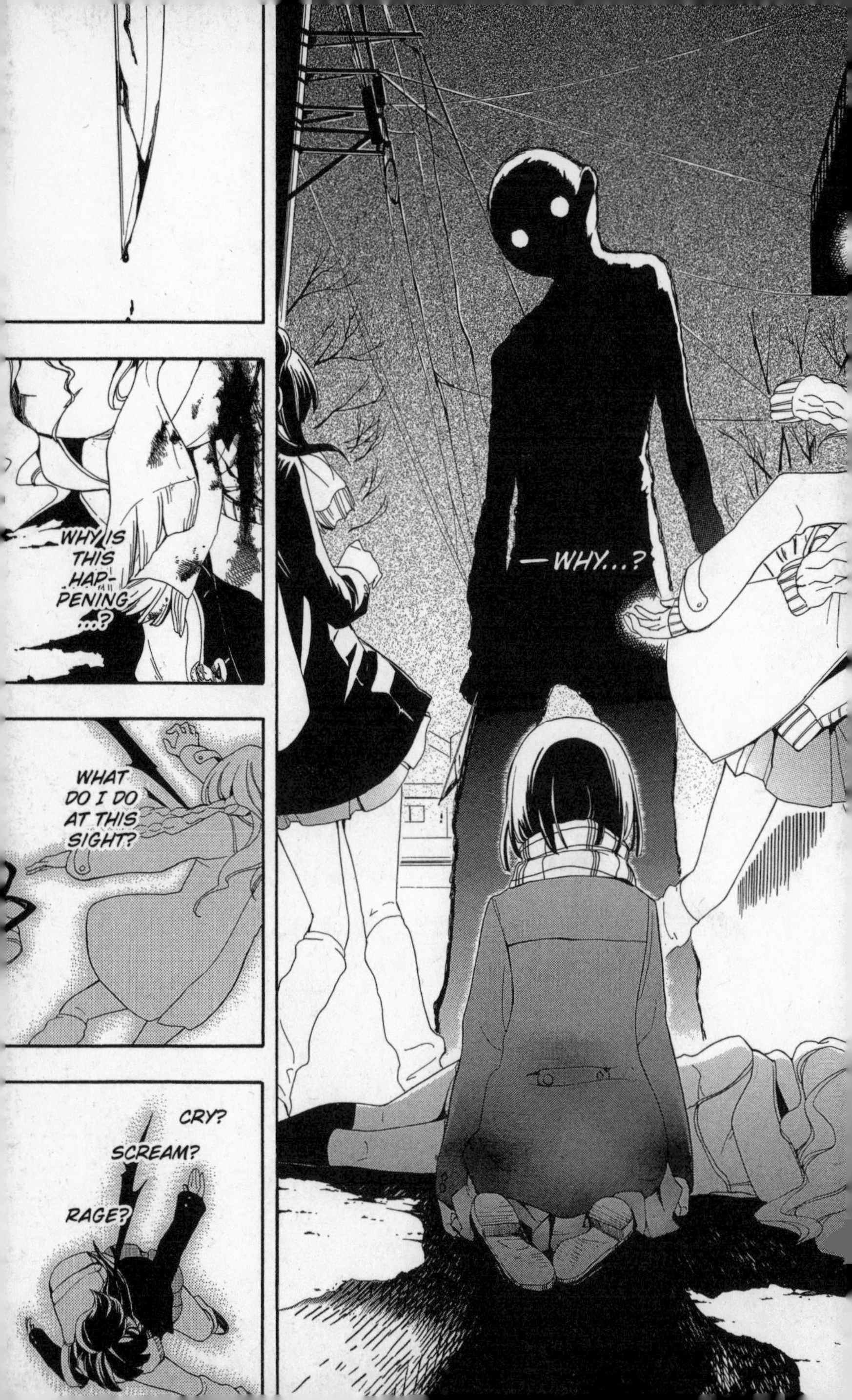
—WHY...?
WHY IS THIS HAPPENING ...?
WHAT DO I DO AT THIS SIGHT?
CRY?
SCREAM?
RAGE?

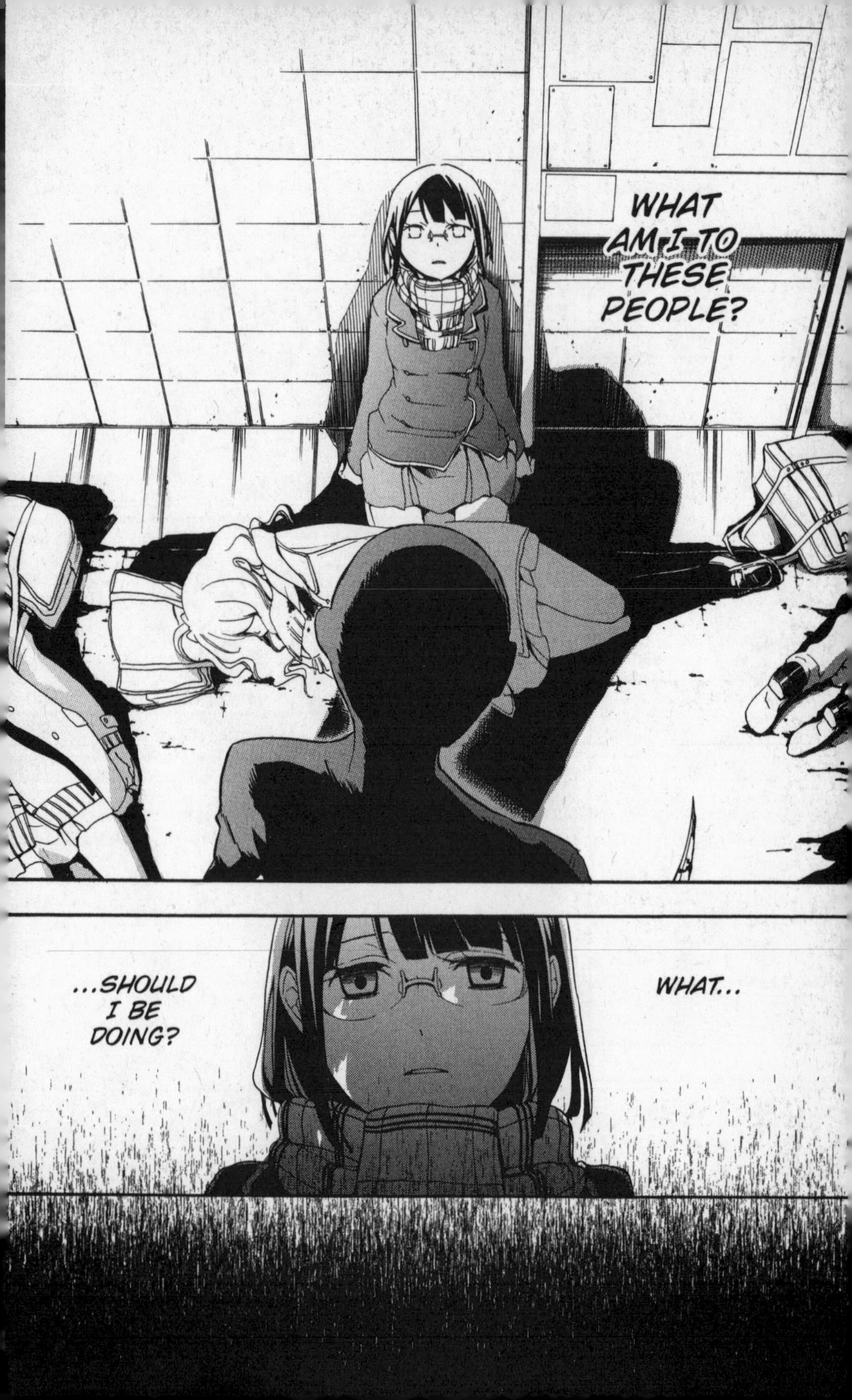
WHAT AM I TO THESE PEOPLE?
WHAT...
...SHOULD I BE DOING?

—SAIKA HAS ENTERED THE CHAT—

Saika: cut

Kanra: Hey, it's that troll again!
Go away! Hmph! (○｀ε´○)

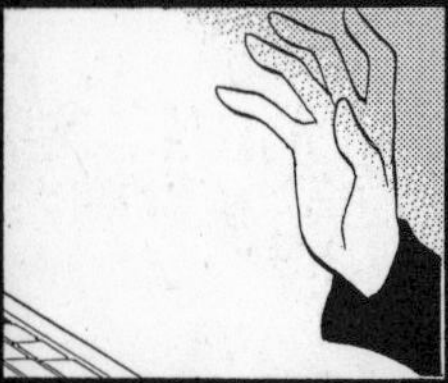

TarouTanaka: They've been trolling
other Ikebukuro
message boards too.

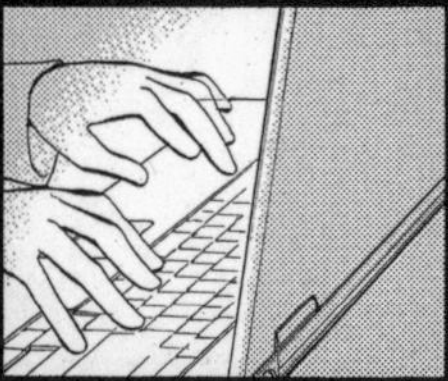

Saika: weak, wrong, rule, cannot

Kanra: Take that...There, I banned 'em.
Tee-hee☆

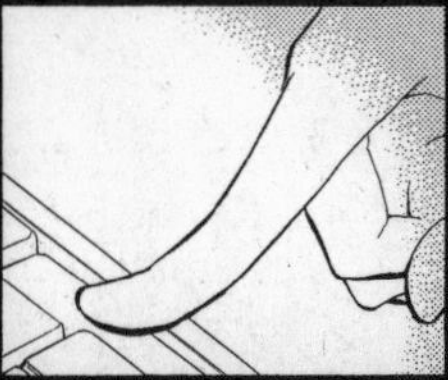

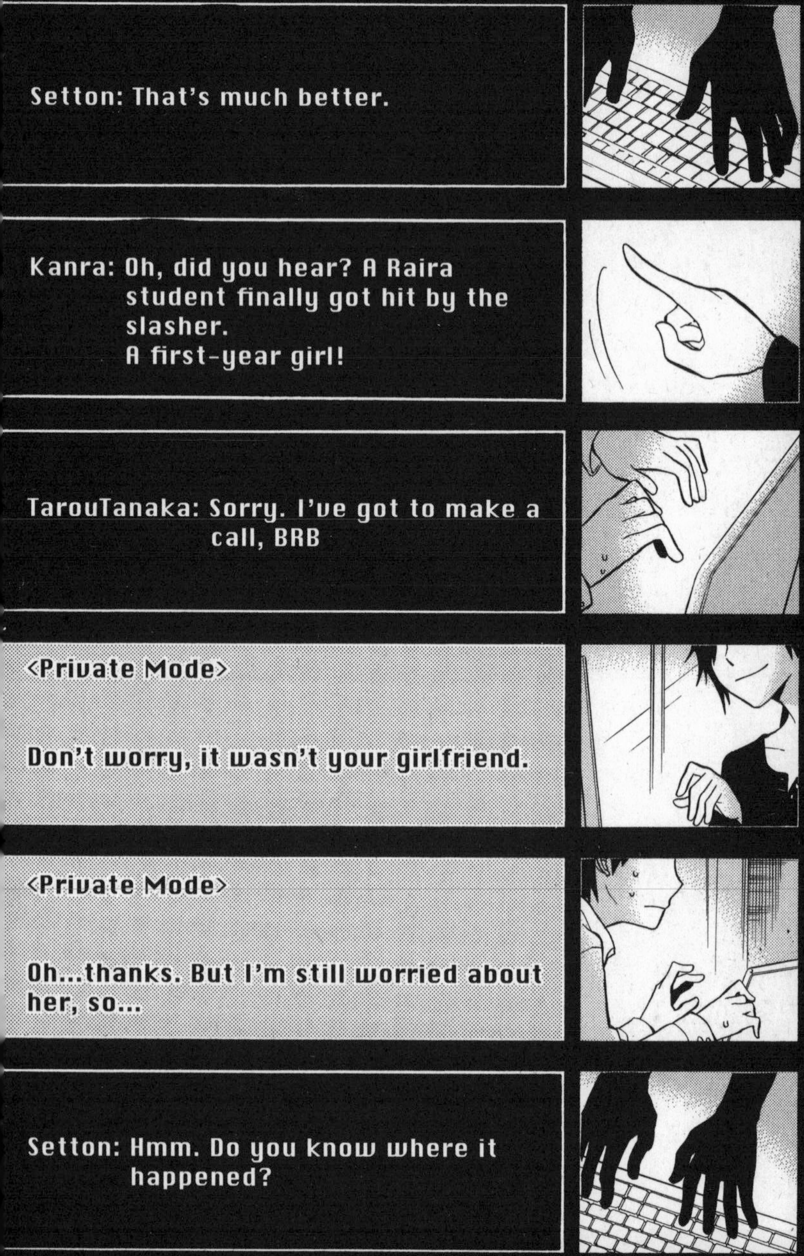
Setton: That's much better.
Kanra: Oh, did you hear? A Raira student finally got hit by the slasher. A first-year girl!
TarouTanaka: Sorry. I've got to make a call, BRB
<Private Mode>
Don't worry, it wasn't your girlfriend.
<Private Mode>
Oh...thanks. But I'm still worried about her, so...
Setton: Hmm. Do you know where it happened?

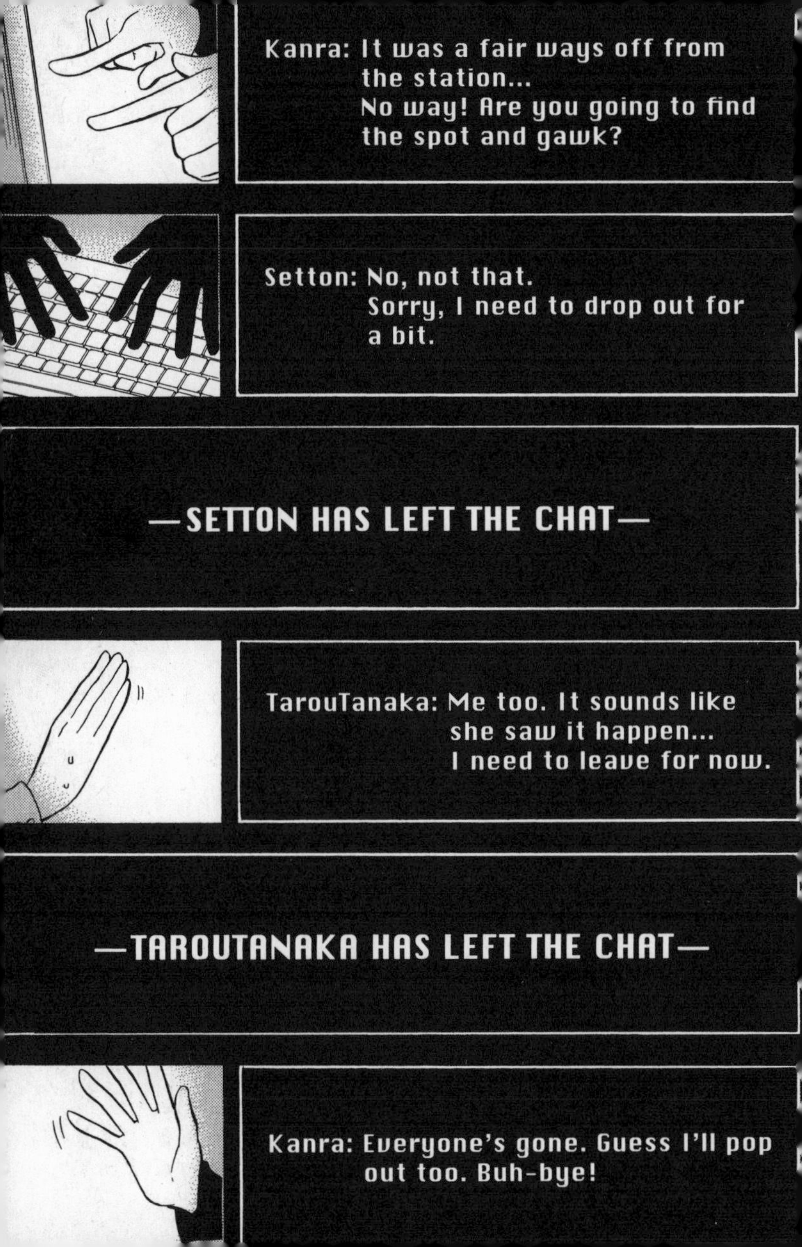
Kanra: It was a fair ways off from the station... No way! Are you going to find the spot and gawk?
Setton: No, not that. Sorry, I need to drop out for a bit.
—SETTON HAS LEFT THE CHAT—
TarouTanaka: Me too. It sounds like she saw it happen... I need to leave for now.
—TAROUTANAKA HAS LEFT THE CHAT—
Kanra: Everyone's gone. Guess I'll pop out too. Buh-bye!

—KANRA HAS LEFT THE CHAT—

—THERE ARE CURRENTLY NO USERS IN THE CHAT ROOM—

—SAIKA HAS ENTERED THE CHAT—

Saika: love, human, strong, who

Saika: wish, me, mother, mother

Saika: mothermothermothermother
mothermothermothermother
mothermothermothermother
mothermothermothermother

nothermothermothermothermothermothermother
nothermothermothermothermothermothermother
nothermothermothermothermothermothermother
nothermothermothermothermothermothermother
nothermothermothermothermothermothermother
nothermothermothermothermothermothermother
nothermothermothermothermothermothermother
nothermothermothermothermothermothermother
nothermothermothermothermothermothermother
nothermothermothermothermothermothermother
nothermothermothermothermothermothermother
nothermothermothermothermothermothermother
nothermothermothermothermothermothermother
nothermothermothermothermothermothermother
nothermothermothermothermothermothermother
nothermothermothermothermothermothermother
nothermothermothermothermothermothermother
nothermothermothermothermothermothermother
nothermothermothermothermothermothermother
nothermothermothermothermothermothermother
nothermothermothermothermothermothermother
nothermothermothermothermothermothermother
nothermothermothermothermothermothermother
nothermothermothermothermothermothermother
nothermothermothermothermothermothermother
nothermothermothermothermothermothermother
nothermothermothermothermothermothermother
nothermothermothermothermothermothermother
nothermothermothermothermothermothermother
nothermothermothermothermothermothermother
nothermothermothermothermothermothermother
nothermothermothermothermothermothermother
nothermothermothermothermothermothermother
nothermothermothermothermothermothermother
nothermothermothermothermothermothermother
nothermothermothermothermothermothermother
nothermothermothermothermothermothermother
nothermothermothermothermothermothermother
nothermothermothermothermothermothermother
nothermothermothermothermothermothermother
nothermothermothermothermothermothermother
nothermothermothermothermothermothermother
nothermothermothermothermothermothermother
nothermothermothermothermothermothermother
nothermothermothermothermothermothermother
nothermothermothermothermothermothermother
nothermothermothermothermothermothermother
nothermothermothermothermothermothermother
nothermothermothermothermothermothermother
nothermothermothermothermothermothermother

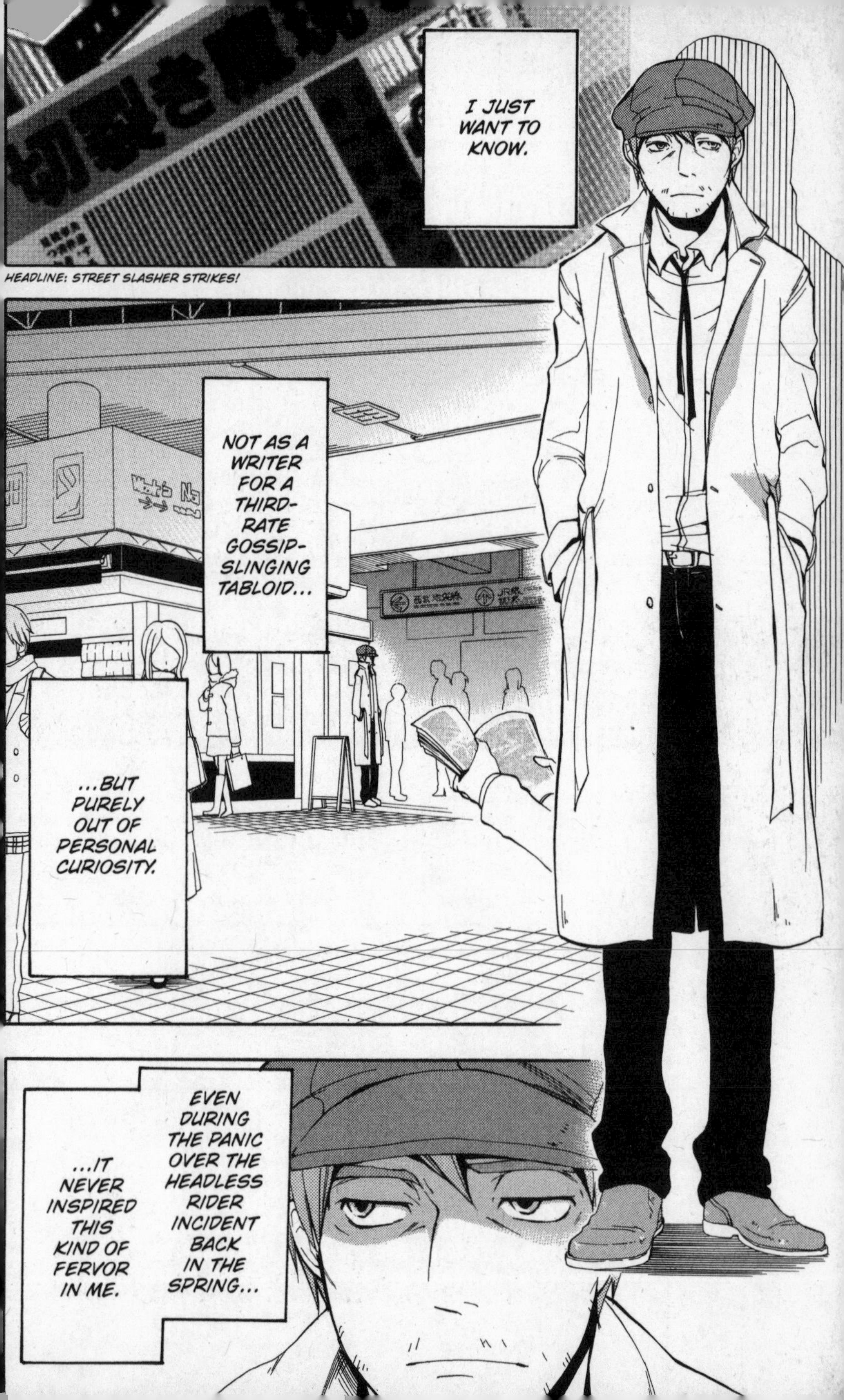
I JUST WANT TO KNOW.
HEADLINE: STREET SLASHER STRIKES!
NOT AS A WRITER FOR A THIRD-RATE GOSSIP-SLINGING TABLOID...
...BUT PURELY OUT OF PERSONAL CURIOSITY.
EVEN DURING THE PANIC OVER THE HEADLESS RIDER INCIDENT BACK IN THE SPRING...
...IT NEVER INSPIRED THIS KIND OF FERVOR IN ME.

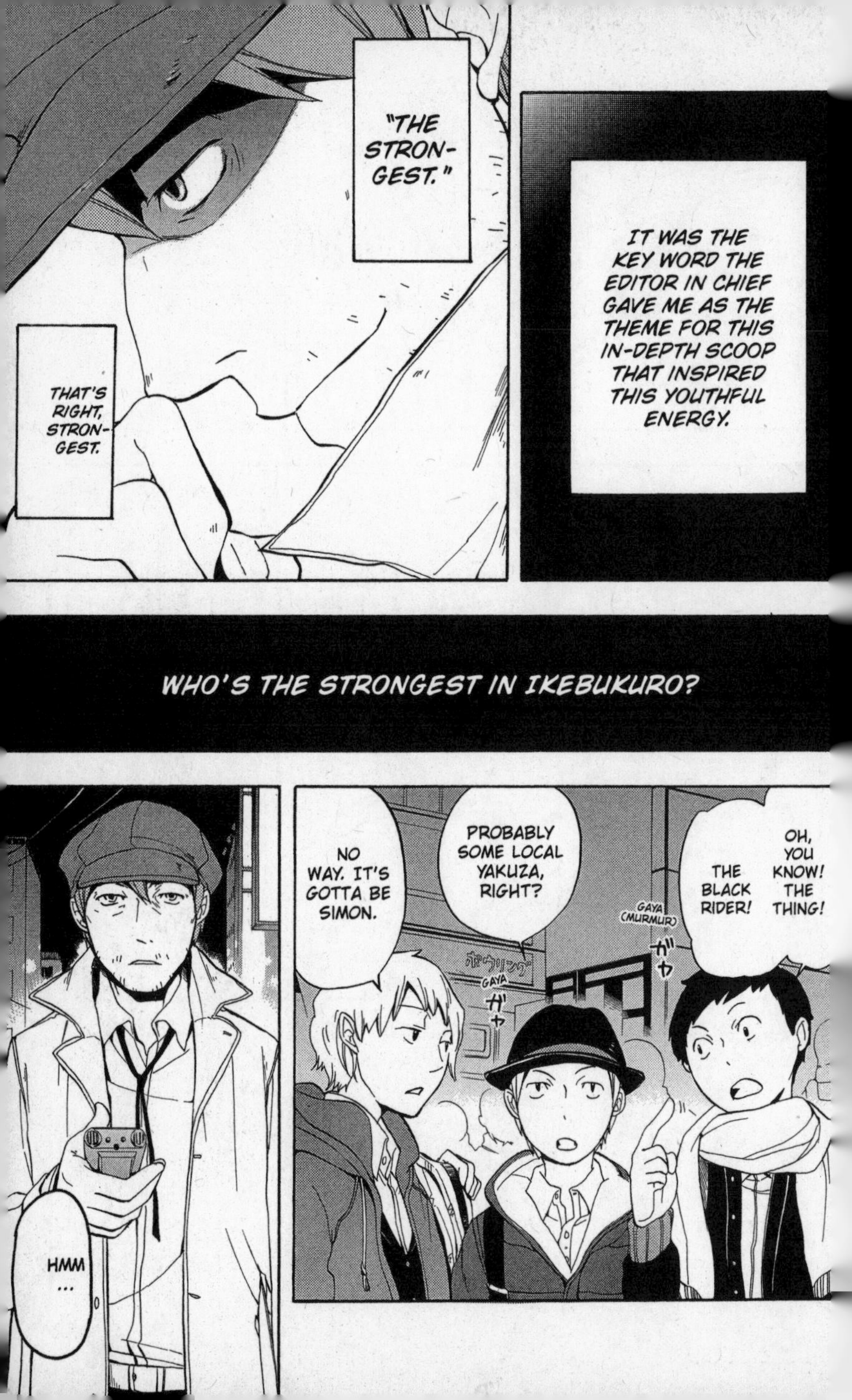
IT WAS THE KEY WORD THE EDITOR IN CHIEF GAVE ME AS THE THEME FOR THIS IN-DEPTH SCOOP THAT INSPIRED THIS YOUTHFUL ENERGY.
"THE STRONGEST."
THAT'S RIGHT, STRONGEST.
WHO'S THE STRONGEST IN IKEBUKURO?
OH, YOU KNOW! THE THING!
THE BLACK RIDER!
GAYA (MURMUR)
ガヤ
PROBABLY SOME LOCAL YAKUZA, RIGHT?
GAYA
ガヤ
NO WAY. IT'S GOTTA BE SIMON.
HMM...

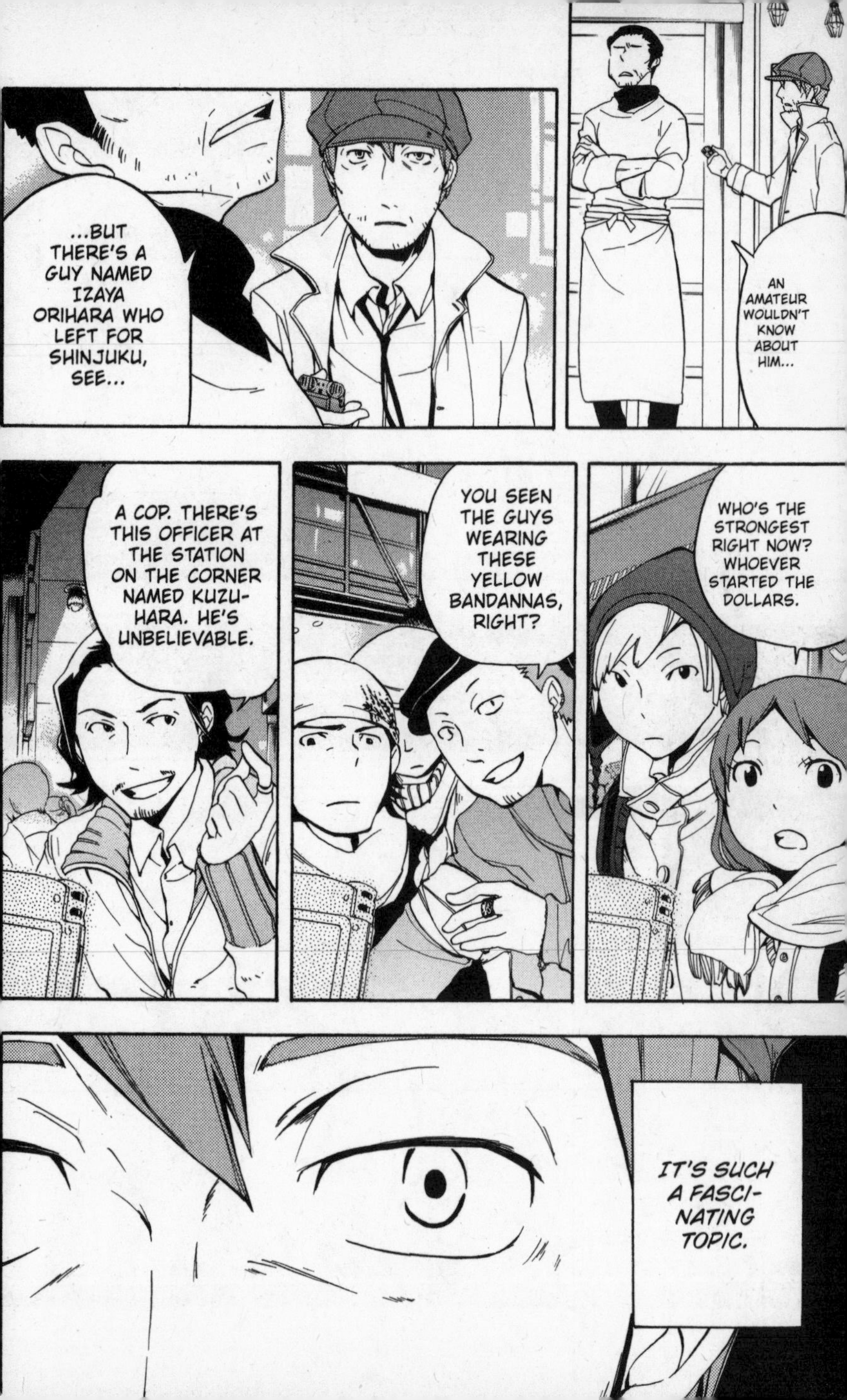
AN AMATEUR WOULDN'T KNOW ABOUT HIM...
...BUT THERE'S A GUY NAMED IZAYA ORIHARA WHO LEFT FOR SHINJUKU, SEE...
WHO'S THE STRONGEST RIGHT NOW? WHOEVER STARTED THE DOLLARS.
YOU SEEN THE GUYS WEARING THESE YELLOW BANDANNAS, RIGHT?
A COP. THERE'S THIS OFFICER AT THE STATION ON THE CORNER NAMED KUZU-HARA. HE'S UNBELIEVABLE.
IT'S SUCH A FASCI-NATING TOPIC.

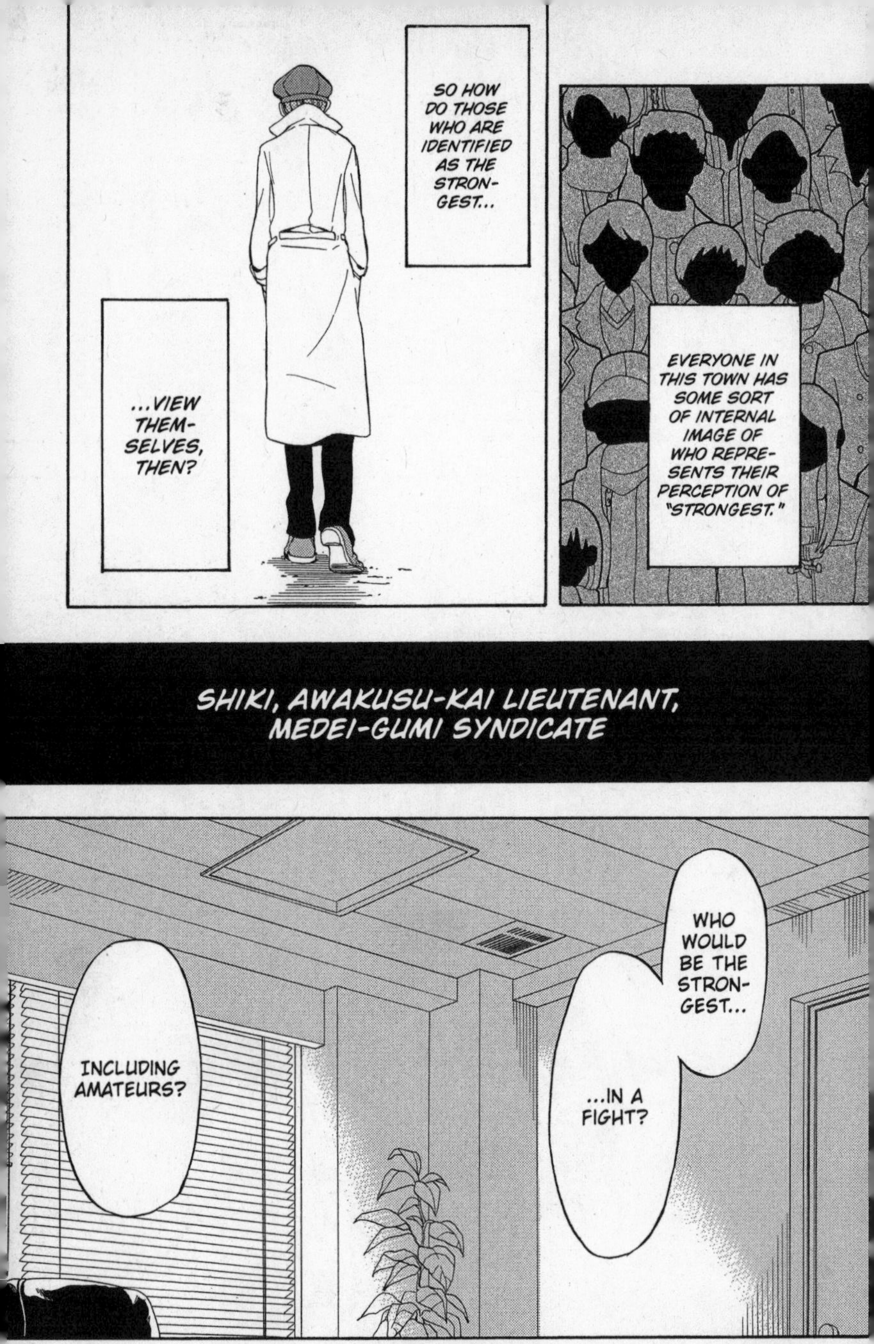
EVERYONE IN THIS TOWN HAS SOME SORT OF INTERNAL IMAGE OF WHO REPRESENTS THEIR PERCEPTION OF "STRONGEST."
SO HOW DO THOSE WHO ARE IDENTIFIED AS THE STRONGEST...
...VIEW THEMSELVES, THEN?
SHIKI, AWAKUSU-KAI LIEUTENANT, MEDEI-GUMI SYNDICATE
WHO WOULD BE THE STRONGEST...
...IN A FIGHT?
INCLUDING AMATEURS?

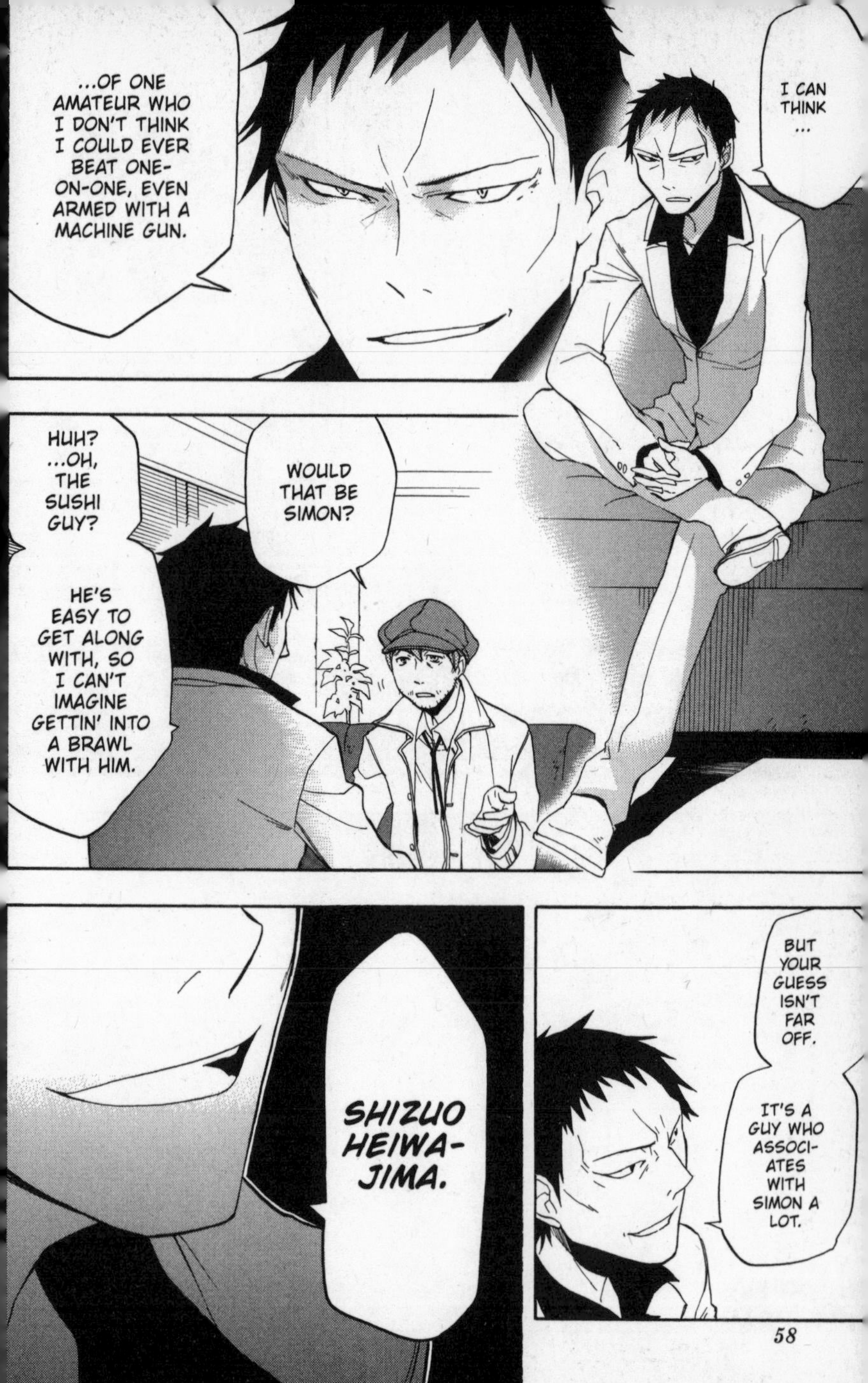
I CAN THINK ...
...OF ONE AMATEUR WHO I DON'T THINK I COULD EVER BEAT ONE-ON-ONE, EVEN ARMED WITH A MACHINE GUN.
WOULD THAT BE SIMON?
HUH? ...OH, THE SUSHI GUY?
HE'S EASY TO GET ALONG WITH, SO I CAN'T IMAGINE GETTIN' INTO A BRAWL WITH HIM.
BUT YOUR GUESS ISN'T FAR OFF.
IT'S A GUY WHO ASSOCIATES WITH SIMON A LOT.
SHIZUO HEIWAJIMA.

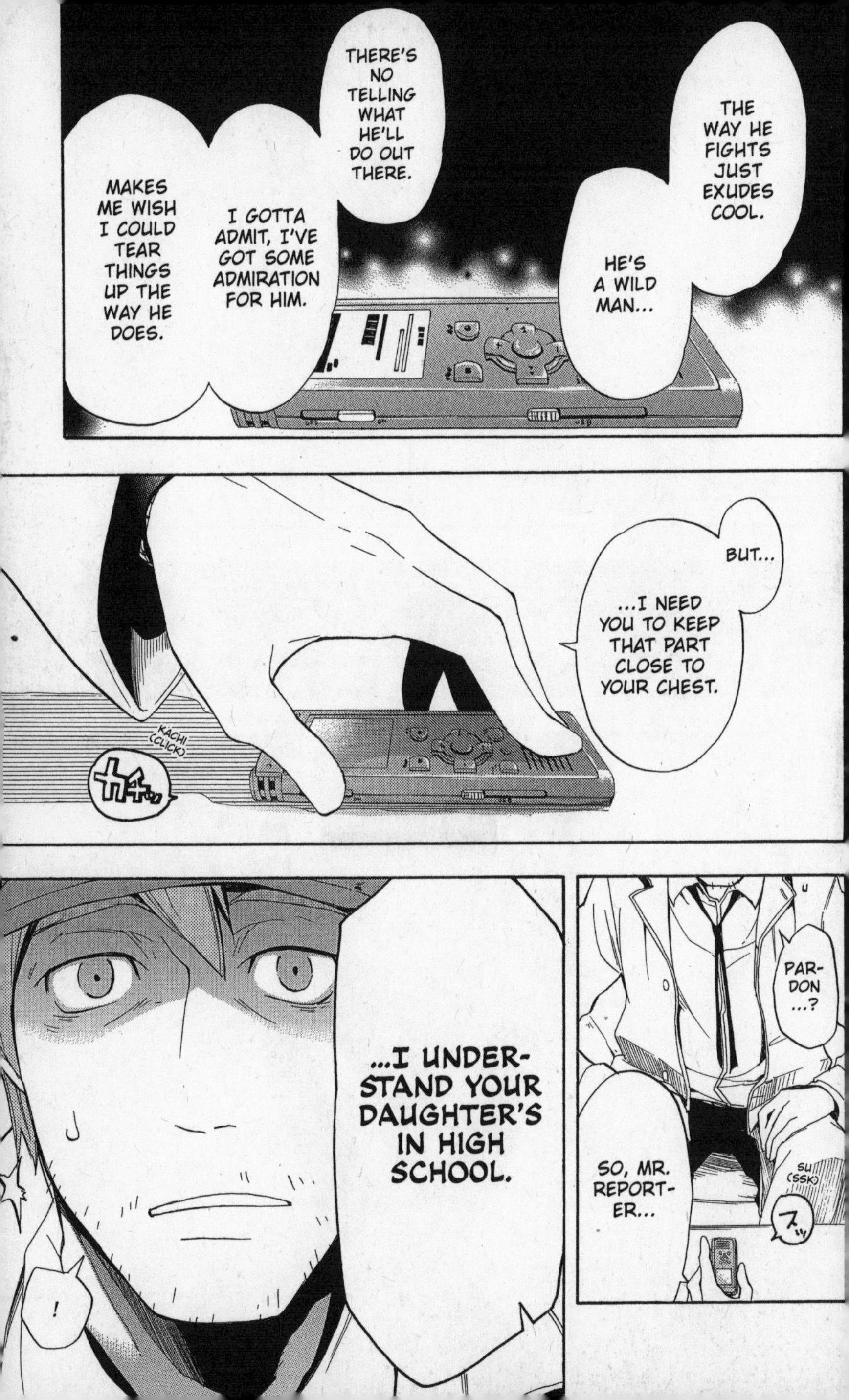
THE WAY HE FIGHTS JUST EXUDES COOL.
HE'S A WILD MAN...
THERE'S NO TELLING WHAT HE'LL DO OUT THERE.
I GOTTA ADMIT, I'VE GOT SOME ADMIRATION FOR HIM.
MAKES ME WISH I COULD TEAR THINGS UP THE WAY HE DOES.
BUT...
...I NEED YOU TO KEEP THAT PART CLOSE TO YOUR CHEST.
KACHI (CLICK)
PAR-DON ...?
SU (SSK)
SO, MR. REPORT-ER...
...I UNDER-STAND YOUR DAUGHTER'S IN HIGH SCHOOL.
!

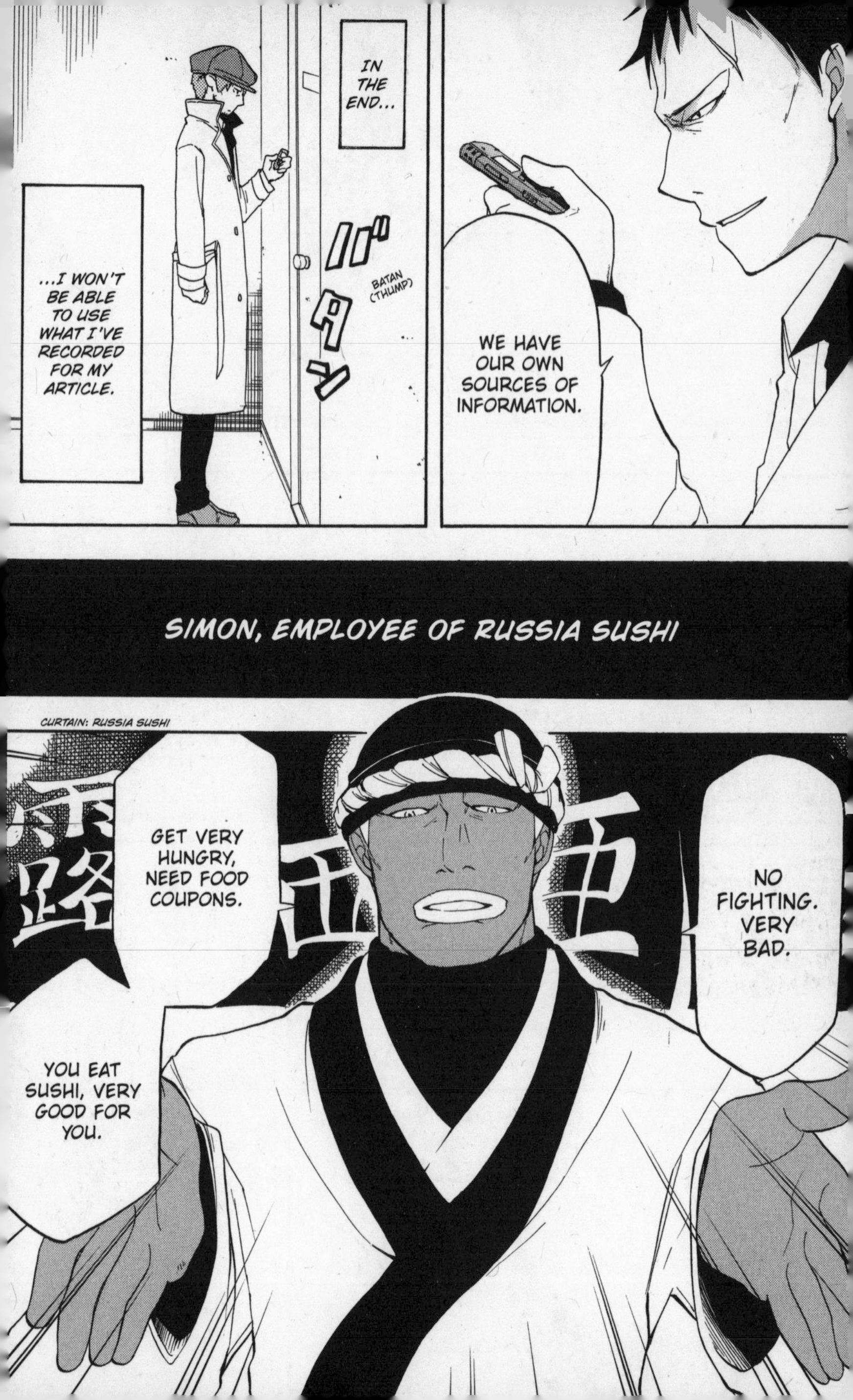
WE HAVE OUR OWN SOURCES OF INFORMATION.
IN THE END...
BATAN (THUMP)
...I WON'T BE ABLE TO USE WHAT I'VE RECORDED FOR MY ARTICLE.
SIMON, EMPLOYEE OF RUSSIA SUSHI
CURTAIN: RUSSIA SUSHI
NO FIGHTING. VERY BAD.
GET VERY HUNGRY, NEED FOOD COUPONS.
YOU EAT SUSHI, VERY GOOD FOR YOU.

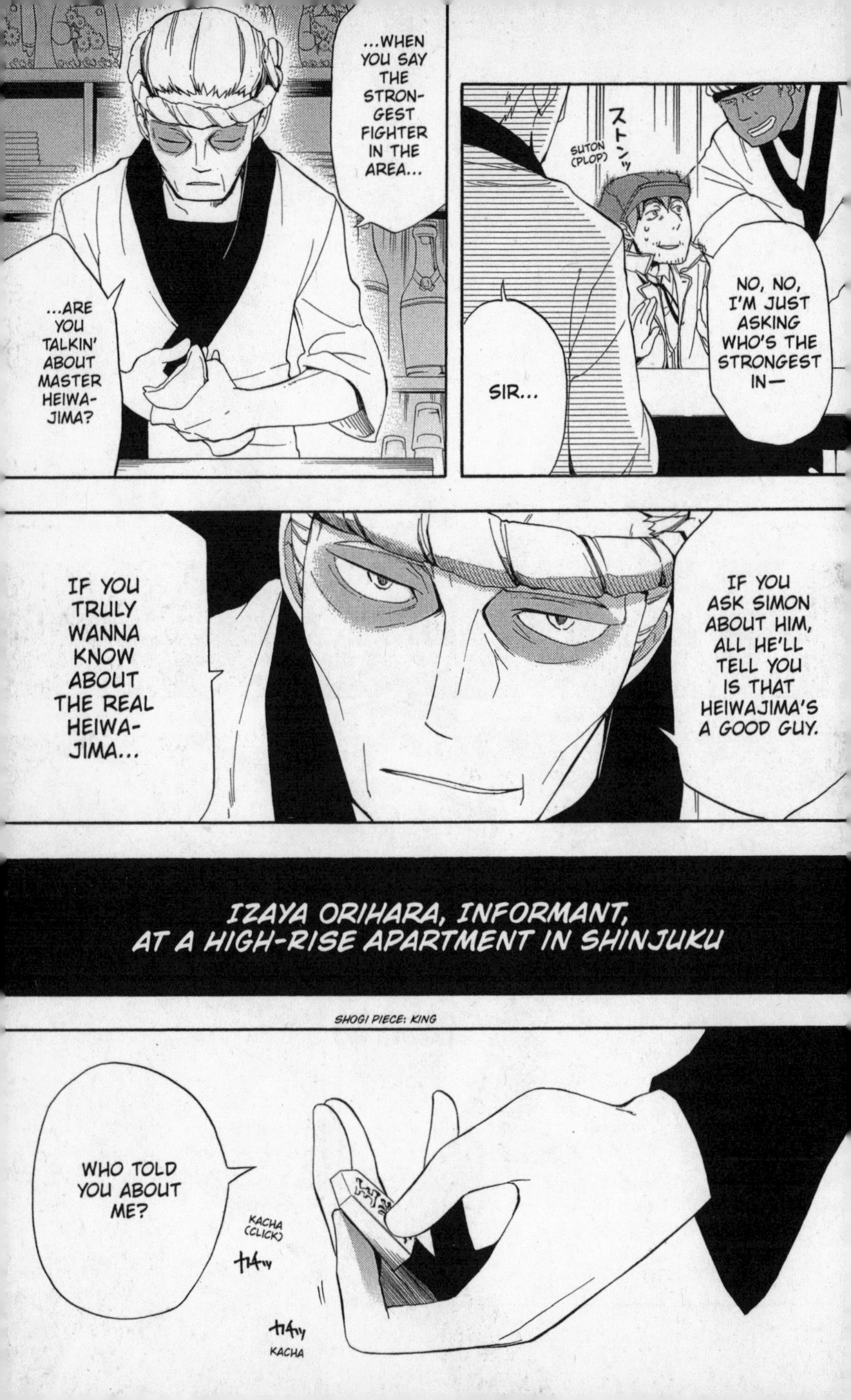
ストンッ
SUTON (PLOP)
NO, NO, I'M JUST ASKING WHO'S THE STRONGEST IN—
SIR...
...WHEN YOU SAY THE STRONGEST FIGHTER IN THE AREA...
...ARE YOU TALKIN' ABOUT MASTER HEIWAJIMA?
IF YOU ASK SIMON ABOUT HIM, ALL HE'LL TELL YOU IS THAT HEIWAJIMA'S A GOOD GUY.
IF YOU TRULY WANNA KNOW ABOUT THE REAL HEIWAJIMA...
IZAYA ORIHARA, INFORMANT, AT A HIGH-RISE APARTMENT IN SHINJUKU
SHOGI PIECE: KING
WHO TOLD YOU ABOUT ME?
KACHA (CLICK)
カチャッ
カチャッ
KACHA

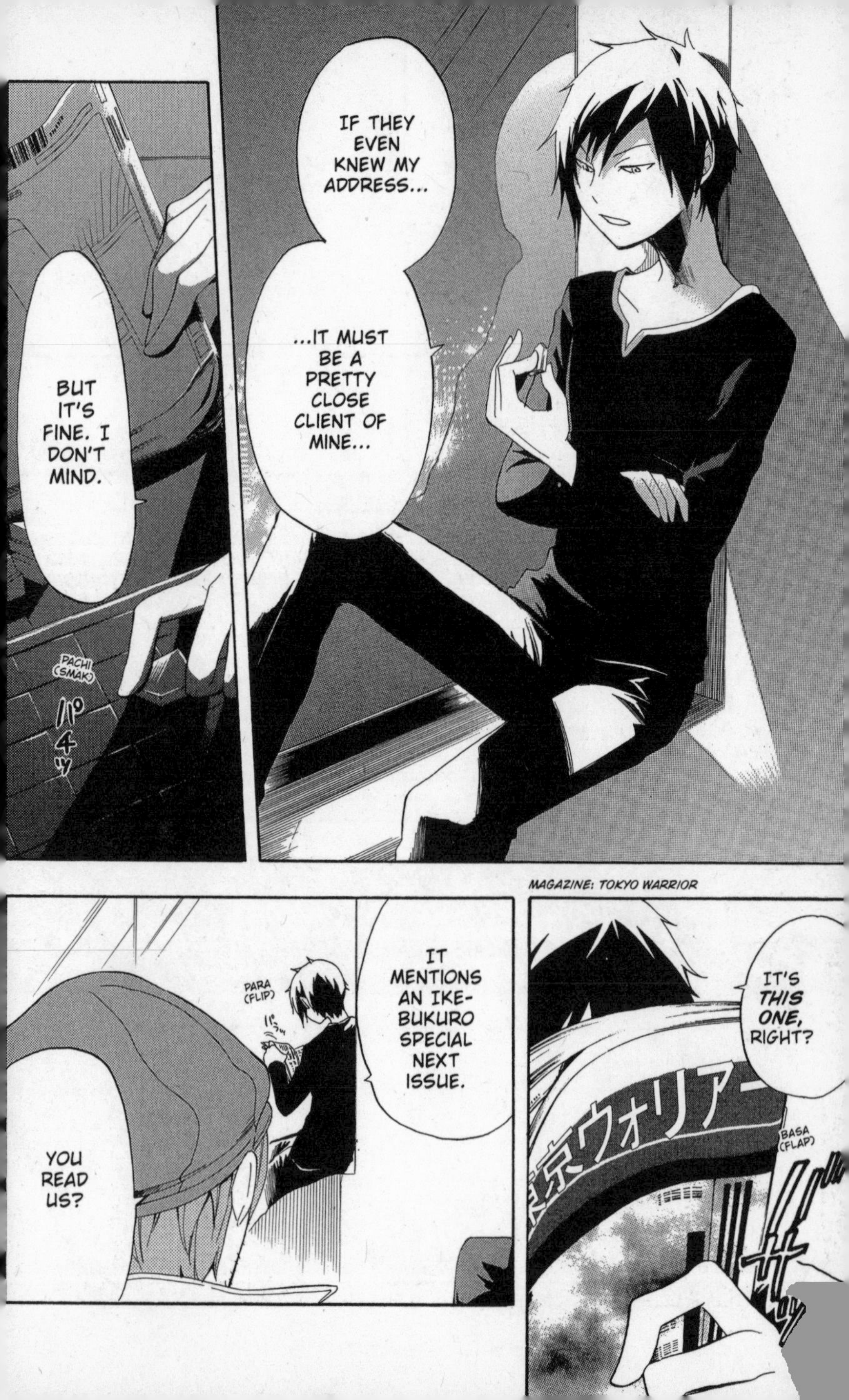
IF THEY EVEN KNEW MY ADDRESS...
...IT MUST BE A PRETTY CLOSE CLIENT OF MINE...
BUT IT'S FINE. I DON'T MIND.
PACHI (SMAK)
パチッ
MAGAZINE: TOKYO WARRIOR
IT'S *THIS ONE*, RIGHT?
東京ウォリアー
BASA (FLAP)
IT MENTIONS AN IKE-BUKURO SPECIAL NEXT ISSUE.
PARA (FLIP)
YOU READ US?

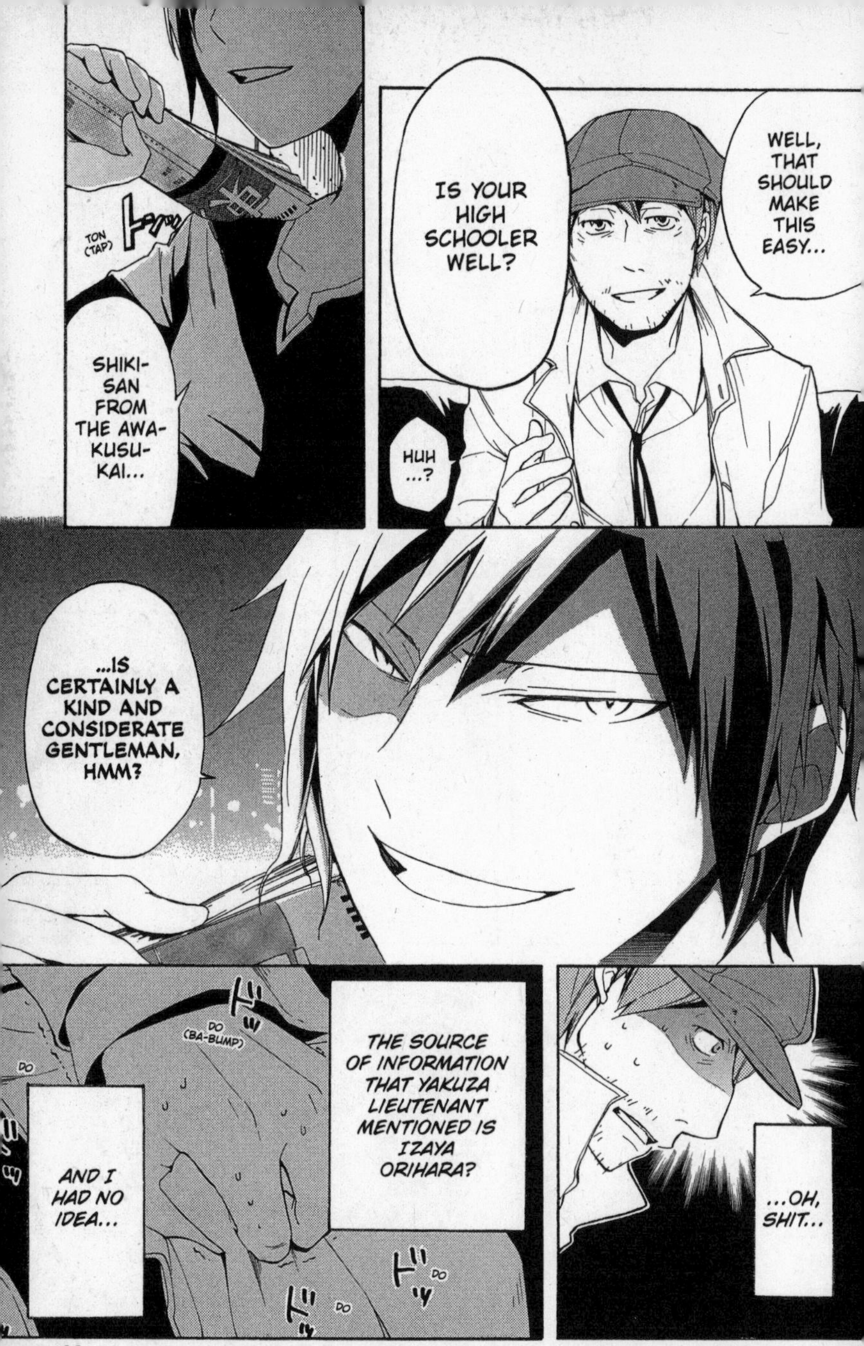
WELL, THAT SHOULD MAKE THIS EASY...
IS YOUR HIGH SCHOOLER WELL?
HUH ...?
TON (TAP)
SHIKI-SAN FROM THE AWA-KUSU-KAI...
...IS CERTAINLY A KIND AND CONSIDERATE GENTLEMAN, HMM?
...OH, SHIT...
DO (BA-BUMP)
DO
THE SOURCE OF INFORMATION THAT YAKUZA LIEUTENANT MENTIONED IS IZAYA ORIHARA?
AND I HAD NO IDEA...
DO
DO

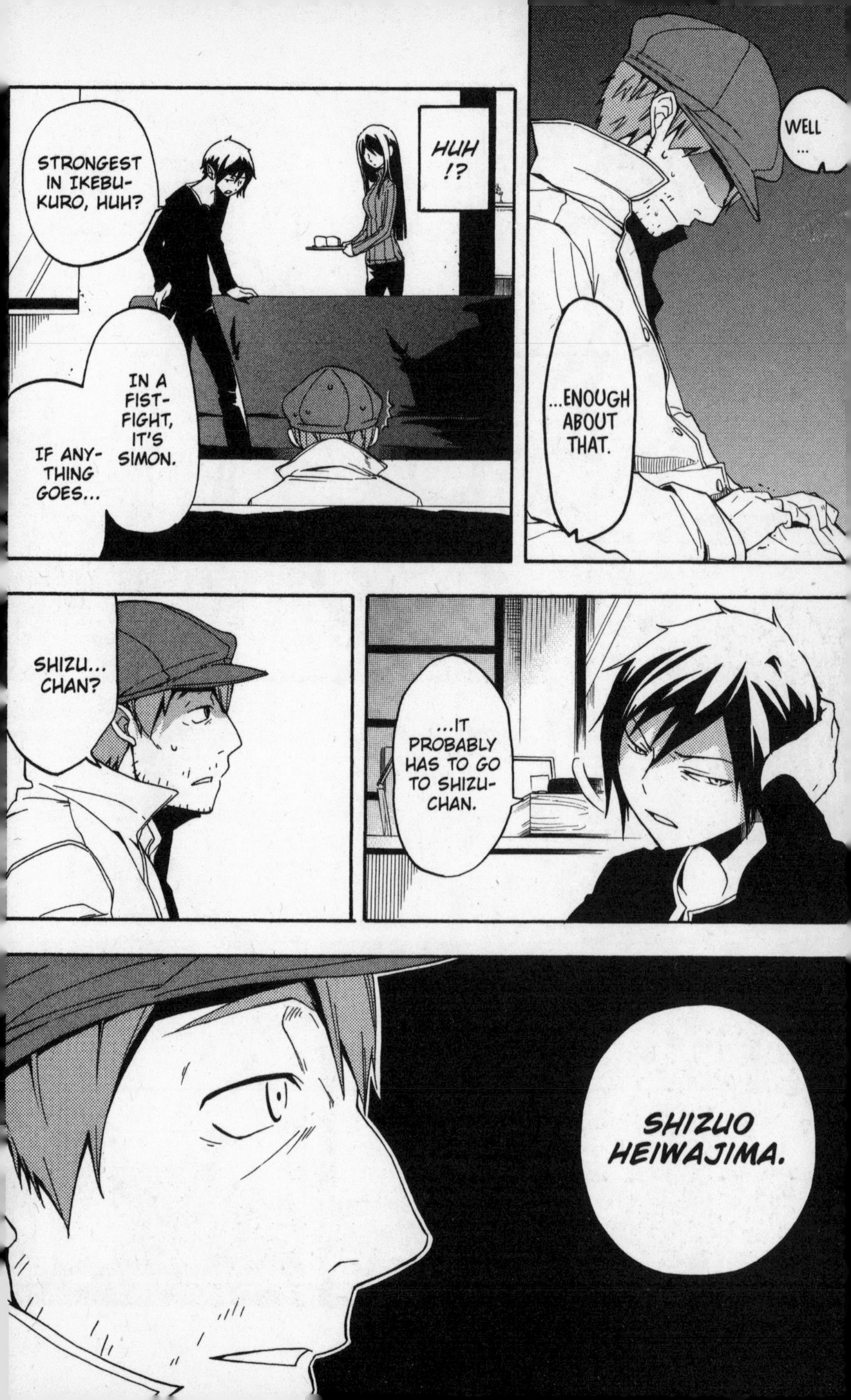
WELL ...
...ENOUGH ABOUT THAT.
HUH !?
STRONGEST IN IKEBU-KURO, HUH?
IN A FIST-FIGHT, IT'S SIMON.
IF ANY-THING GOES...
...IT PROBABLY HAS TO GO TO SHIZU-CHAN.
SHIZU... CHAN?
SHIZUO HEIWAJIMA.

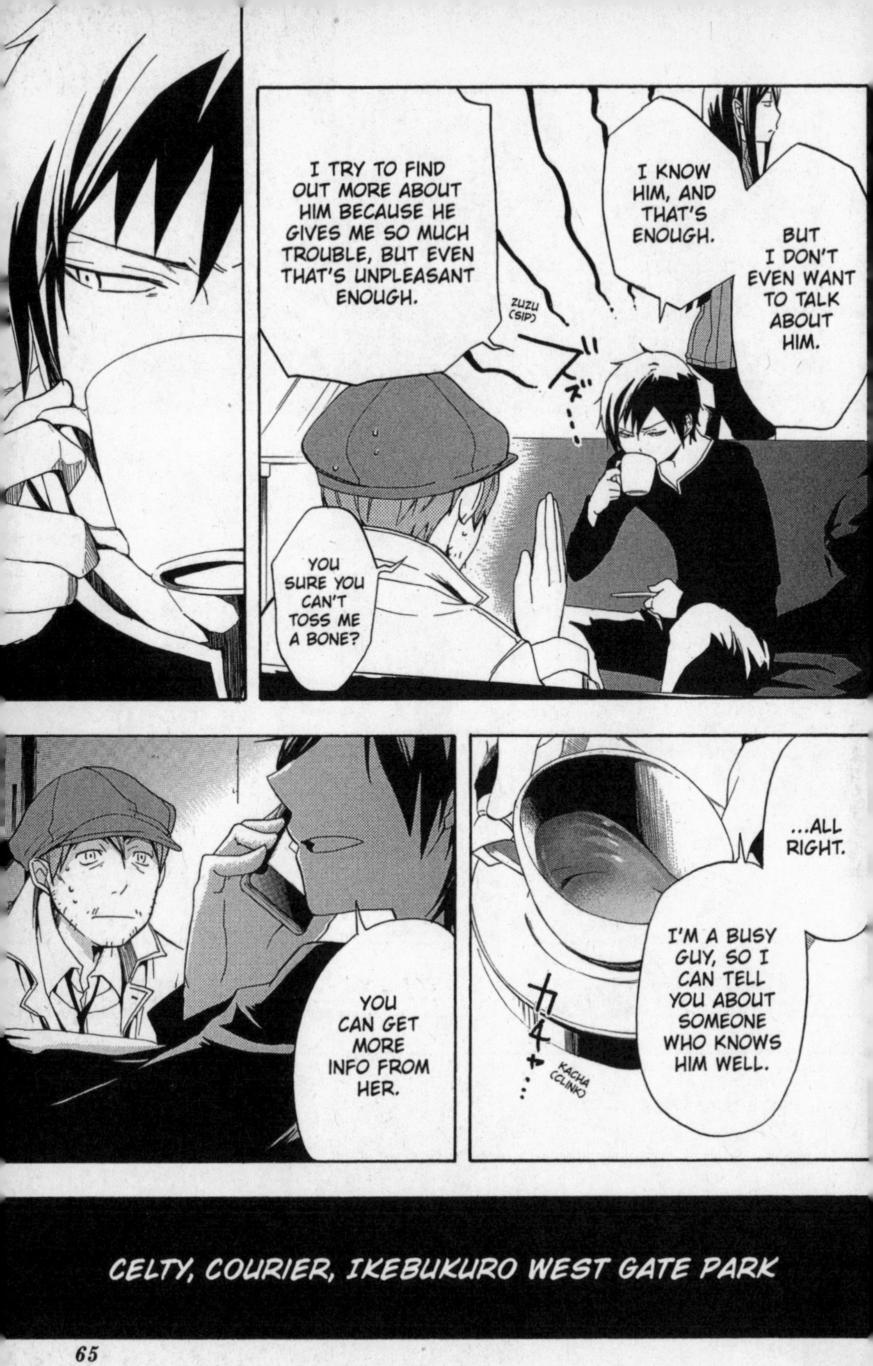
I KNOW HIM, AND THAT'S ENOUGH.
BUT I DON'T EVEN WANT TO TALK ABOUT HIM.
I TRY TO FIND OUT MORE ABOUT HIM BECAUSE HE GIVES ME SO MUCH TROUBLE, BUT EVEN THAT'S UNPLEASANT ENOUGH.
ZUZU (SIP)
YOU SURE YOU CAN'T TOSS ME A BONE?
...ALL RIGHT.
I'M A BUSY GUY, SO I CAN TELL YOU ABOUT SOMEONE WHO KNOWS HIM WELL.
KACHA (CLINK)
YOU CAN GET MORE INFO FROM HER.
CELTY, COURIER, IKEBUKURO WEST GATE PARK

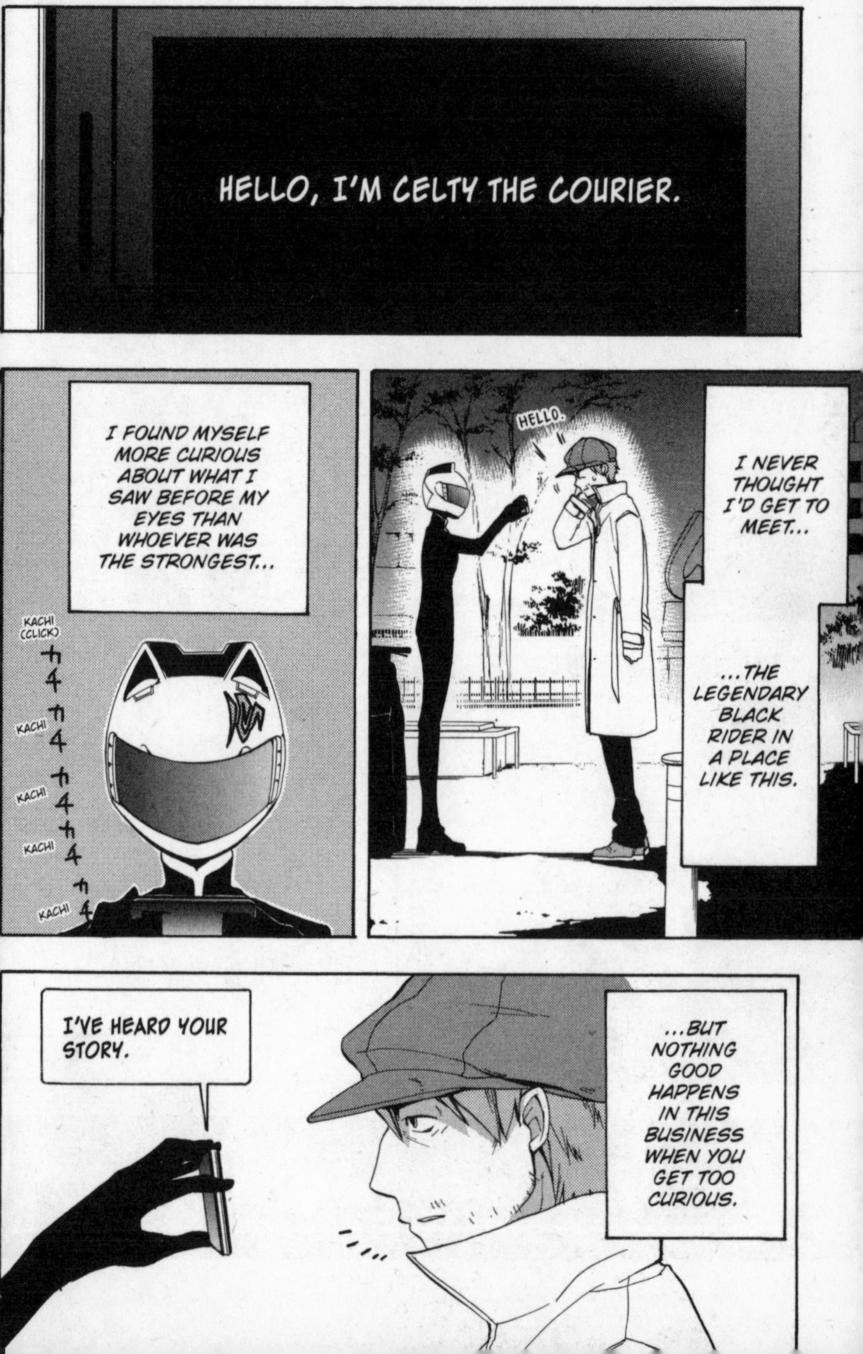
HELLO, I'M CELTY THE COURIER.
HELLO.
I NEVER THOUGHT I'D GET TO MEET...
...THE LEGENDARY BLACK RIDER IN A PLACE LIKE THIS.
I FOUND MYSELF MORE CURIOUS ABOUT WHAT I SAW BEFORE MY EYES THAN WHOEVER WAS THE STRONGEST...
KACHI (CLICK)
KACHI
KACHI
KACHI
KACHI
...BUT NOTHING GOOD HAPPENS IN THIS BUSINESS WHEN YOU GET TOO CURIOUS.
I'VE HEARD YOUR STORY.
...

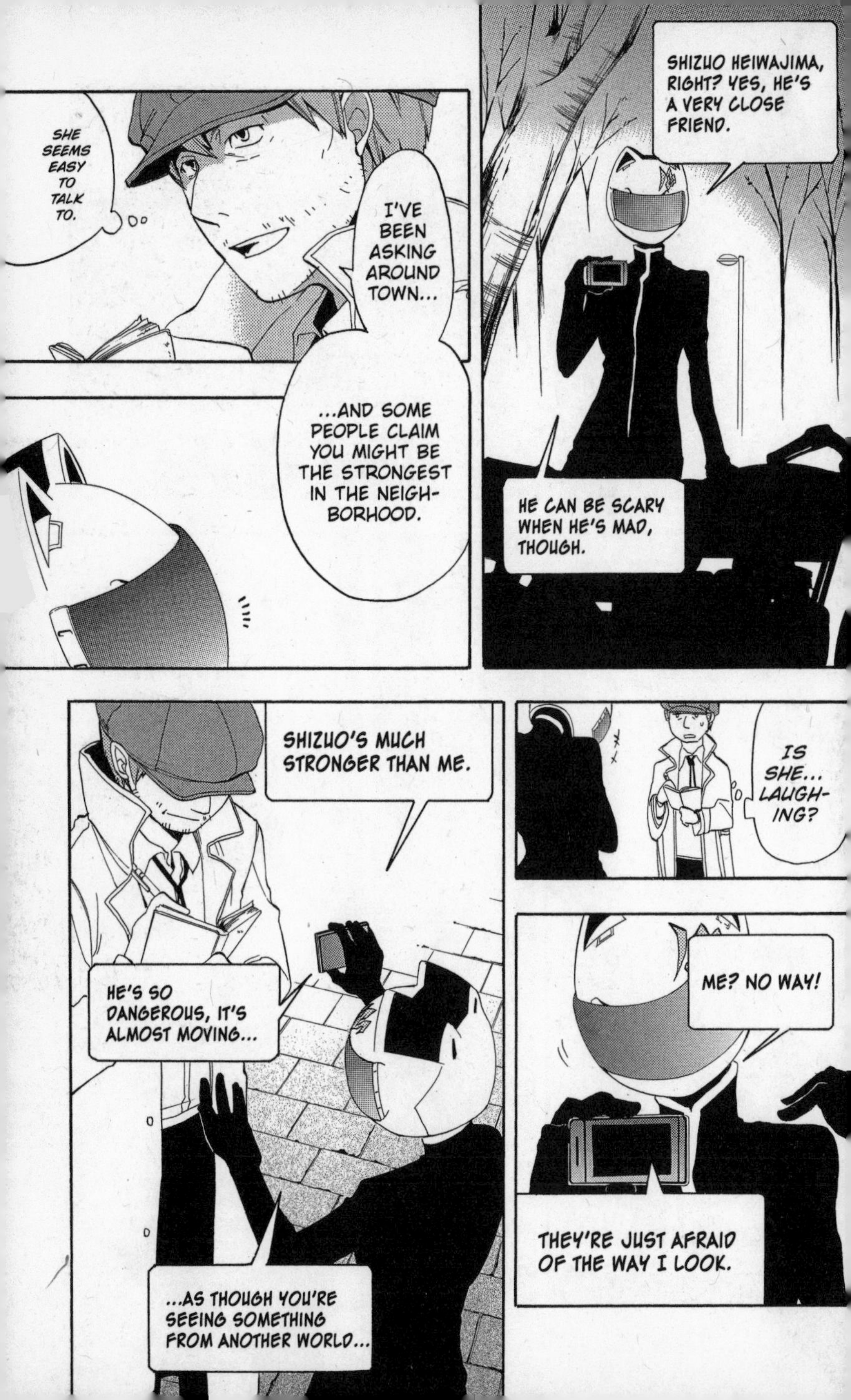
SHIZUO HEIWAJIMA, RIGHT? YES, HE'S A VERY CLOSE FRIEND.
HE CAN BE SCARY WHEN HE'S MAD, THOUGH.
SHE SEEMS EASY TO TALK TO.
I'VE BEEN ASKING AROUND TOWN...
...AND SOME PEOPLE CLAIM YOU MIGHT BE THE STRONGEST IN THE NEIGH-BORHOOD.
IS SHE... LAUGH-ING?
ME? NO WAY!
THEY'RE JUST AFRAID OF THE WAY I LOOK.
SHIZUO'S MUCH STRONGER THAN ME.
HE'S SO DANGEROUS, IT'S ALMOST MOVING...
...AS THOUGH YOU'RE SEEING SOMETHING FROM ANOTHER WORLD...

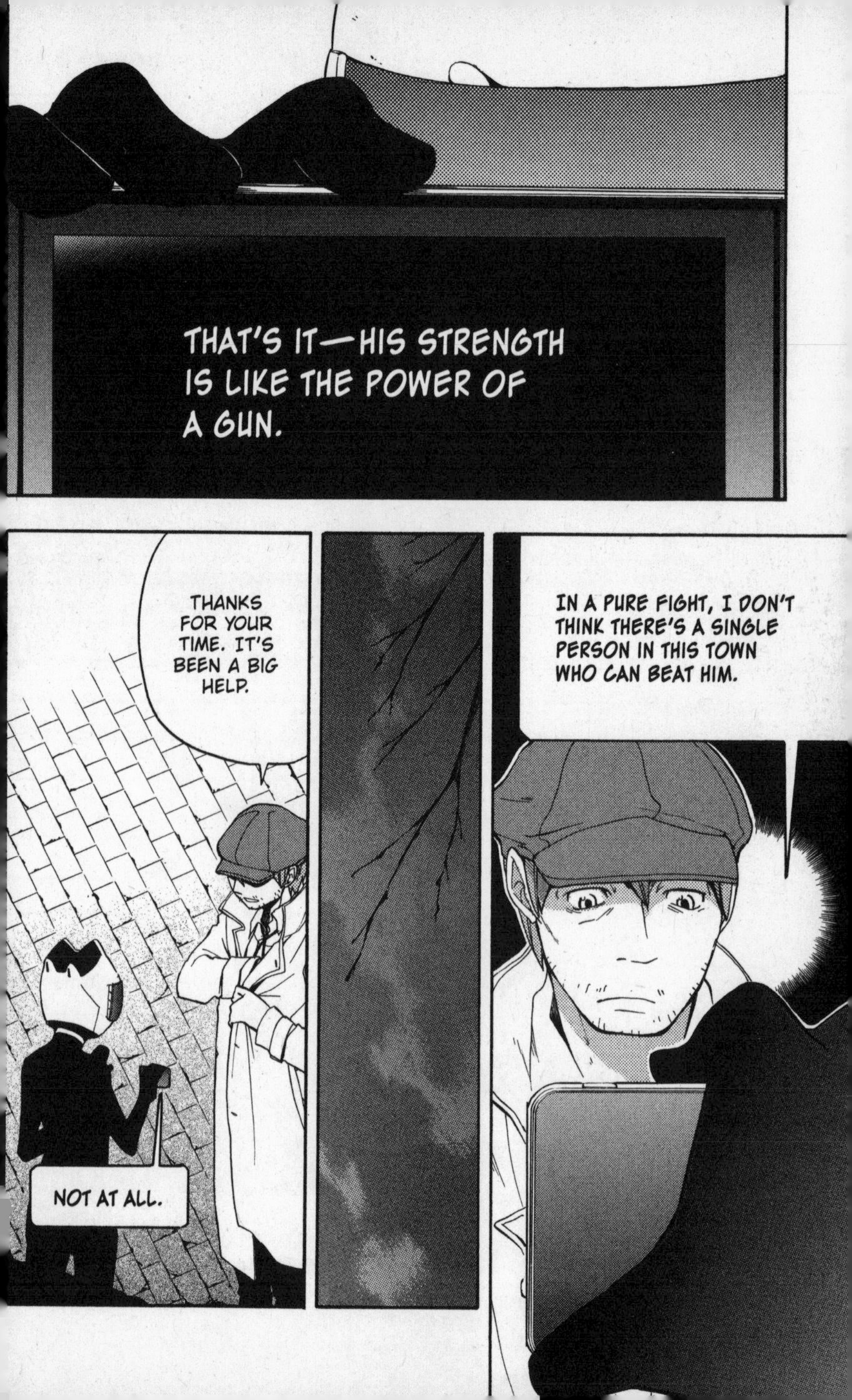
THAT'S IT—HIS STRENGTH IS LIKE THE POWER OF A GUN.
IN A PURE FIGHT, I DON'T THINK THERE'S A SINGLE PERSON IN THIS TOWN WHO CAN BEAT HIM.
THANKS FOR YOUR TIME. IT'S BEEN A BIG HELP.
NOT AT ALL.

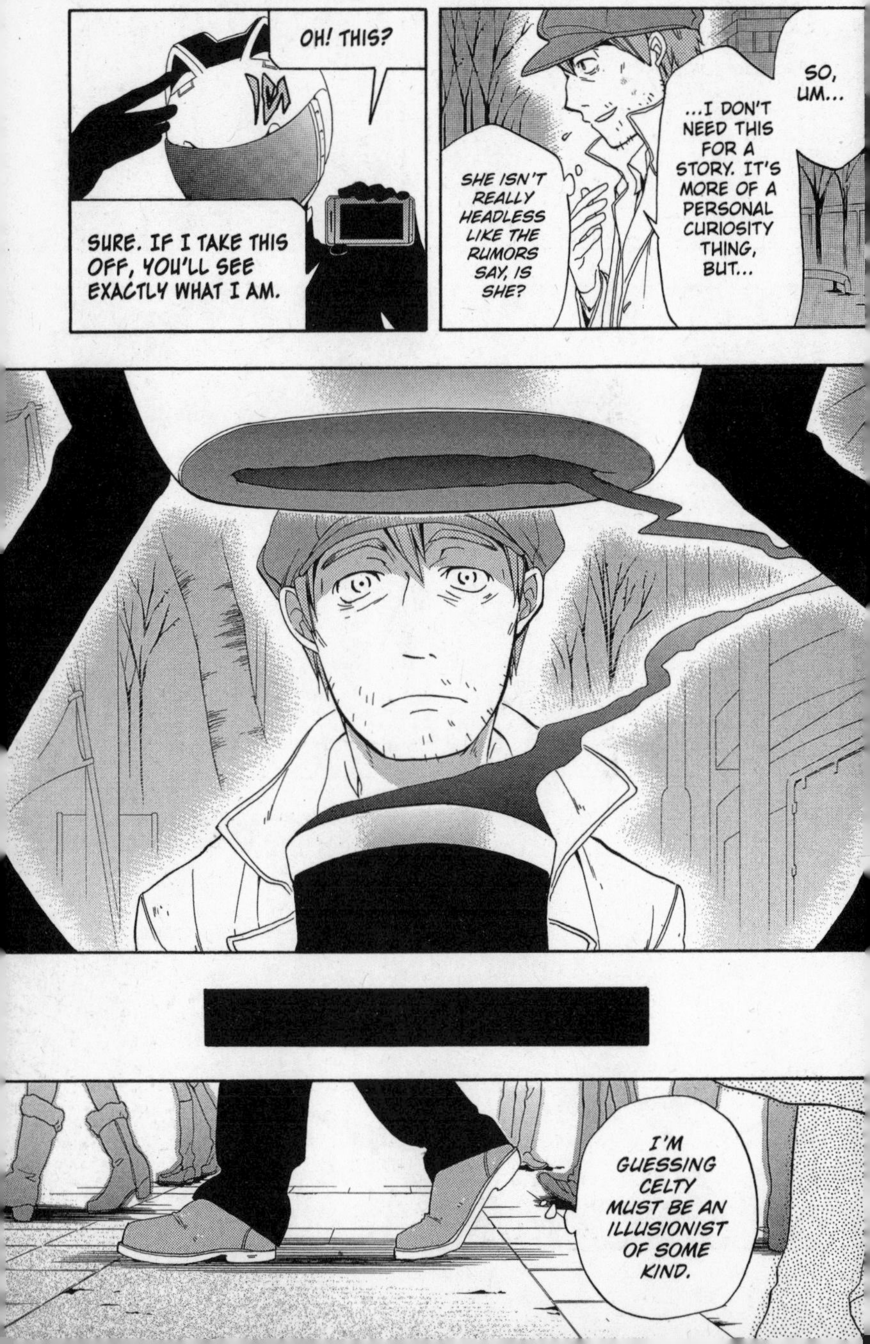
SO, UM...
...I DON'T NEED THIS FOR A STORY. IT'S MORE OF A PERSONAL CURIOSITY THING, BUT...
SHE ISN'T REALLY HEADLESS LIKE THE RUMORS SAY, IS SHE?
OH! THIS?
SURE. IF I TAKE THIS OFF, YOU'LL SEE EXACTLY WHAT I AM.
I'M GUESSING CELTY MUST BE AN ILLUSIONIST OF SOME KIND.

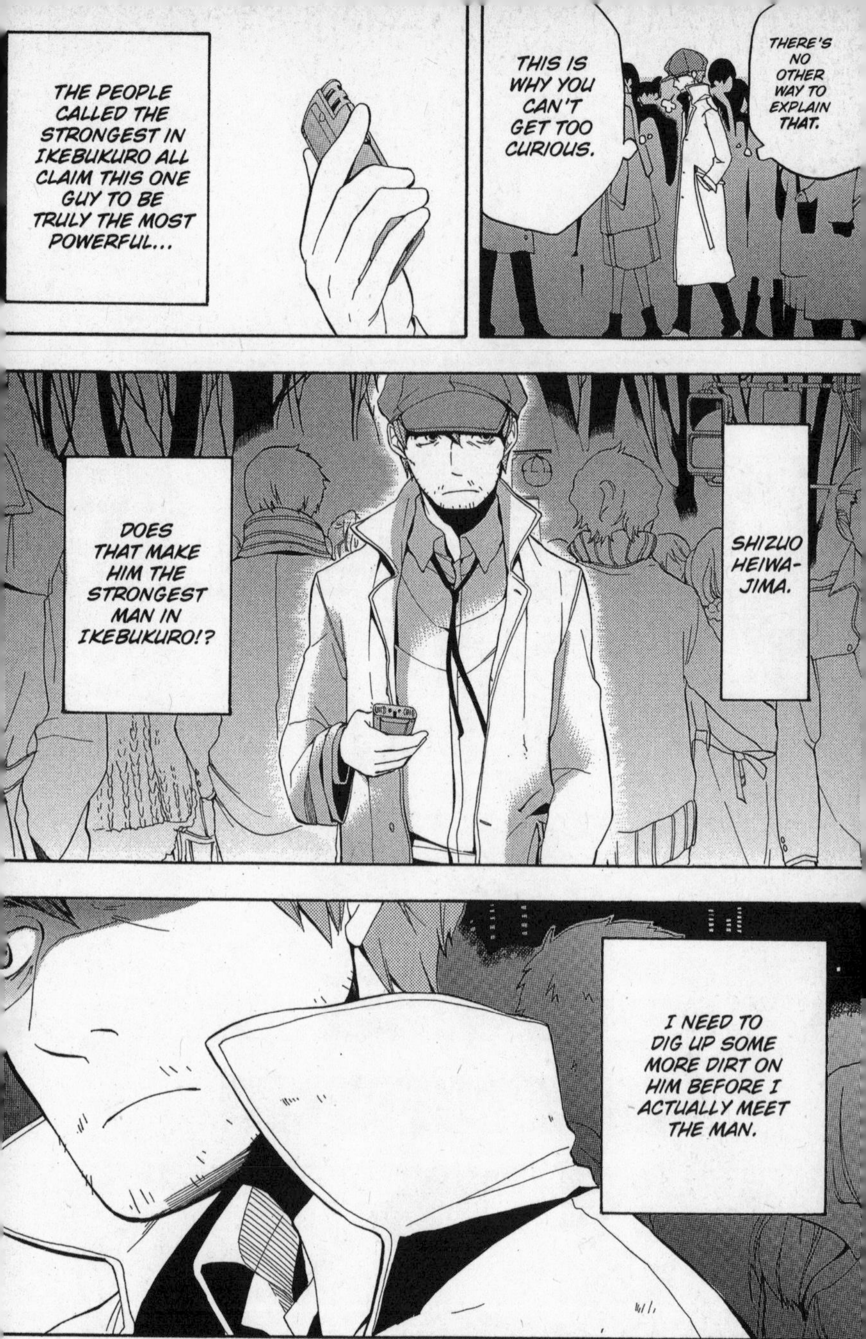
THERE'S NO OTHER WAY TO EXPLAIN THAT.
THIS IS WHY YOU CAN'T GET TOO CURIOUS.
THE PEOPLE CALLED THE STRONGEST IN IKEBUKURO ALL CLAIM THIS ONE GUY TO BE TRULY THE MOST POWERFUL...
SHIZUO HEIWA-JIMA.
DOES THAT MAKE HIM THE STRONGEST MAN IN IKEBUKURO!?
I NEED TO DIG UP SOME MORE DIRT ON HIM BEFORE I ACTUALLY MEET THE MAN.

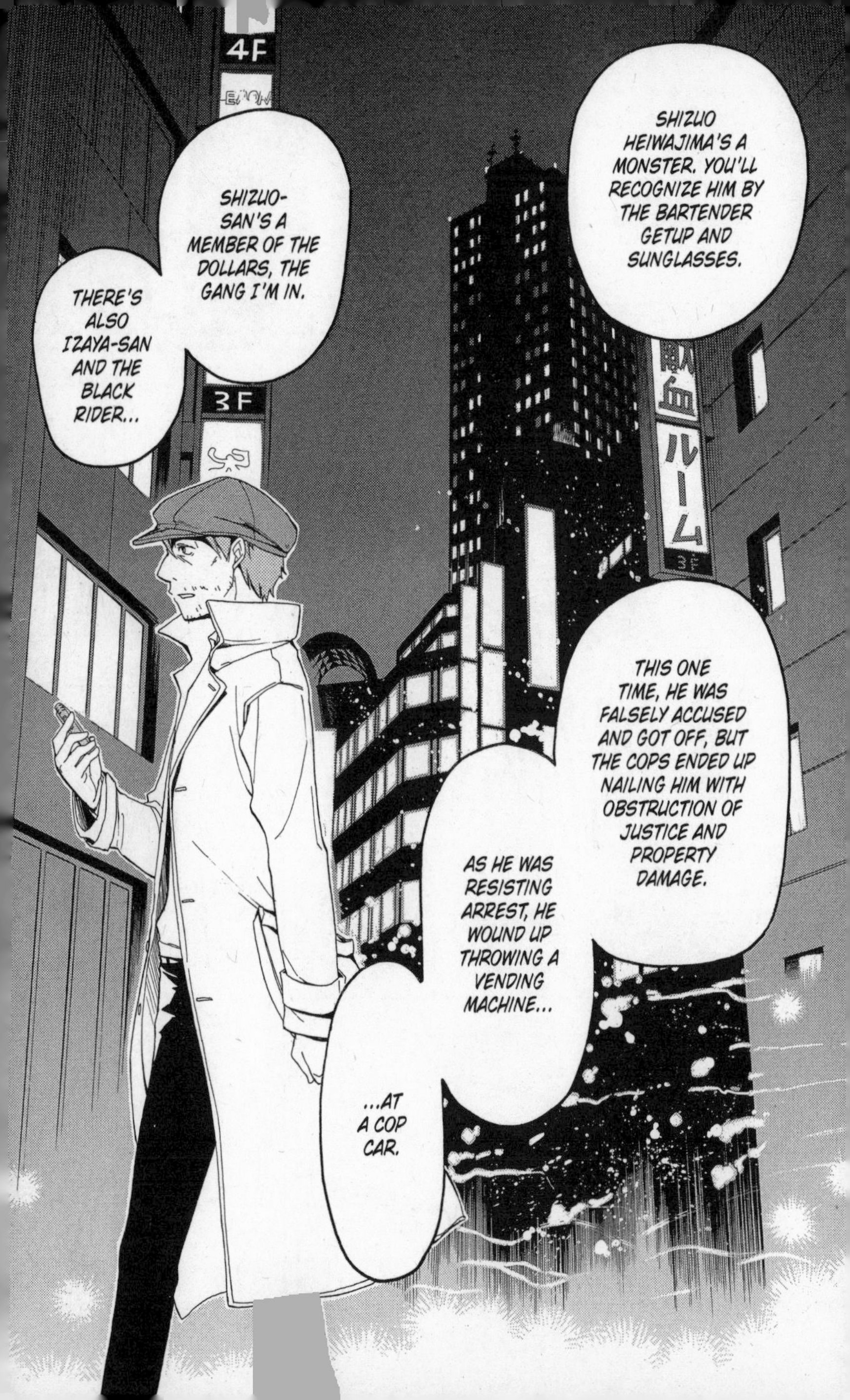
SHIZUO HEIWAJIMA'S A MONSTER. YOU'LL RECOGNIZE HIM BY THE BARTENDER GETUP AND SUNGLASSES.
SHIZUO-SAN'S A MEMBER OF THE DOLLARS, THE GANG I'M IN.
THERE'S ALSO IZAYA-SAN AND THE BLACK RIDER...
THIS ONE TIME, HE WAS FALSELY ACCUSED AND GOT OFF, BUT THE COPS ENDED UP NAILING HIM WITH OBSTRUCTION OF JUSTICE AND PROPERTY DAMAGE.
AS HE WAS RESISTING ARREST, HE WOUND UP THROWING A VENDING MACHINE...
...AT A COP CAR.

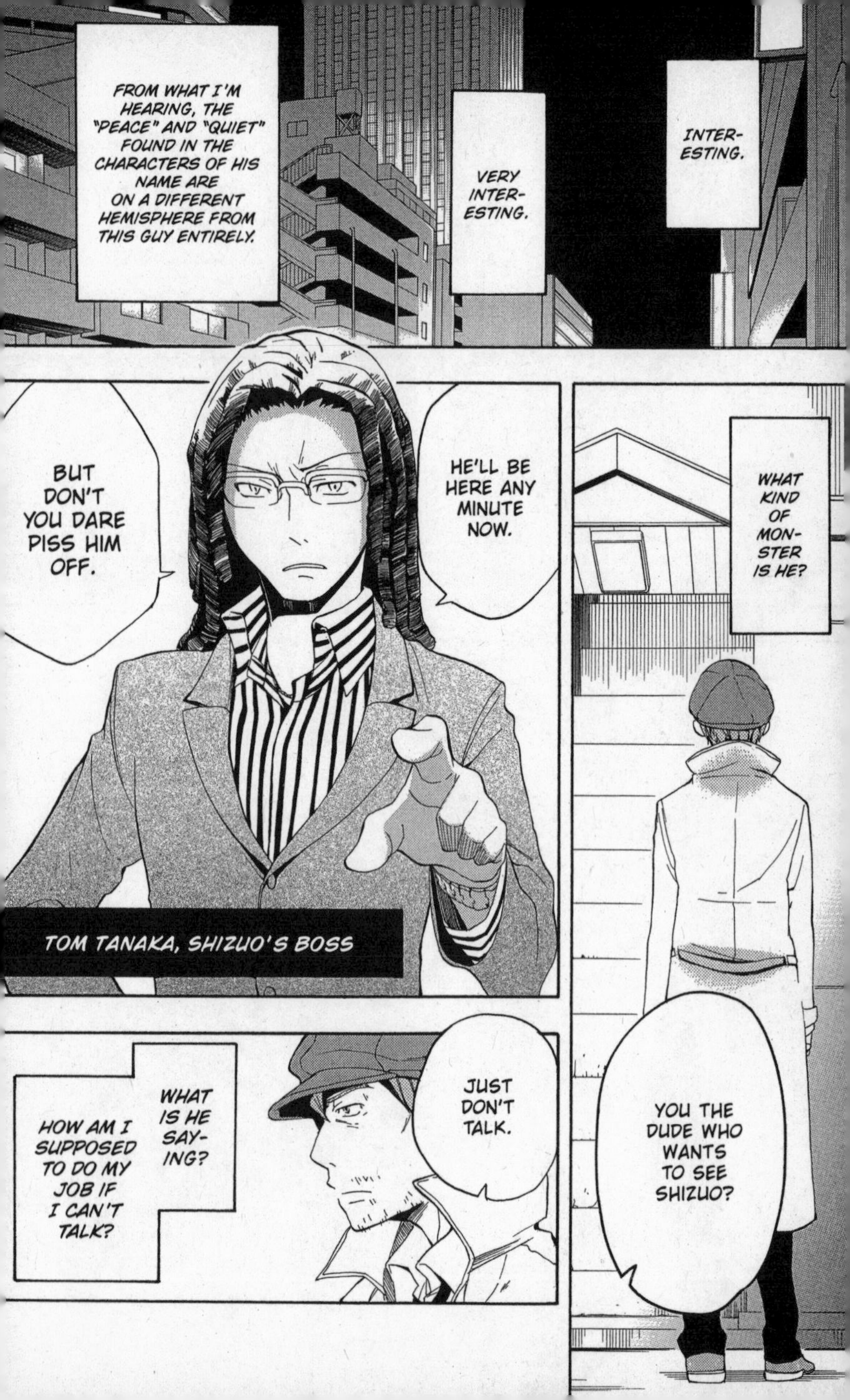
INTERESTING.
VERY INTERESTING.
FROM WHAT I'M HEARING, THE "PEACE" AND "QUIET" FOUND IN THE CHARACTERS OF HIS NAME ARE ON A DIFFERENT HEMISPHERE FROM THIS GUY ENTIRELY.
WHAT KIND OF MONSTER IS HE?
YOU THE DUDE WHO WANTS TO SEE SHIZUO?
HE'LL BE HERE ANY MINUTE NOW.
BUT DON'T YOU DARE PISS HIM OFF.
TOM TANAKA, SHIZUO'S BOSS
JUST DON'T TALK.
WHAT IS HE SAYING?
HOW AM I SUPPOSED TO DO MY JOB IF I CAN'T TALK?

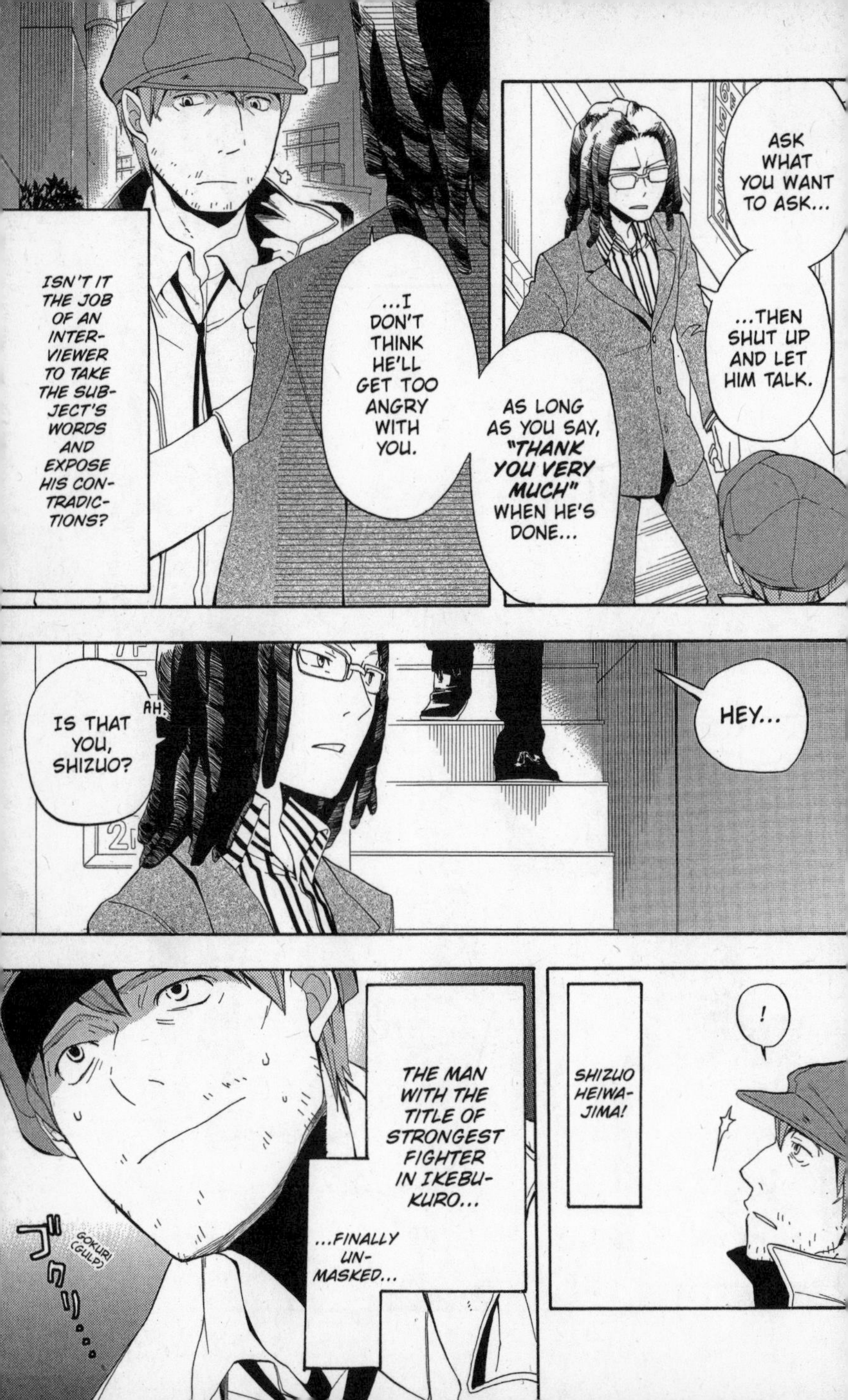
ASK WHAT YOU WANT TO ASK...
...THEN SHUT UP AND LET HIM TALK.
AS LONG AS YOU SAY, "THANK YOU VERY MUCH" WHEN HE'S DONE...
...I DON'T THINK HE'LL GET TOO ANGRY WITH YOU.
ISN'T IT THE JOB OF AN INTERVIEWER TO TAKE THE SUBJECT'S WORDS AND EXPOSE HIS CONTRADICTIONS?
HEY...
AH.
IS THAT YOU, SHIZUO?
!
SHIZUO HEIWAJIMA!
THE MAN WITH THE TITLE OF STRONGEST FIGHTER IN IKEBUKURO...
...FINALLY UNMASKED...
GOKURI (GULP)

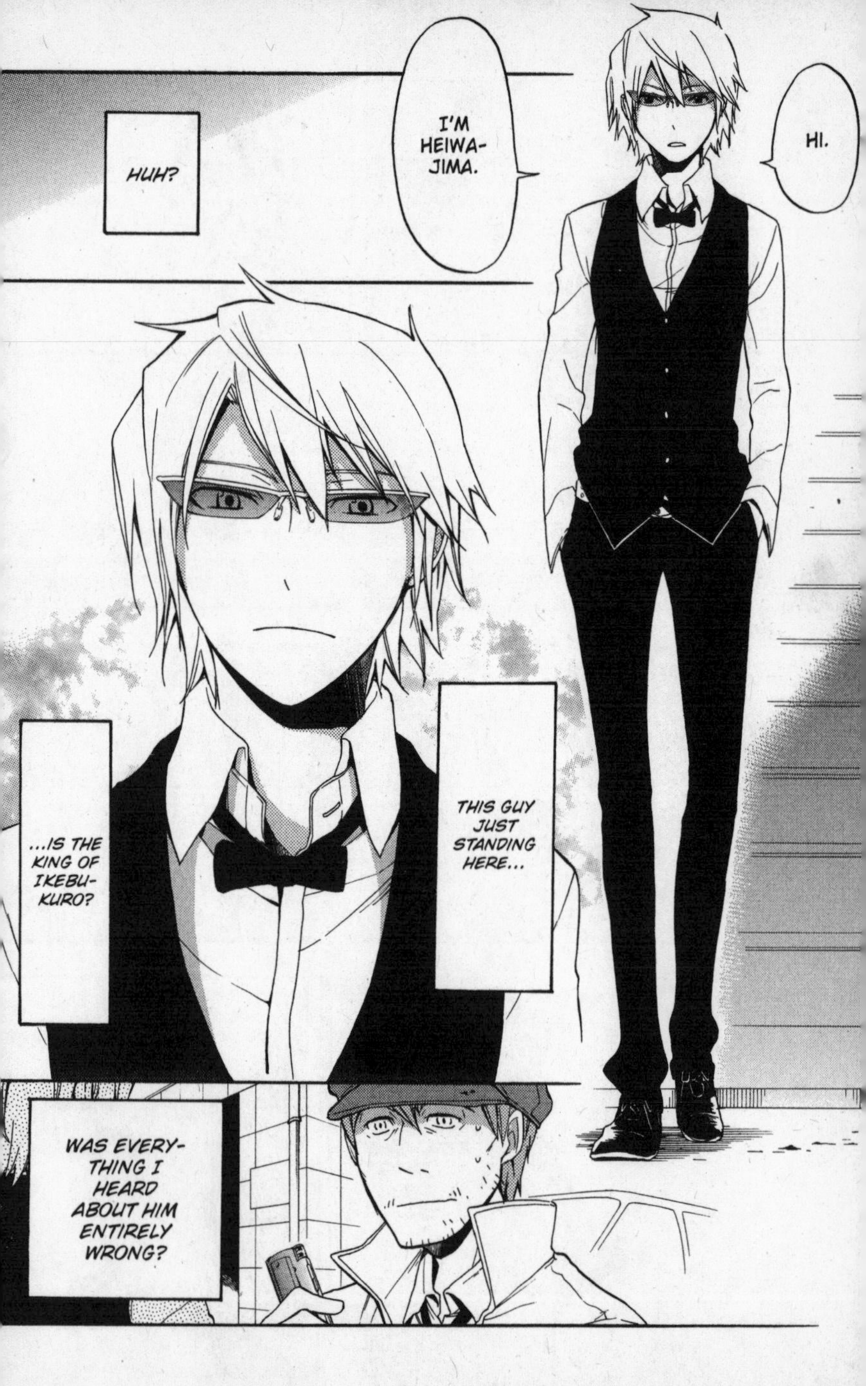
HI.
I'M HEIWAJIMA.
HUH?
THIS GUY JUST STANDING HERE...
...IS THE KING OF IKEBUKURO?
WAS EVERYTHING I HEARD ABOUT HIM ENTIRELY WRONG?

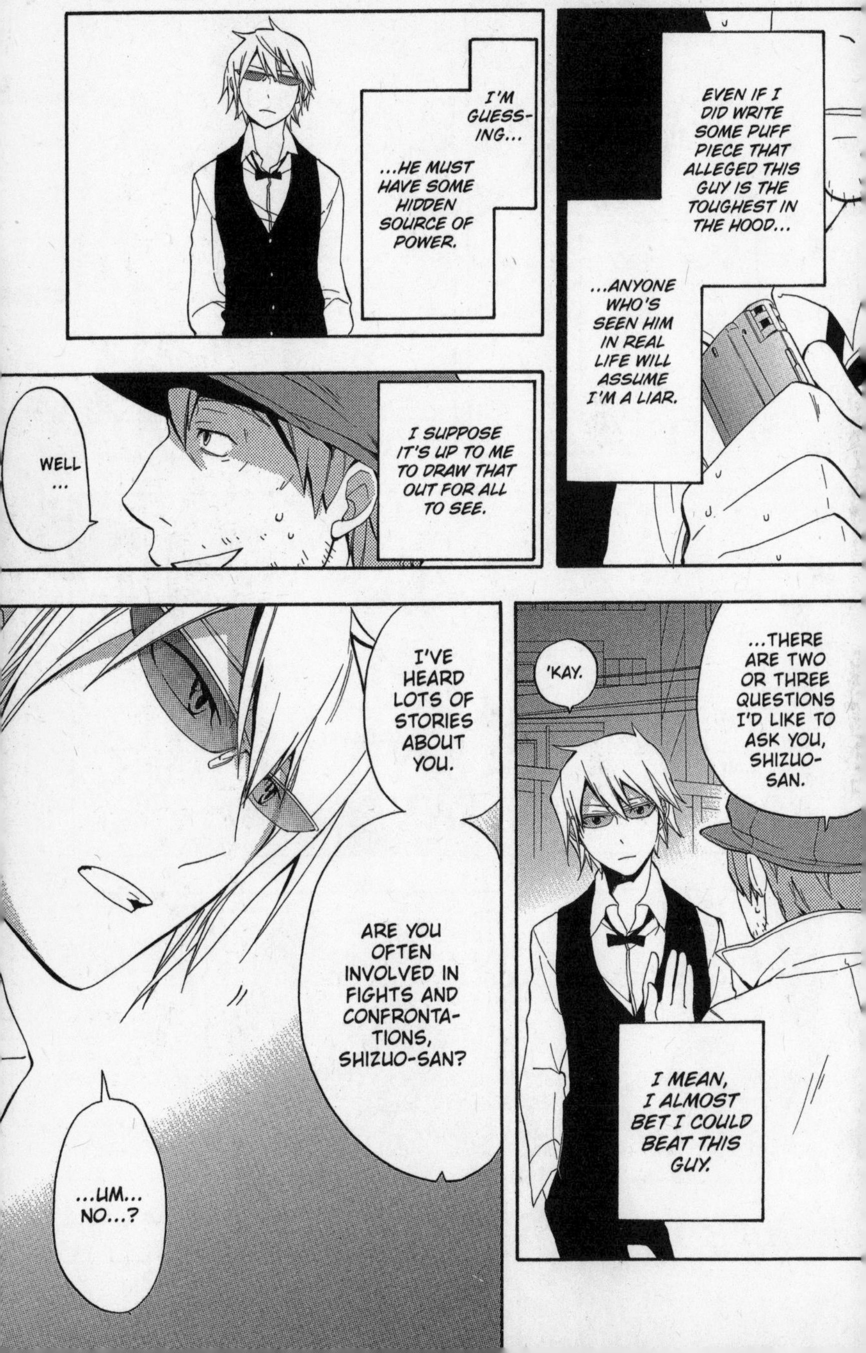
EVEN IF I DID WRITE SOME PUFF PIECE THAT ALLEGED THIS GUY IS THE TOUGHEST IN THE HOOD...
...ANYONE WHO'S SEEN HIM IN REAL LIFE WILL ASSUME I'M A LIAR.
I'M GUESSING-ING...
...HE MUST HAVE SOME HIDDEN SOURCE OF POWER.
I SUPPOSE IT'S UP TO ME TO DRAW THAT OUT FOR ALL TO SEE.
WELL ...
...THERE ARE TWO OR THREE QUESTIONS I'D LIKE TO ASK YOU, SHIZUO-SAN.
'KAY.
I MEAN, I ALMOST BET I COULD BEAT THIS GUY.
I'VE HEARD LOTS OF STORIES ABOUT YOU.
ARE YOU OFTEN INVOLVED IN FIGHTS AND CONFRONTATIONS, SHIZUO-SAN?
...UM... NO...?

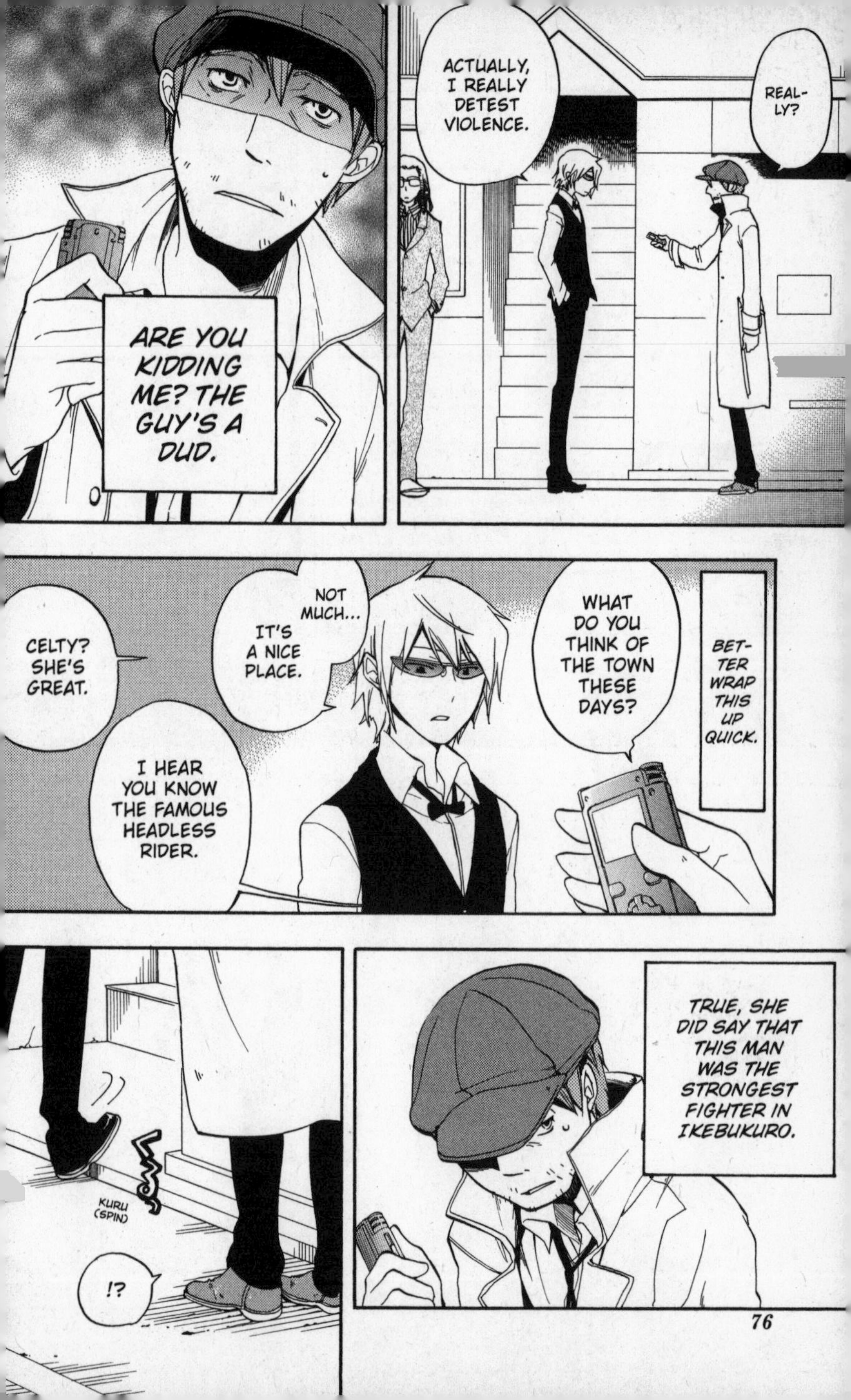
REAL-LY?
ACTUALLY, I REALLY DETEST VIOLENCE.
ARE YOU KIDDING ME? THE GUY'S A DUD.
BET-TER WRAP THIS UP QUICK.
WHAT DO YOU THINK OF THE TOWN THESE DAYS?
NOT MUCH...
IT'S A NICE PLACE.
I HEAR YOU KNOW THE FAMOUS HEADLESS RIDER.
CELTY? SHE'S GREAT.
TRUE, SHE DID SAY THAT THIS MAN WAS THE STRONGEST FIGHTER IN IKEBUKURO.
KURU (SPIN)
!?

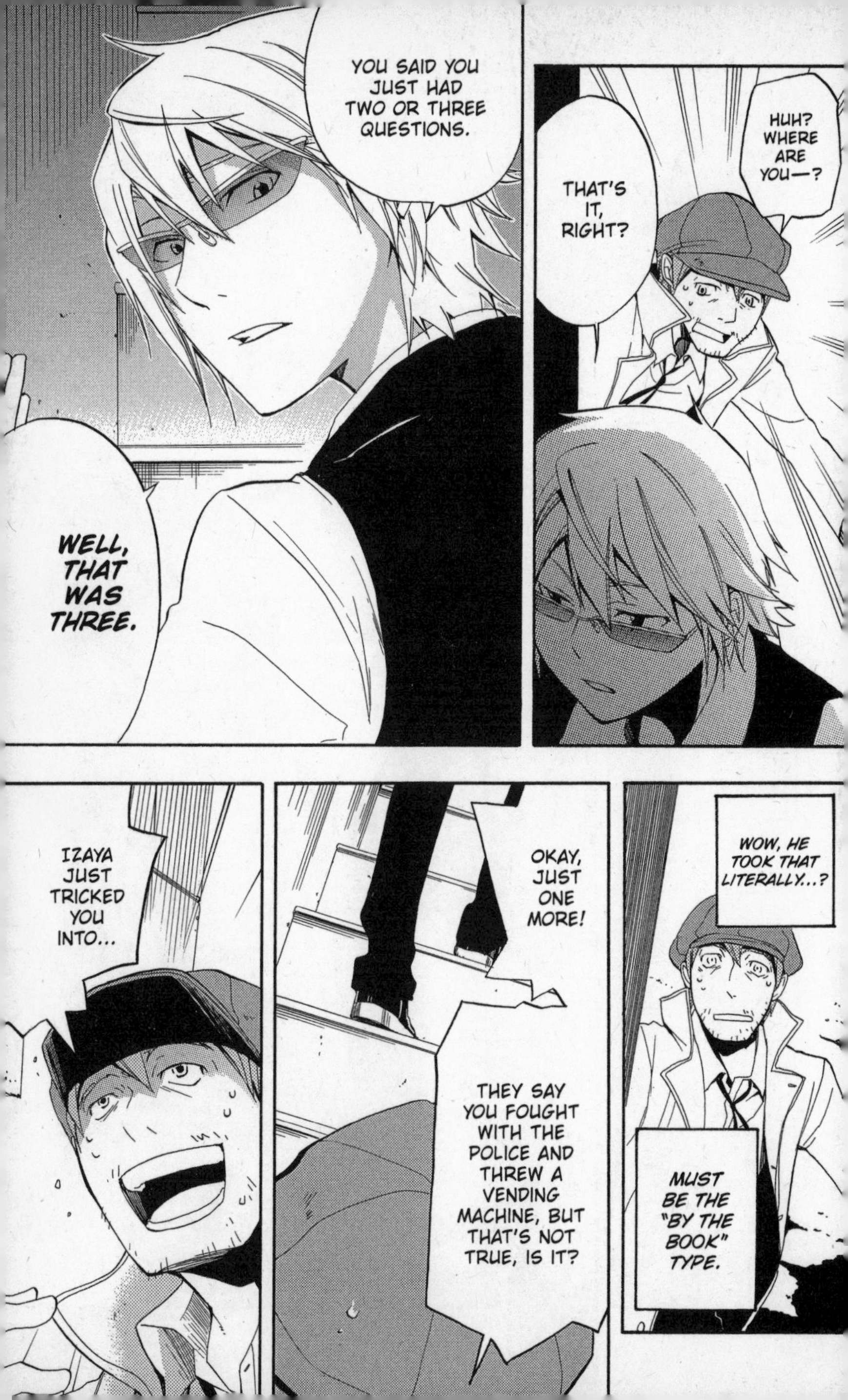
HUH? WHERE ARE YOU—?
THAT'S IT, RIGHT?
YOU SAID YOU JUST HAD TWO OR THREE QUESTIONS.
WELL, THAT WAS THREE.
WOW, HE TOOK THAT LITERALLY...?
MUST BE THE "BY THE BOOK" TYPE.
OKAY, JUST ONE MORE!
THEY SAY YOU FOUGHT WITH THE POLICE AND THREW A VENDING MACHINE, BUT THAT'S NOT TRUE, IS IT?
IZAYA JUST TRICKED YOU INTO...

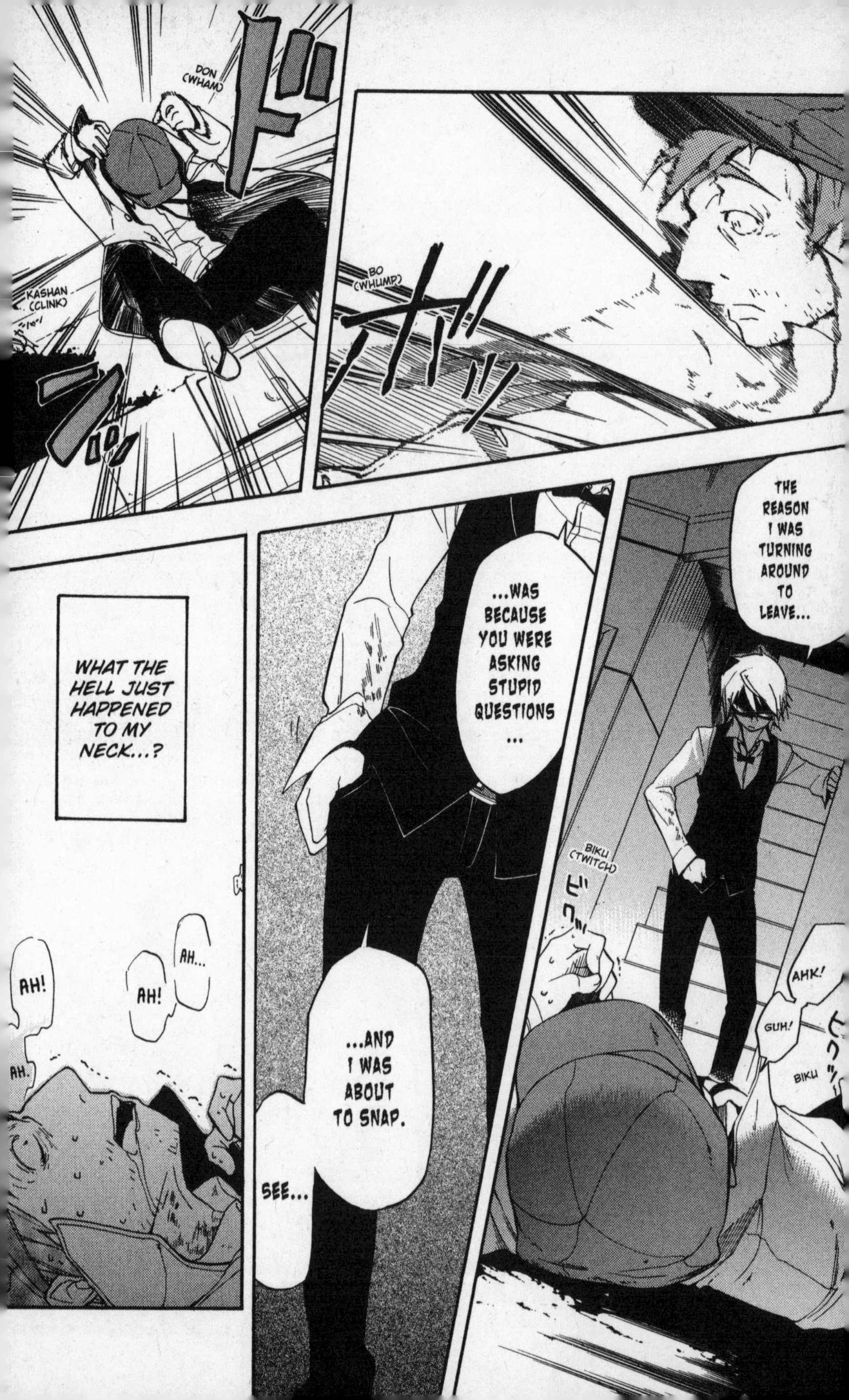
BO (WHUMP)
DON (WHAM)
KASHAN (CLINK)
THE REASON I WAS TURNING AROUND TO LEAVE...
BIKU (TWITCH)
AHK!
GUH!
BIKU
...WAS BECAUSE YOU WERE ASKING STUPID QUESTIONS...
...AND I WAS ABOUT TO SNAP.
SEE...
WHAT THE HELL JUST HAPPENED TO MY NECK...?
AH...
AH!
AH!
AH.

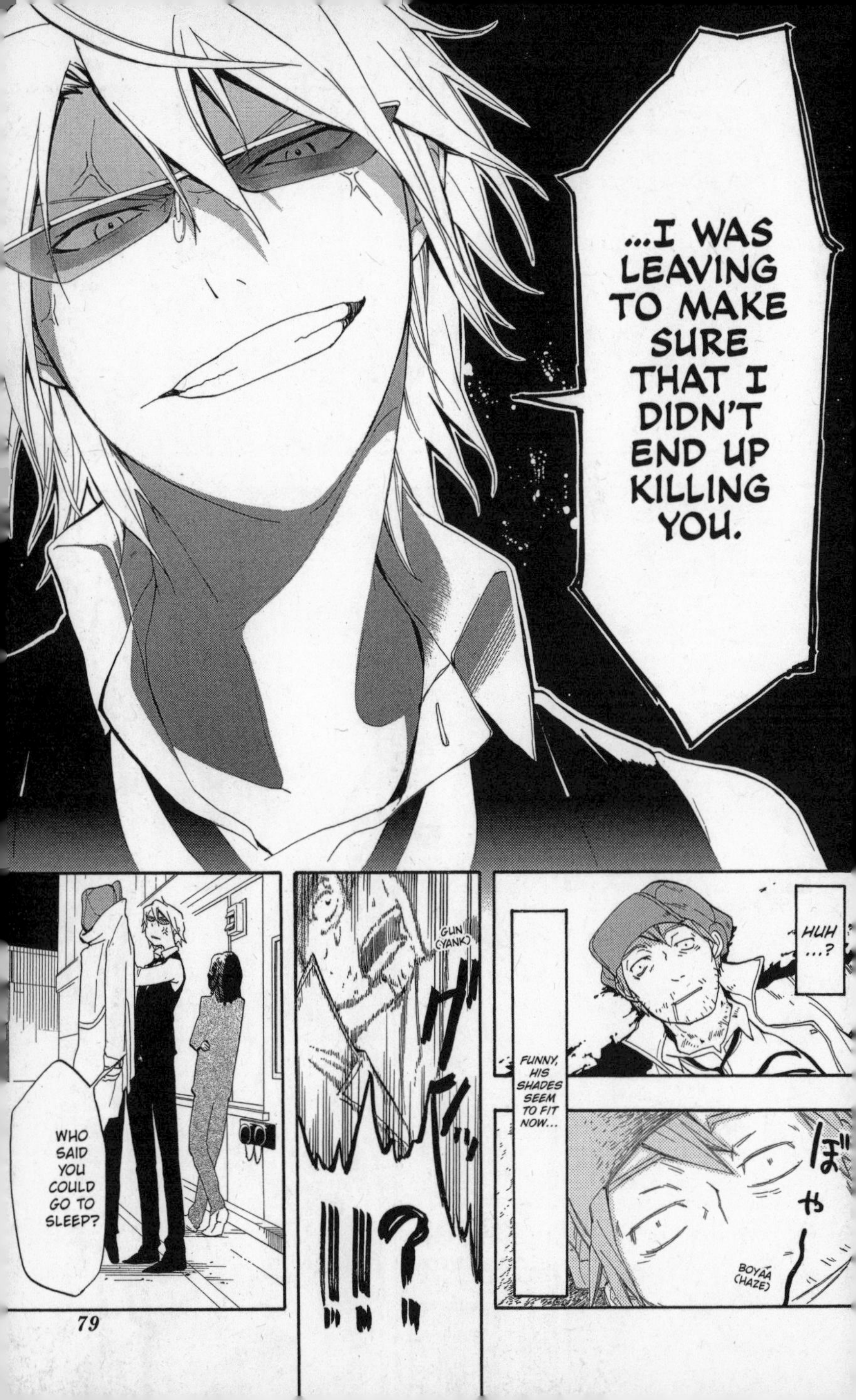
...I WAS LEAVING TO MAKE SURE THAT I DIDN'T END UP KILLING YOU.
HUH ...?
FUNNY, HIS SHADES SEEM TO FIT NOW...
ぼやー
BOYĀA (HAZE)
GUN (YANK)
!!!?
WHO SAID YOU COULD GO TO SLEEP?

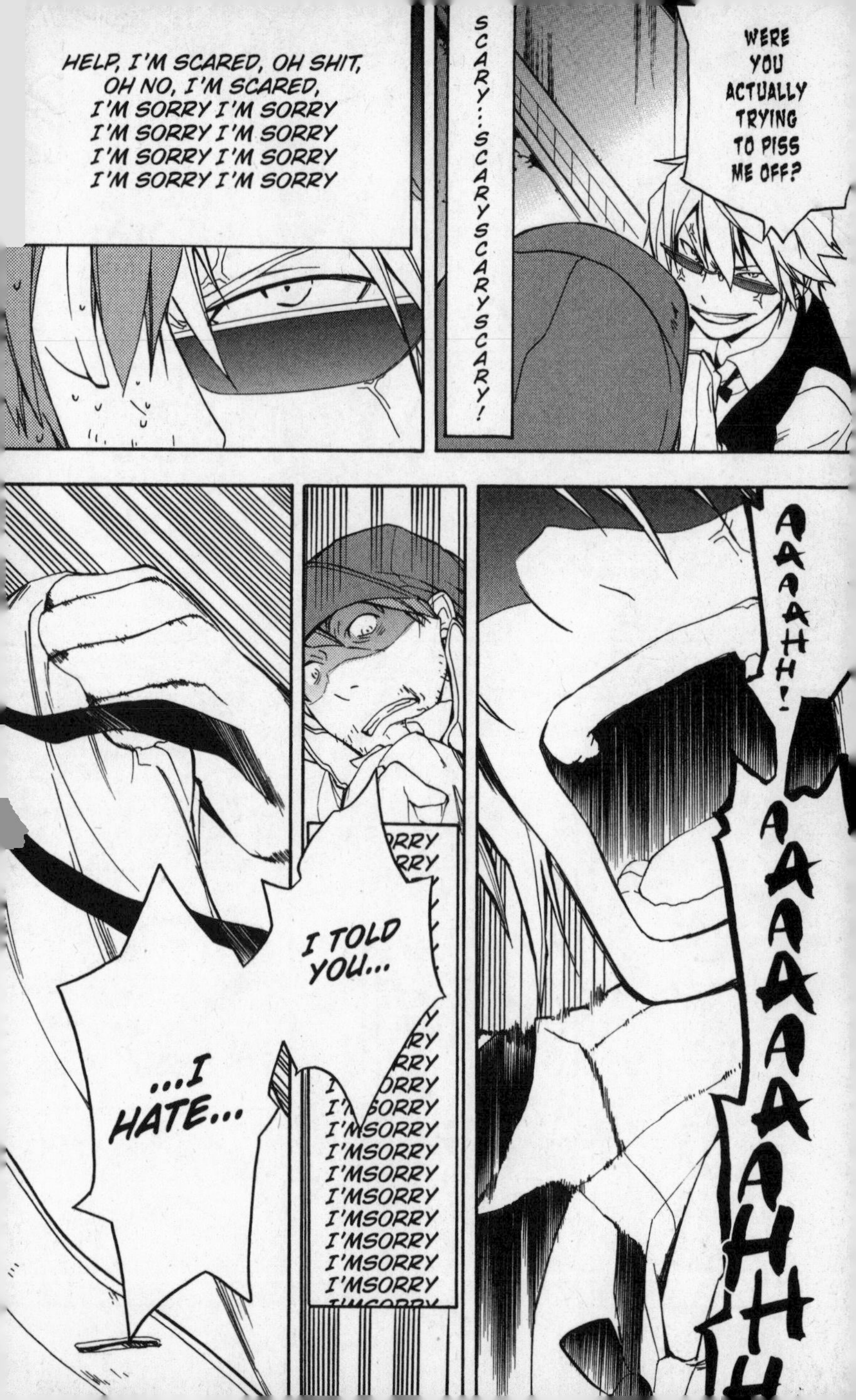
WERE YOU ACTUALLY TRYING TO PISS ME OFF?
SCARY...SCARYSCARYSCARY!
HELP, I'M SCARED, OH SHIT, OH NO, I'M SCARED, I'M SORRY I'M SORRY I'M SORRY I'M SORRY I'M SORRY I'M SORRY I'M SORRY I'M SORRY
AAAAAH!
AAAAAAAAHHH
I'MSORRY I'MSORRY I'MSORRY I'MSORRY I'MSORRY I'MSORRY I'MSORRY
I TOLD YOU...
...I HATE...

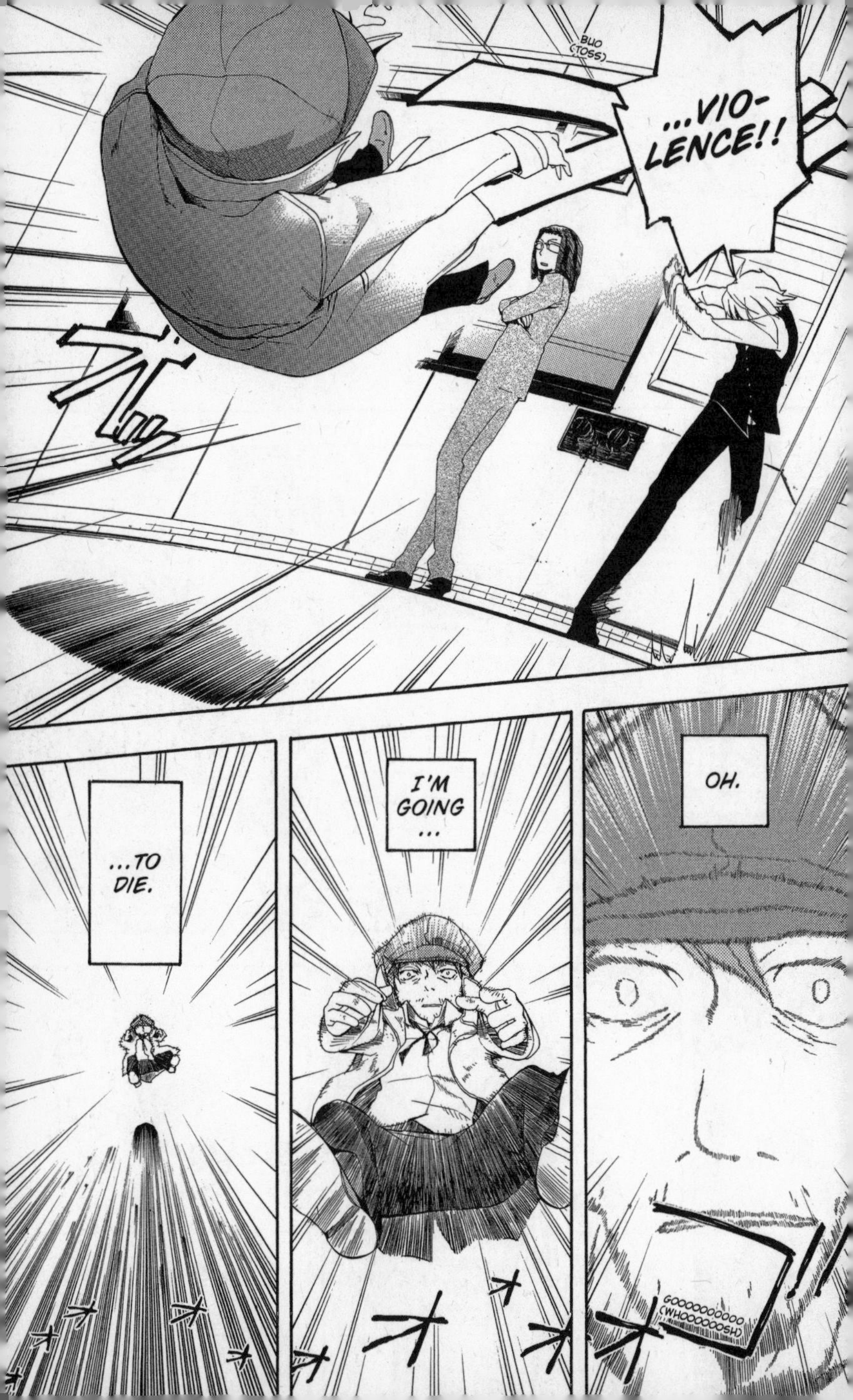
...VIO-
LENCE!!
BUO
(TOSS)
OH.
I'M
GOING
...
...TO
DIE.
GOOOOOOOOOO
(WHOOOOOOSH)

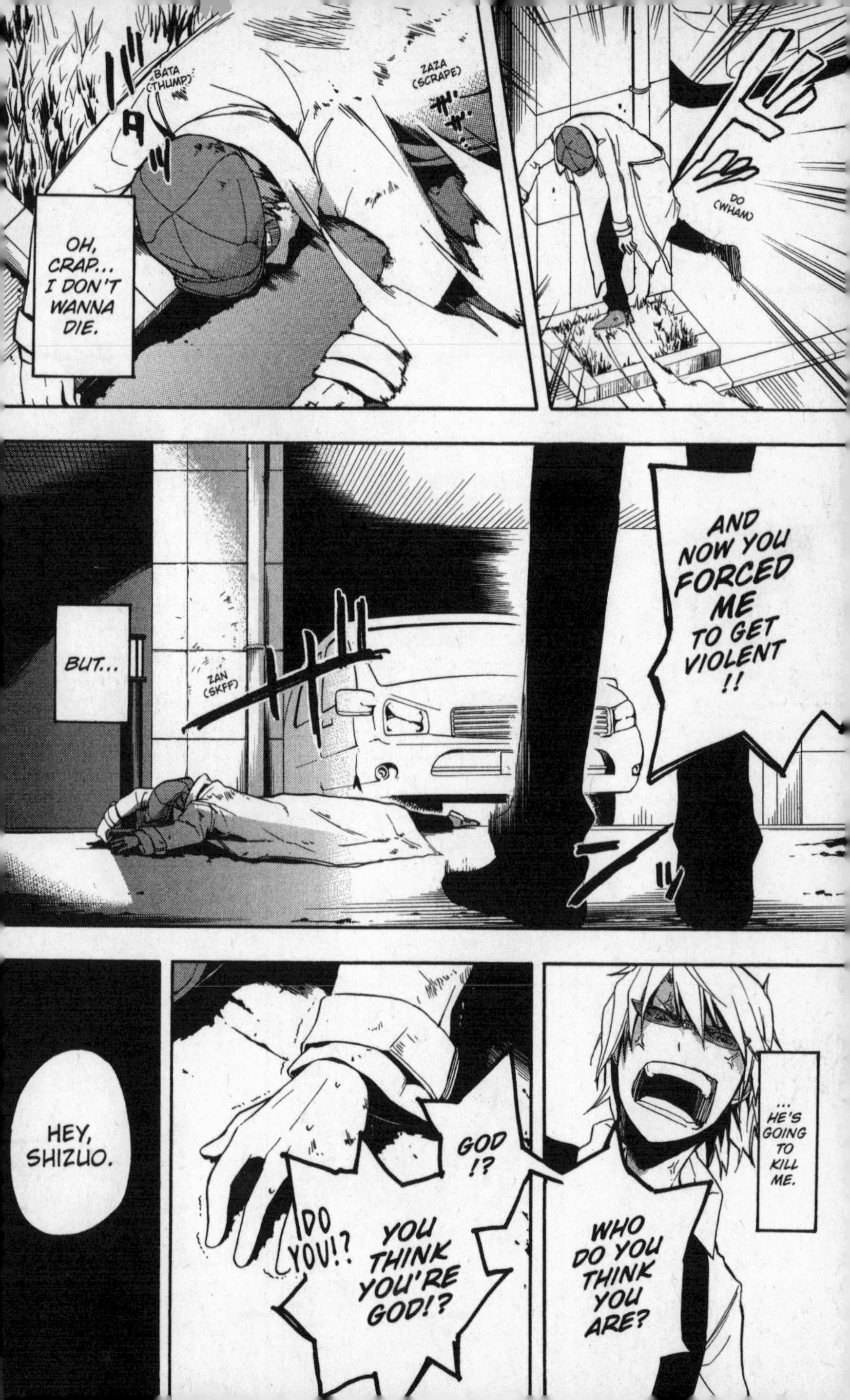
DO (WHAM)
ZAZA (SCRAPE)
BATA (THUMP)
OH, CRAP... I DON'T WANNA DIE.
AND NOW YOU FORCED ME TO GET VIOLENT!!
ZAN (SKFF)
BUT...
...HE'S GOING TO KILL ME.
WHO DO YOU THINK YOU ARE?
GOD!?
YOU THINK YOU'RE GOD!?
DO YOU!?
HEY, SHIZUO.

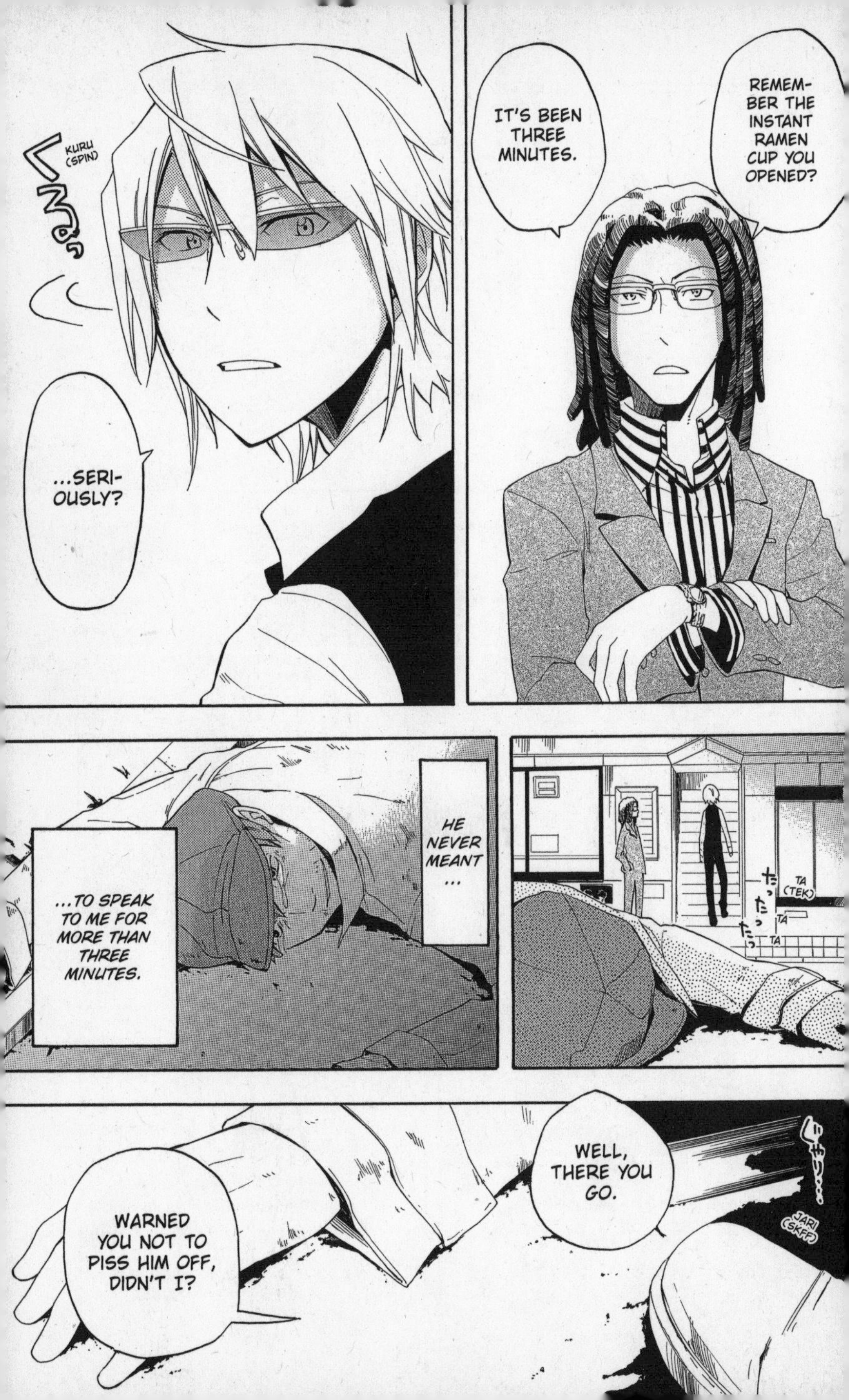
REMEMBER THE INSTANT RAMEN CUP YOU OPENED?
IT'S BEEN THREE MINUTES.
KURU (SPIN)
...SERIOUSLY?
TA (TEK)
TA
TA
HE NEVER MEANT...
...TO SPEAK TO ME FOR MORE THAN THREE MINUTES.
JARI (SKFF)
WELL, THERE YOU GO.
WARNED YOU NOT TO PISS HIM OFF, DIDN'T I?

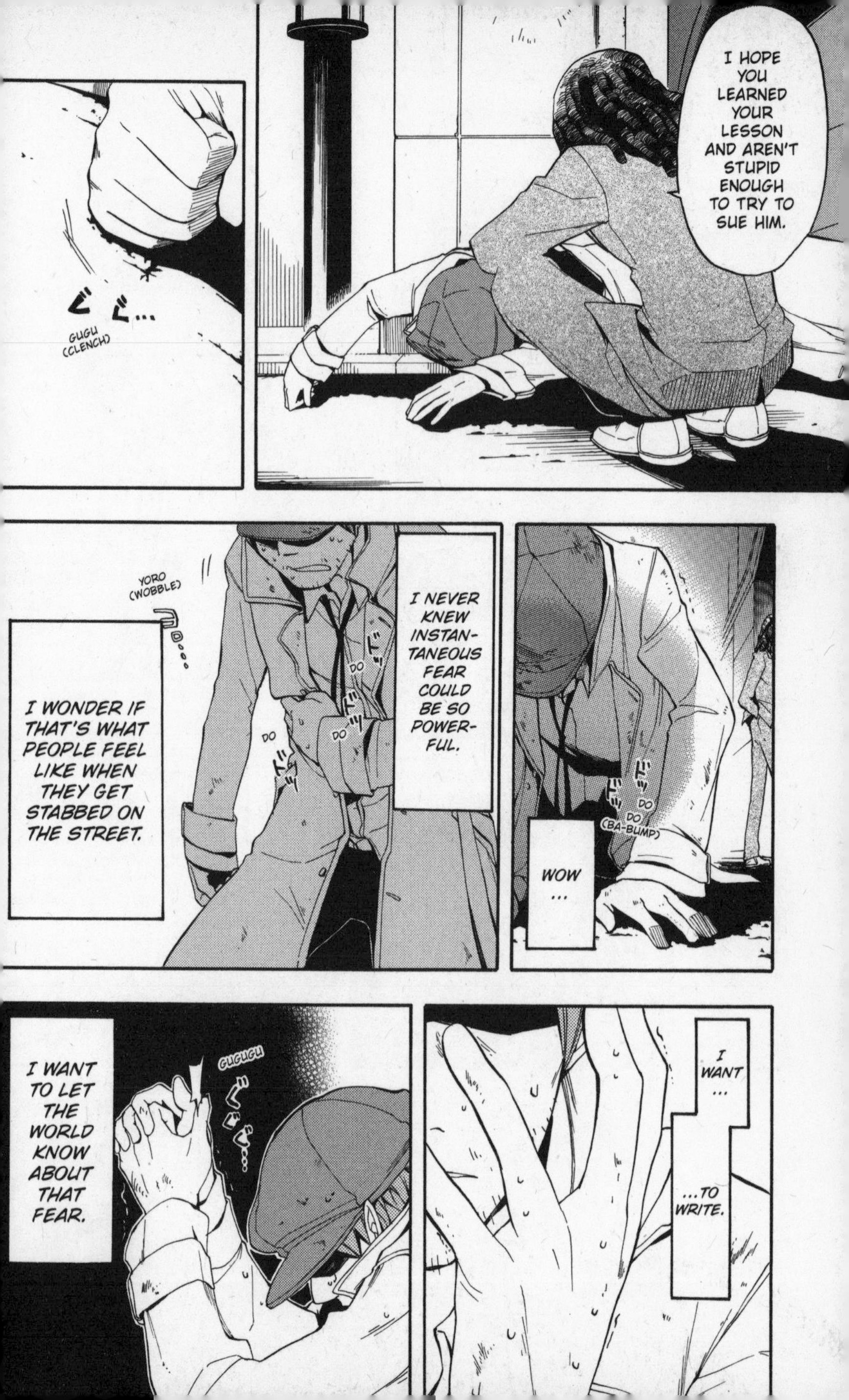
I HOPE YOU LEARNED YOUR LESSON AND AREN'T STUPID ENOUGH TO TRY TO SUE HIM.
GUGU (CLENCH)
DO
DO (BA-BUMP)
WOW ...
I NEVER KNEW INSTANTANEOUS FEAR COULD BE SO POWERFUL.
DO
DO
DO
YORO (WOBBLE)
I WONDER IF THAT'S WHAT PEOPLE FEEL LIKE WHEN THEY GET STABBED ON THE STREET.
I WANT ...
...TO WRITE.
GUGUGU
I WANT TO LET THE WORLD KNOW ABOUT THAT FEAR.

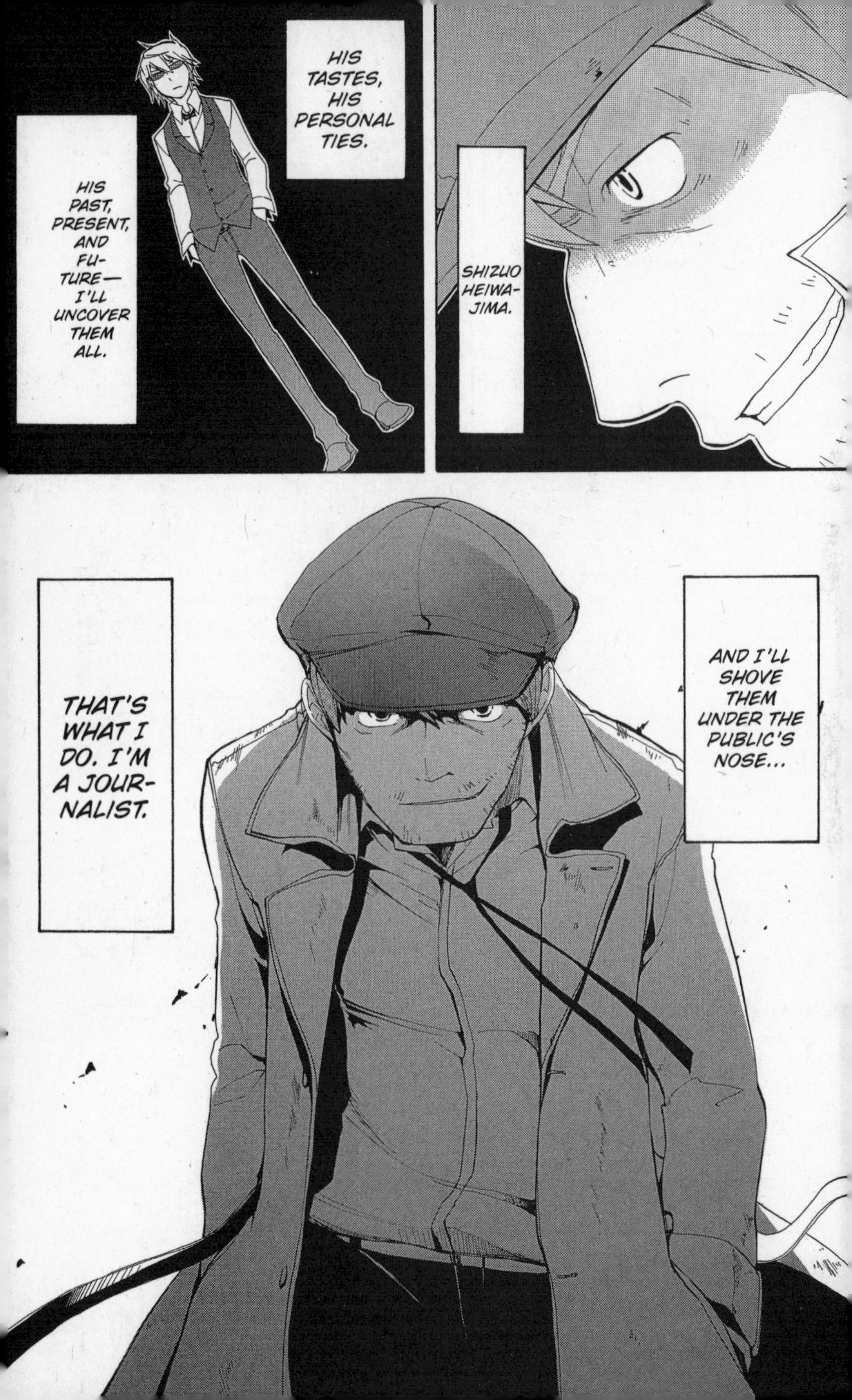
SHIZUO HEIWA-JIMA.
HIS TASTES, HIS PERSONAL TIES.
HIS PAST, PRESENT, AND FU-TURE—I'LL UNCOVER THEM ALL.
AND I'LL SHOVE THEM UNDER THE PUBLIC'S NOSE...
THAT'S WHAT I DO. I'M A JOUR-NALIST.

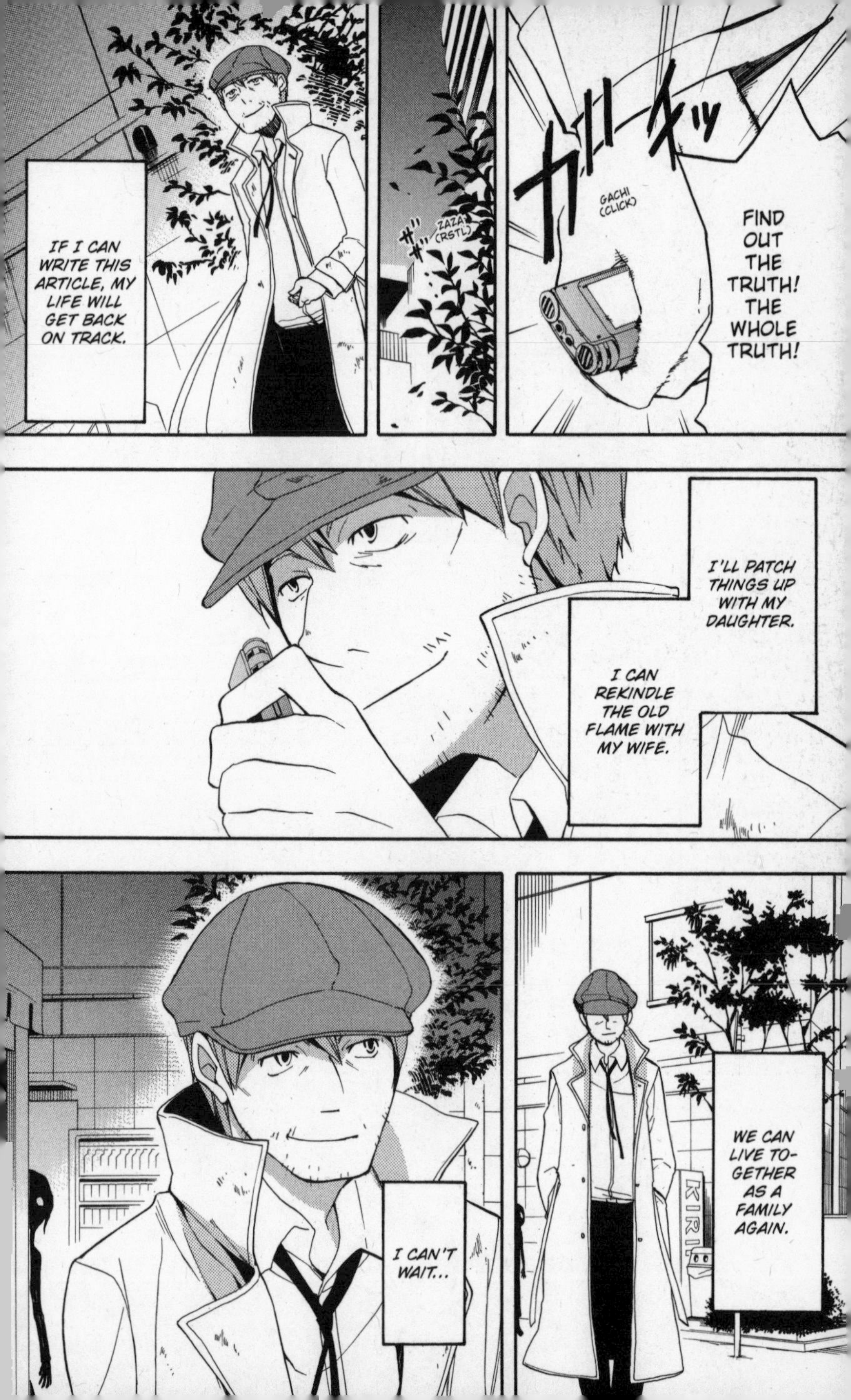
GACHI (CLICK)
FIND OUT THE TRUTH! THE WHOLE TRUTH!
ZAZA (RSTL)
IF I CAN WRITE THIS ARTICLE, MY LIFE WILL GET BACK ON TRACK.
I'LL PATCH THINGS UP WITH MY DAUGHTER.
I CAN REKINDLE THE OLD FLAME WITH MY WIFE.
WE CAN LIVE TO-GETHER AS A FAMILY AGAIN.
KIRI
I CAN'T WAIT...

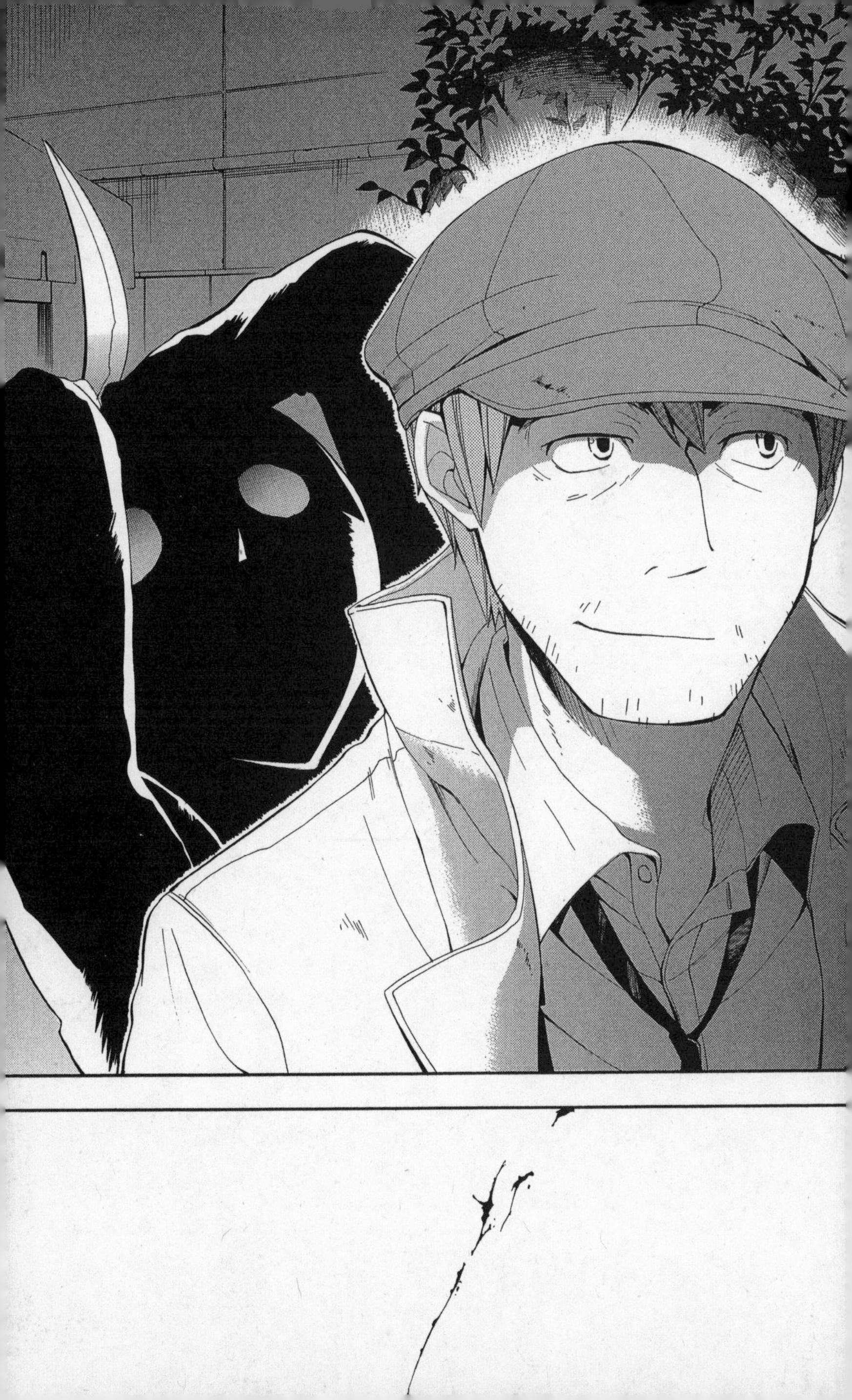

—SAIKA HAS ENTERED THE CHAT—

Saika: found it

Saika: goal, love, found

KA: Shizuo

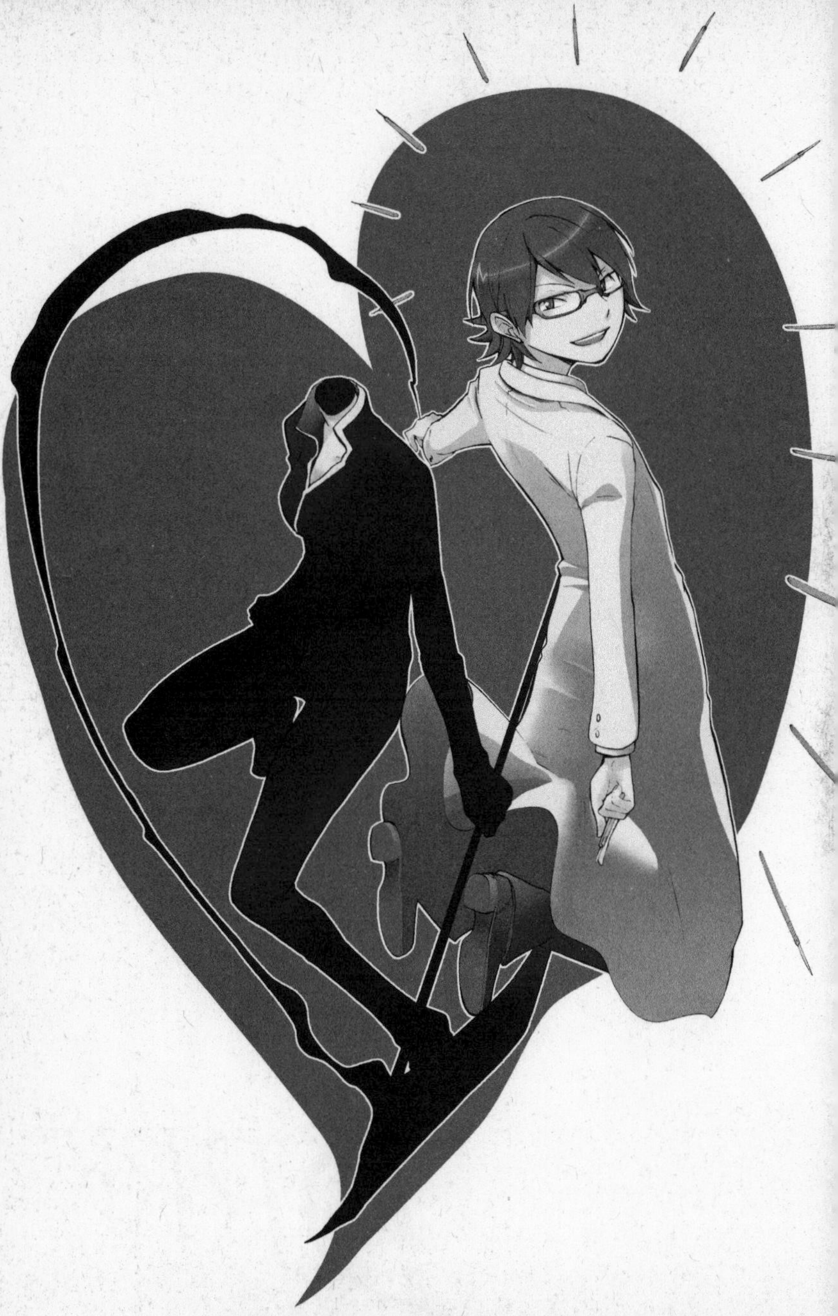

CHAPTER 2: DEMON BLADE, DOG MEAT

DRRR!!

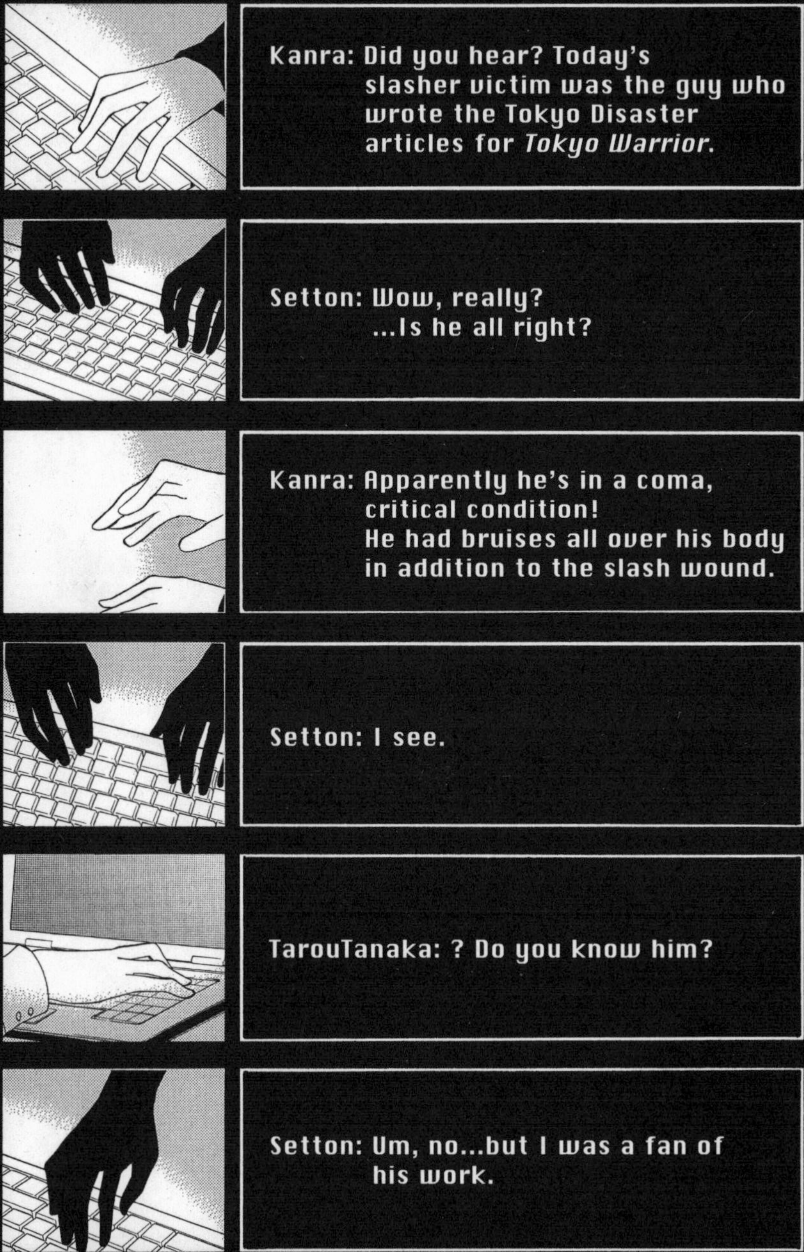

Kanra: Did you hear? Today's slasher victim was the guy who wrote the Tokyo Disaster articles for *Tokyo Warrior*.

Setton: Wow, really?
...Is he all right?

Kanra: Apparently he's in a coma, critical condition!
He had bruises all over his body in addition to the slash wound.

Setton: I see.

TarouTanaka: ? Do you know him?

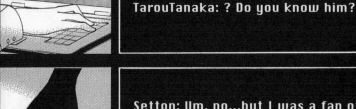

Setton: Um, no...but I was a fan of his work.

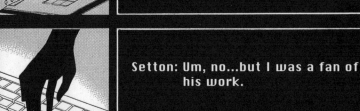

—SAIKA HAS ENTERED THE CHAT—

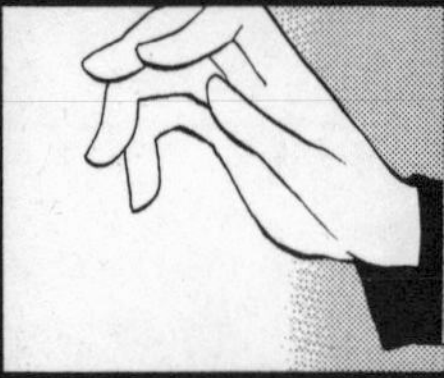

Kanra: Here we gooooo!!

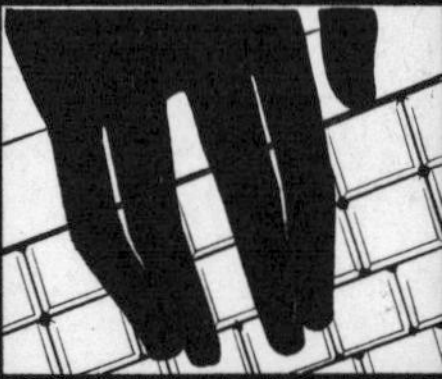

Setton: Evening, Troll-san.

Saika: cut, person, but, still, bad

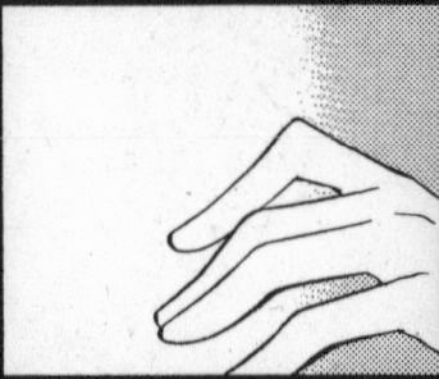

Kanra: Don't bother, Setton-san.
It won't respond to our
messages.

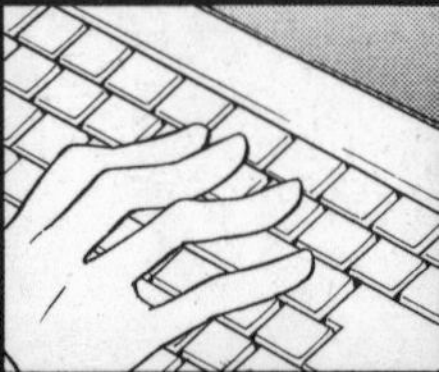

TarouTanaka: I'm guessing it's a bot of
some kind.
Kinda creepy, isn't it?

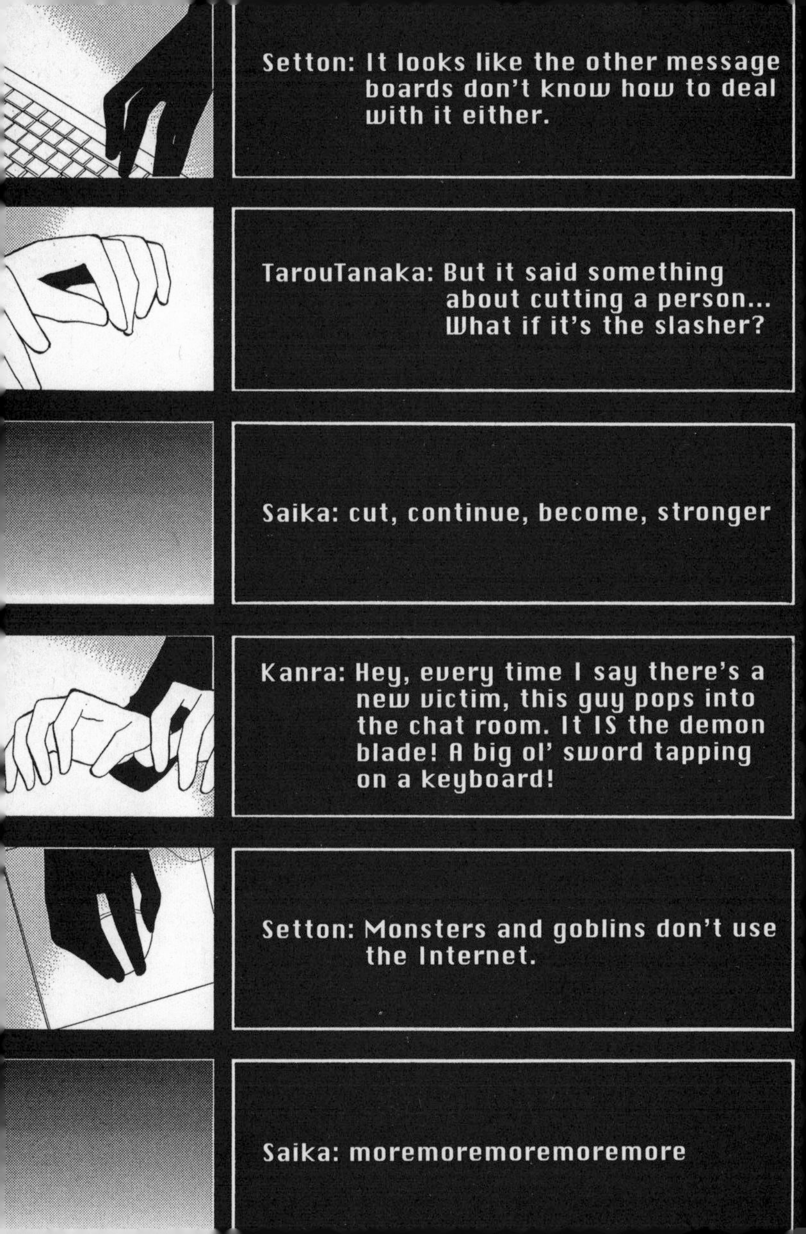
Setton: It looks like the other message boards don't know how to deal with it either.
TarouTanaka: But it said something about cutting a person... What if it's the slasher?
Saika: cut, continue, become, stronger
Kanra: Hey, every time I say there's a new victim, this guy pops into the chat room. It IS the demon blade! A big ol' sword tapping on a keyboard!
Setton: Monsters and goblins don't use the Internet.
Saika: moremoremoremoremore

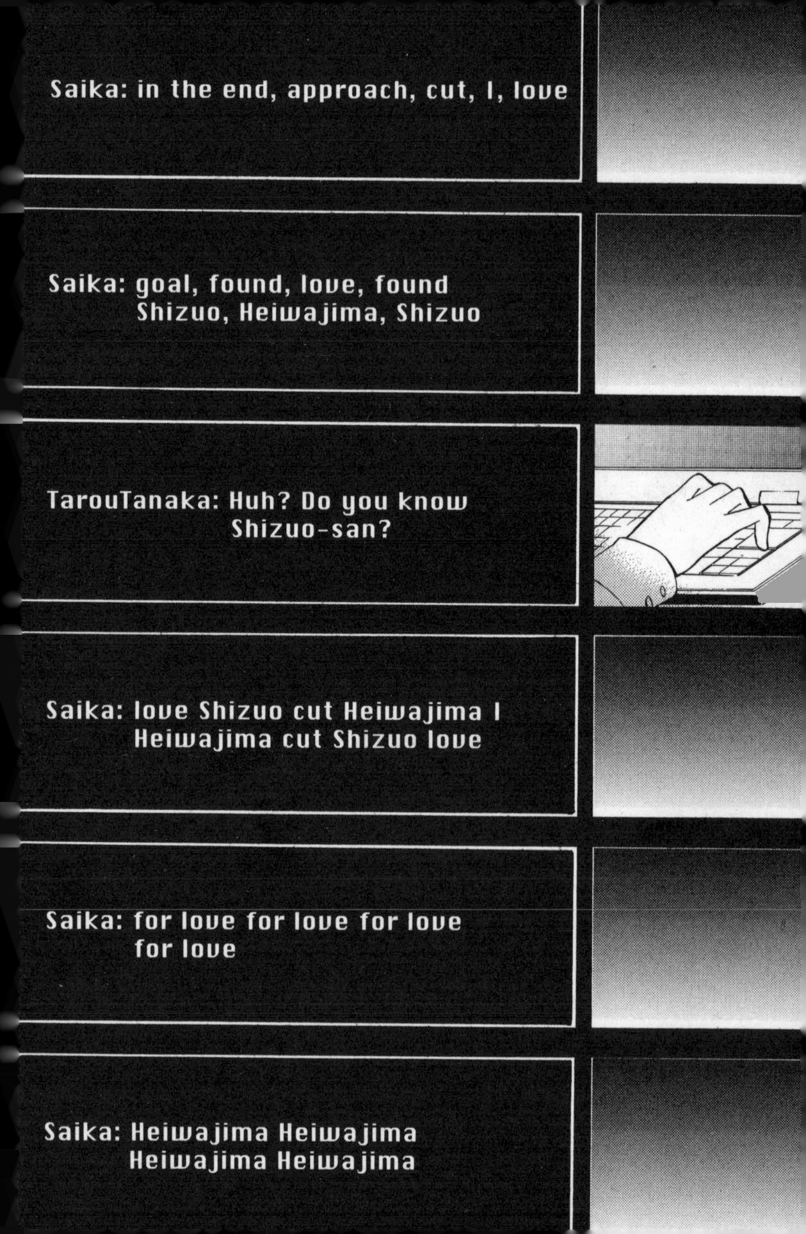
Saika: in the end, approach, cut, I, love
Saika: goal, found, love, found Shizuo, Heiwajima, Shizuo
TarouTanaka: Huh? Do you know Shizuo-san?
Saika: love Shizuo cut Heiwajima I Heiwajima cut Shizuo love
Saika: for love for love for love for love
Saika: Heiwajima Heiwajima Heiwajima Heiwajima

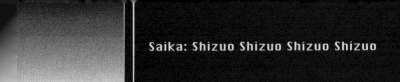

Saika: Shizuo Shizuo Shizuo Shizuo

<Private Mode>

TarouTanaka: ...Izaya-san.

<Private Mode>

Kanra: Damn, is this someone Shizu-chan knows?
No way Shizu-chan would let someone this annoying live.

TarouTanaka: I think we should just leave the chat room until it calms down.
See you guys later.

Setton: Okay, me too.

Kanra: I guess that's it for today.

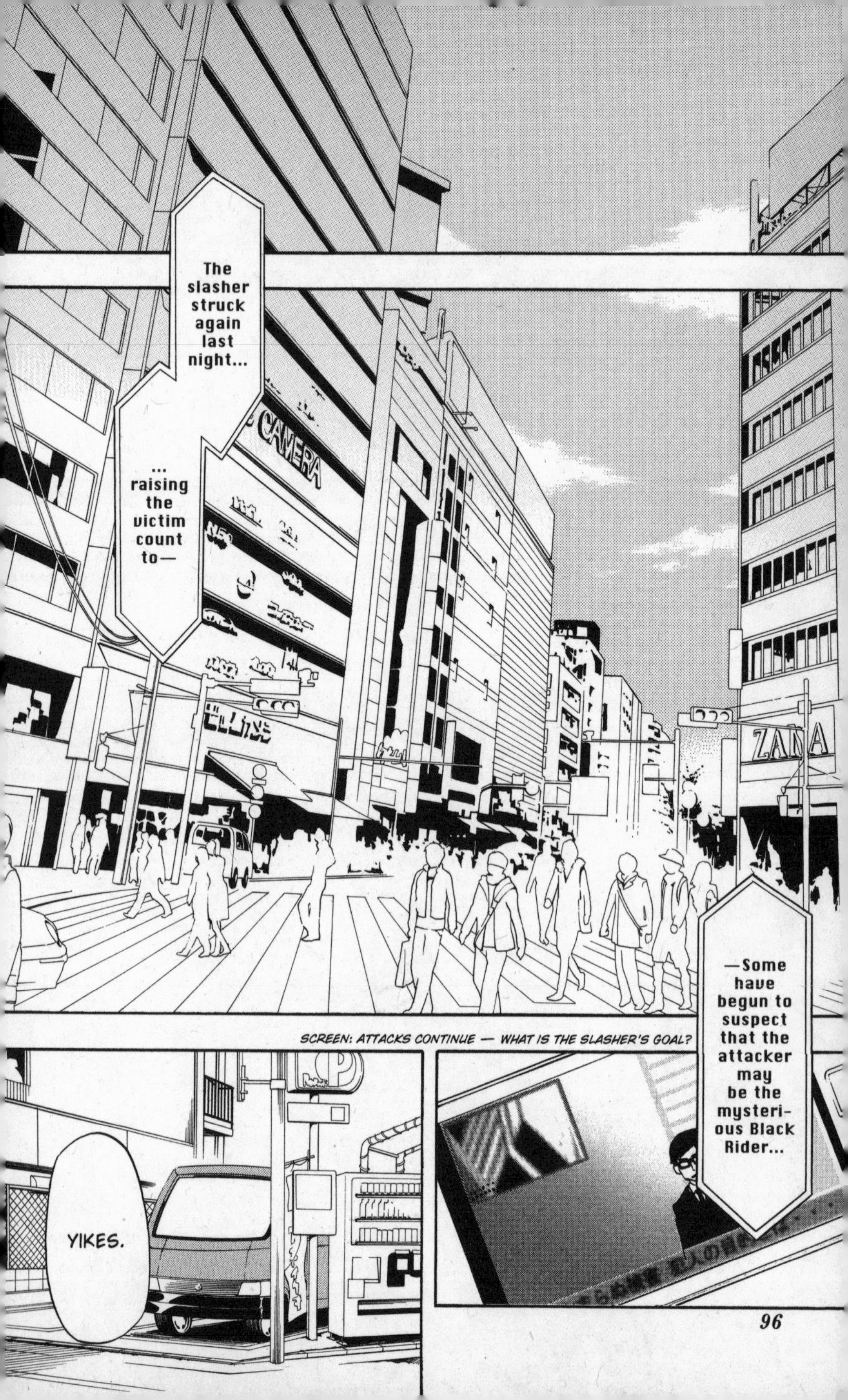
The slasher struck again last night...
... raising the victim count to—
SCREEN: ATTACKS CONTINUE — WHAT IS THE SLASHER'S GOAL?
—Some have begun to suspect that the attacker may be the mysterious Black Rider...
YIKES.

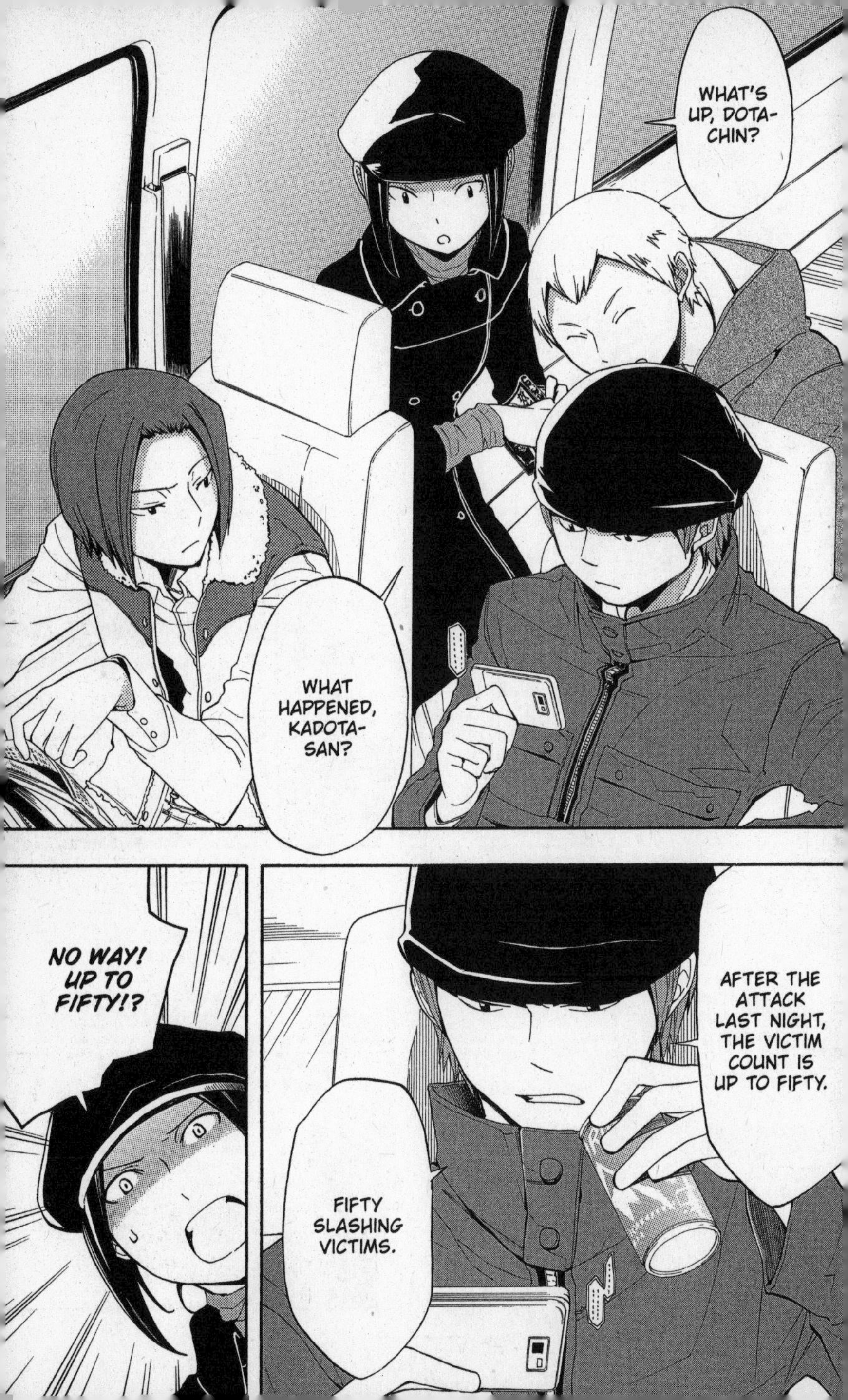
WHAT'S UP, DOTA-CHIN?
WHAT HAPPENED, KADOTA-SAN?
AFTER THE ATTACK LAST NIGHT, THE VICTIM COUNT IS UP TO FIFTY.
FIFTY SLASHING VICTIMS.
NO WAY! UP TO FIFTY!?

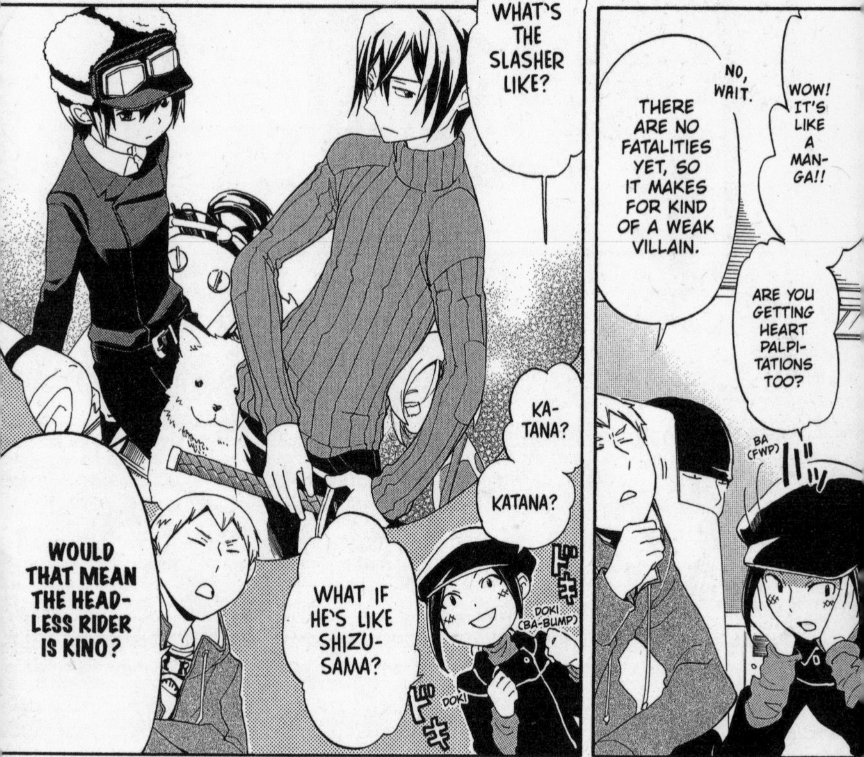
WOW! IT'S LIKE A MAN-GA!!
NO, WAIT.
THERE ARE NO FATALITIES YET, SO IT MAKES FOR KIND OF A WEAK VILLAIN.
ARE YOU GETTING HEART PALPI-TATIONS TOO?
BA (FWP)
WHAT'S THE SLASHER LIKE?
KA-TANA?
KATANA?
DOKI (BA-BUMP)
WHAT IF HE'S LIKE SHIZU-SAMA?
DOKI
WOULD THAT MEAN THE HEAD-LESS RIDER IS KINO?

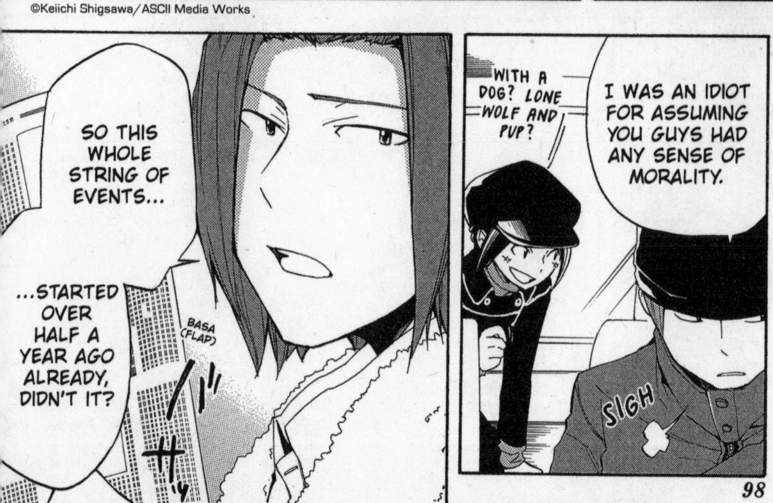
I WAS AN IDIOT FOR ASSUMING YOU GUYS HAD ANY SENSE OF MORALITY.
WITH A DOG? LONE WOLF AND PUP?
SIGH
SO THIS WHOLE STRING OF EVENTS...
...STARTED OVER HALF A YEAR AGO ALREADY, DIDN'T IT?
BASA (FLAP)

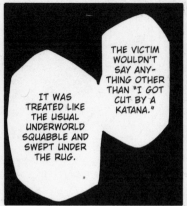

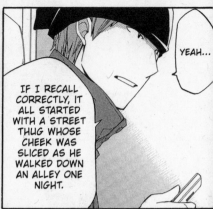

YEAH...
IF I RECALL CORRECTLY, IT ALL STARTED WITH A STREET THUG WHOSE CHEEK WAS SLICED AS HE WALKED DOWN AN ALLEY ONE NIGHT.
THE VICTIM WOULDN'T SAY ANY-THING OTHER THAN "I GOT CUT BY A KATANA."
IT WAS TREATED LIKE THE USUAL UNDERWORLD SQUABBLE AND SWEPT UNDER THE RUG.
BUT TWO MONTHS LATER, A TYPICAL SALARYMAN WITH NO HISTORY OF VIOLENCE GOT SLASHED.
THEN THERE WAS THE COUPLE ON CHRISTMAS.
ONCE IT WAS ANNOUNCED THAT THESE WERE ALL THE WORK OF THE SAME ATTACKER, THE STORY STARTED PICKING UP STEAM.
NOW EVERY SINGLE CHANNEL AND MAGAZINE IS DEDICATED TO COVERING THE SLASHER.
BASA
LATELY, THE PACE HAS PICKED UP TO ABOUT ONE VICTIM PER DAY.

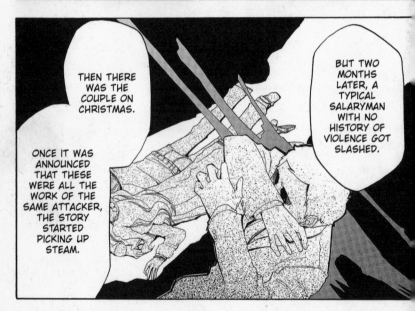

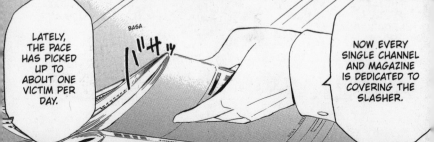

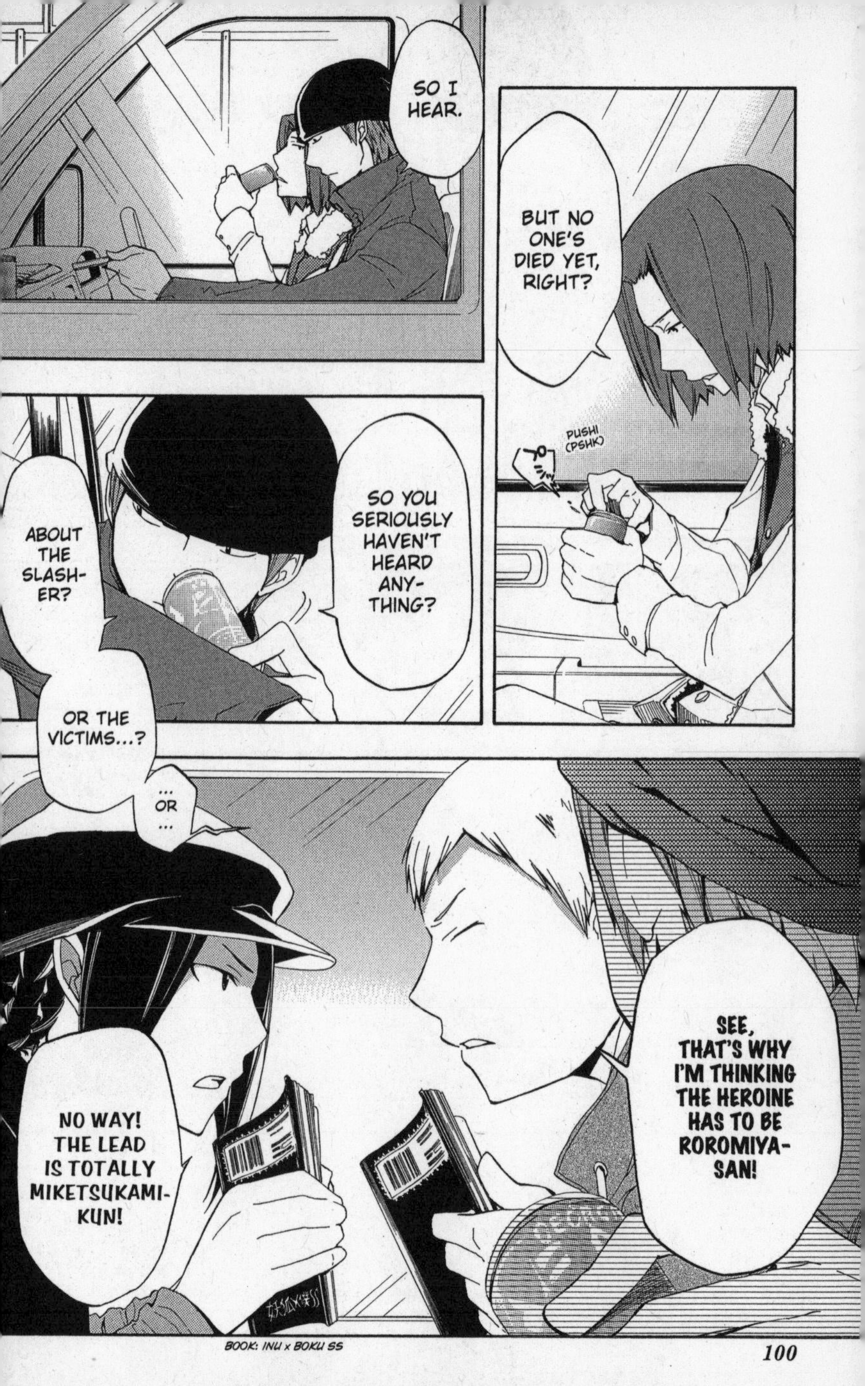
SO I HEAR.
BUT NO ONE'S DIED YET, RIGHT?
PUSHI (PSHK)
SO YOU SERIOUSLY HAVEN'T HEARD ANYTHING?
ABOUT THE SLASHER?
OR THE VICTIMS...?
...OR...
SEE, THAT'S WHY I'M THINKING THE HEROINE HAS TO BE ROROMIYA-SAN!
NO WAY! THE LEAD IS TOTALLY MIKETSUKAMI-KUN!

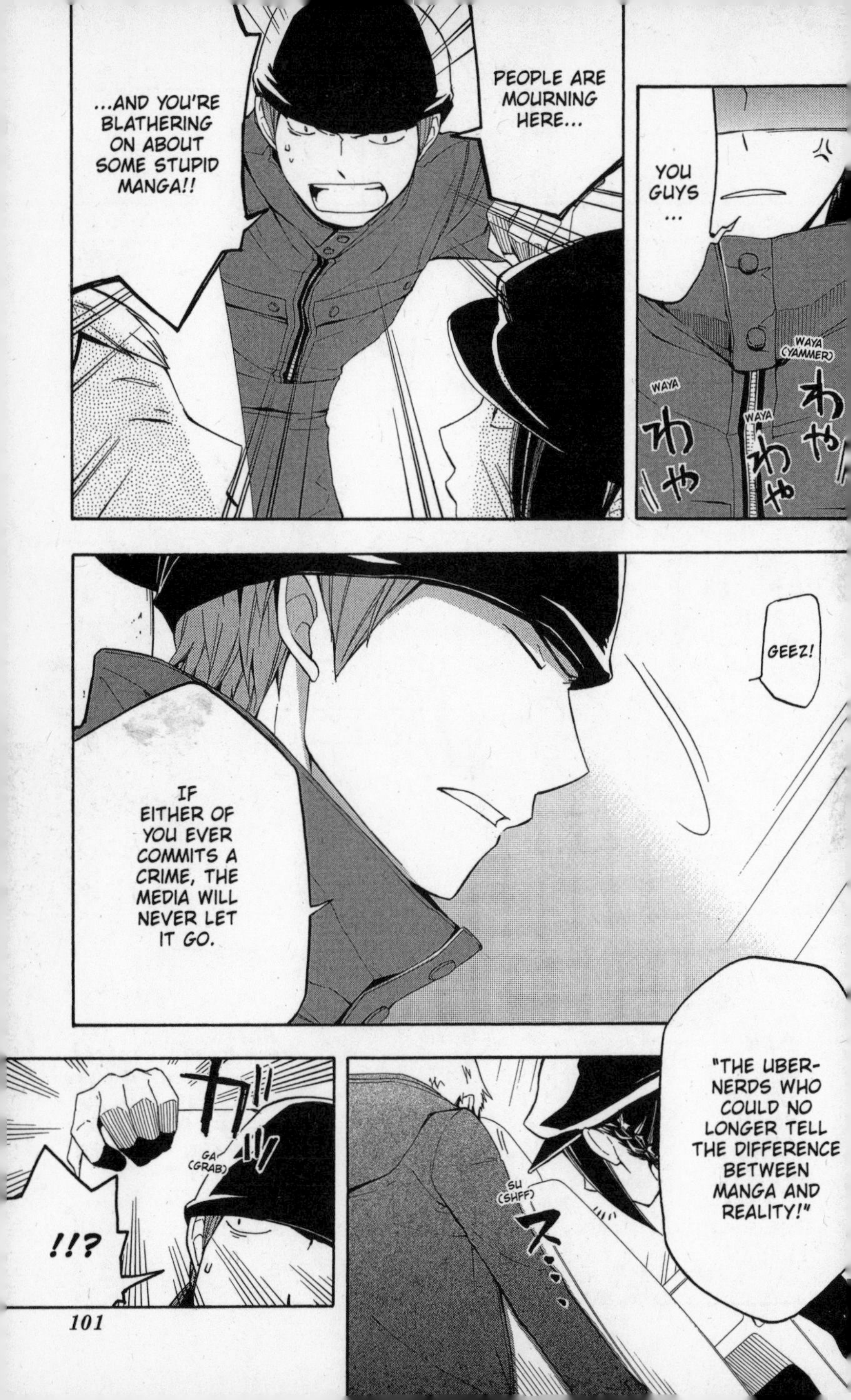
YOU GUYS...
WAYA (YAMMER)
わや
WAYA
わやわや
WAYA
わやわや
PEOPLE ARE MOURNING HERE...
...AND YOU'RE BLATHERING ON ABOUT SOME STUPID MANGA!!
GEEZ!
IF EITHER OF YOU EVER COMMITS A CRIME, THE MEDIA WILL NEVER LET IT GO.
"THE UBER-NERDS WHO COULD NO LONGER TELL THE DIFFERENCE BETWEEN MANGA AND REALITY!"
SU (SHFF)
ス...
GA (GRAB)
ガッ
!!?

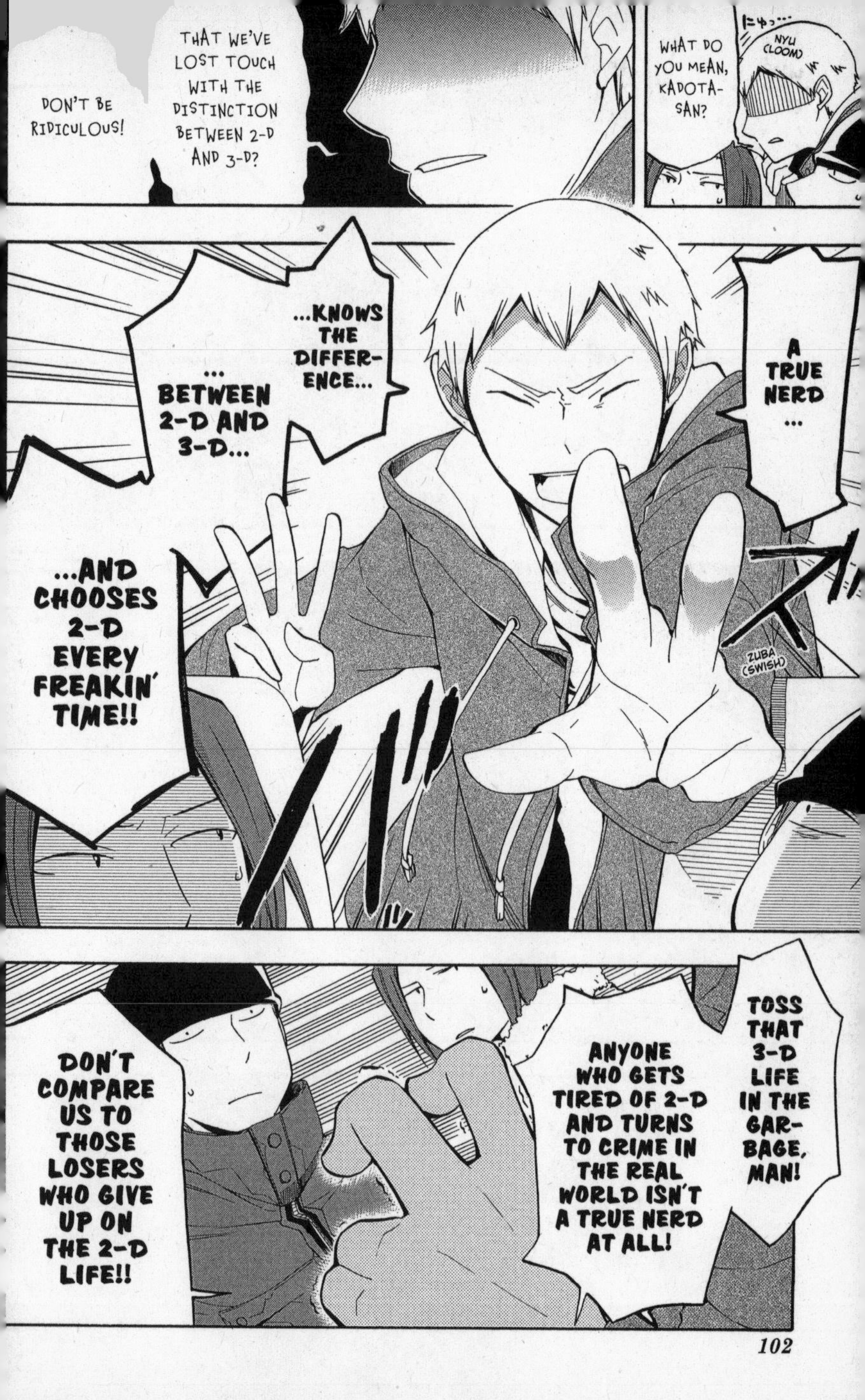
にゅっ
NYU (LOOM)
WHAT DO YOU MEAN, KADOTA-SAN?
THAT WE'VE LOST TOUCH WITH THE DISTINCTION BETWEEN 2-D AND 3-D?
DON'T BE RIDICULOUS!
A TRUE NERD...
...KNOWS THE DIFFER-ENCE...
...BETWEEN 2-D AND 3-D...
ZUBA (SWISH)
...AND CHOOSES 2-D EVERY FREAKIN' TIME!!
TOSS THAT 3-D LIFE IN THE GAR-BAGE, MAN!
ANYONE WHO GETS TIRED OF 2-D AND TURNS TO CRIME IN THE REAL WORLD ISN'T A TRUE NERD AT ALL!
DON'T COMPARE US TO THOSE LOSERS WHO GIVE UP ON THE 2-D LIFE!!

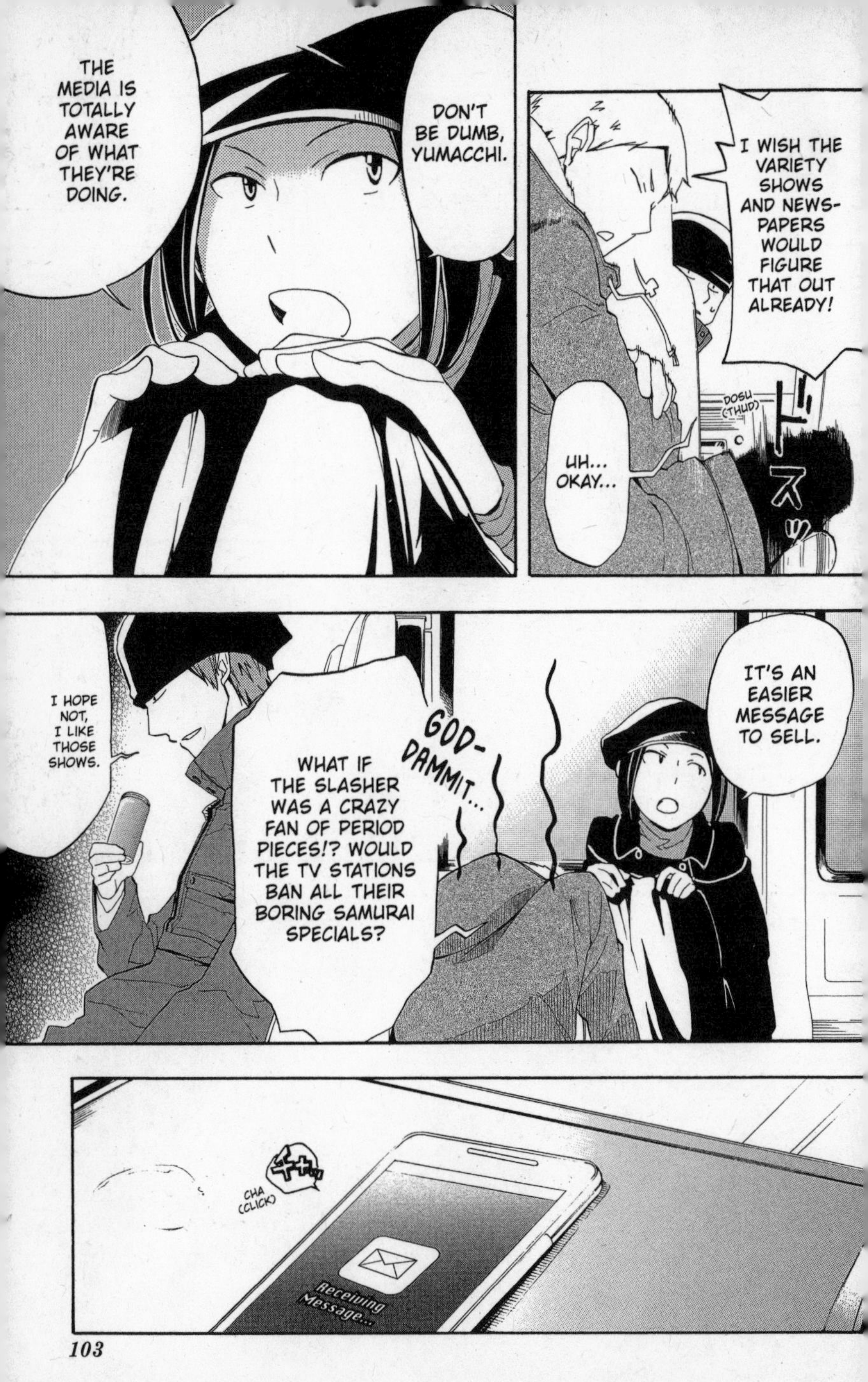
I WISH THE VARIETY SHOWS AND NEWS-PAPERS WOULD FIGURE THAT OUT ALREADY!
DOSU (THUD)
UH... OKAY...
DON'T BE DUMB, YUMACCHI.
THE MEDIA IS TOTALLY AWARE OF WHAT THEY'RE DOING.
IT'S AN EASIER MESSAGE TO SELL.
GOD-DAMMIT...
WHAT IF THE SLASHER WAS A CRAZY FAN OF PERIOD PIECES!? WOULD THE TV STATIONS BAN ALL THEIR BORING SAMURAI SPECIALS?
I HOPE NOT, I LIKE THOSE SHOWS.
CHA (CLICK)
Receiving Message...

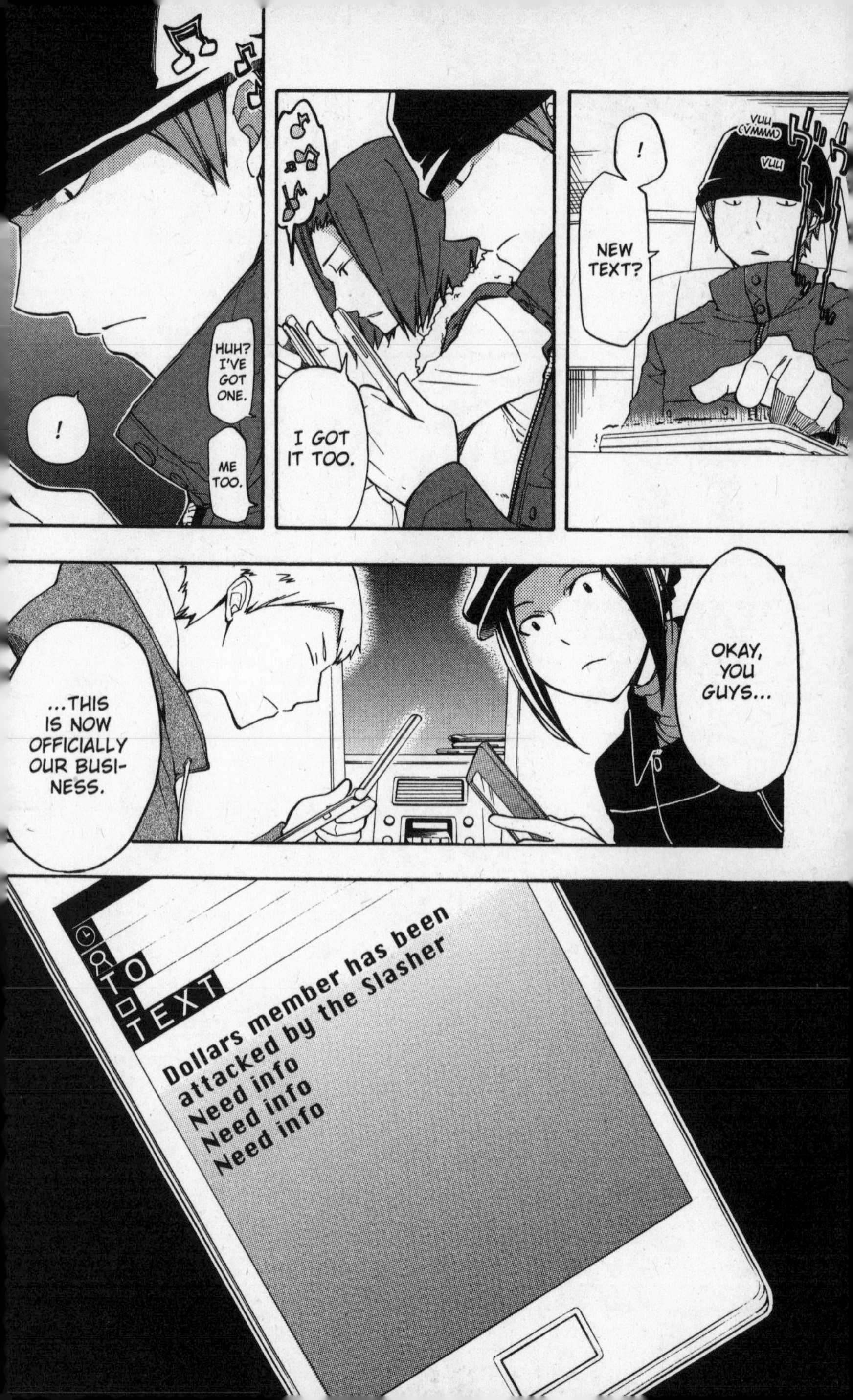

VUU (VMMM)
VUU
!
NEW TEXT?
I GOT IT TOO.
HUH? I'VE GOT ONE.
ME TOO.
!
OKAY, YOU GUYS...
...THIS IS NOW OFFICIALLY OUR BUSINESS.
TO
TEXT
Dollars member has been attacked by the Slasher
Need info
Need info
Need info

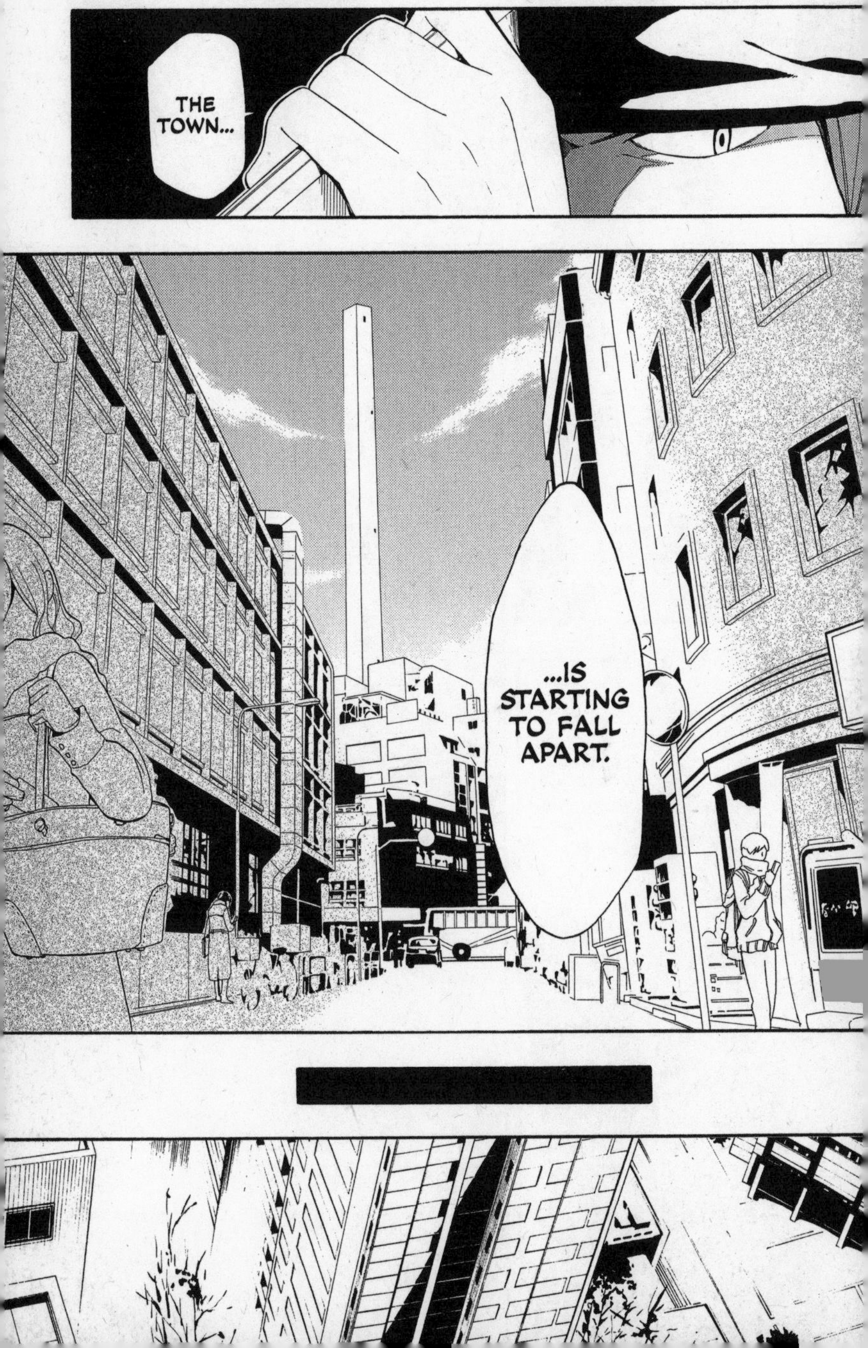

THE TOWN...
...IS STARTING TO FALL APART.
[redacted]

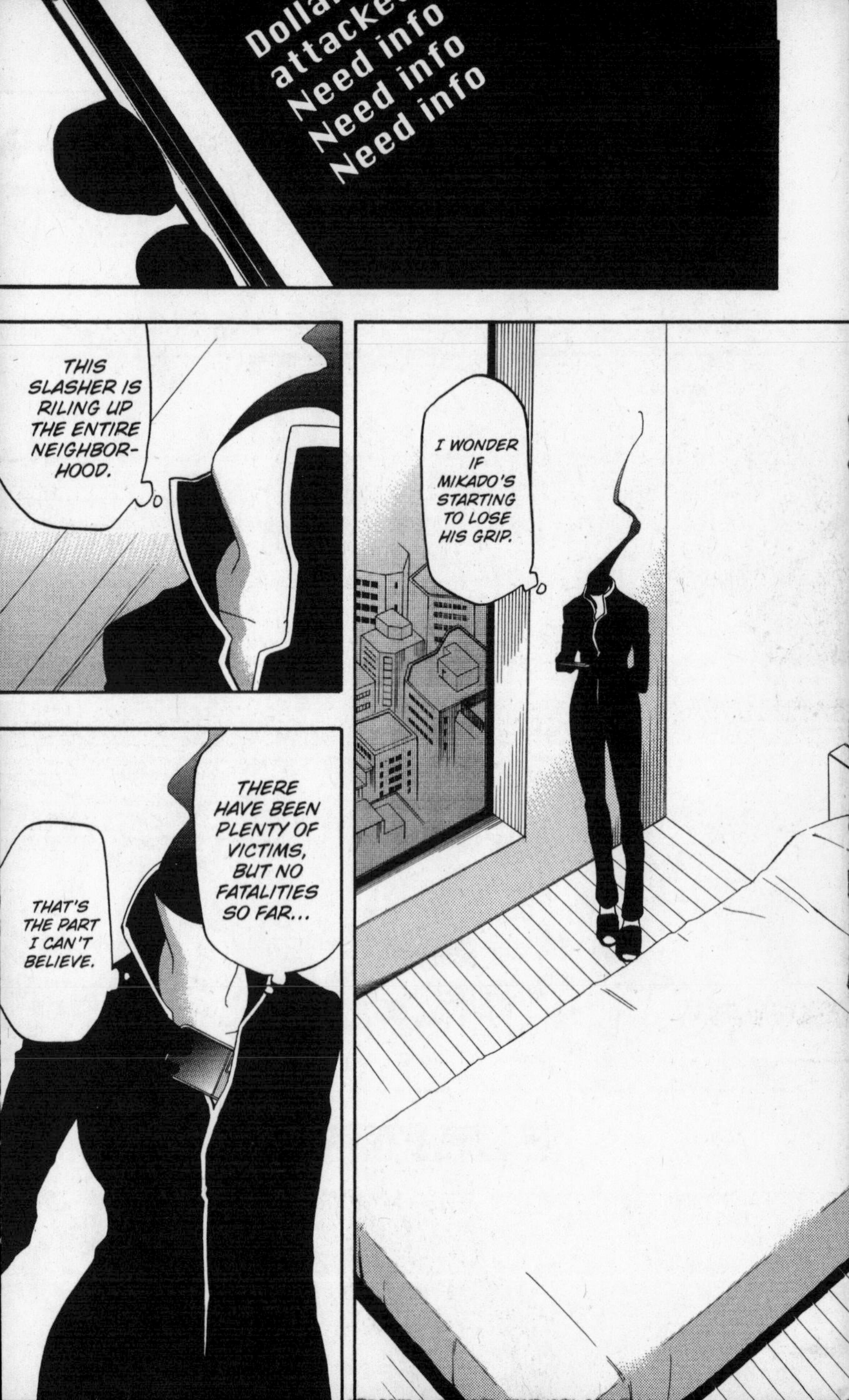
Need info
Need info
Need info
I WONDER IF MIKADO'S STARTING TO LOSE HIS GRIP.
THIS SLASHER IS RILING UP THE ENTIRE NEIGHBOR-HOOD.
THERE HAVE BEEN PLENTY OF VICTIMS, BUT NO FATALITIES SO FAR...
THAT'S THE PART I CAN'T BELIEVE.

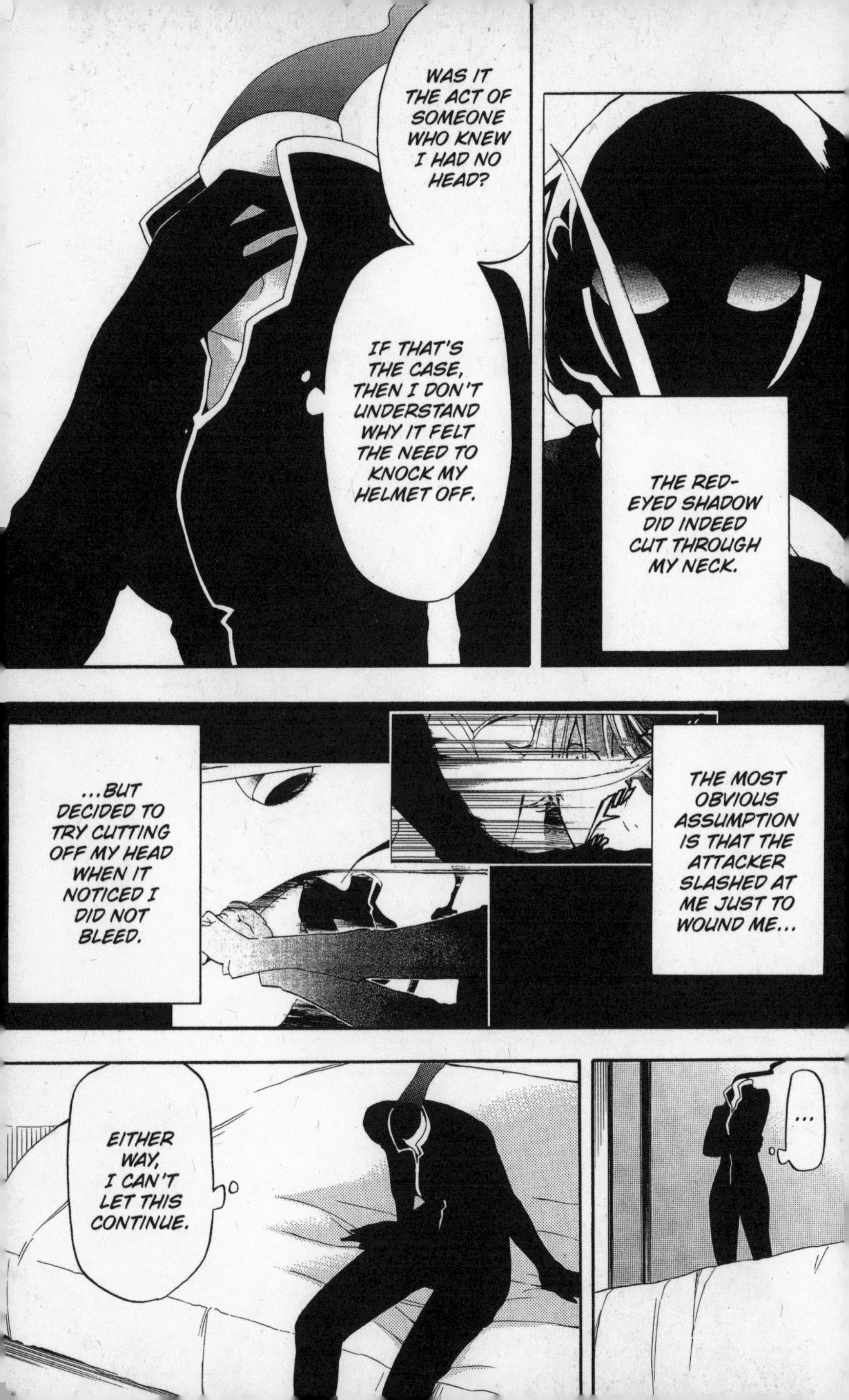
THE RED-EYED SHADOW DID INDEED CUT THROUGH MY NECK.
WAS IT THE ACT OF SOMEONE WHO KNEW I HAD NO HEAD?
IF THAT'S THE CASE, THEN I DON'T UNDERSTAND WHY IT FELT THE NEED TO KNOCK MY HELMET OFF.
THE MOST OBVIOUS ASSUMPTION IS THAT THE ATTACKER SLASHED AT ME JUST TO WOUND ME...
...BUT DECIDED TO TRY CUTTING OFF MY HEAD WHEN IT NOTICED I DID NOT BLEED.
...
EITHER WAY, I CAN'T LET THIS CONTINUE.

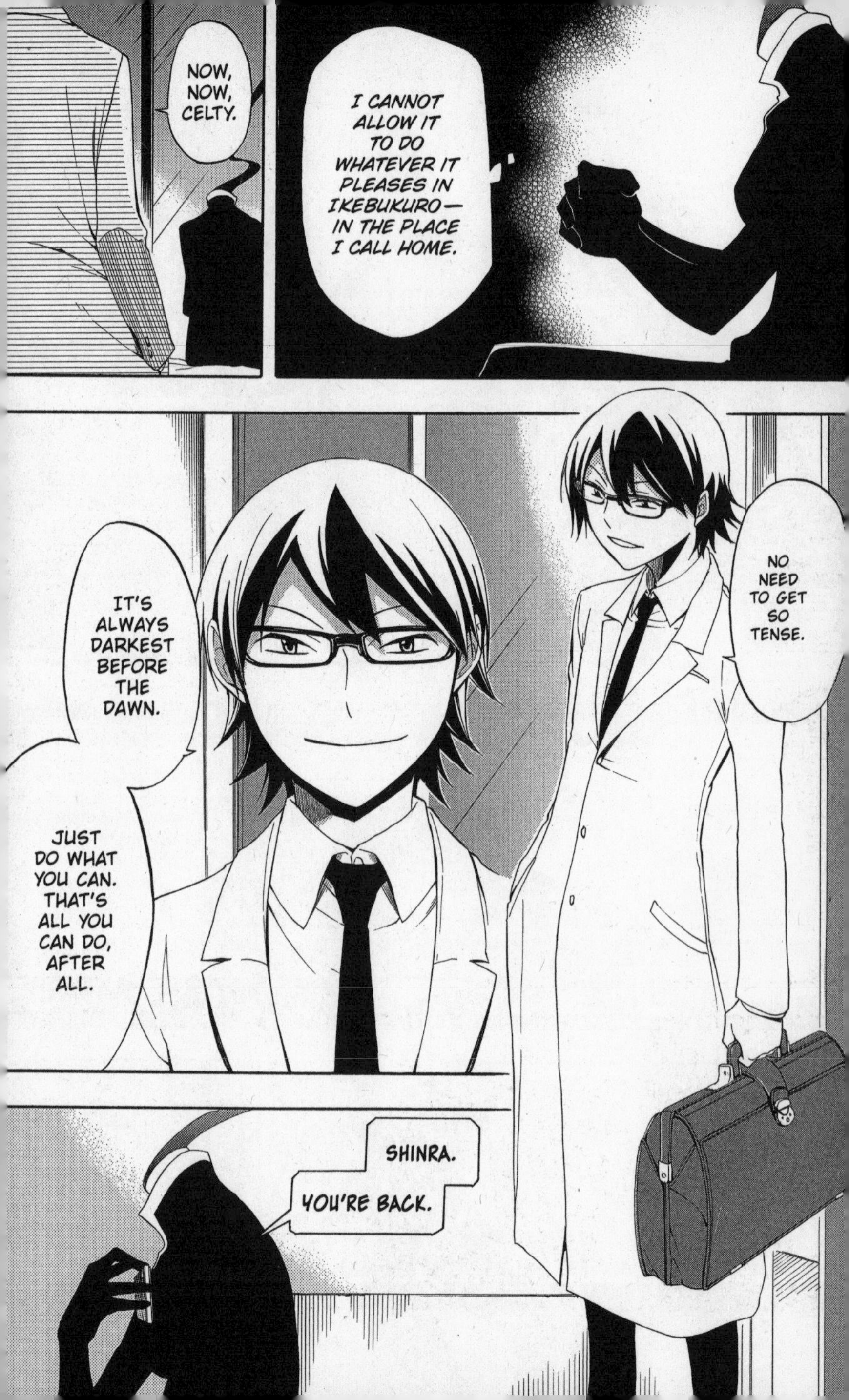
I CANNOT ALLOW IT TO DO WHATEVER IT PLEASES IN IKEBUKURO— IN THE PLACE I CALL HOME.
NOW, NOW, CELTY.
NO NEED TO GET SO TENSE.
IT'S ALWAYS DARKEST BEFORE THE DAWN.
JUST DO WHAT YOU CAN. THAT'S ALL YOU CAN DO, AFTER ALL.
SHINRA.
YOU'RE BACK.

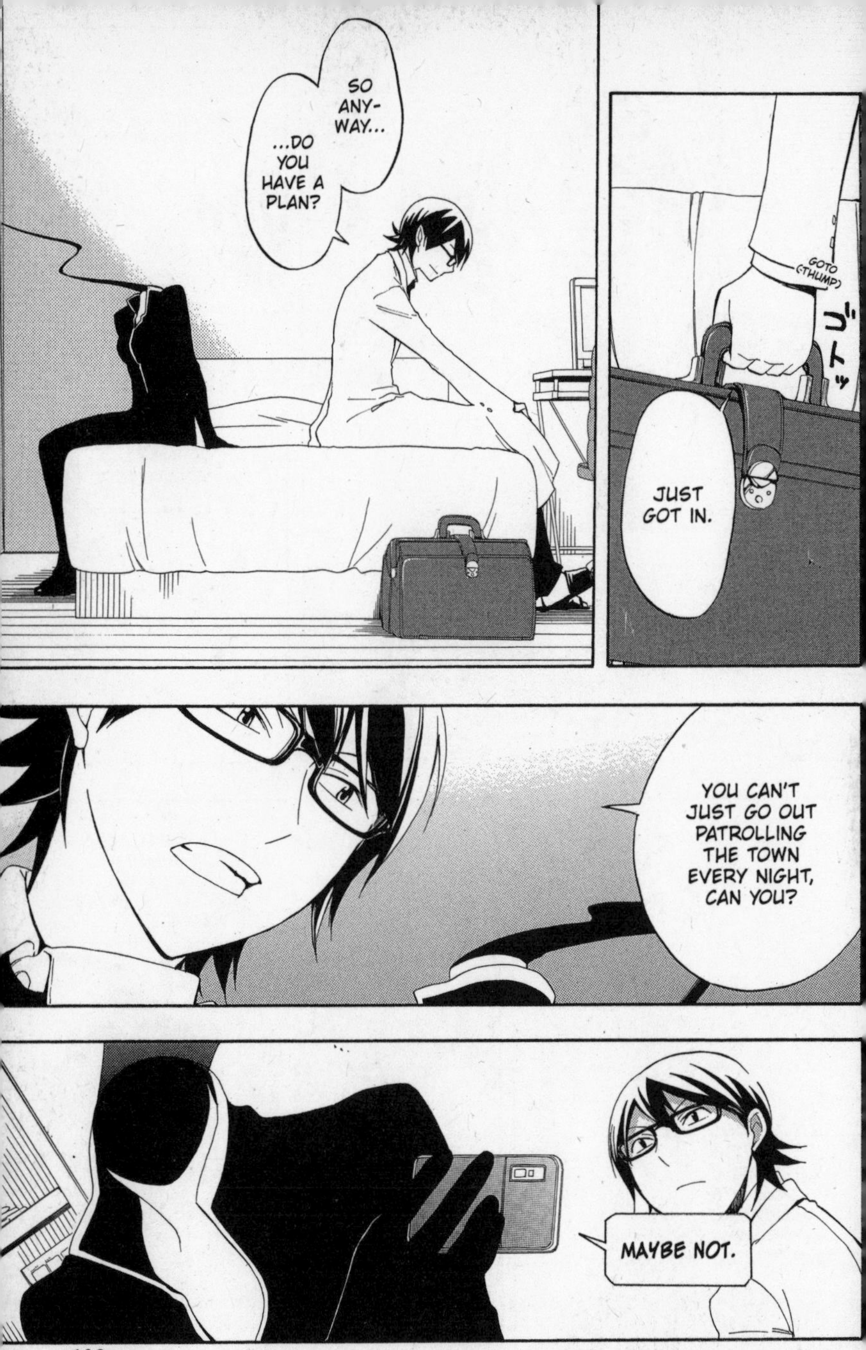
GOTO (THUMP)
ゴトッ
JUST GOT IN.
SO ANYWAY...
...DO YOU HAVE A PLAN?
YOU CAN'T JUST GO OUT PATROLLING THE TOWN EVERY NIGHT, CAN YOU?
...
MAYBE NOT.

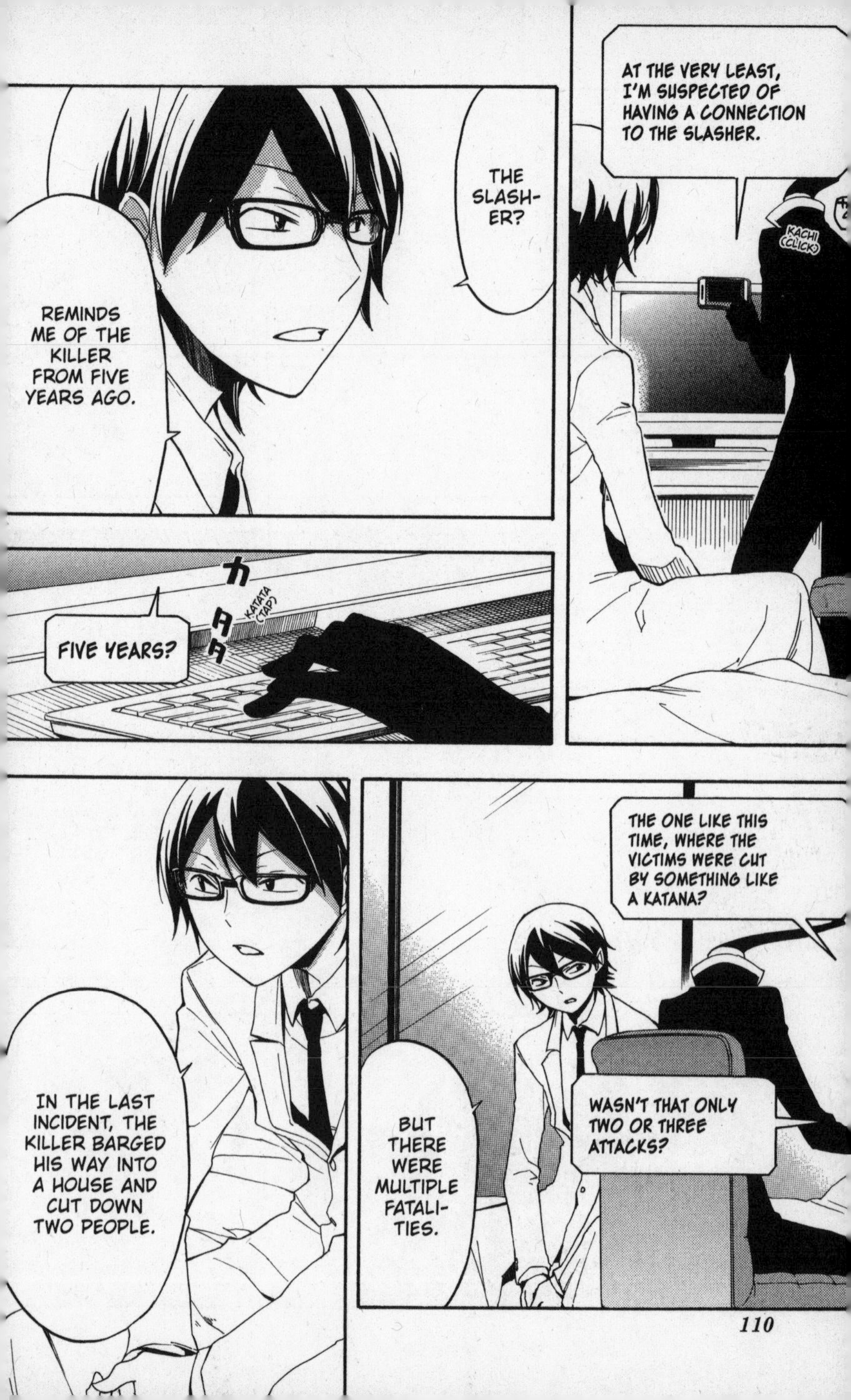
AT THE VERY LEAST, I'M SUSPECTED OF HAVING A CONNECTION TO THE SLASHER.
KACHI (CLICK)
THE SLASH-ER?
REMINDS ME OF THE KILLER FROM FIVE YEARS AGO.
KATATA (TAP)
FIVE YEARS?
THE ONE LIKE THIS TIME, WHERE THE VICTIMS WERE CUT BY SOMETHING LIKE A KATANA?
WASN'T THAT ONLY TWO OR THREE ATTACKS?
BUT THERE WERE MULTIPLE FATALI-TIES.
IN THE LAST INCIDENT, THE KILLER BARGED HIS WAY INTO A HOUSE AND CUT DOWN TWO PEOPLE.

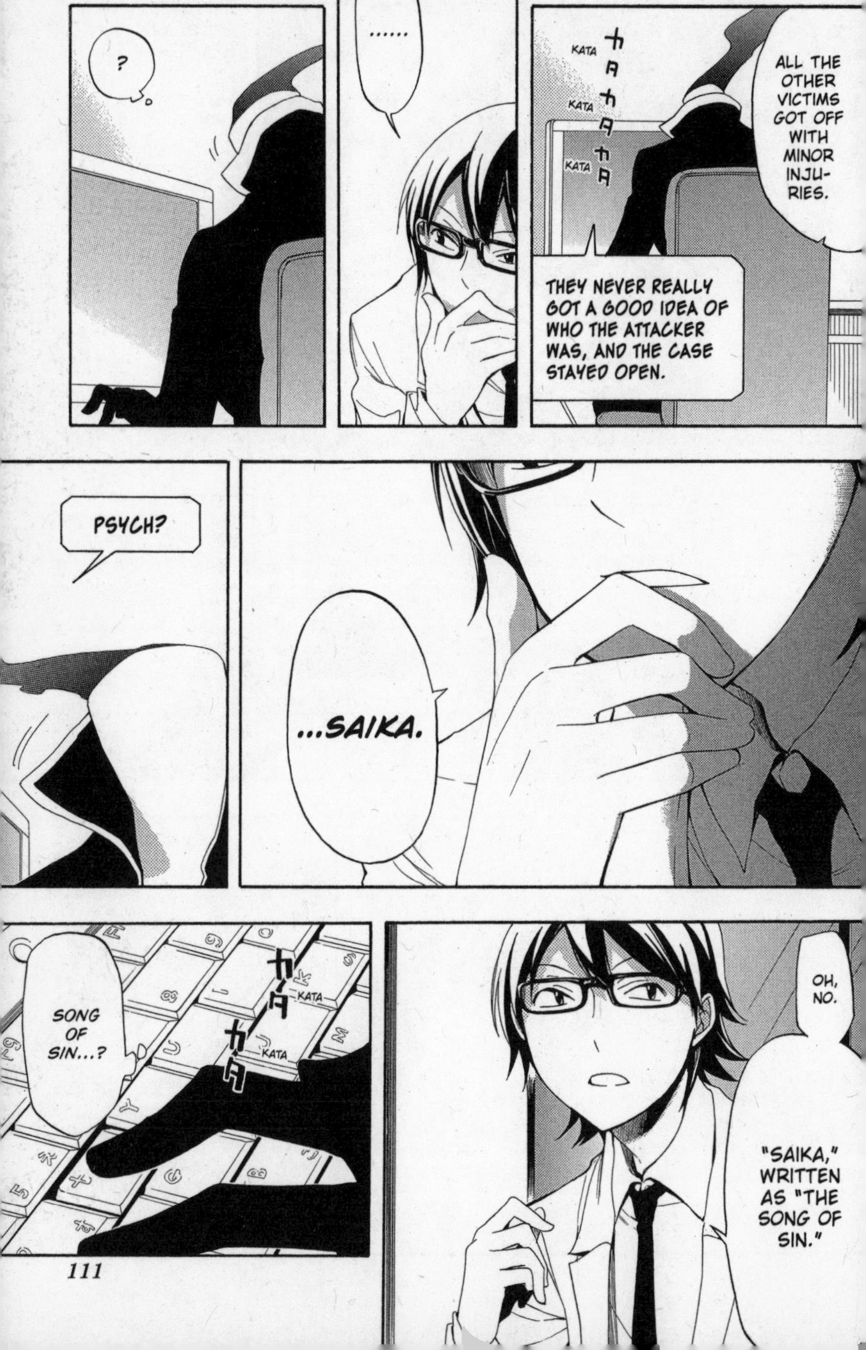
ALL THE OTHER VICTIMS GOT OFF WITH MINOR INJURIES.
KATA KATA KATA
THEY NEVER REALLY GOT A GOOD IDEA OF WHO THE ATTACKER WAS, AND THE CASE STAYED OPEN.
......
?
...SAIKA.
PSYCH?
OH, NO.
"SAIKA," WRITTEN AS "THE SONG OF SIN."
KATA KATA
SONG OF SIN...?

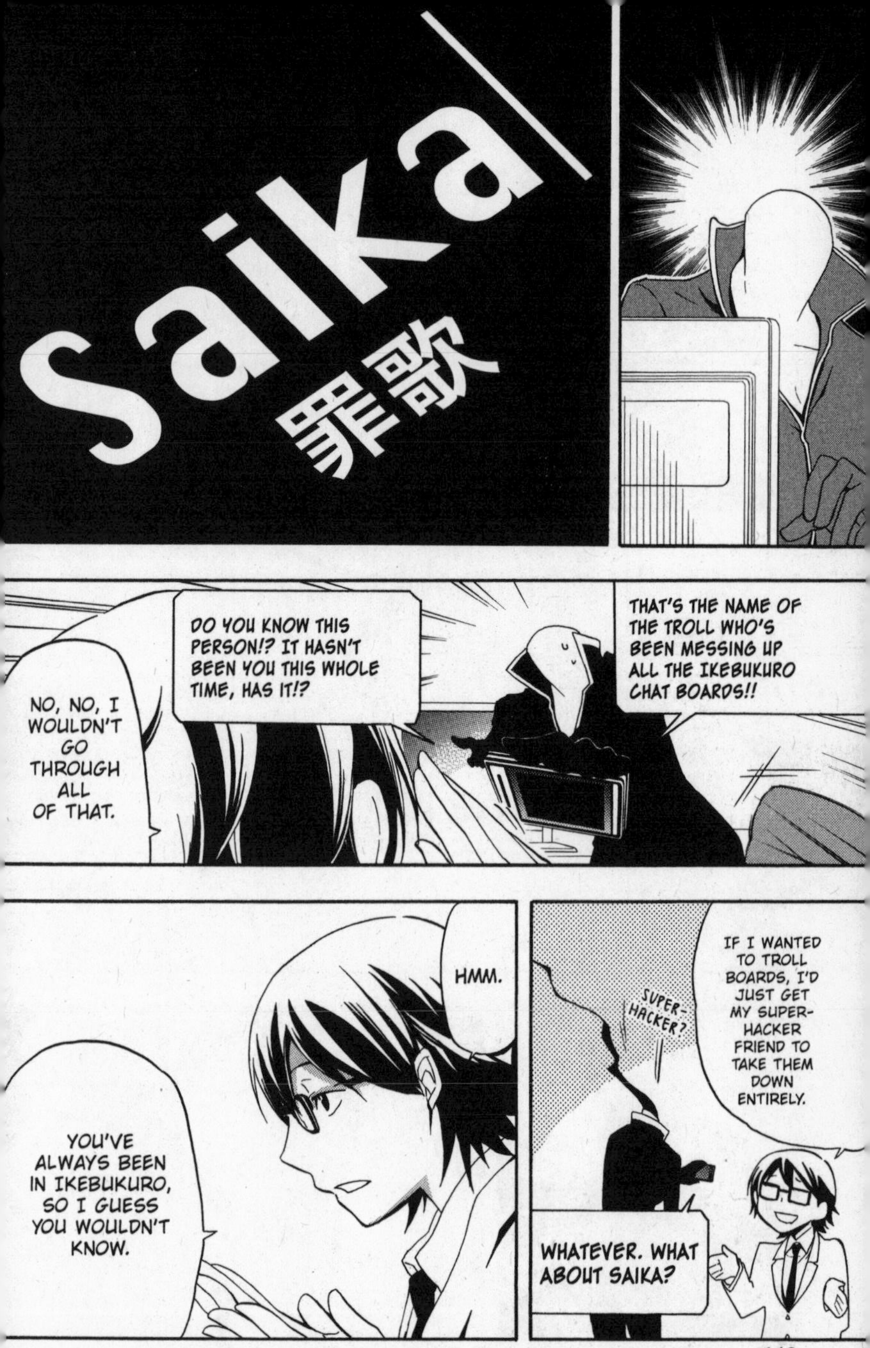
Saika
罪歌
THAT'S THE NAME OF THE TROLL WHO'S BEEN MESSING UP ALL THE IKEBUKURO CHAT BOARDS!!
DO YOU KNOW THIS PERSON!? IT HASN'T BEEN YOU THIS WHOLE TIME, HAS IT!?
NO, NO, I WOULDN'T GO THROUGH ALL OF THAT.
IF I WANTED TO TROLL BOARDS, I'D JUST GET MY SUPER-HACKER FRIEND TO TAKE THEM DOWN ENTIRELY.
SUPER-HACKER?
WHATEVER. WHAT ABOUT SAIKA?
HMM.
YOU'VE ALWAYS BEEN IN IKEBUKURO, SO I GUESS YOU WOULDN'T KNOW.

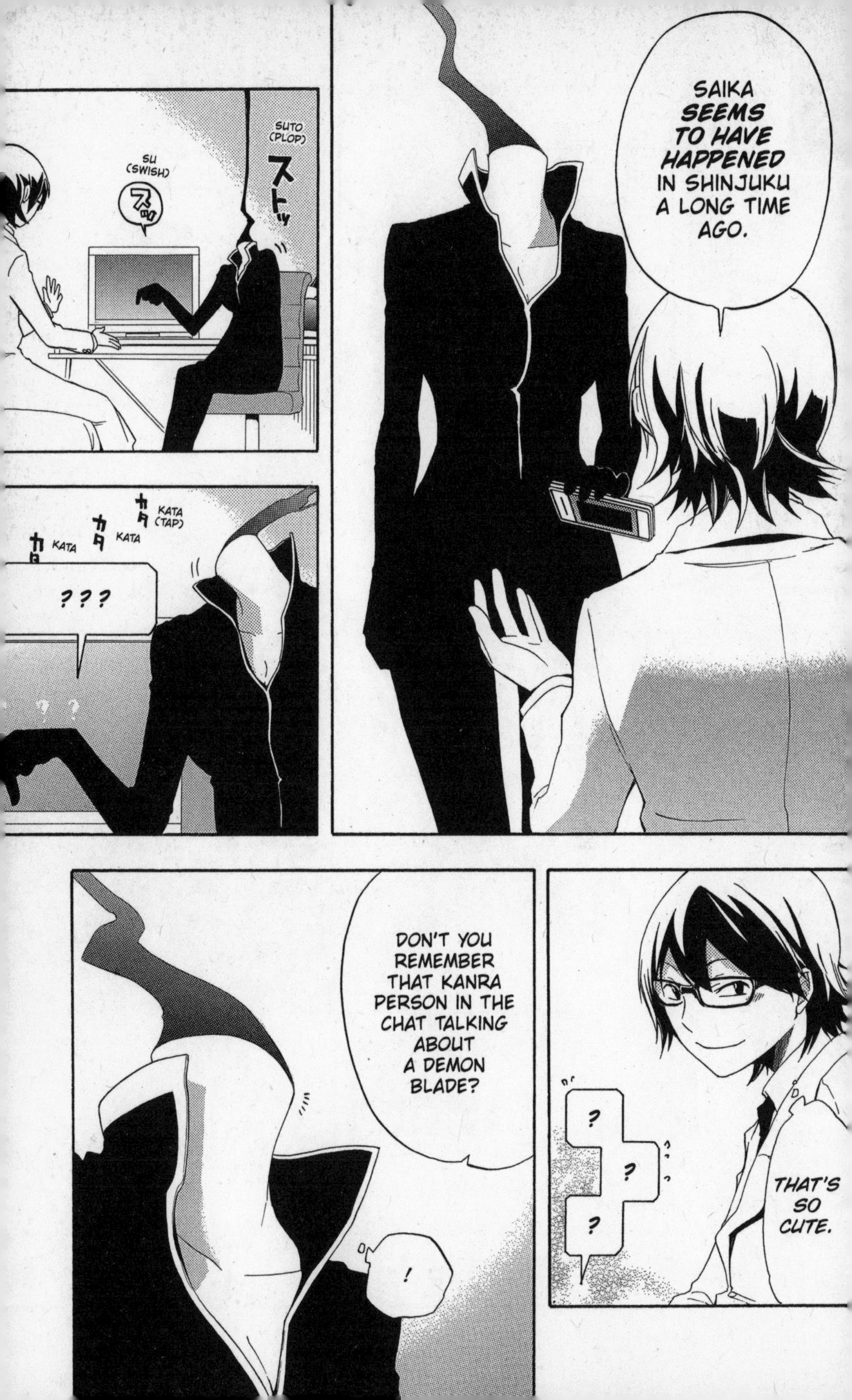
SAIKA SEEMS TO HAVE HAPPENED IN SHINJUKU A LONG TIME AGO.
ストッ
SUTO (PLOP)
スッ
SU (SWISH)
カタ
KATA (TAP)
カタ
KATA
カタ
KATA
???
??
THAT'S SO CUTE.
?
?
?
DON'T YOU REMEMBER THAT KANRA PERSON IN THE CHAT TALKING ABOUT A DEMON BLADE?
!

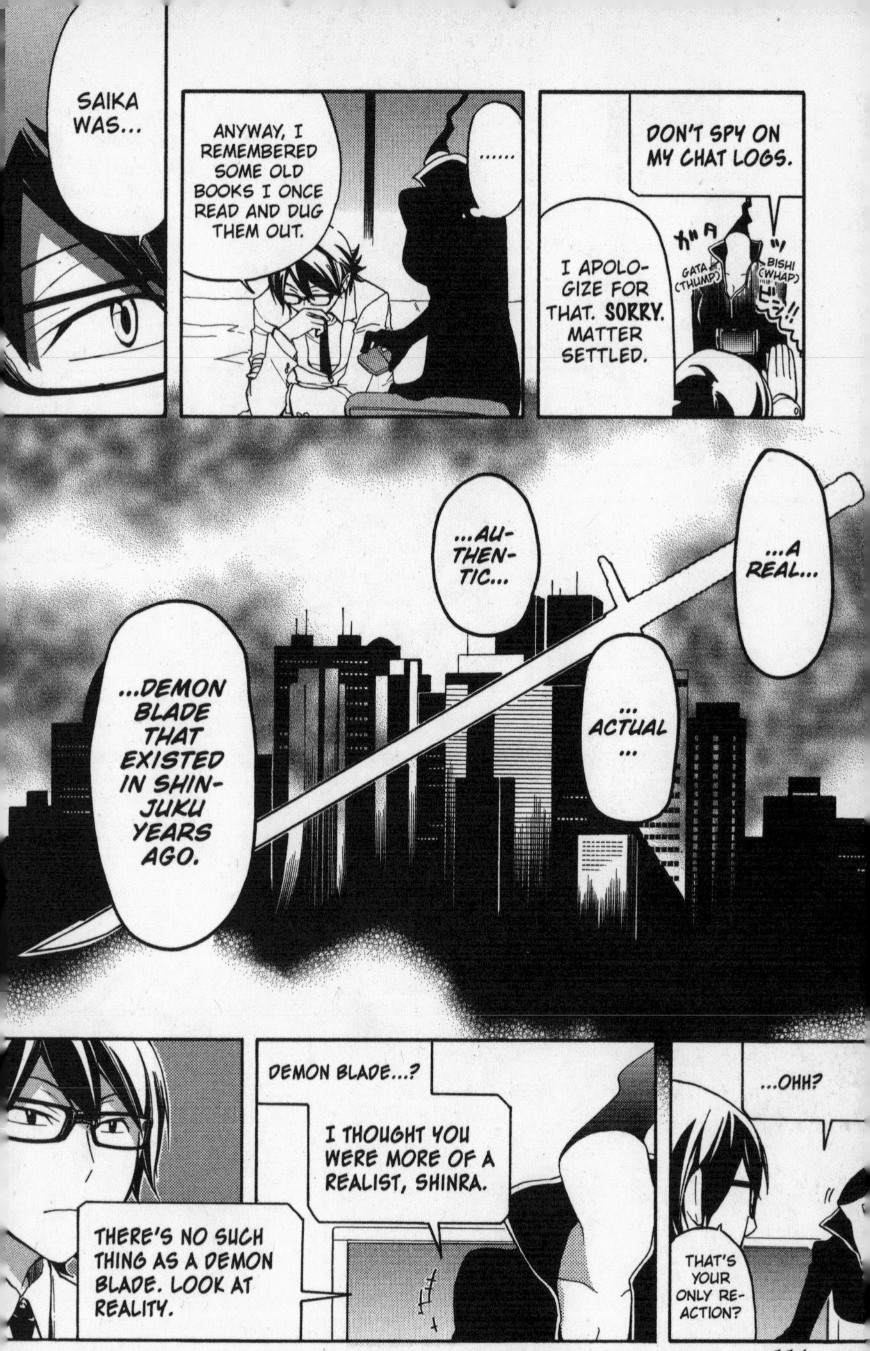
DON'T SPY ON MY CHAT LOGS.
BISHI (WHAP)
GATA (THUMP)
I APOLOGIZE FOR THAT. SORRY. MATTER SETTLED.
......
ANYWAY, I REMEMBERED SOME OLD BOOKS I ONCE READ AND DUG THEM OUT.
SAIKA WAS...
...A REAL...
...AUTHENTIC...
...ACTUAL...
...DEMON BLADE THAT EXISTED IN SHINJUKU YEARS AGO.
...OHH?
THAT'S YOUR ONLY REACTION?
DEMON BLADE...?
I THOUGHT YOU WERE MORE OF A REALIST, SHINRA.
THERE'S NO SUCH THING AS A DEMON BLADE. LOOK AT REALITY.

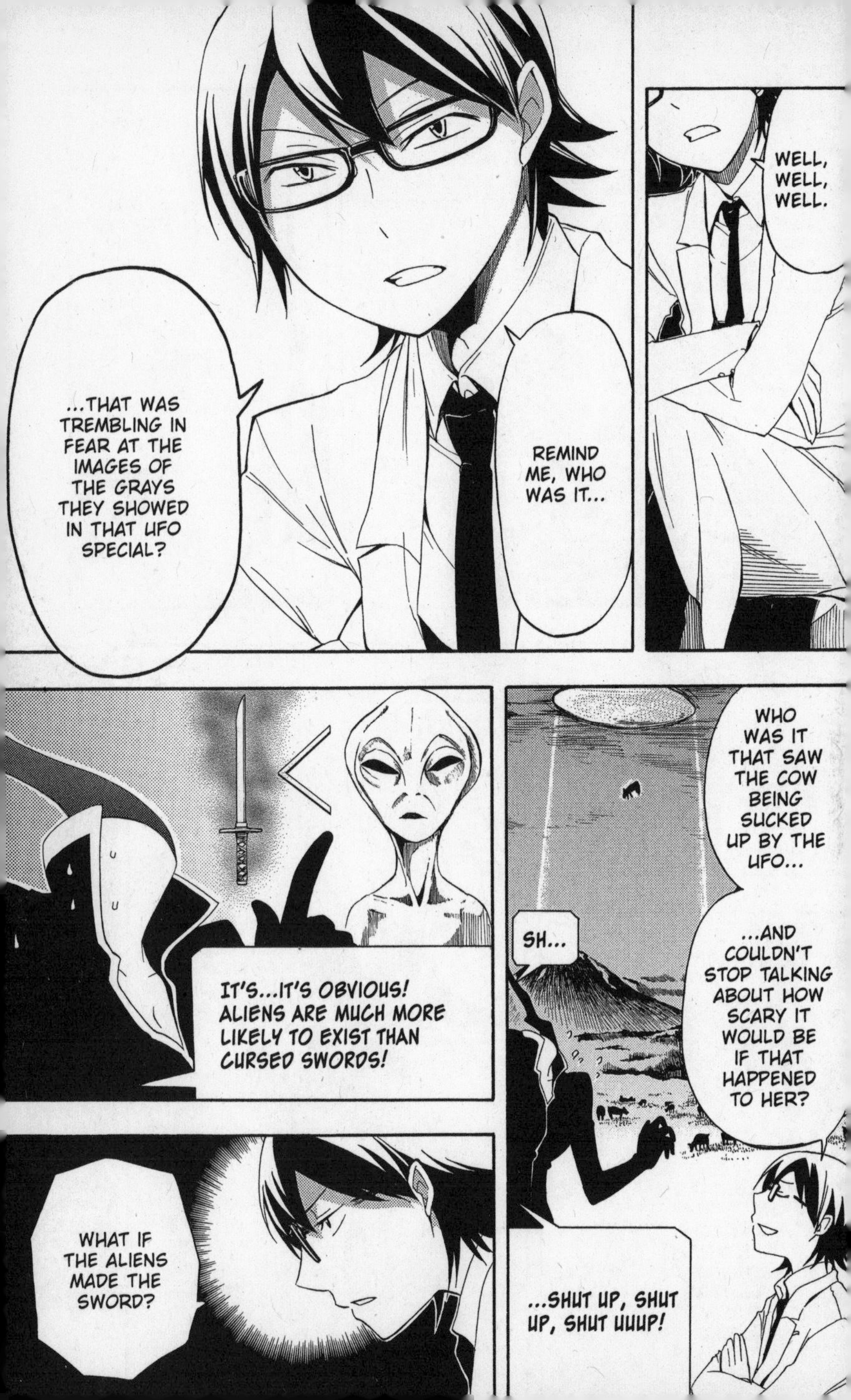
WELL, WELL, WELL.
REMIND ME, WHO WAS IT...
...THAT WAS TREMBLING IN FEAR AT THE IMAGES OF THE GRAYS THEY SHOWED IN THAT UFO SPECIAL?
WHO WAS IT THAT SAW THE COW BEING SUCKED UP BY THE UFO...
SH...
...AND COULDN'T STOP TALKING ABOUT HOW SCARY IT WOULD BE IF THAT HAPPENED TO HER?
IT'S...IT'S OBVIOUS! ALIENS ARE MUCH MORE LIKELY TO EXIST THAN CURSED SWORDS!
...SHUT UP, SHUT UP, SHUT UUUP!
WHAT IF THE ALIENS MADE THE SWORD?

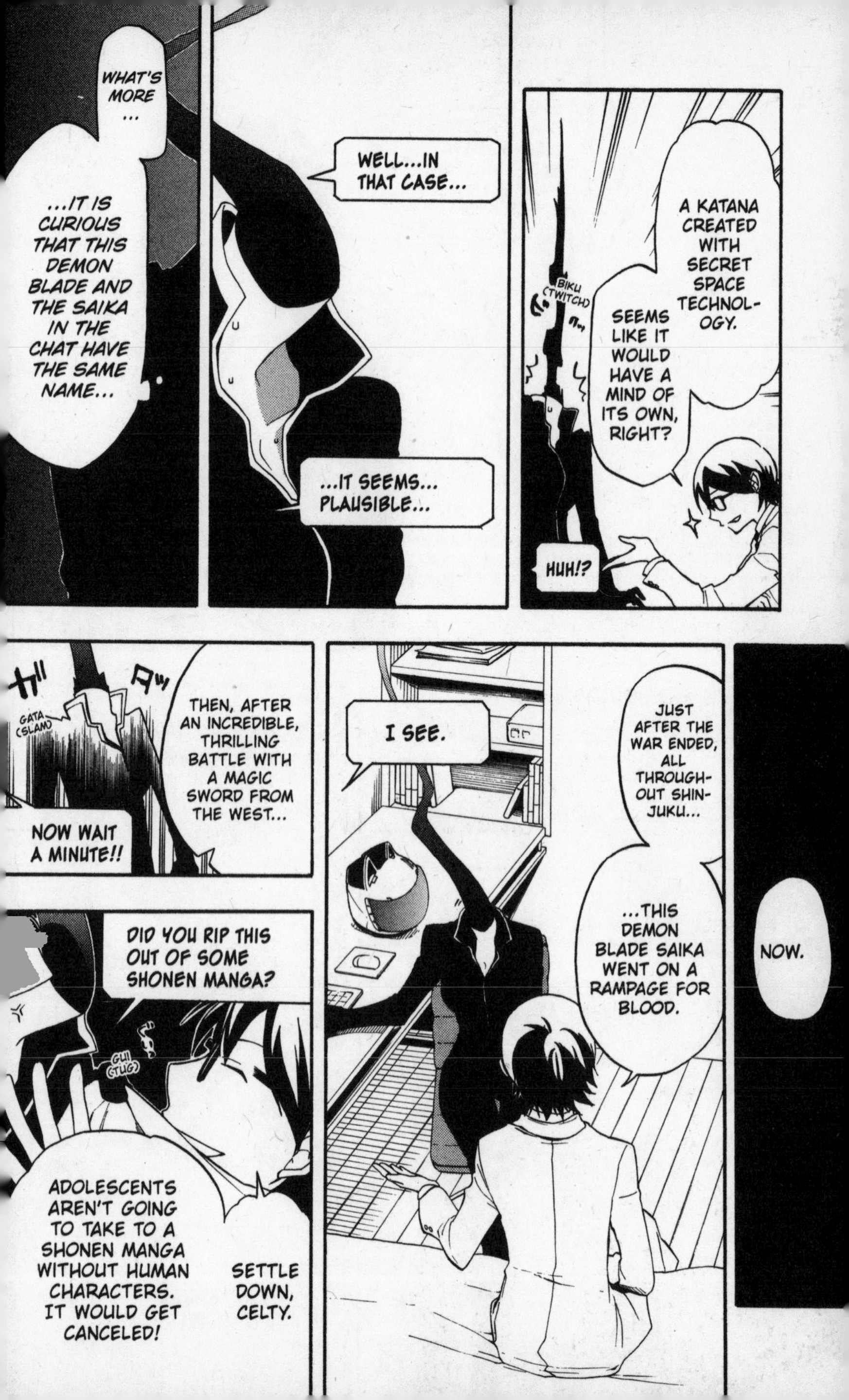
A KATANA CREATED WITH SECRET SPACE TECHNOLOGY.
SEEMS LIKE IT WOULD HAVE A MIND OF ITS OWN, RIGHT?
BIKU (TWITCH)
HUH!?
WELL...IN THAT CASE...
...IT SEEMS... PLAUSIBLE...
WHAT'S MORE...
...IT IS CURIOUS THAT THIS DEMON BLADE AND THE SAIKA IN THE CHAT HAVE THE SAME NAME...
NOW.
JUST AFTER THE WAR ENDED, ALL THROUGHOUT SHINJUKU...
I SEE.
...THIS DEMON BLADE SAIKA WENT ON A RAMPAGE FOR BLOOD.
THEN, AFTER AN INCREDIBLE, THRILLING BATTLE WITH A MAGIC SWORD FROM THE WEST...
GATA (SLAM)
NOW WAIT A MINUTE!!
DID YOU RIP THIS OUT OF SOME SHONEN MANGA?
GUI (TUG)
ADOLESCENTS AREN'T GOING TO TAKE TO A SHONEN MANGA WITHOUT HUMAN CHARACTERS. IT WOULD GET CANCELED!
SETTLE DOWN, CELTY.

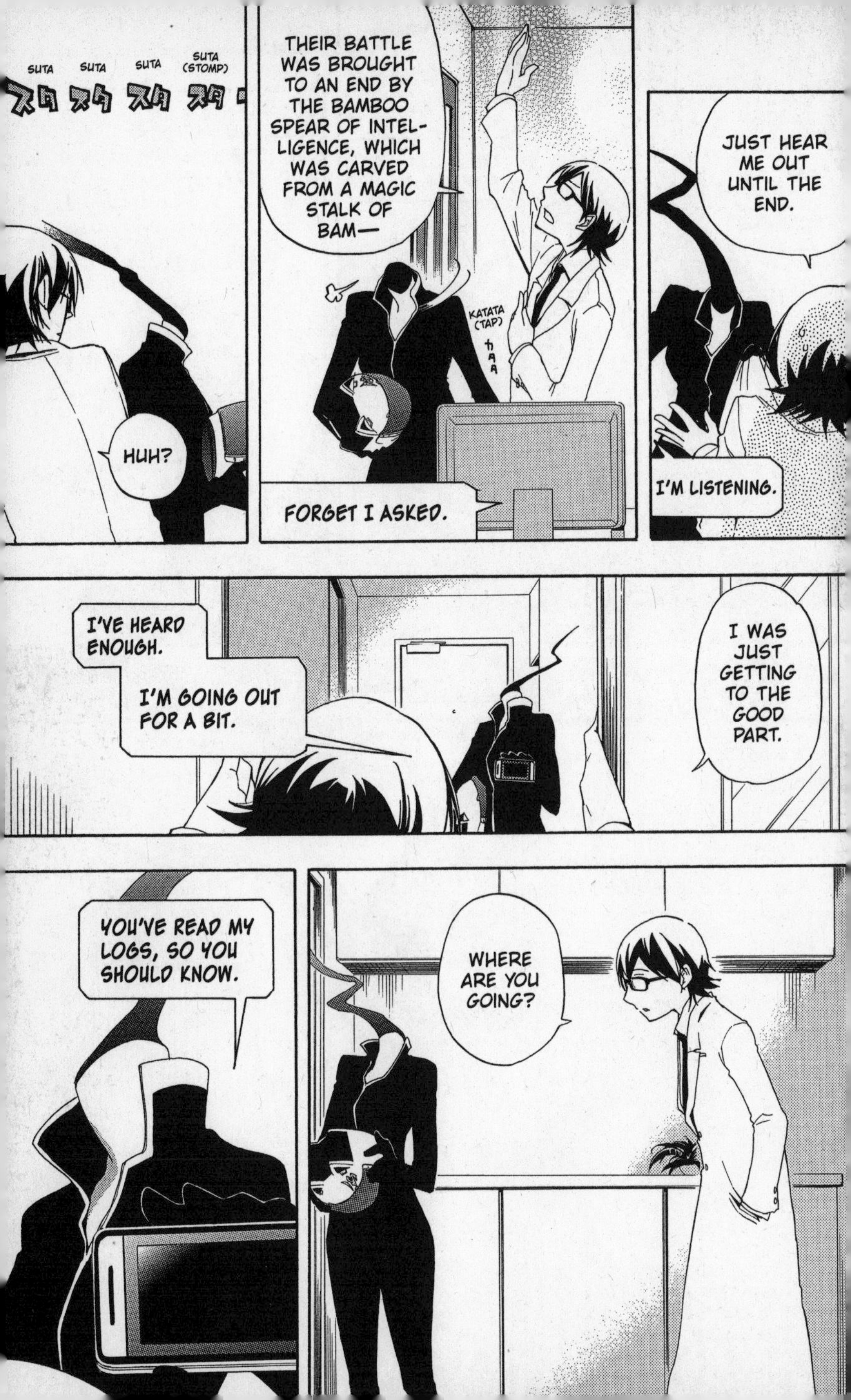
JUST HEAR ME OUT UNTIL THE END.
I'M LISTENING.
THEIR BATTLE WAS BROUGHT TO AN END BY THE BAMBOO SPEAR OF INTEL-LIGENCE, WHICH WAS CARVED FROM A MAGIC STALK OF BAM—
KATATA (TAP)
カタタ
FORGET I ASKED.
SUTA SUTA SUTA SUTA (STOMP)
スタ スタ スタ スタ
HUH?
I WAS JUST GETTING TO THE GOOD PART.
I'VE HEARD ENOUGH.
I'M GOING OUT FOR A BIT.
WHERE ARE YOU GOING?
YOU'VE READ MY LOGS, SO YOU SHOULD KNOW.

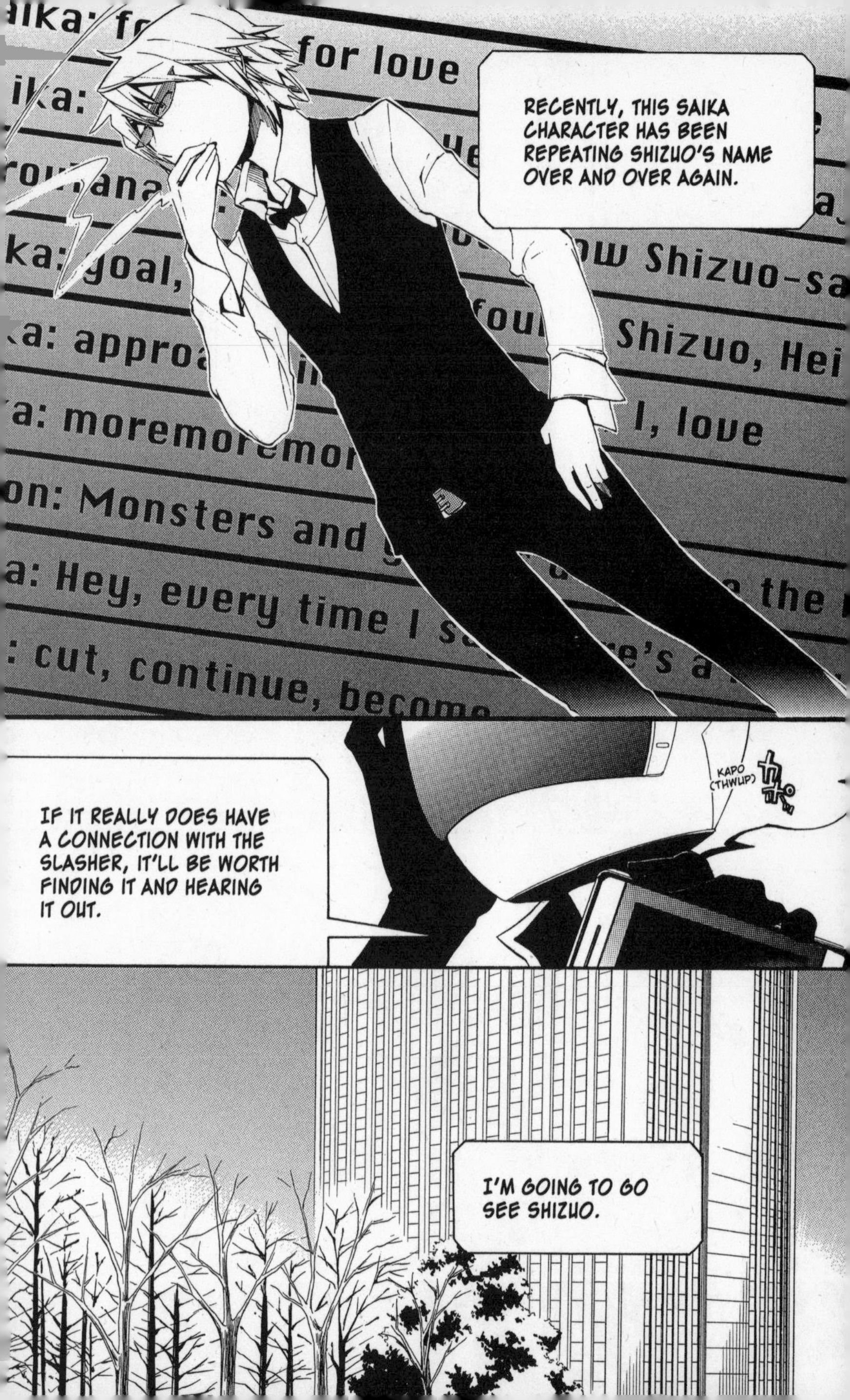
RECENTLY, THIS SAIKA CHARACTER HAS BEEN REPEATING SHIZUO'S NAME OVER AND OVER AGAIN.
for love
ka: goal,
Shizuo-sa
a: approa
Shizuo, Hei
a: moremoremor
I, love
on: Monsters and
a: Hey, every time I s
the
: cut, continue, become
KAPO (THWUP)
IF IT REALLY DOES HAVE A CONNECTION WITH THE SLASHER, IT'LL BE WORTH FINDING IT AND HEARING IT OUT.
I'M GOING TO GO SEE SHIZUO.

Durarara!! Saika Arc

DRRR!!

CHAPTER 3: IKEBUKURO'S MOST DANGEROUS

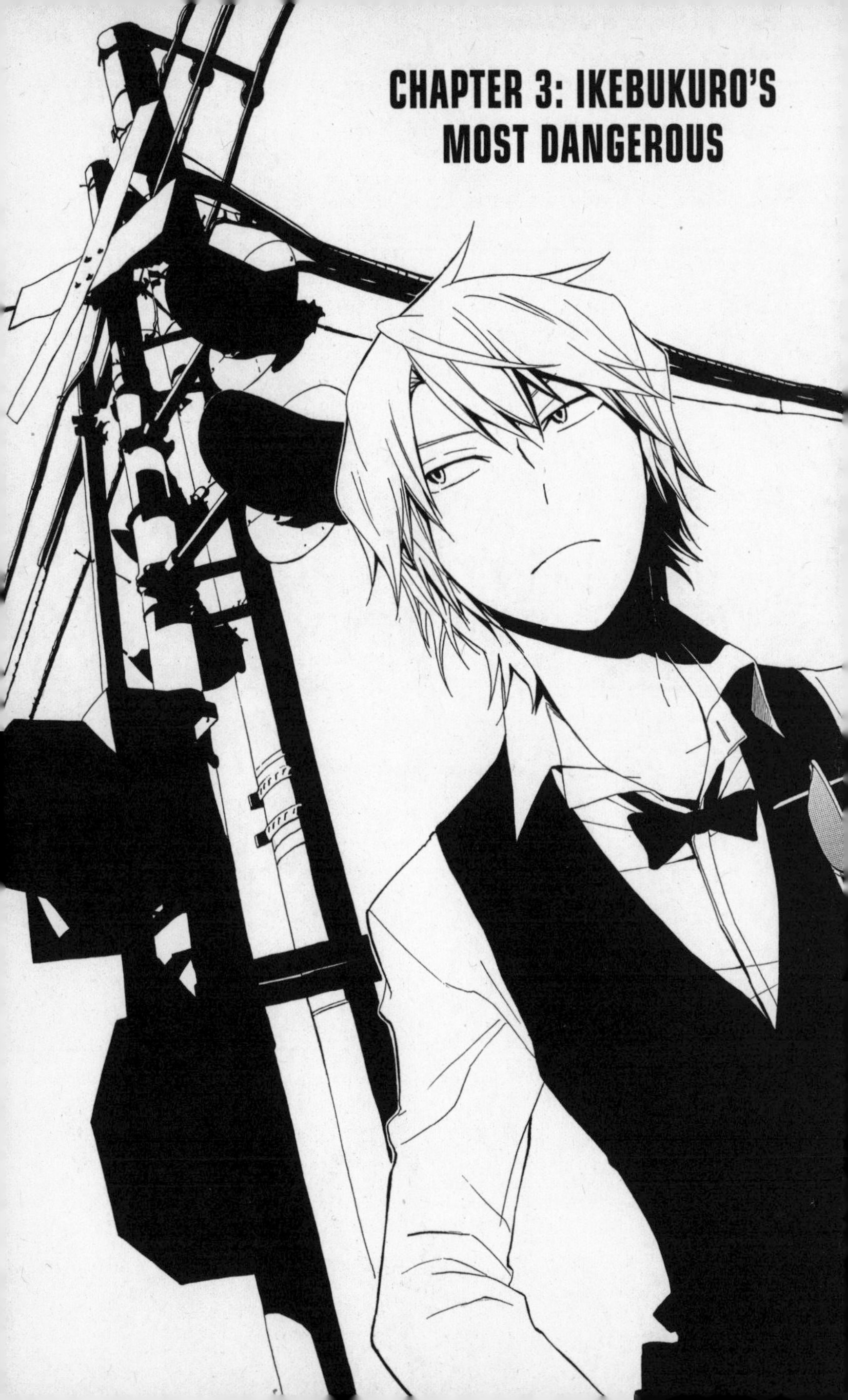

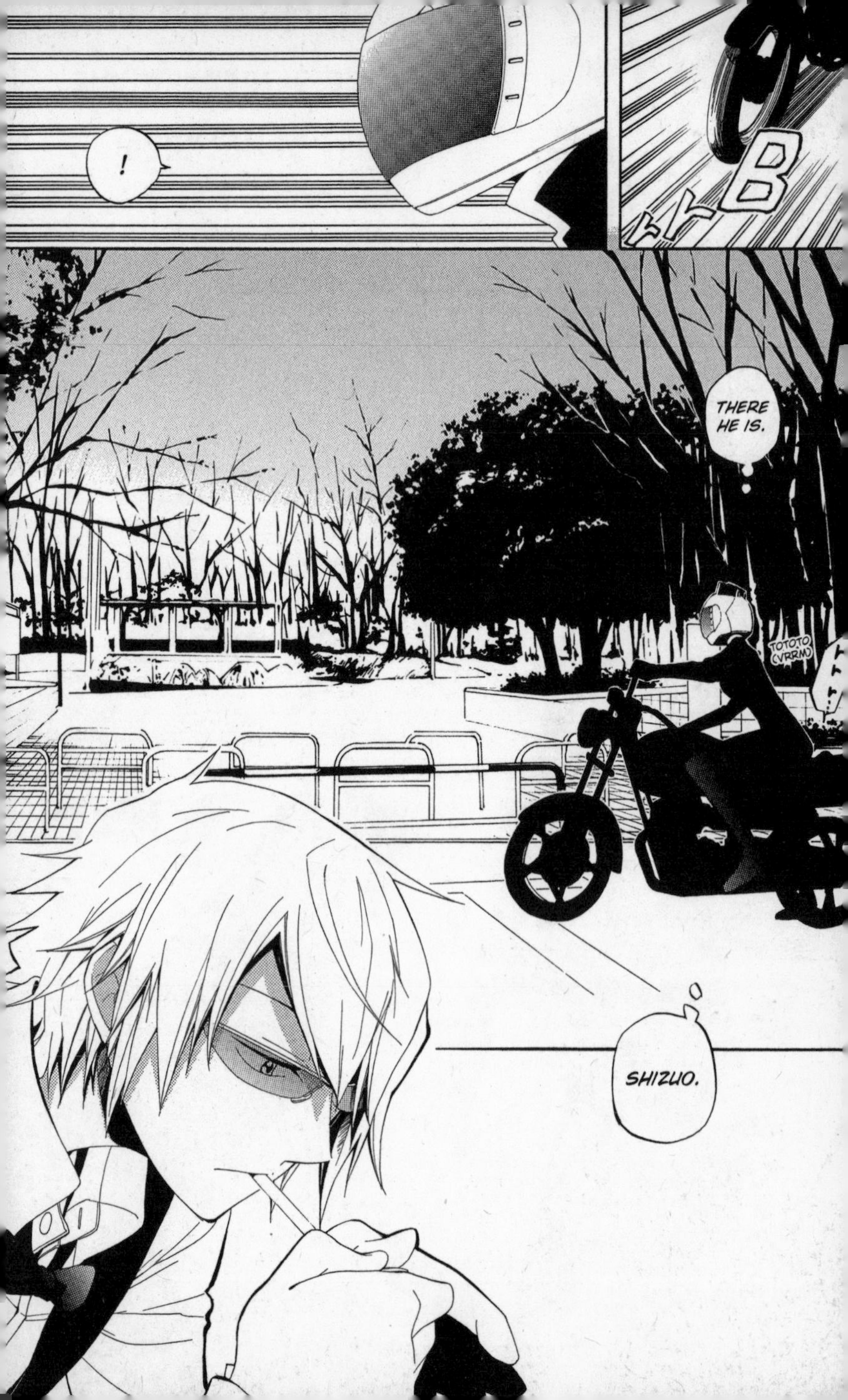
!
THERE HE IS.
TOTOTO (VRRM)
SHIZUO.

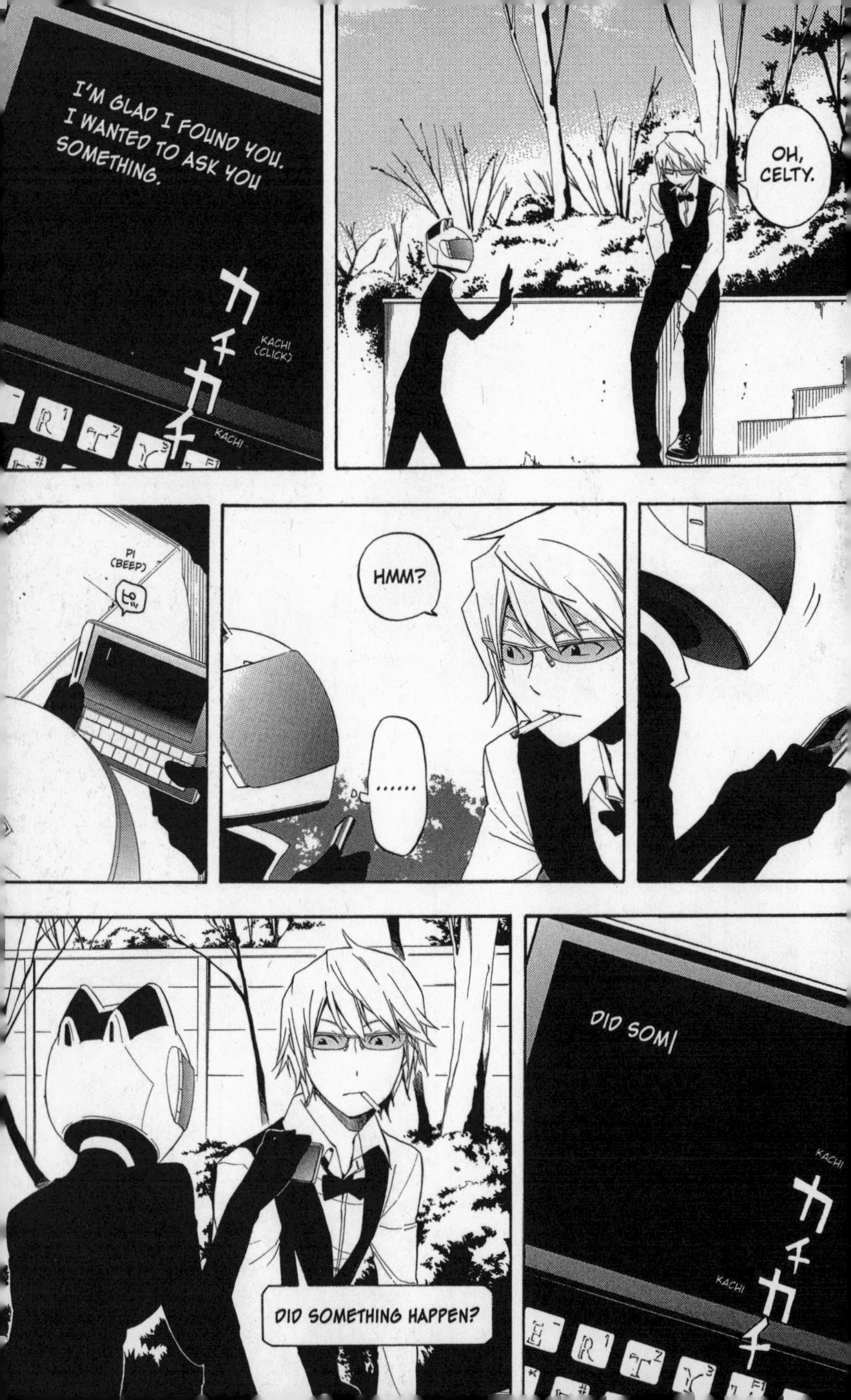
OH, CELTY.
I'M GLAD I FOUND YOU. I WANTED TO ASK YOU SOMETHING.
カチカチ
KACHI (CLICK)
KACHI
HMM?
......
ピッ
PI (BEEP)
DID SOM
カチカチ
KACHI
KACHI
DID SOMETHING HAPPEN?

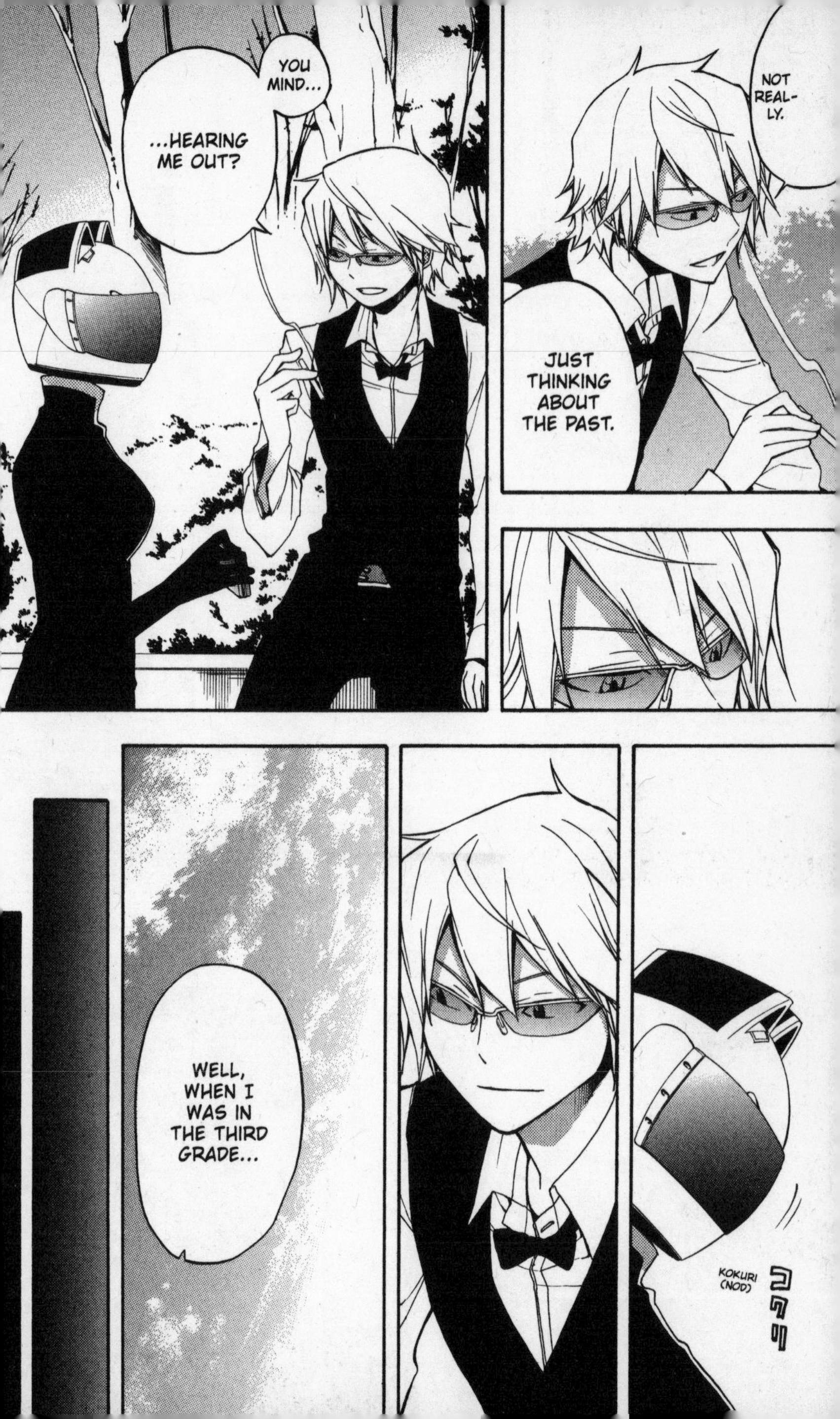

NOT REALLY.
JUST THINKING ABOUT THE PAST.
YOU MIND...
...HEARING ME OUT?
KOKURI (NOD)
WELL, WHEN I WAS IN THE THIRD GRADE...

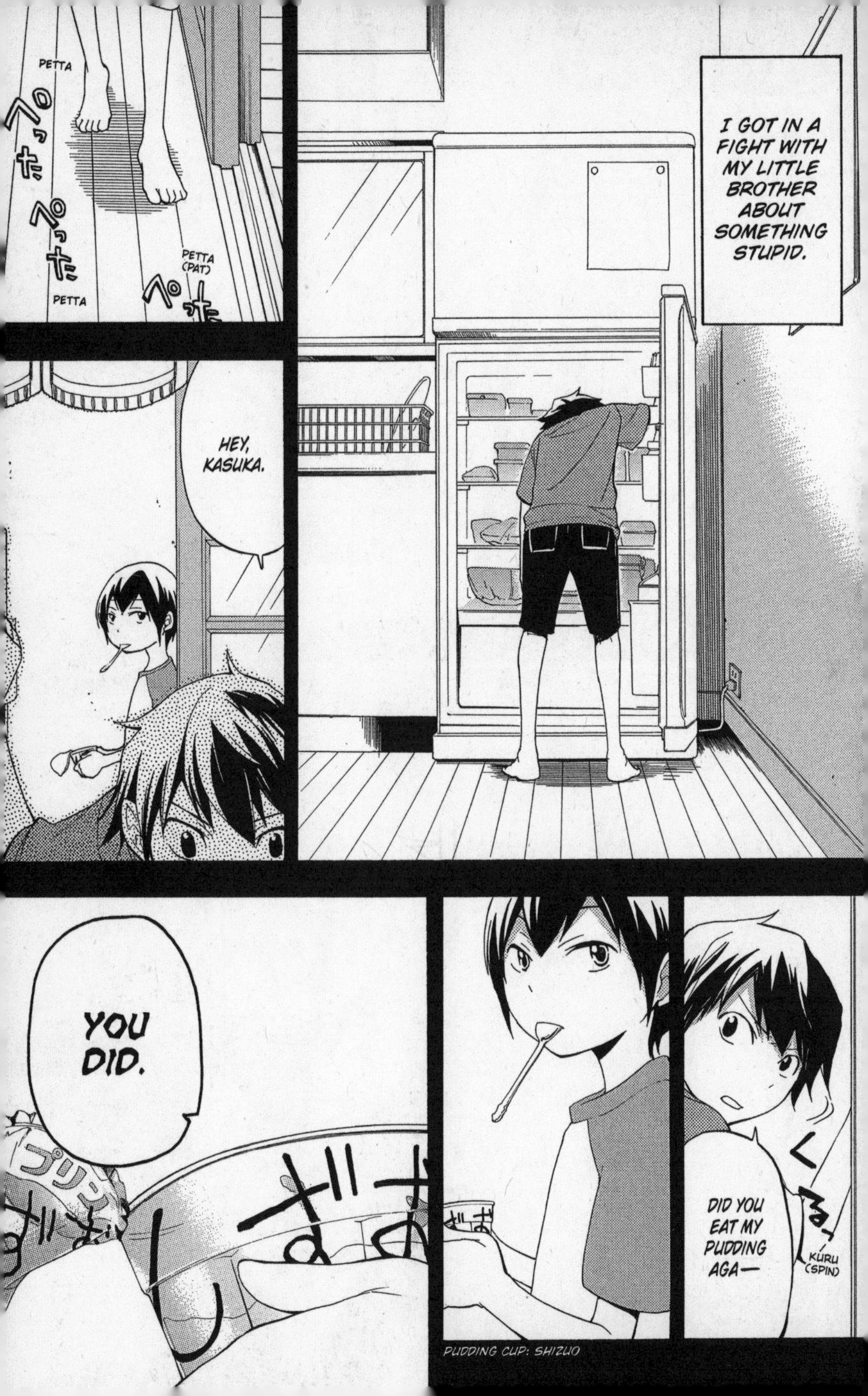
I GOT IN A FIGHT WITH MY LITTLE BROTHER ABOUT SOMETHING STUPID.
PETTA
PETTA
PETTA (PAT)
HEY, KASUKA.
KURU (SPIN)
DID YOU EAT MY PUDDING AGA—
PUDDING CUP: SHIZUO
YOU DID.

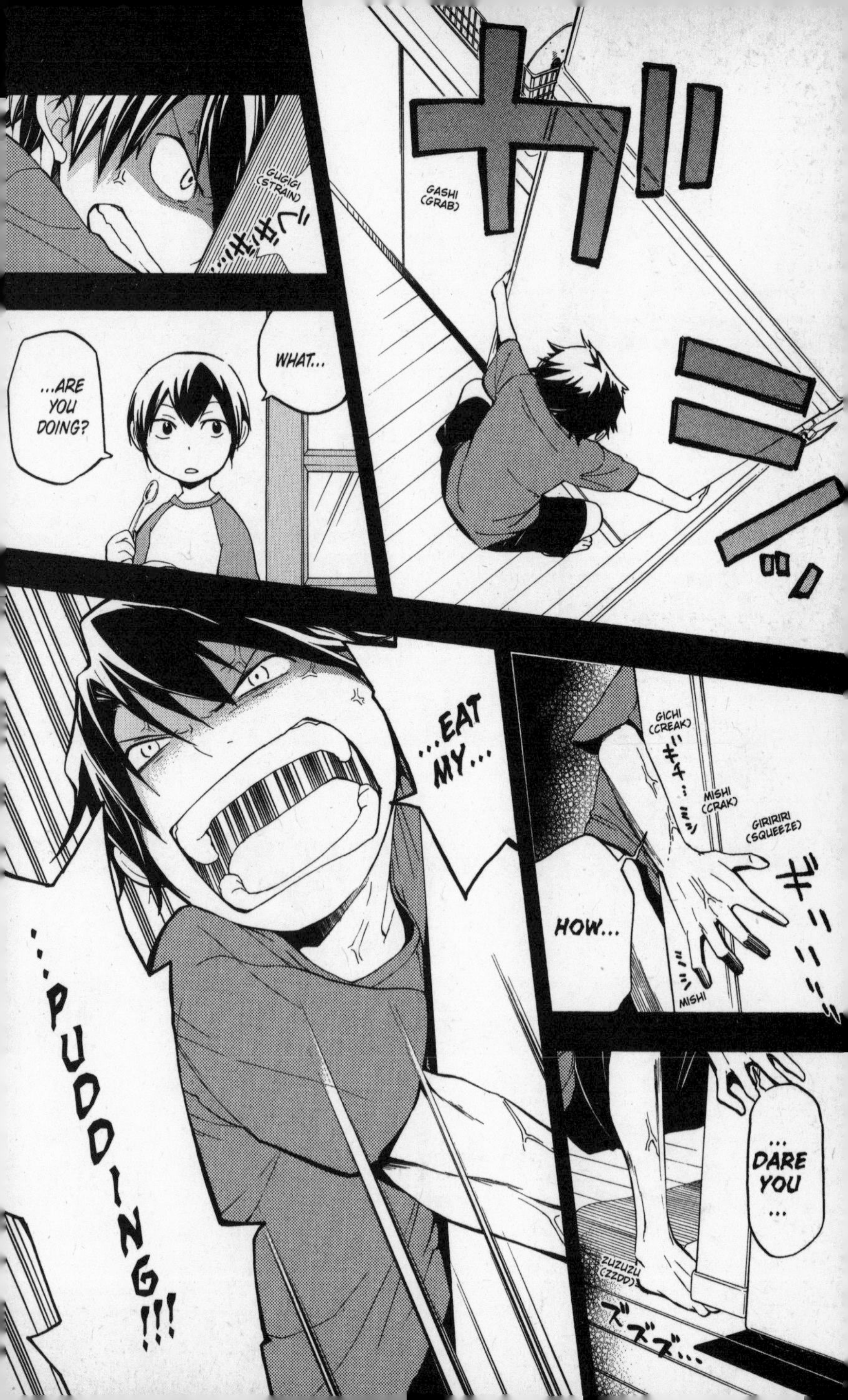

GASHI (GRAB)
GUGIGI (STRAIN)
WHAT...
...ARE YOU DOING?
GICHI (CREAK)
MISHI (CRAK)
GIRIRIRI (SQUEEZE)
HOW...
MISHI
... DARE YOU ...
ZUZUZU (ZZDD)
...EAT MY...
...PUDDING!!!

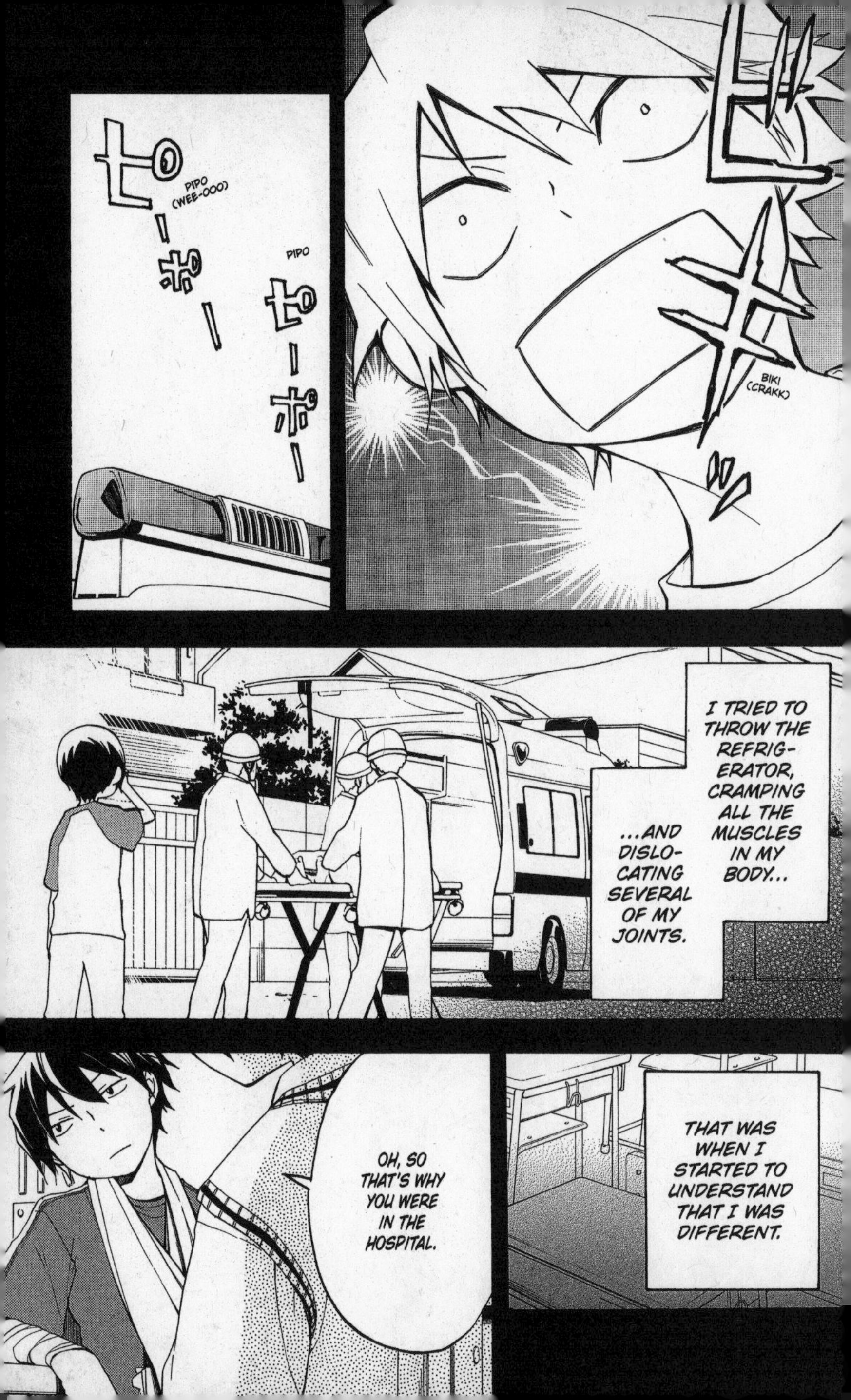
BIKI (CRAKK)
PIPO
PIPO (WEE-OOO)
I TRIED TO THROW THE REFRIGERATOR, CRAMPING ALL THE MUSCLES IN MY BODY...
...AND DISLOCATING SEVERAL OF MY JOINTS.
THAT WAS WHEN I STARTED TO UNDERSTAND THAT I WAS DIFFERENT.
OH, SO THAT'S WHY YOU WERE IN THE HOSPITAL.

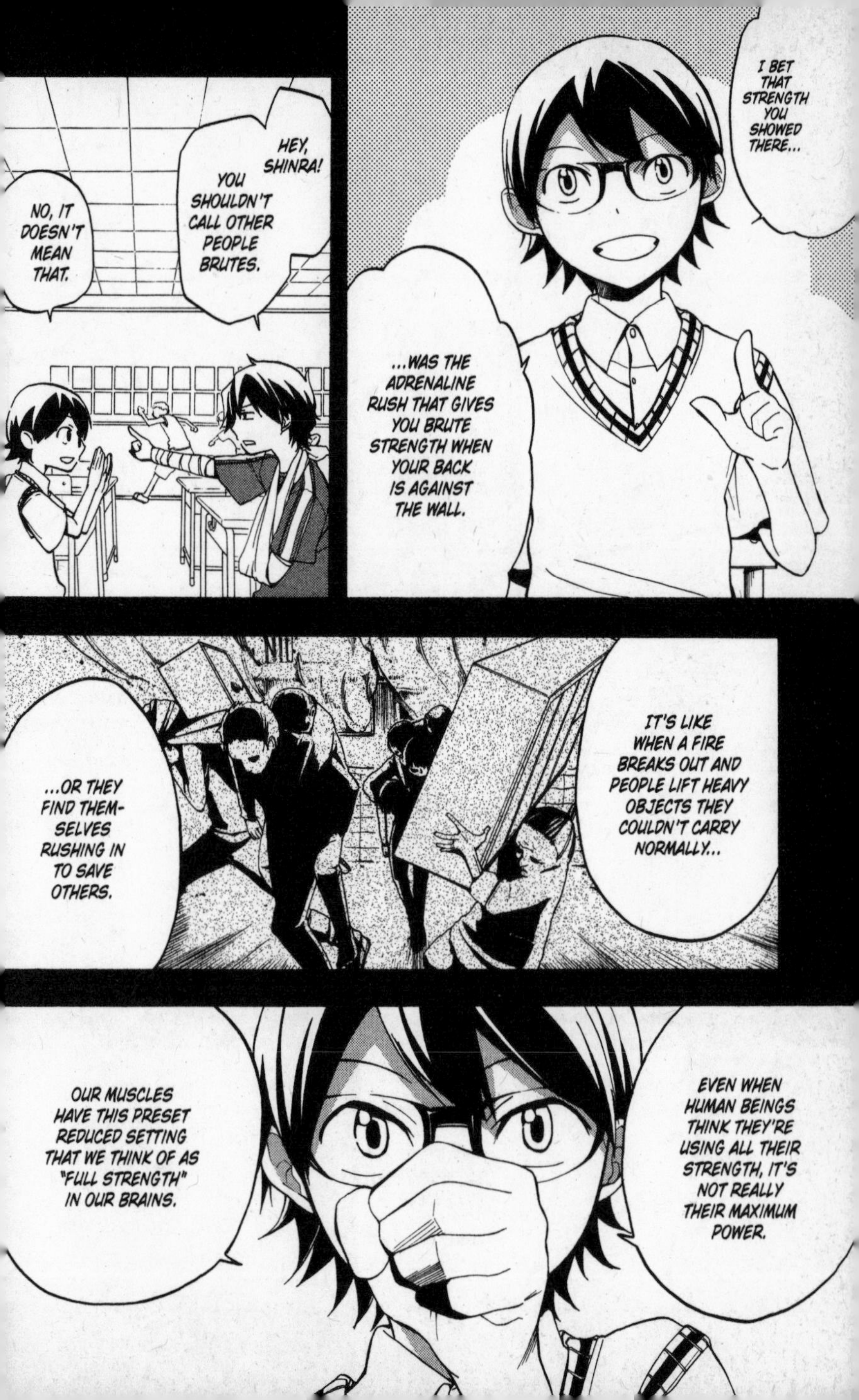
I BET THAT STRENGTH YOU SHOWED THERE...
...WAS THE ADRENALINE RUSH THAT GIVES YOU BRUTE STRENGTH WHEN YOUR BACK IS AGAINST THE WALL.
HEY, SHINRA! YOU SHOULDN'T CALL OTHER PEOPLE BRUTES.
NO, IT DOESN'T MEAN THAT.
IT'S LIKE WHEN A FIRE BREAKS OUT AND PEOPLE LIFT HEAVY OBJECTS THEY COULDN'T CARRY NORMALLY...
...OR THEY FIND THEM-SELVES RUSHING IN TO SAVE OTHERS.
EVEN WHEN HUMAN BEINGS THINK THEY'RE USING ALL THEIR STRENGTH, IT'S NOT REALLY THEIR MAXIMUM POWER.
OUR MUSCLES HAVE THIS PRESET REDUCED SETTING THAT WE THINK OF AS "FULL STRENGTH" IN OUR BRAINS.

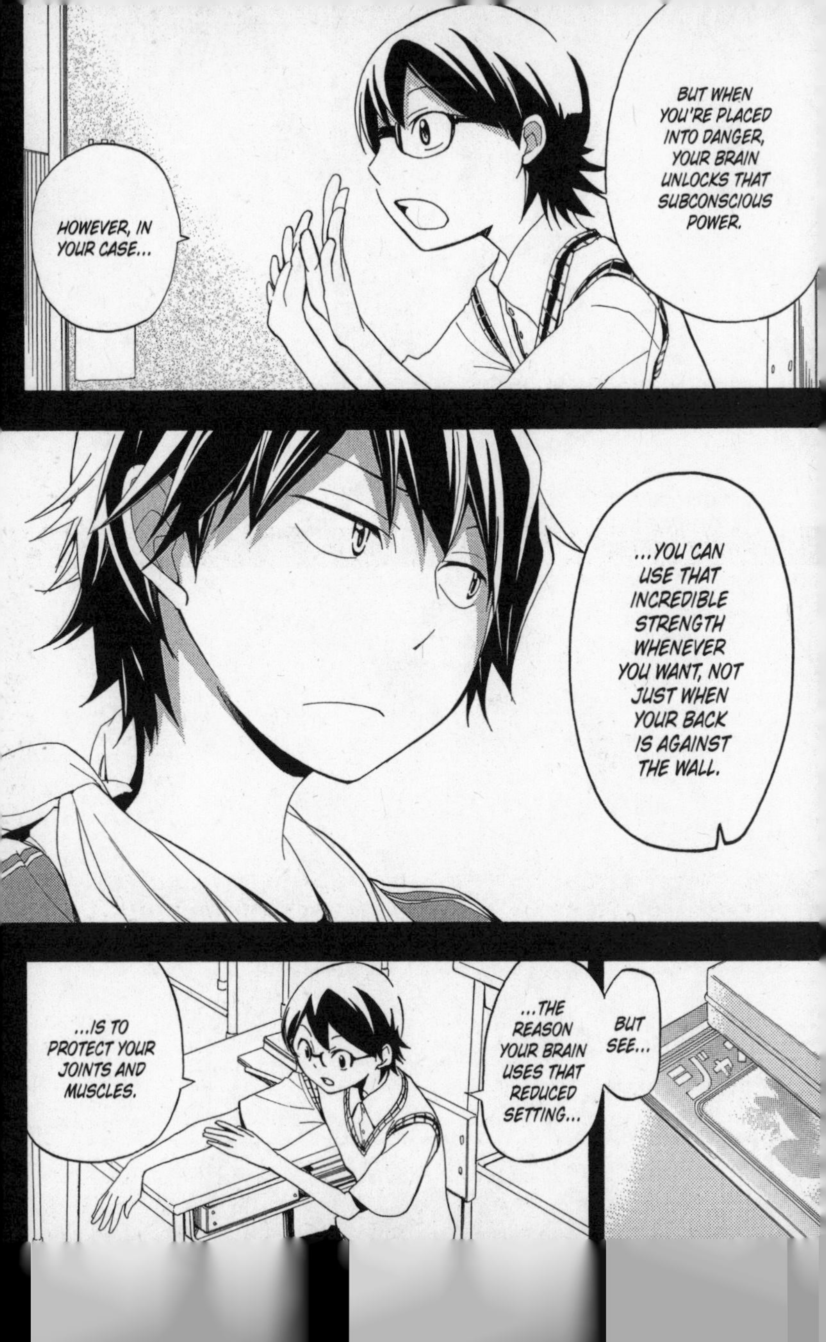
BUT WHEN YOU'RE PLACED INTO DANGER, YOUR BRAIN UNLOCKS THAT SUBCONSCIOUS POWER.
HOWEVER, IN YOUR CASE...
...YOU CAN USE THAT INCREDIBLE STRENGTH WHENEVER YOU WANT, NOT JUST WHEN YOUR BACK IS AGAINST THE WALL.
BUT SEE...
...THE REASON YOUR BRAIN USES THAT REDUCED SETTING...
...IS TO PROTECT YOUR JOINTS AND MUSCLES.

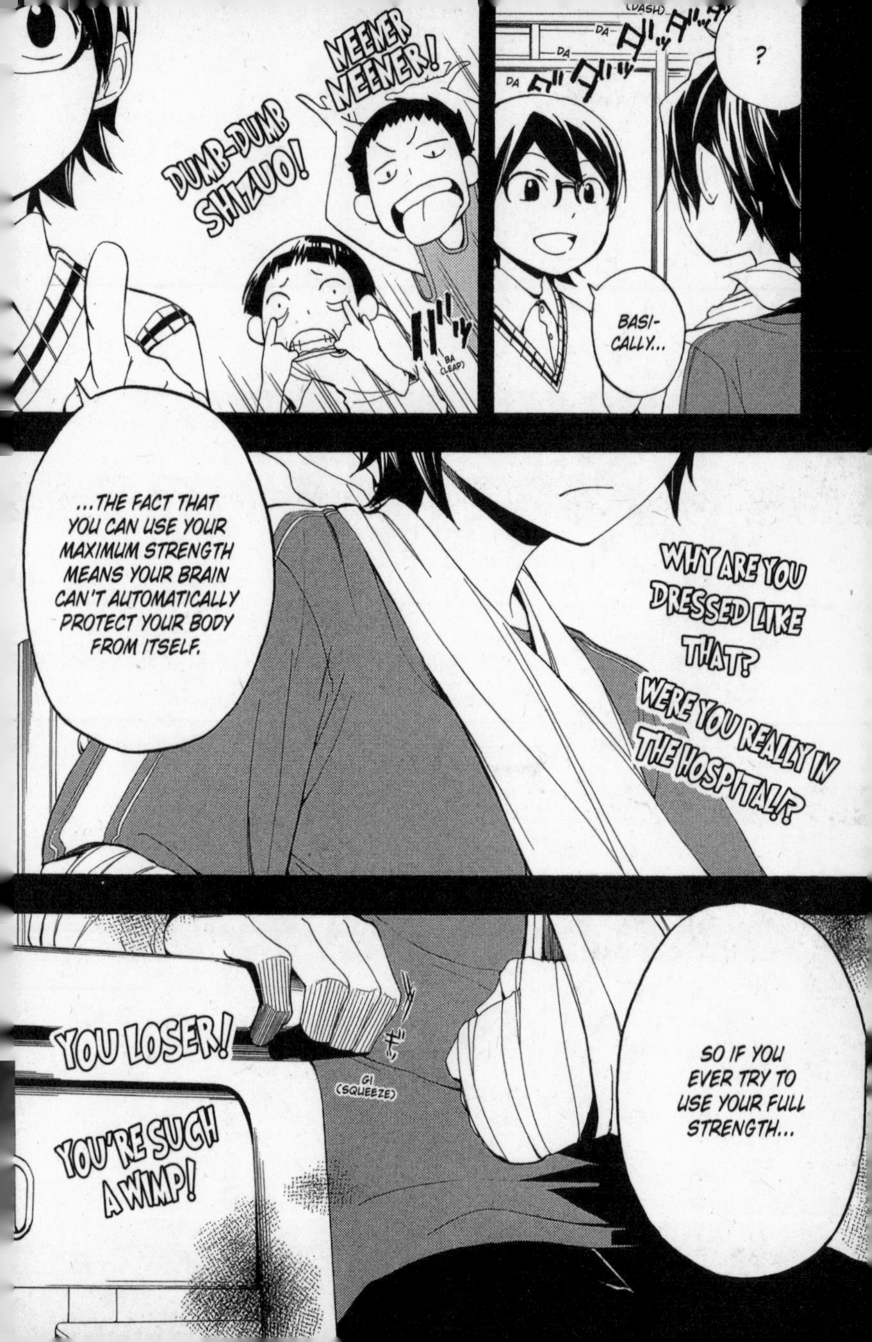
(DASH)
DA
DA
DA
?
BASI-CALLY...
NEENER NEENER!
DUMB-DUMB SHIZUO!
BA (LEAP)
...THE FACT THAT YOU CAN USE YOUR MAXIMUM STRENGTH MEANS YOUR BRAIN CAN'T AUTOMATICALLY PROTECT YOUR BODY FROM ITSELF.
WHY ARE YOU DRESSED LIKE THAT?
WERE YOU REALLY IN THE HOSPITAL!?
SO IF YOU EVER TRY TO USE YOUR FULL STRENGTH...
GI (SQUEEZE)
YOU LOSER!
YOU'RE SUCH A WIMP!

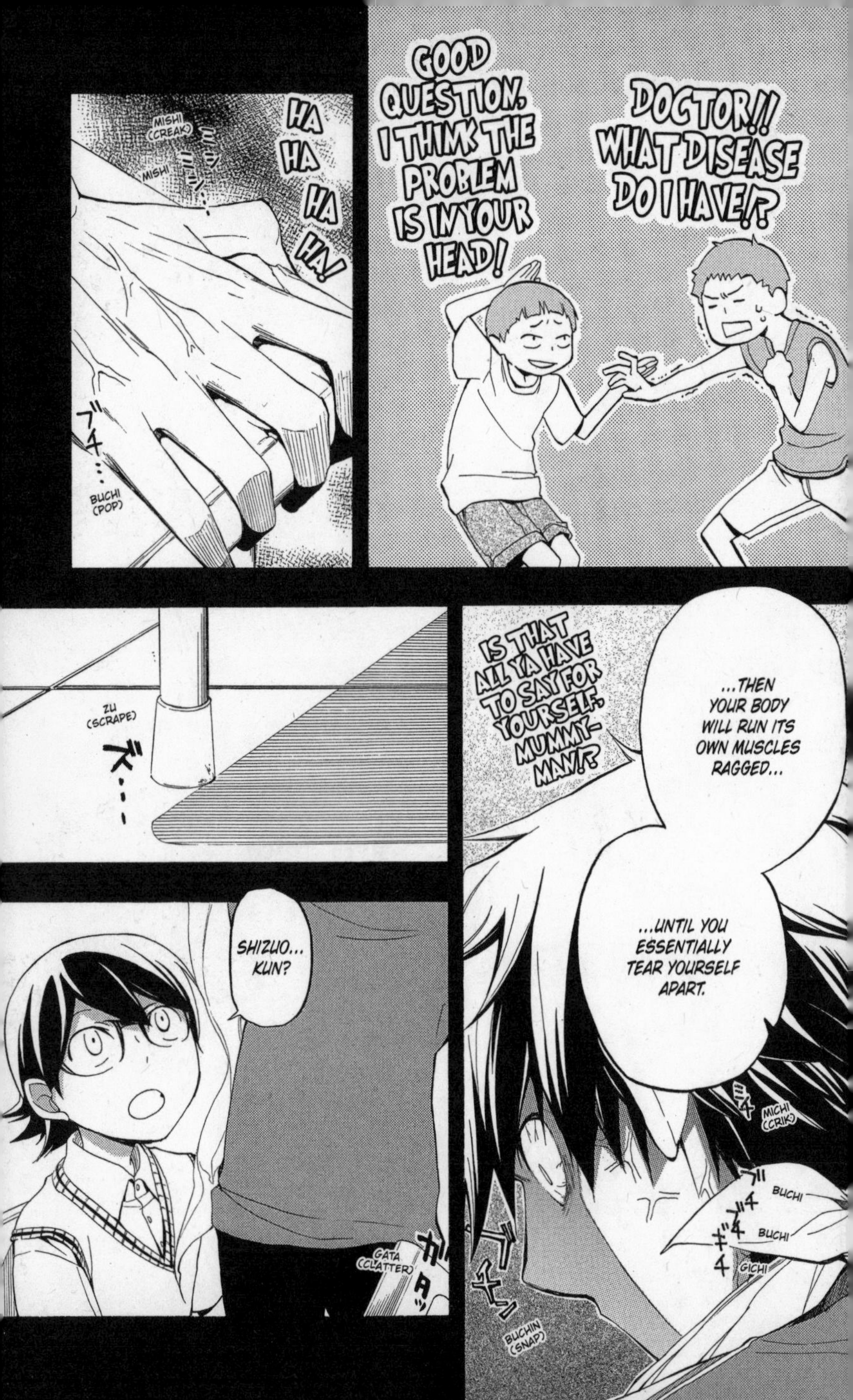
DOCTOR!! WHAT DISEASE DO I HAVE!?
GOOD QUESTION. I THINK THE PROBLEM IS IN YOUR HEAD!
HA HA HA HA!
MISHI (CREAK)
ミシ
MISHI
ミシ…
ブチ…
BUCHI (POP)
...THEN YOUR BODY WILL RUN ITS OWN MUSCLES RAGGED...
IS THAT ALL YA HAVE TO SAY FOR YOURSELF, MUMMY-MAN!?
...UNTIL YOU ESSENTIALLY TEAR YOURSELF APART.
ミチ
MICHI (CRIK)
ブチ
BUCHI
ブチ
BUCHI
ギチ
GICHI
ブチン!
BUCHIN (SNAP)
ZU (SCRAPE)
ズ…
SHIZUO... KUN?
ガタッ
GATA (CLATTER)

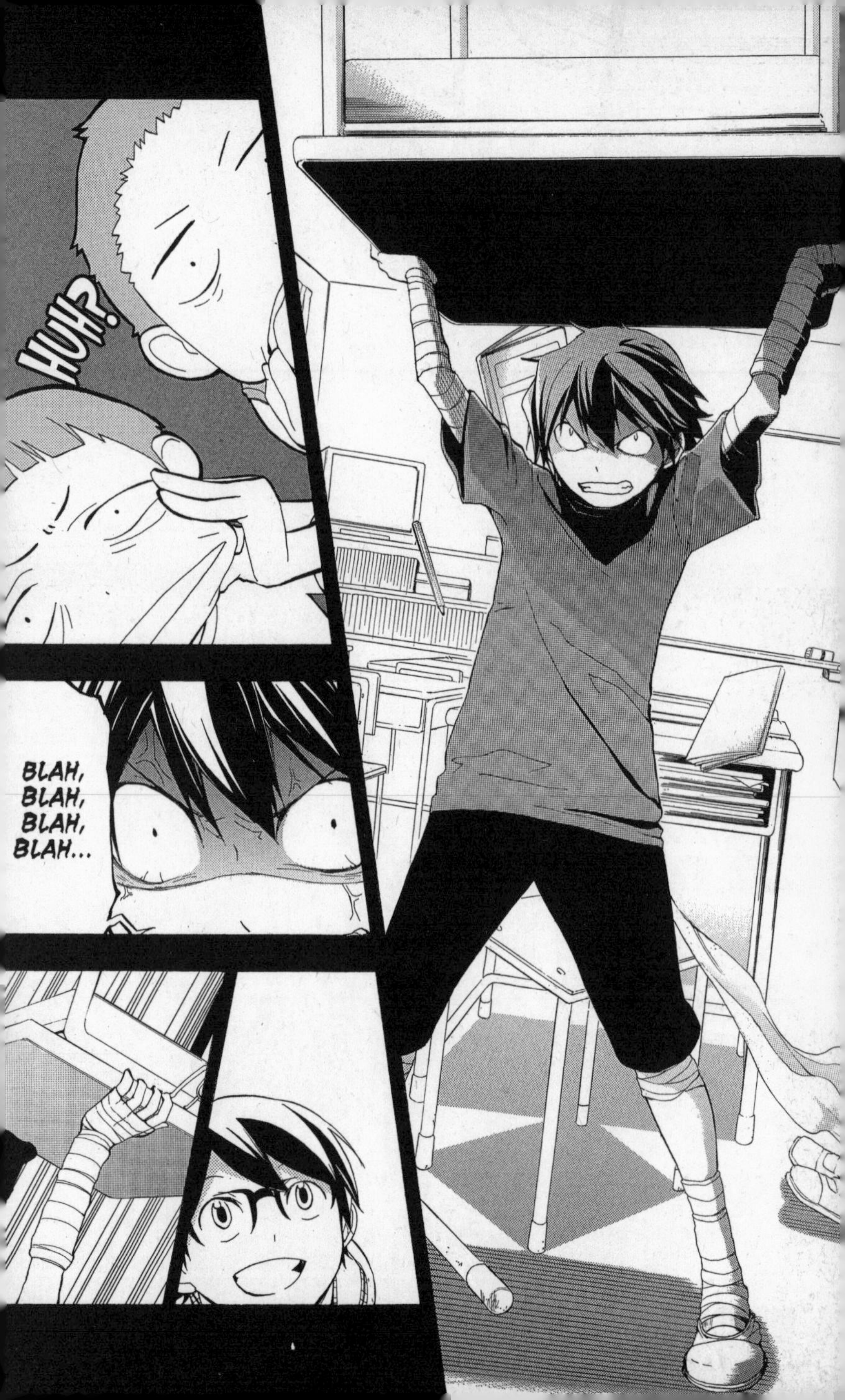
HUH?
BLAH, BLAH, BLAH, BLAH...

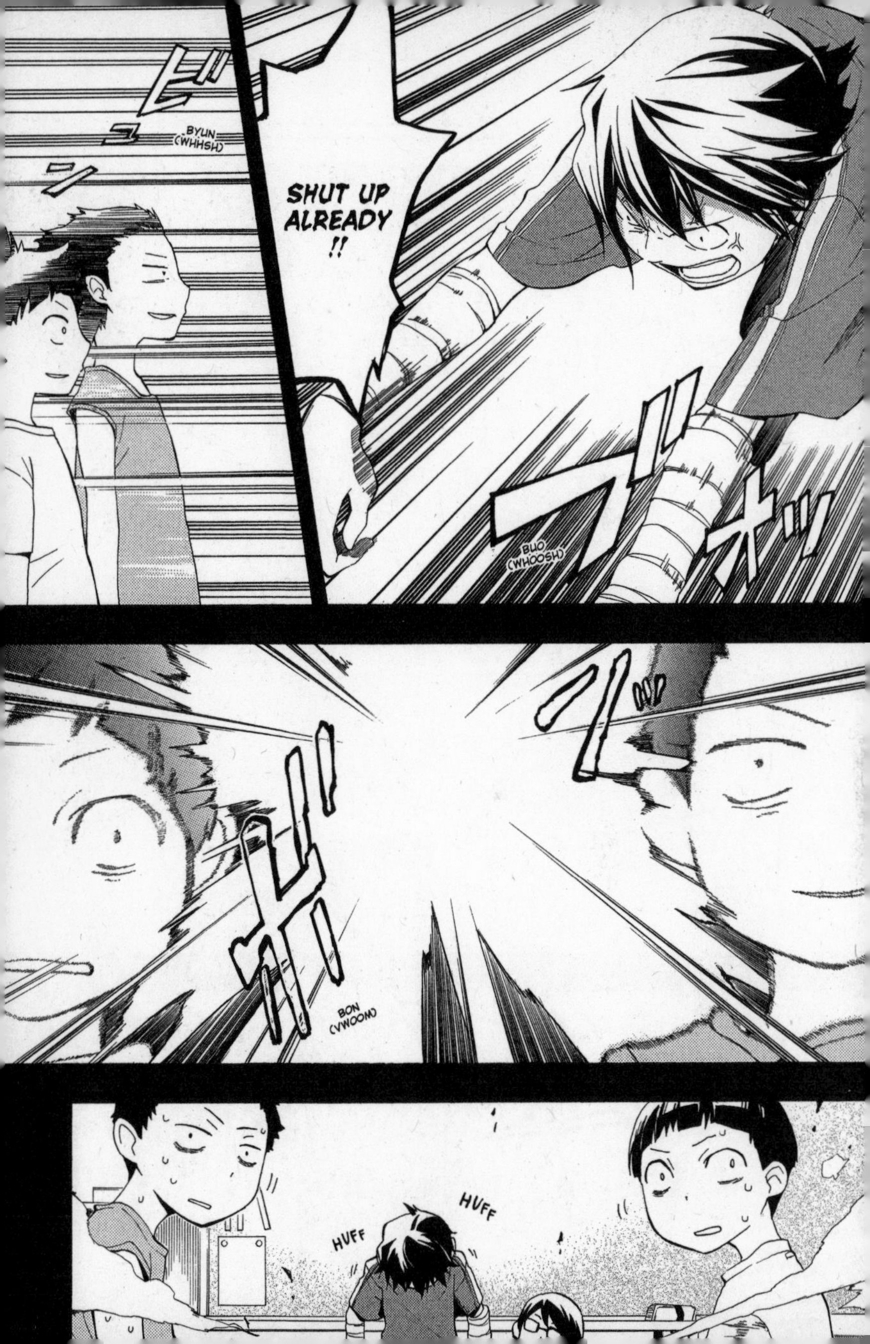
SHUT UP ALREADY !!
BUO (WHOOSH)
BYUN (WHHSH)
BON (VWOOM)
HUFF
HUFF

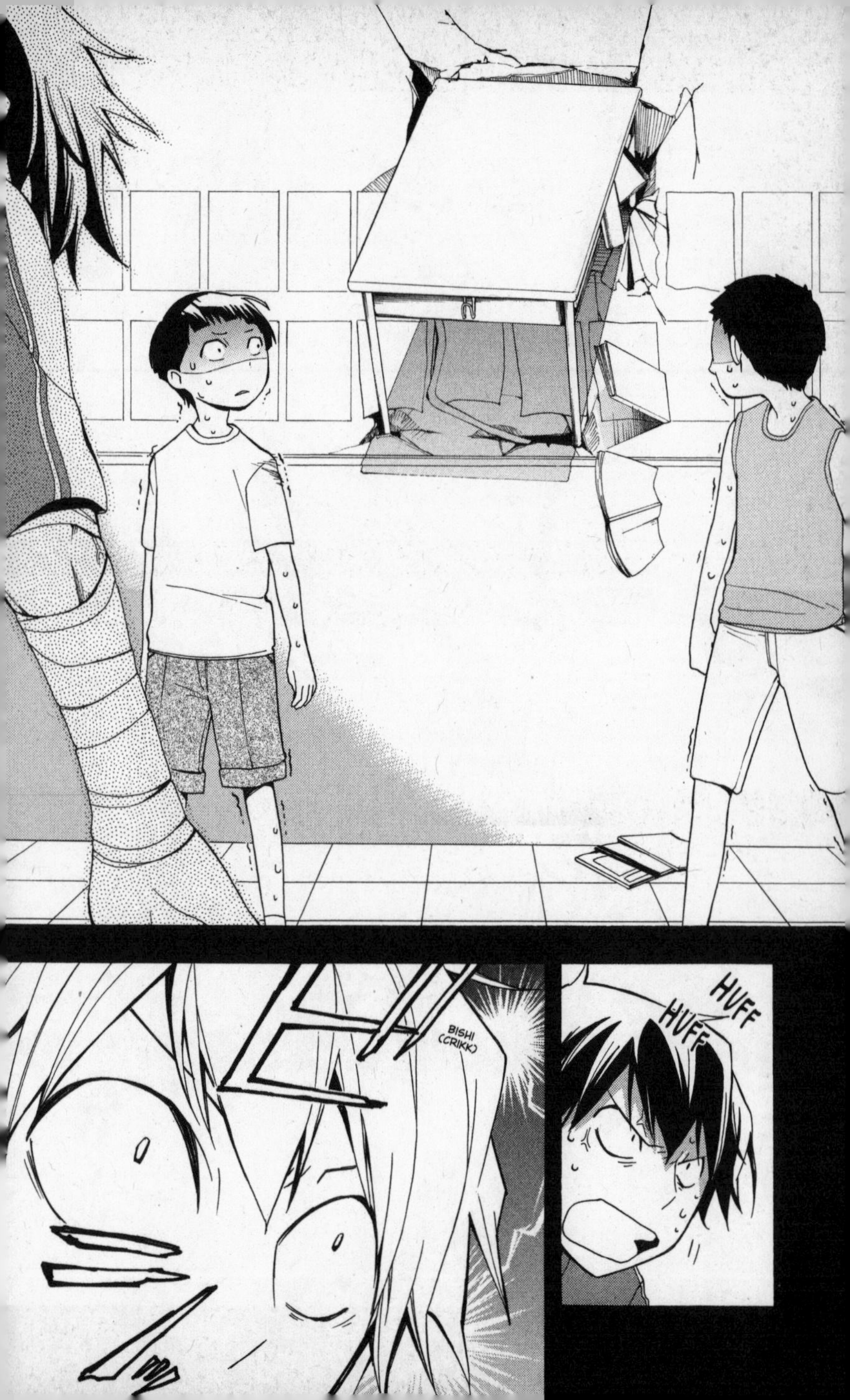
HUFF
HUFF
BISHI (CRIKK)

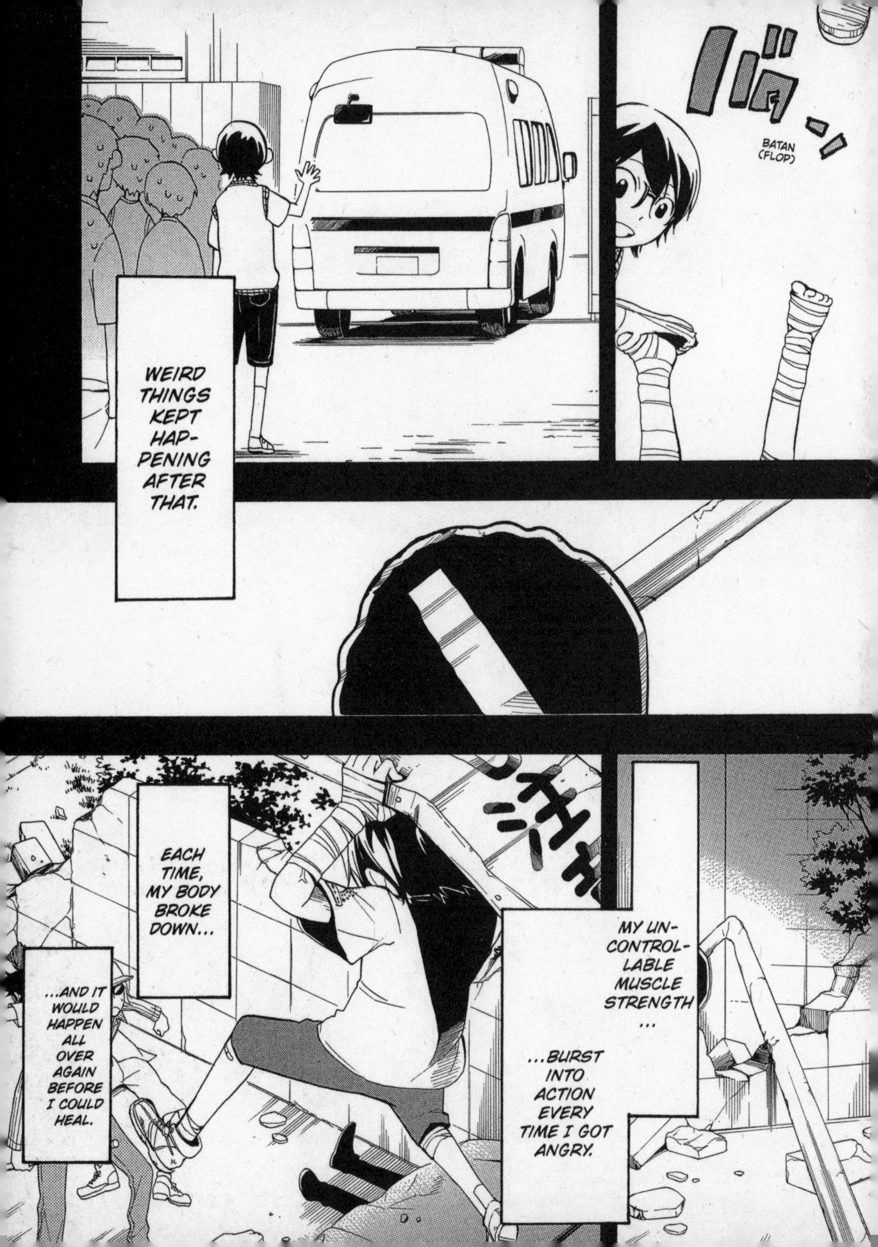
BATAN (FLOP)
WEIRD THINGS KEPT HAP-PENING AFTER THAT.
MY UN-CONTROL-LABLE MUSCLE STRENGTH ...
...BURST INTO ACTION EVERY TIME I GOT ANGRY.
EACH TIME, MY BODY BROKE DOWN...
...AND IT WOULD HAPPEN ALL OVER AGAIN BEFORE I COULD HEAL.

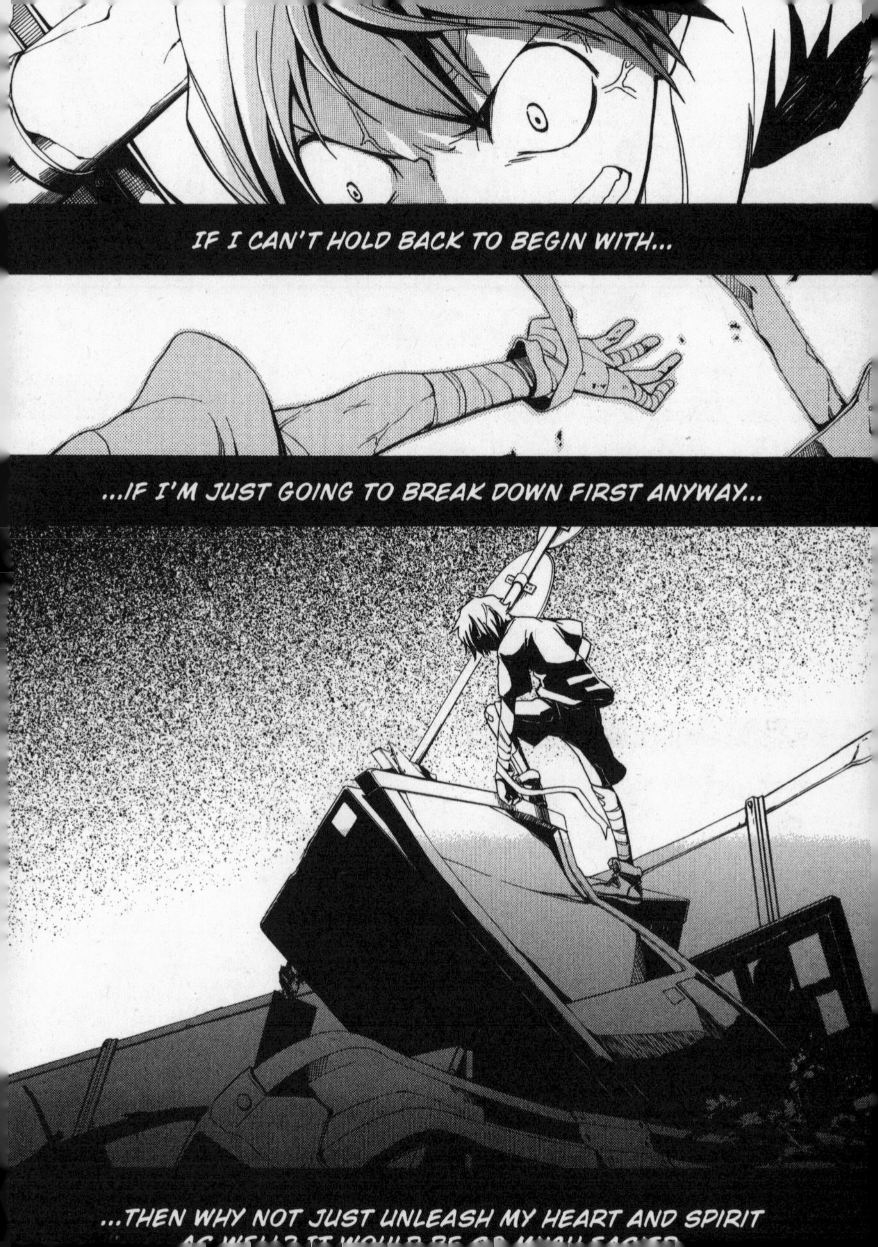
IF I CAN'T HOLD BACK TO BEGIN WITH...
...IF I'M JUST GOING TO BREAK DOWN FIRST ANYWAY...
...THEN WHY NOT JUST UNLEASH MY HEART AND SPIRIT

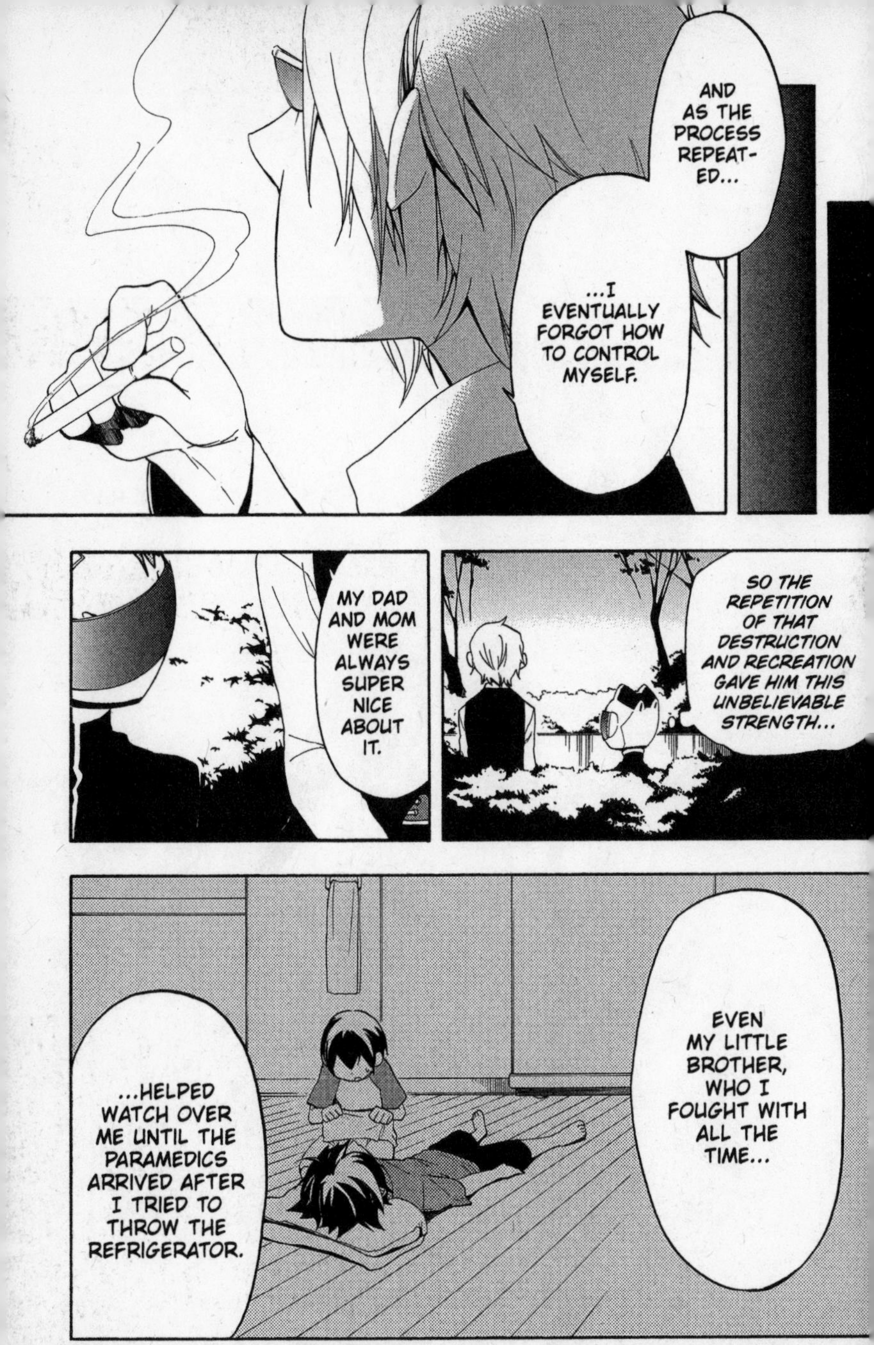
AND AS THE PROCESS REPEAT-ED...
...I EVENTUALLY FORGOT HOW TO CONTROL MYSELF.
SO THE REPETITION OF THAT DESTRUCTION AND RECREATION GAVE HIM THIS UNBELIEVABLE STRENGTH...
MY DAD AND MOM WERE ALWAYS SUPER NICE ABOUT IT.
EVEN MY LITTLE BROTHER, WHO I FOUGHT WITH ALL THE TIME...
...HELPED WATCH OVER ME UNTIL THE PARAMEDICS ARRIVED AFTER I TRIED TO THROW THE REFRIGERATOR.

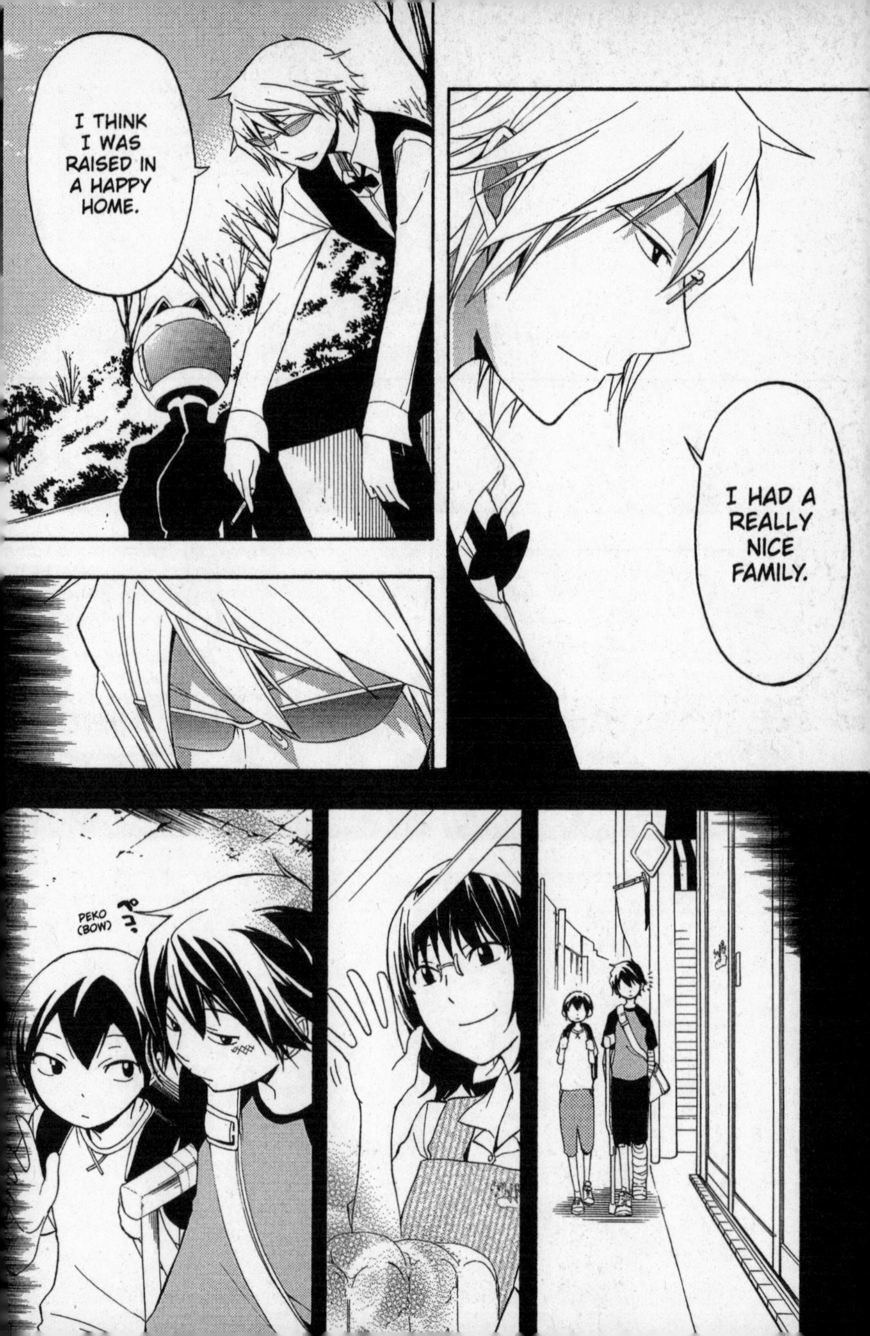
I HAD A REALLY NICE FAMILY.
I THINK I WAS RAISED IN A HAPPY HOME.
PEKO (BOW)

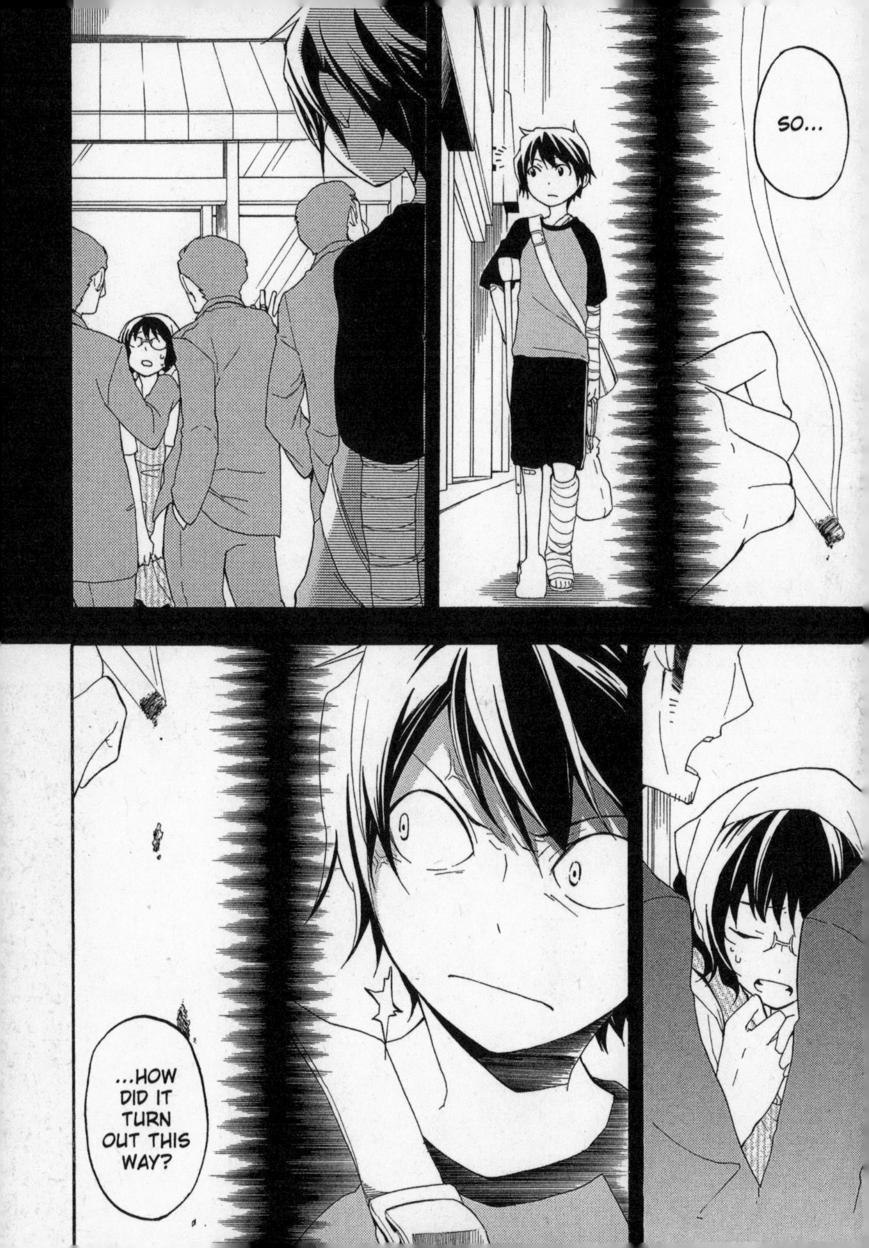
SO...
...HOW DID IT TURN OUT THIS WAY?

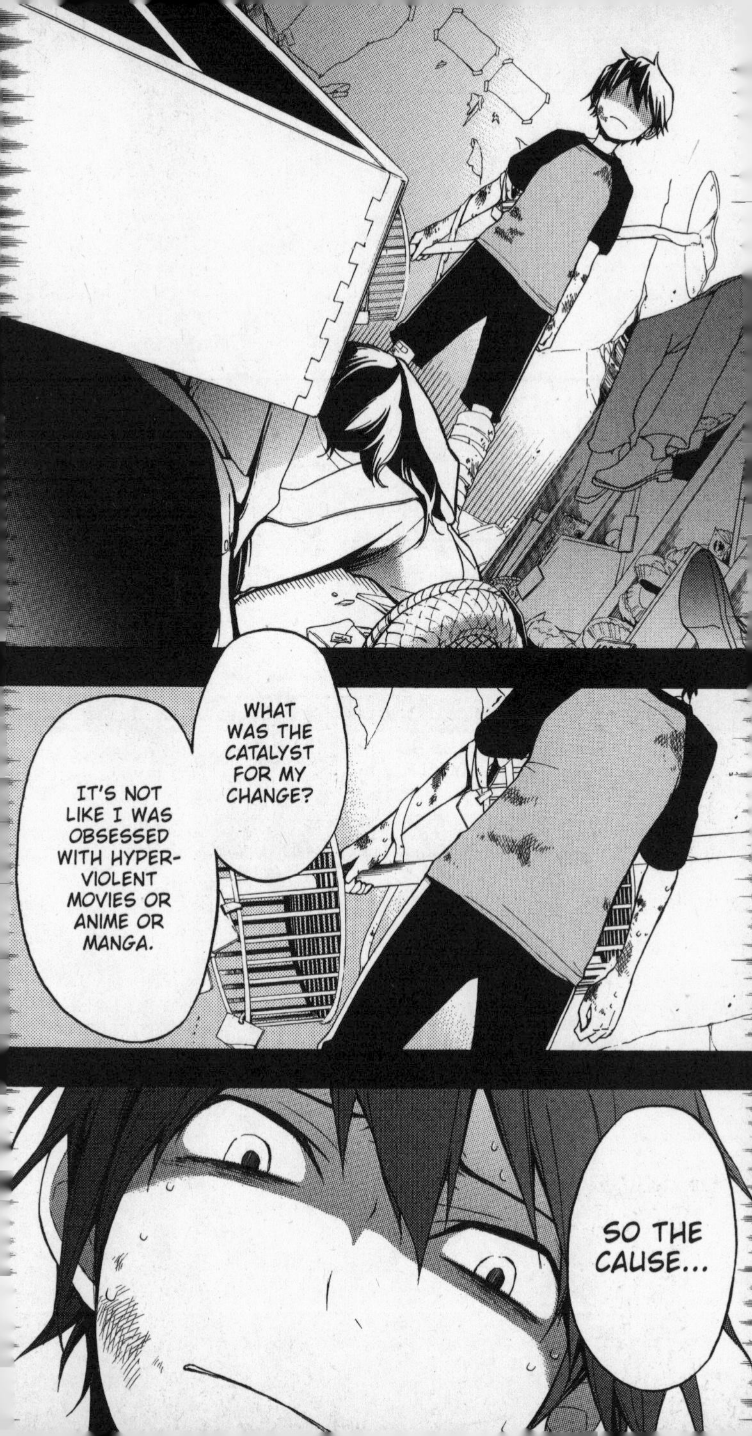
WHAT WAS THE CATALYST FOR MY CHANGE?
IT'S NOT LIKE I WAS OBSESSED WITH HYPER-VIOLENT MOVIES OR ANIME OR MANGA.
SO THE CAUSE...

...IS
ME.

IT COULDN'T HAVE COME FROM ANYTHING BUT ME.

THAT MEANS I HAVE NO ONE TO BLAME BUT MYSELF.

I DON'T CARE ABOUT THE FIGHTING.

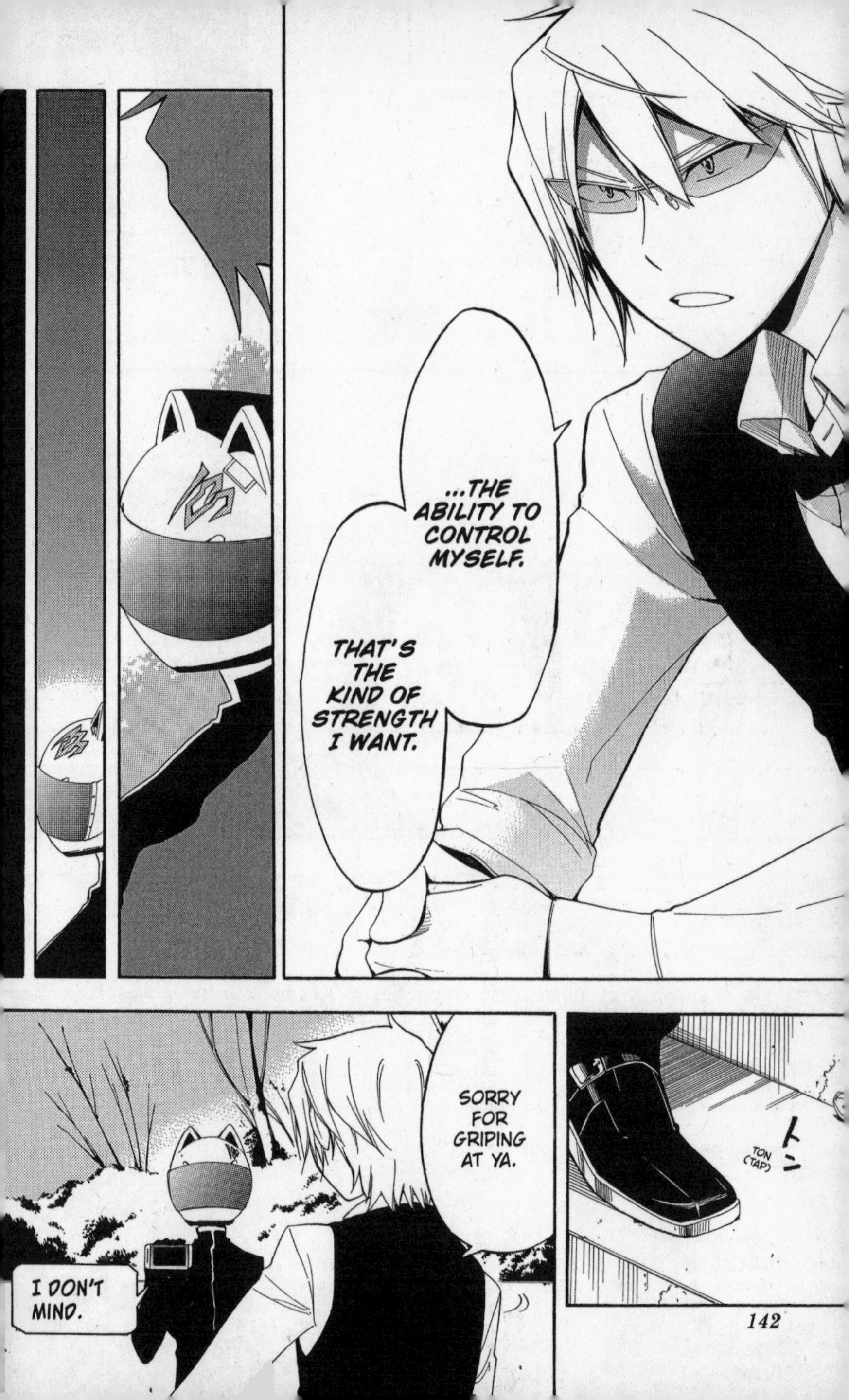
...THE ABILITY TO CONTROL MYSELF.
THAT'S THE KIND OF STRENGTH I WANT.
トン
TON (TAP)
SORRY FOR GRIPING AT YA.
I DON'T MIND.

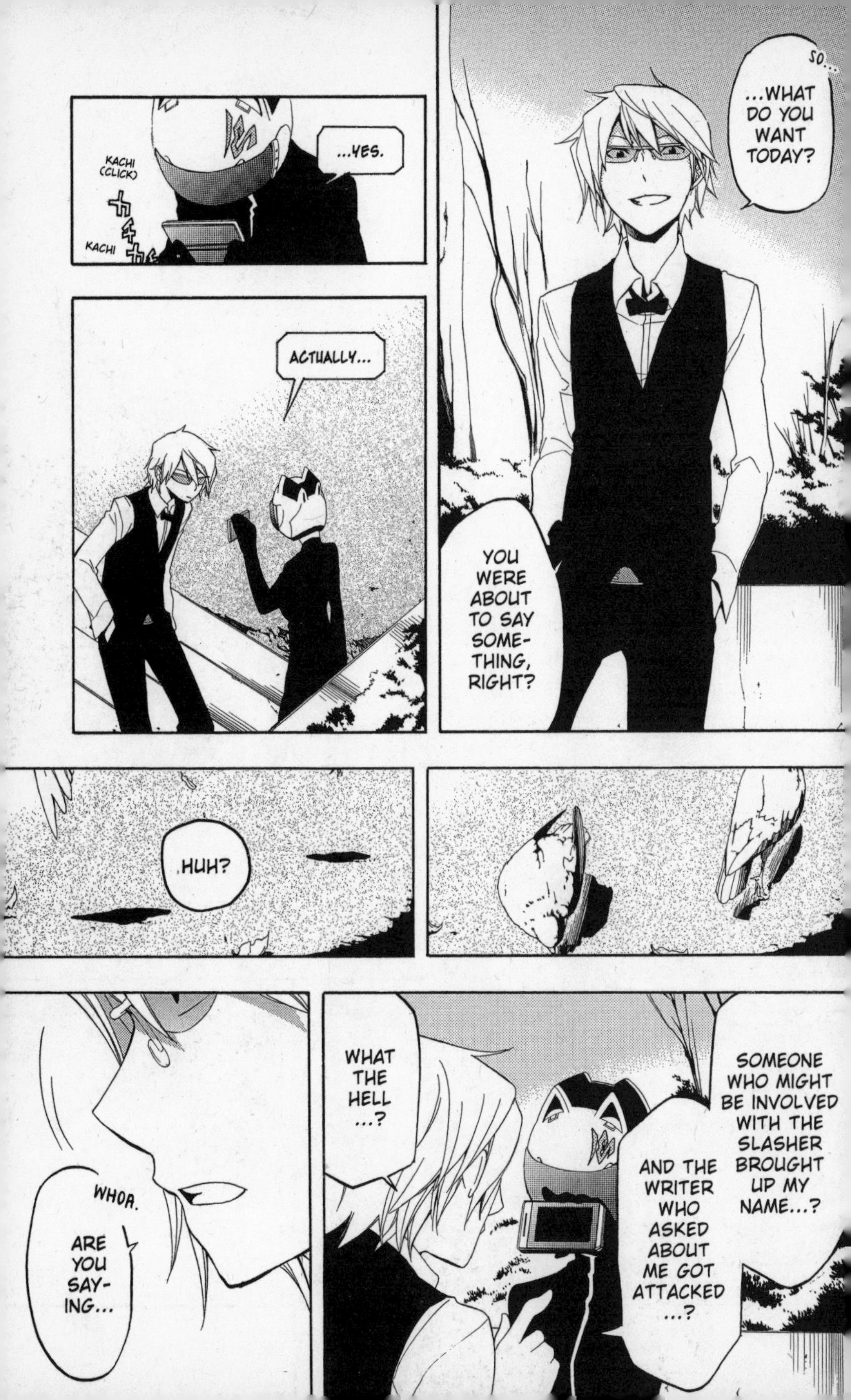
SO...
...WHAT DO YOU WANT TODAY?
YOU WERE ABOUT TO SAY SOME-THING, RIGHT?
...YES.
KACHI (CLICK)
KACHI
ACTUALLY...
HUH?
SOMEONE WHO MIGHT BE INVOLVED WITH THE SLASHER BROUGHT UP MY NAME...?
AND THE WRITER WHO ASKED ABOUT ME GOT ATTACKED...?
WHAT THE HELL...?
WHOA.
ARE YOU SAY-ING...

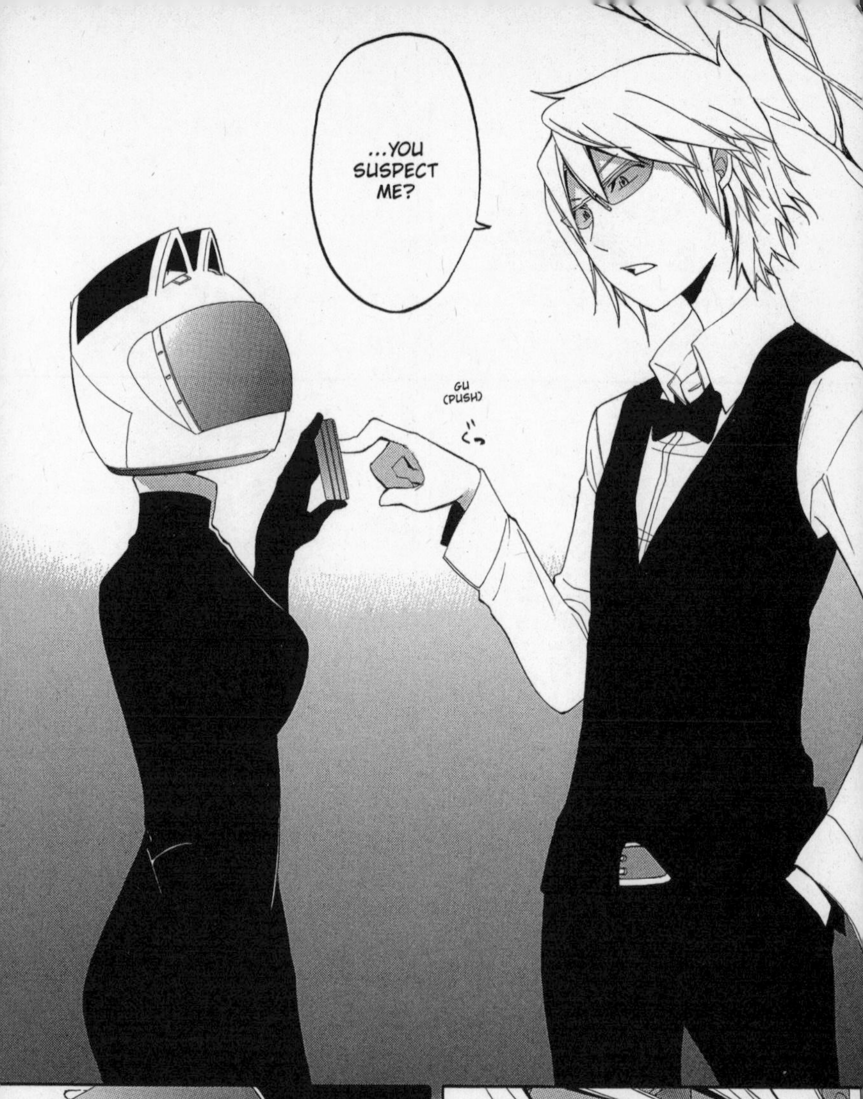
...YOU SUSPECT ME?
GU (PUSH)
ぐっ

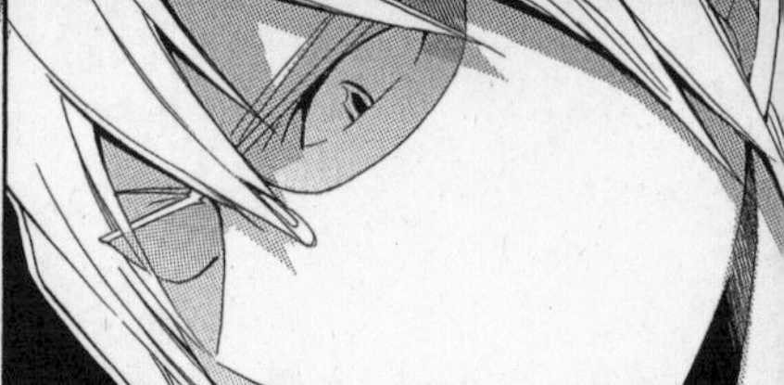

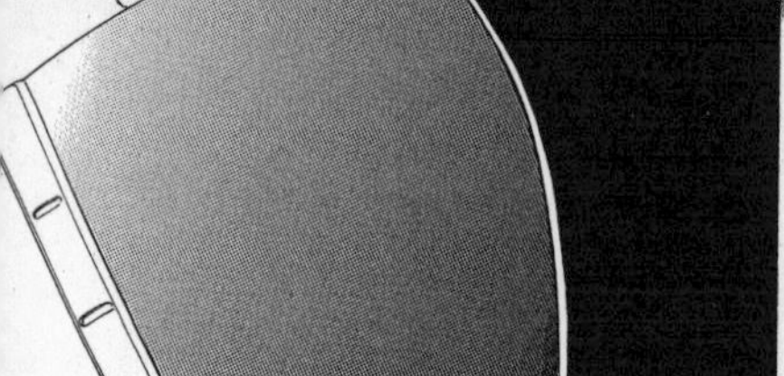

Durarara!! Saika Arc

DRRR!!

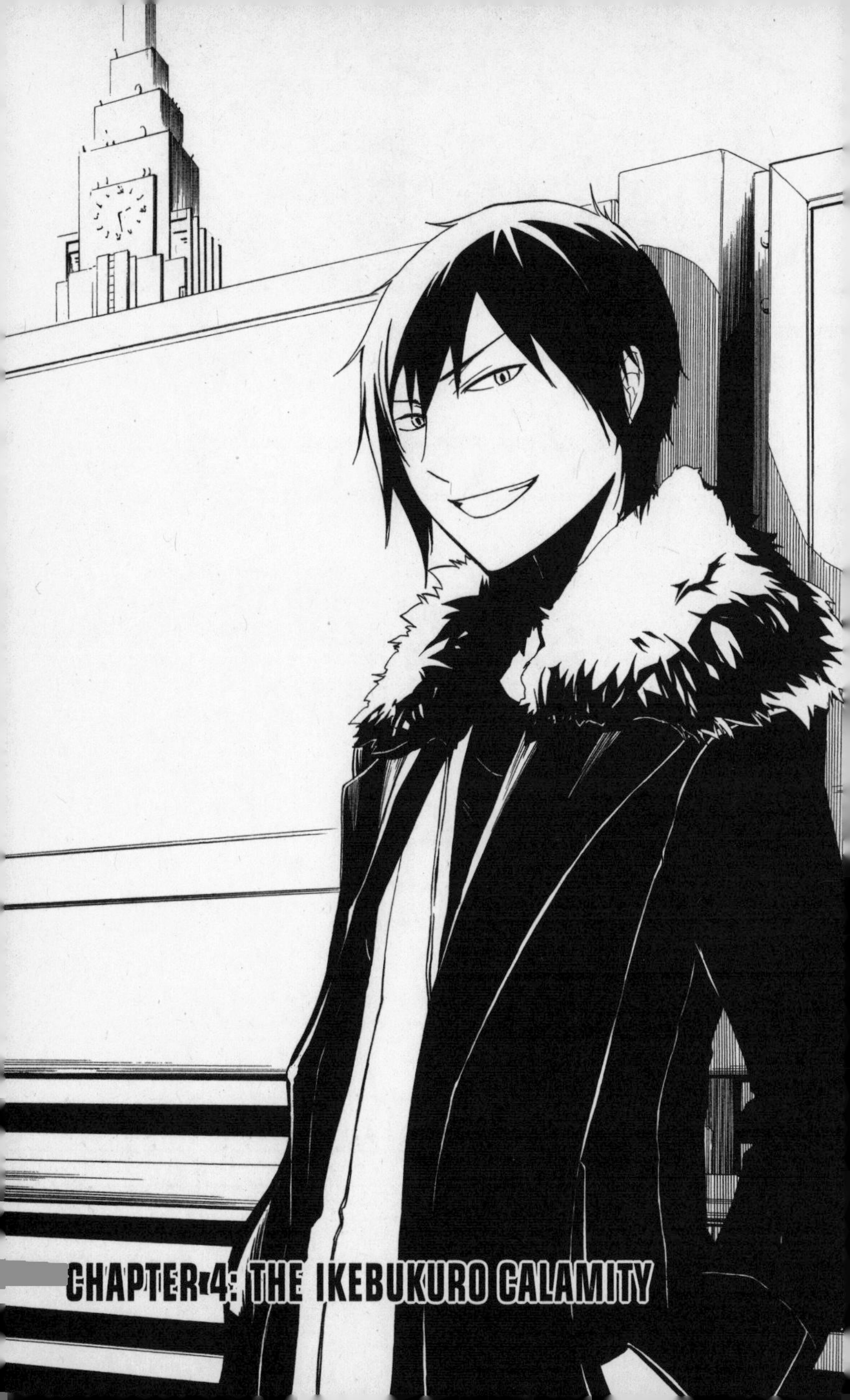
CHAPTER 4: THE IKEBUKURO CALAMITY

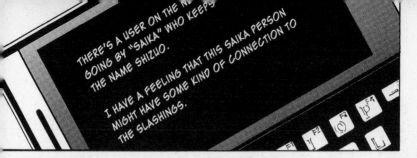

THERE'S A USER ON THE N[...] GOING BY "SAIKA" WHO KEEPS [...] THE NAME SHIZUO.

I HAVE A FEELING THAT THIS SAIKA PERSON MIGHT HAVE SOME KIND OF CONNECTION TO THE SLASHINGS.

AND THE NIGHT MY NAME POPPED UP IN CHAT WAS THE NIGHT THE WRITER WAS HIT?

ARE YOU SAYING YOU SUSPECT ME?

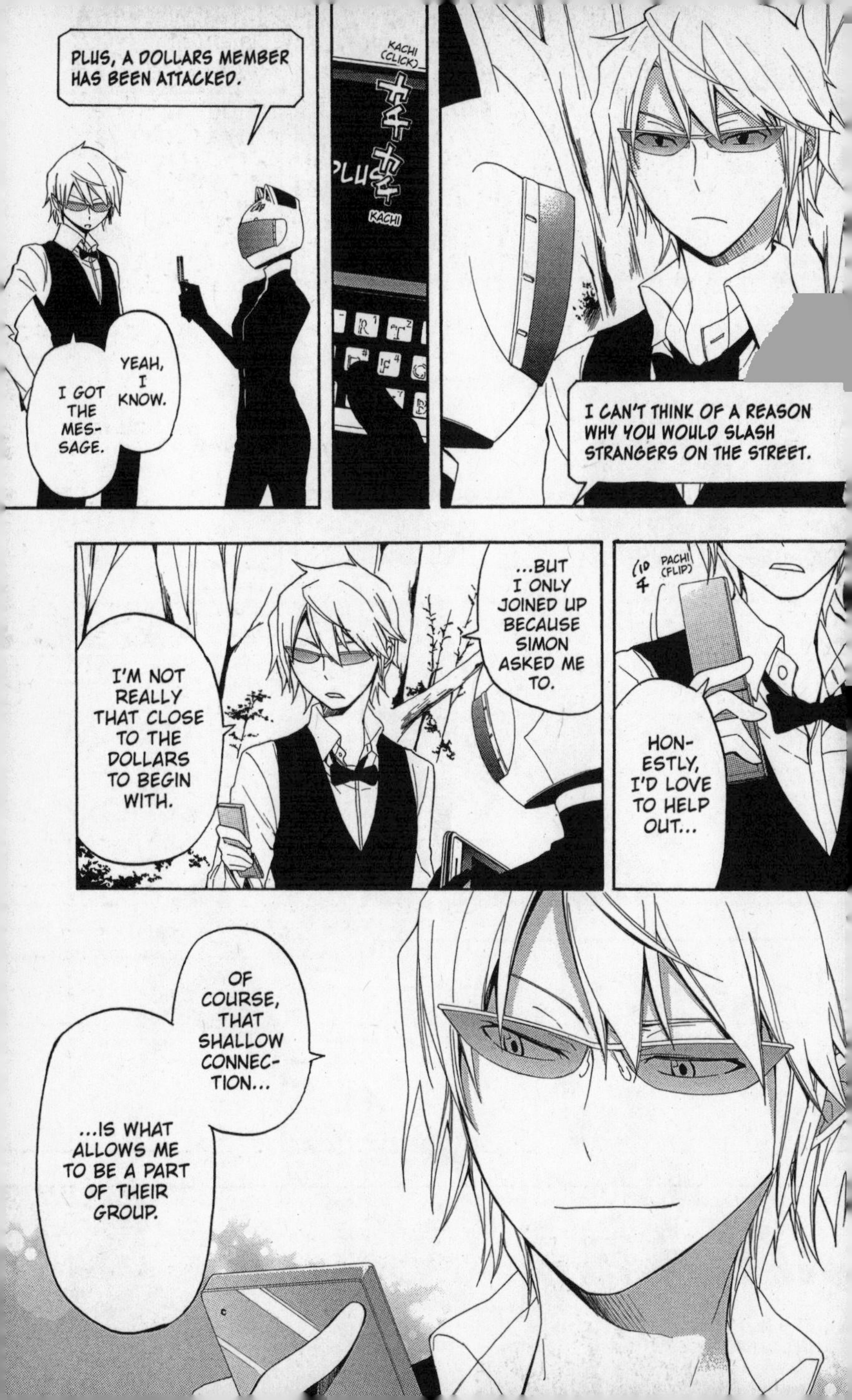
I CAN'T THINK OF A REASON WHY YOU WOULD SLASH STRANGERS ON THE STREET.
KACHI (CLICK)
PLUS
KACHI
PLUS, A DOLLARS MEMBER HAS BEEN ATTACKED.
YEAH, I KNOW.
I GOT THE MESSAGE.
PACHI (FLIP)
HONESTLY, I'D LOVE TO HELP OUT...
...BUT I ONLY JOINED UP BECAUSE SIMON ASKED ME TO.
I'M NOT REALLY THAT CLOSE TO THE DOLLARS TO BEGIN WITH.
OF COURSE, THAT SHALLOW CONNECTION...
...IS WHAT ALLOWS ME TO BE A PART OF THEIR GROUP.

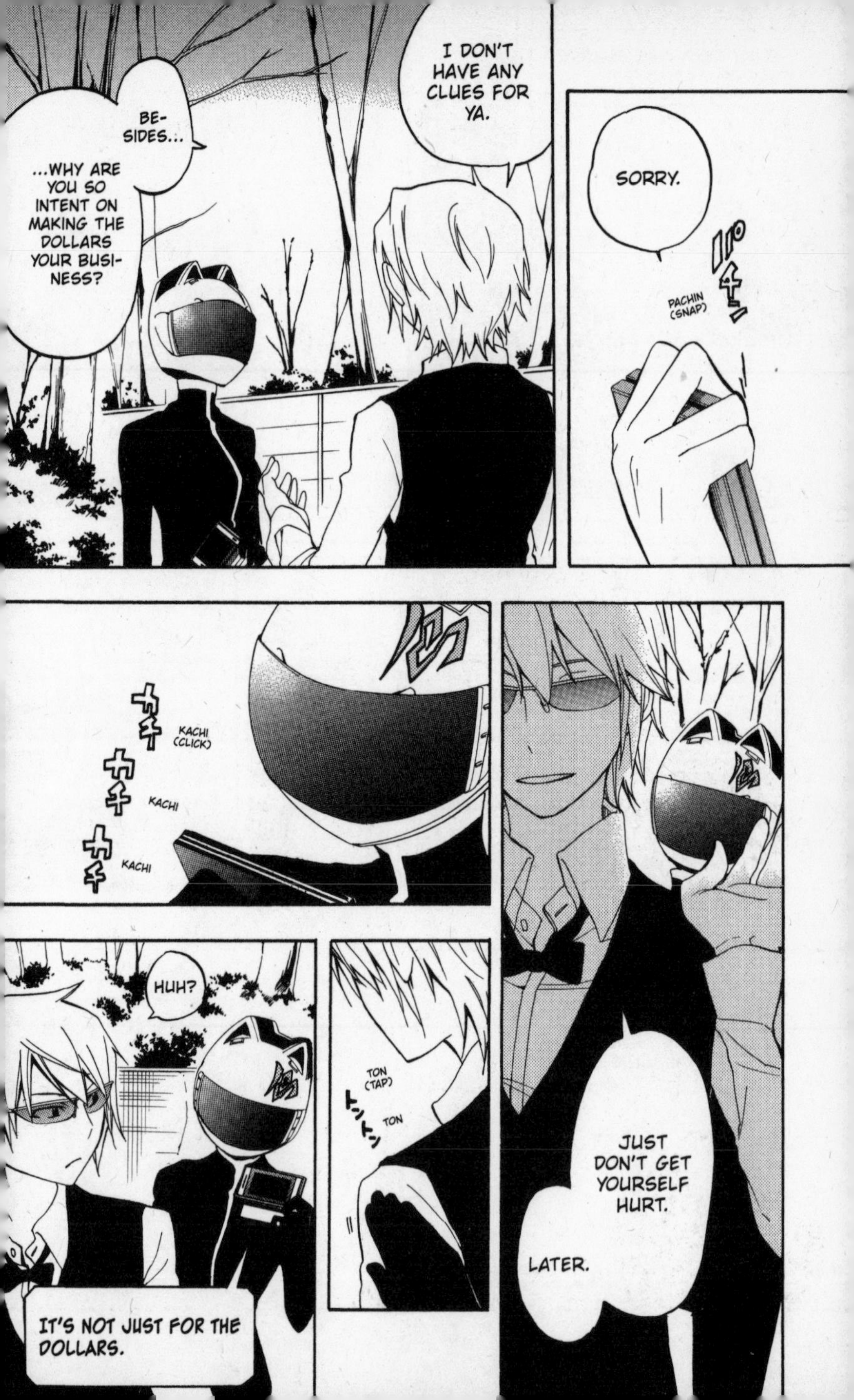
SORRY.
PACHIN (SNAP)
I DON'T HAVE ANY CLUES FOR YA.
BE- SIDES...
...WHY ARE YOU SO INTENT ON MAKING THE DOLLARS YOUR BUSI- NESS?
JUST DON'T GET YOURSELF HURT.
LATER.
KACHI (CLICK)
KACHI
KACHI
TON (TAP)
TON
HUH?
IT'S NOT JUST FOR THE DOLLARS.

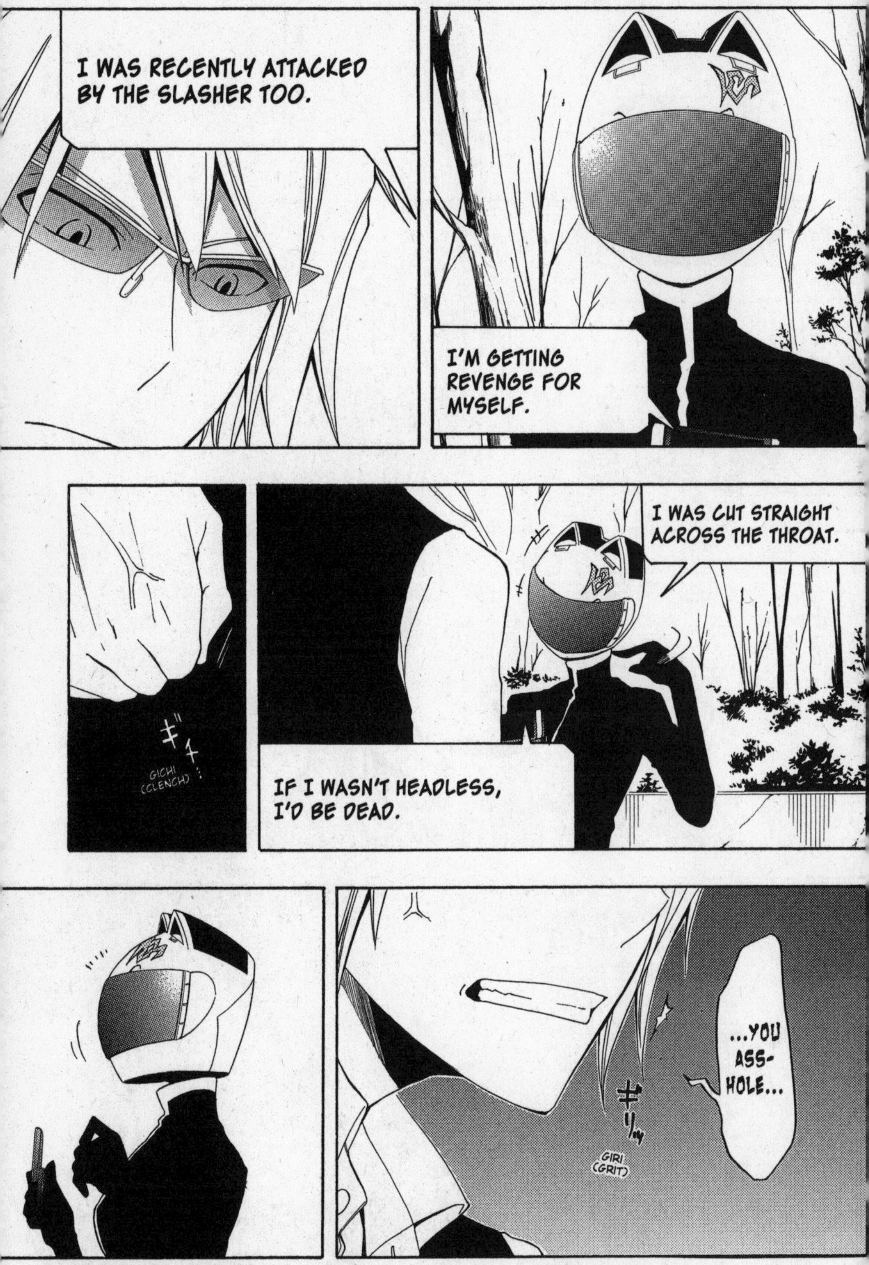
I'M GETTING REVENGE FOR MYSELF.
I WAS RECENTLY ATTACKED BY THE SLASHER TOO.
I WAS CUT STRAIGHT ACROSS THE THROAT.
IF I WASN'T HEADLESS, I'D BE DEAD.
GICHI (CLENCH)
...YOU ASS-HOLE...
GIRI (GRIT)

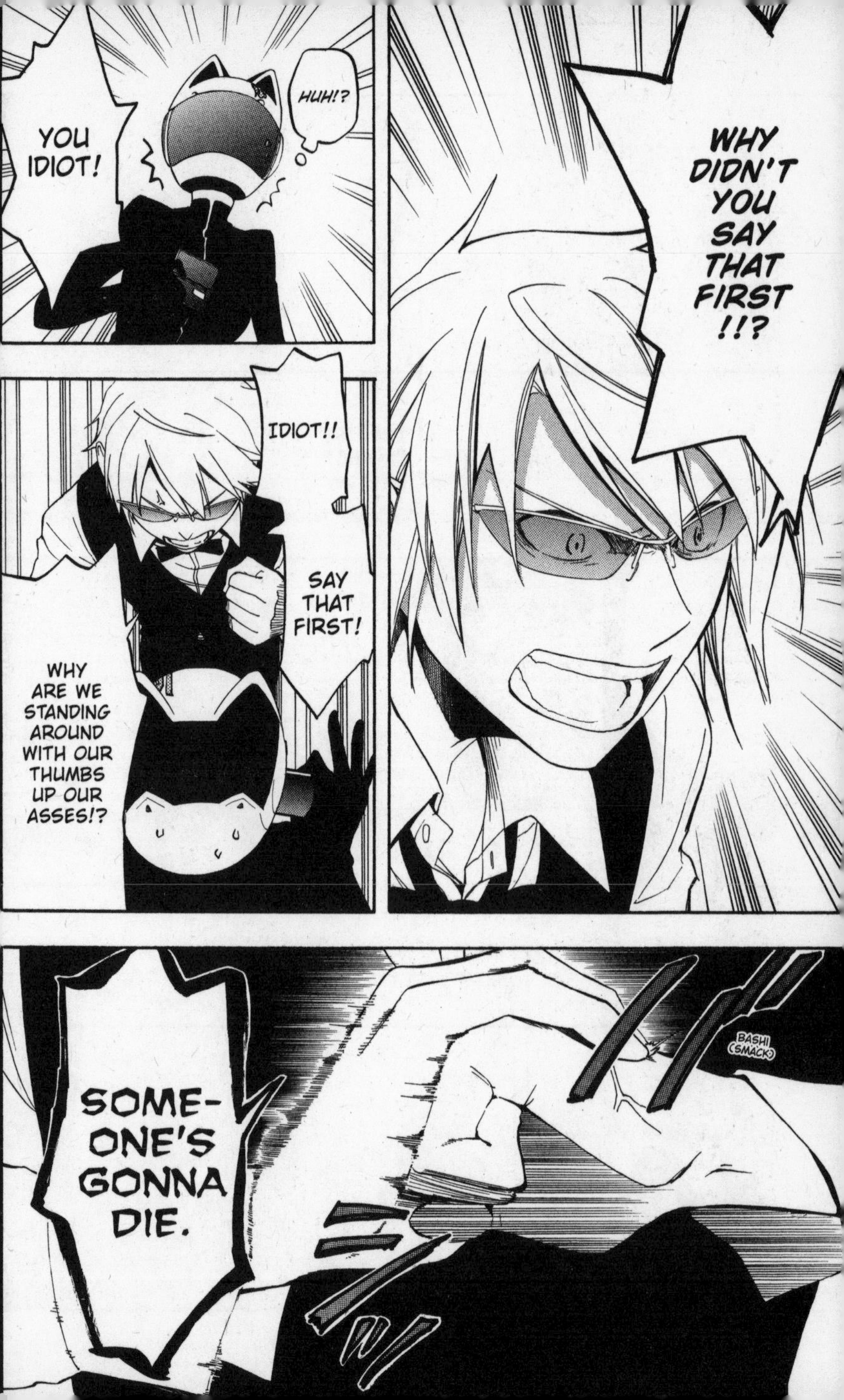
WHY DIDN'T YOU SAY THAT FIRST!!?
HUH!?
YOU IDIOT!
IDIOT!!
SAY THAT FIRST!
WHY ARE WE STANDING AROUND WITH OUR THUMBS UP OUR ASSES!?
BASHI (SMACK)
SOME-ONE'S GONNA DIE.

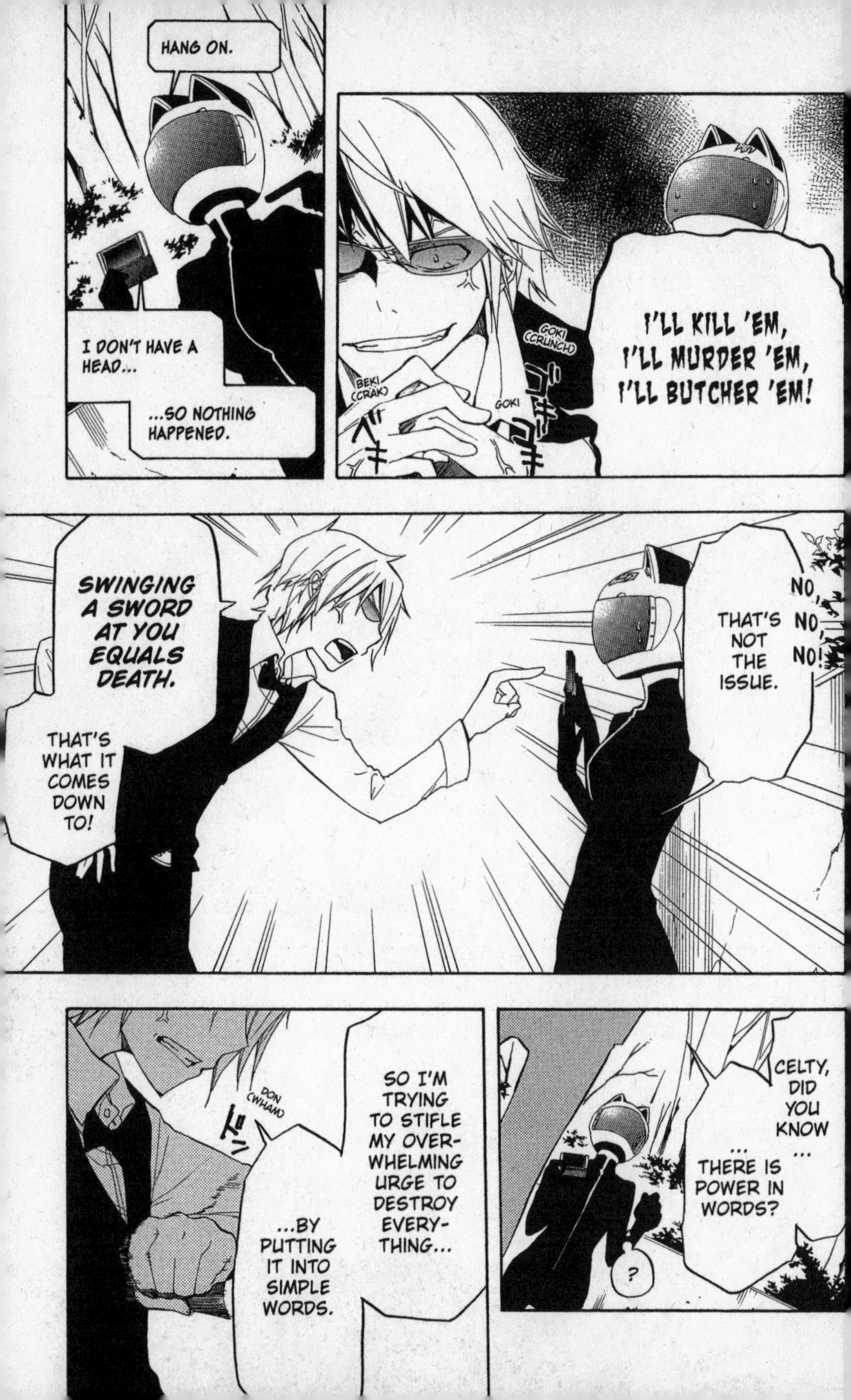
GOKI (CRUNCH)
BEKI (CRAK)
GOKI
I'LL KILL 'EM, I'LL MURDER 'EM, I'LL BUTCHER 'EM!
HANG ON.
I DON'T HAVE A HEAD...
...SO NOTHING HAPPENED.
NO, NO, NO!
THAT'S NOT THE ISSUE.
SWINGING A SWORD AT YOU EQUALS DEATH.
THAT'S WHAT IT COMES DOWN TO!
CELTY, DID YOU KNOW...
...THERE IS POWER IN WORDS?
?
SO I'M TRYING TO STIFLE MY OVER-WHELMING URGE TO DESTROY EVERY-THING...
DON (WHAM)
...BY PUTTING IT INTO SIMPLE WORDS.

SFX: BUTSU (MUTTER) BUTSU BUTSU BUTSU BUTSU BUTSU BUTSU BUTSU BUTSU BUTSU...

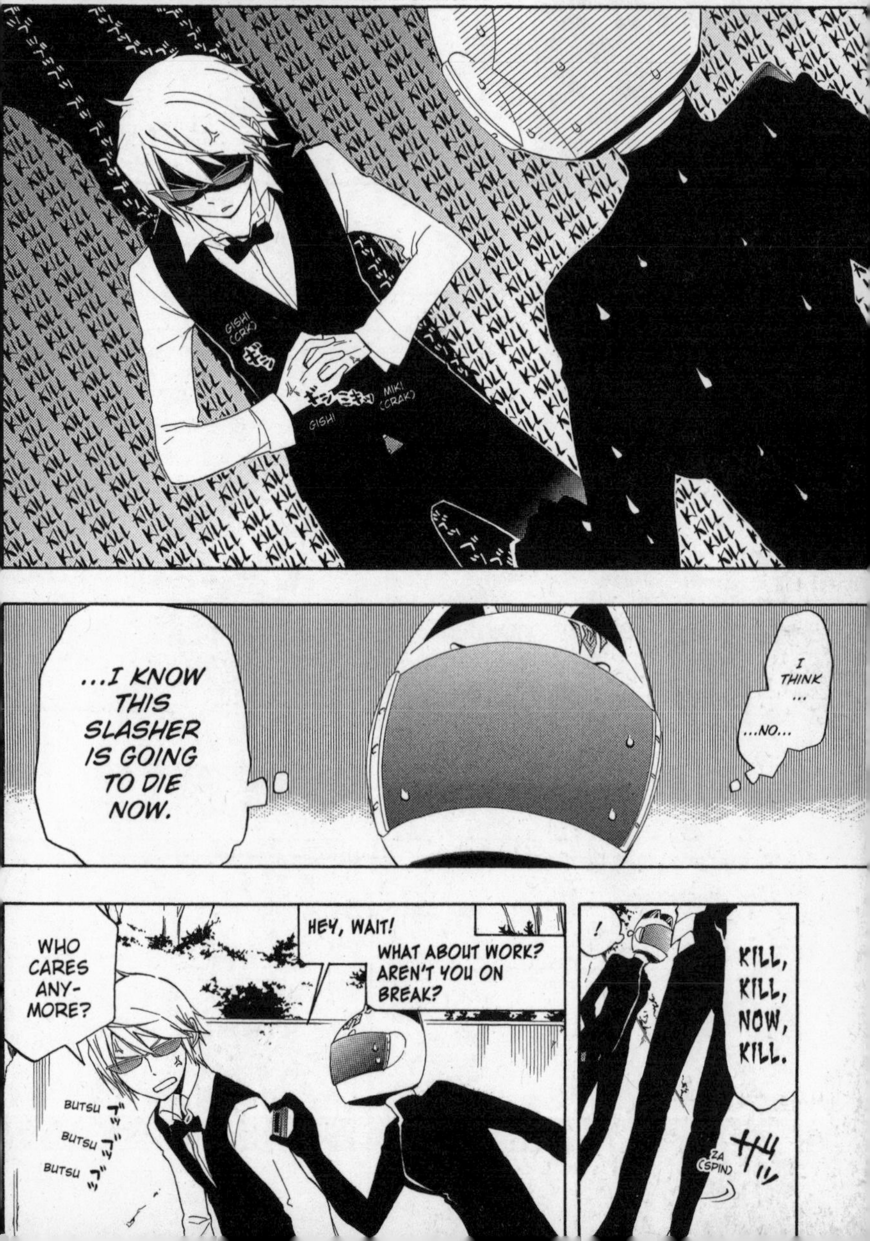
KILL KILL KILL KILL
GISHI (CRK)
MIKI (CRAK)
GISHI
I THINK...
...NO...
...I KNOW THIS SLASHER IS GOING TO DIE NOW.
!
KILL, KILL, NOW, KILL.
ZA (SPIN)
HEY, WAIT!
WHAT ABOUT WORK? AREN'T YOU ON BREAK?
WHO CARES ANYMORE?
BUTSU
BUTSU
BUTSU

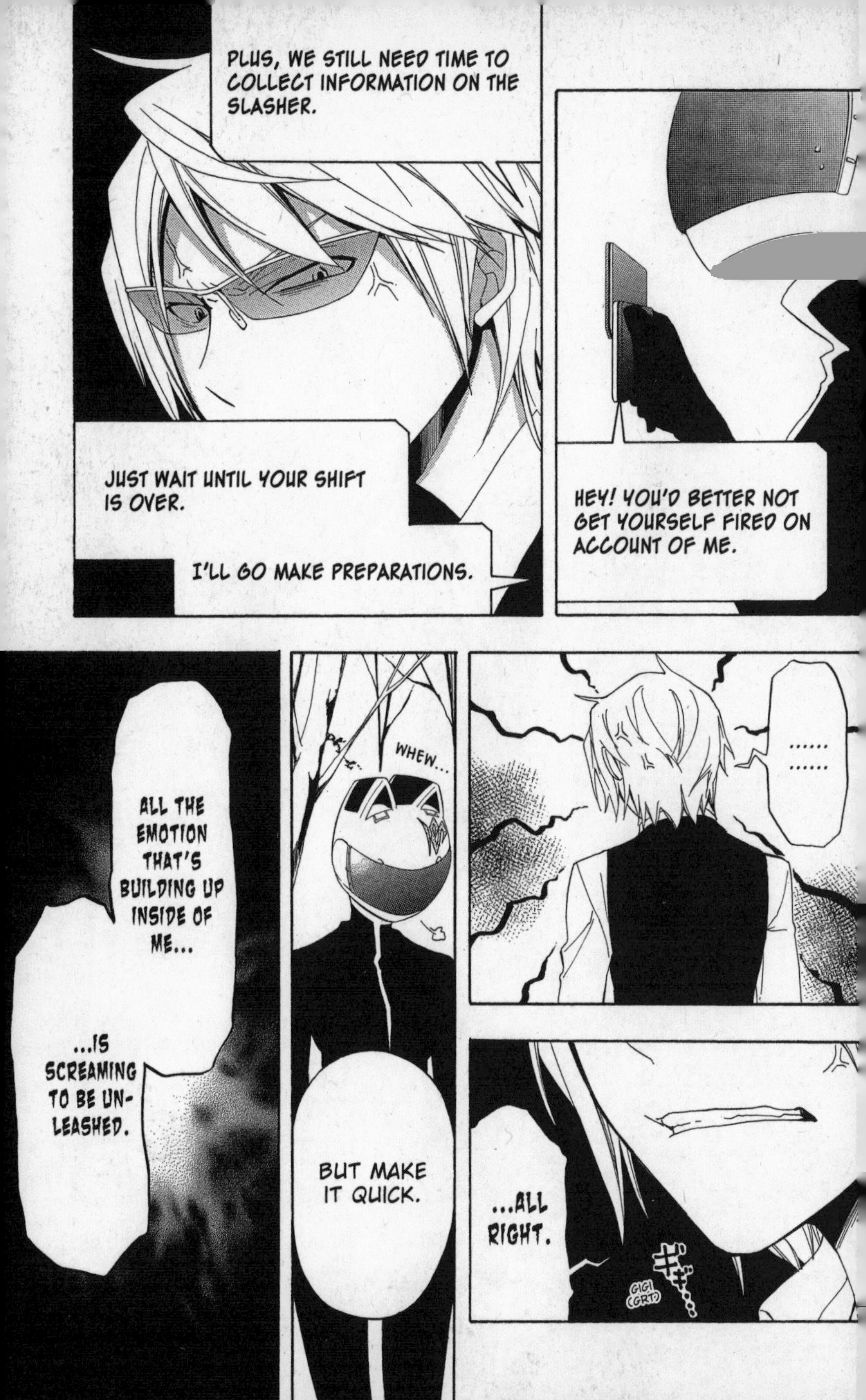
HEY! YOU'D BETTER NOT GET YOURSELF FIRED ON ACCOUNT OF ME.
PLUS, WE STILL NEED TIME TO COLLECT INFORMATION ON THE SLASHER.
JUST WAIT UNTIL YOUR SHIFT IS OVER.
I'LL GO MAKE PREPARATIONS.
....
...ALL RIGHT.
GIGI (GRT)
WHEW...
BUT MAKE IT QUICK.
ALL THE EMOTION THAT'S BUILDING UP INSIDE OF ME...
...IS SCREAMING TO BE UN-LEASHED.

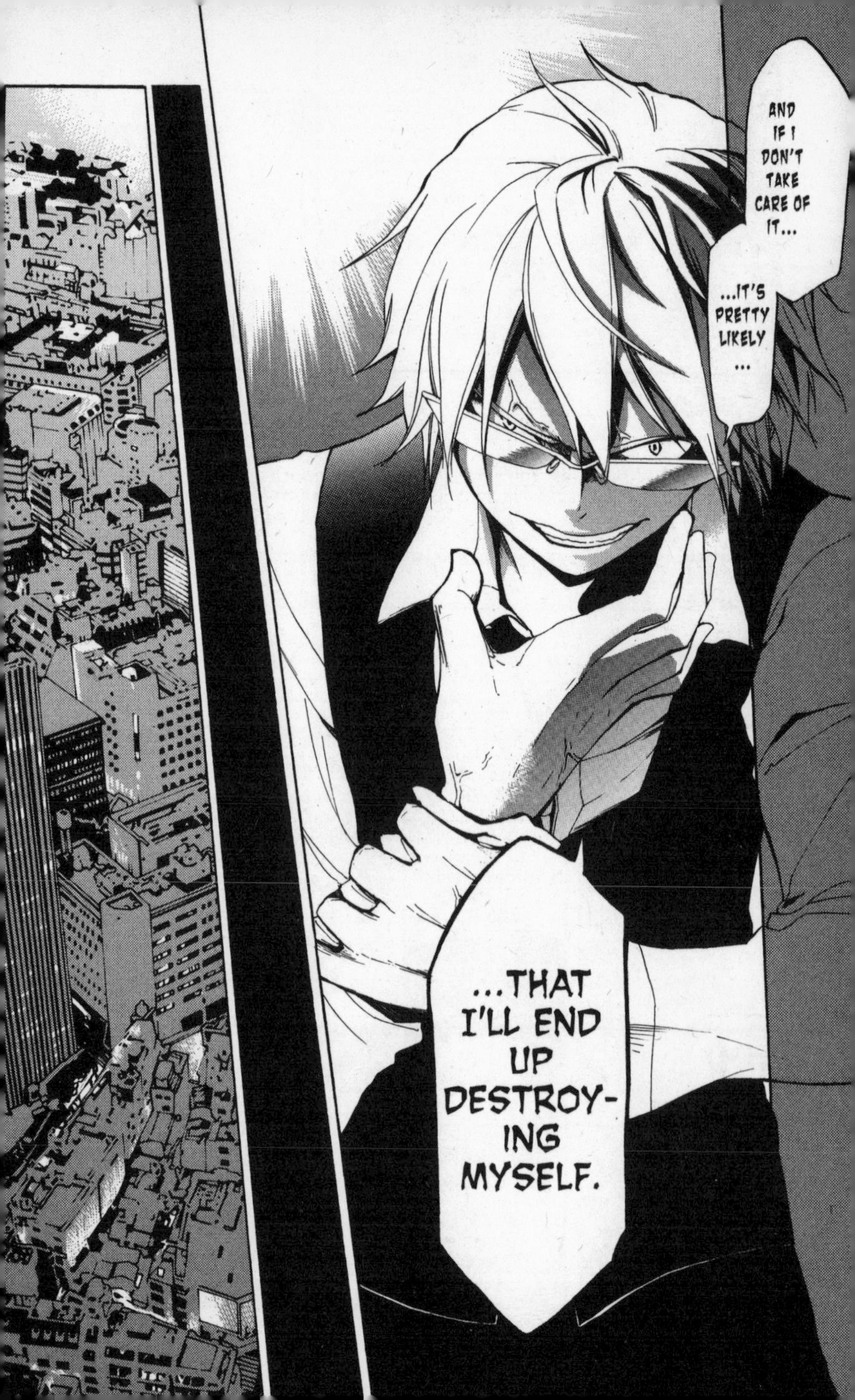
AND IF I DON'T TAKE CARE OF IT...
...IT'S PRETTY LIKELY ...
...THAT I'LL END UP DESTROY-ING MYSELF.

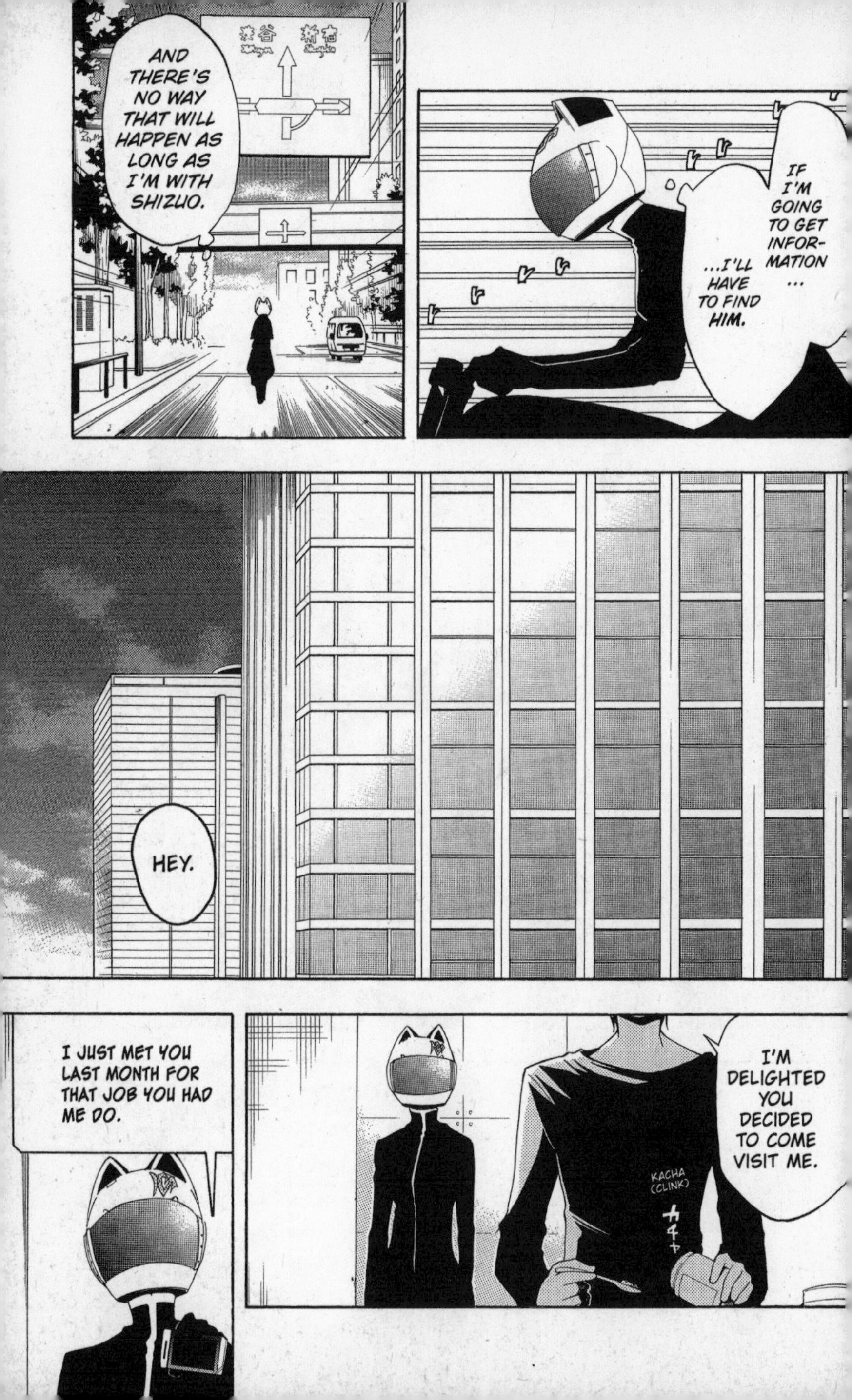
IF I'M GOING TO GET INFOR-MATION...
...I'LL HAVE TO FIND HIM.
AND THERE'S NO WAY THAT WILL HAPPEN AS LONG AS I'M WITH SHIZUO.
HEY.
I'M DELIGHTED YOU DECIDED TO COME VISIT ME.
KACHA (CLINK)
カチャ
I JUST MET YOU LAST MONTH FOR THAT JOB YOU HAD ME DO.

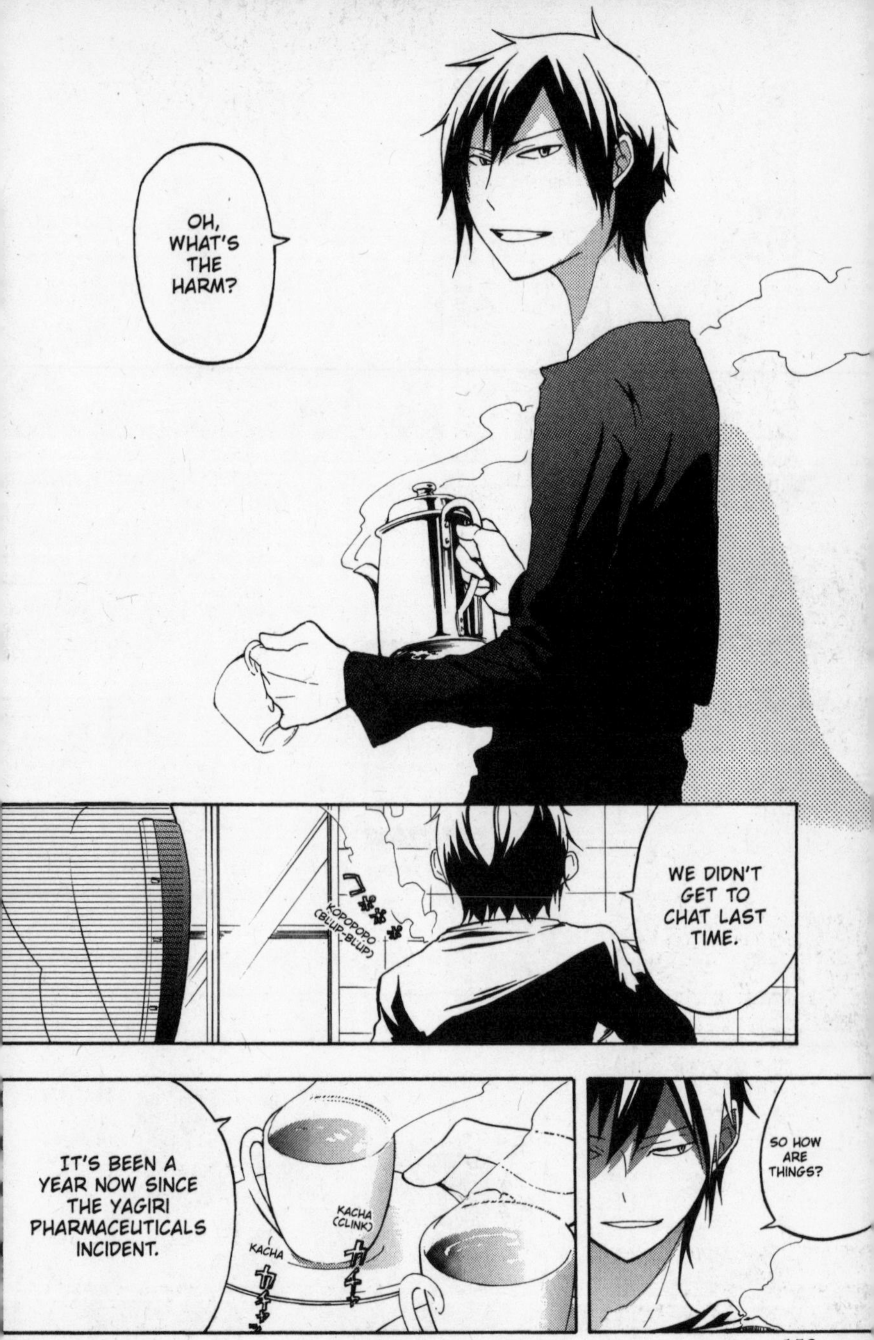
OH, WHAT'S THE HARM?
WE DIDN'T GET TO CHAT LAST TIME.
KOPOPOPO (BLUP-BLUP)
SO HOW ARE THINGS?
IT'S BEEN A YEAR NOW SINCE THE YAGIRI PHARMACEUTICALS INCIDENT.
KACHA (CLINK)
KACHA

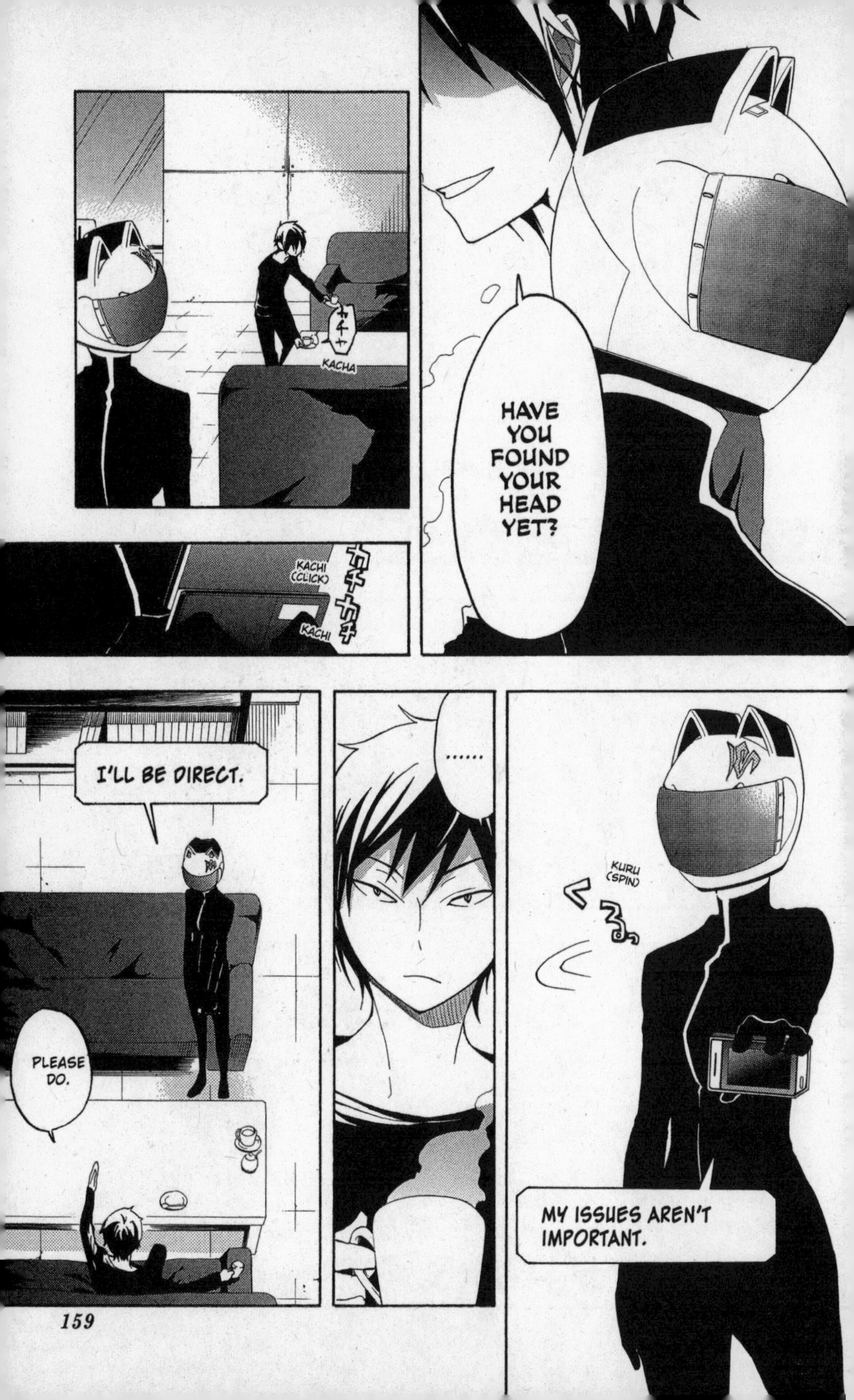
HAVE YOU FOUND YOUR HEAD YET?
KACHA
KACHI (CLICK)
KACHI
KURU (SPIN)
MY ISSUES AREN'T IMPORTANT.
......
I'LL BE DIRECT.
PLEASE DO.

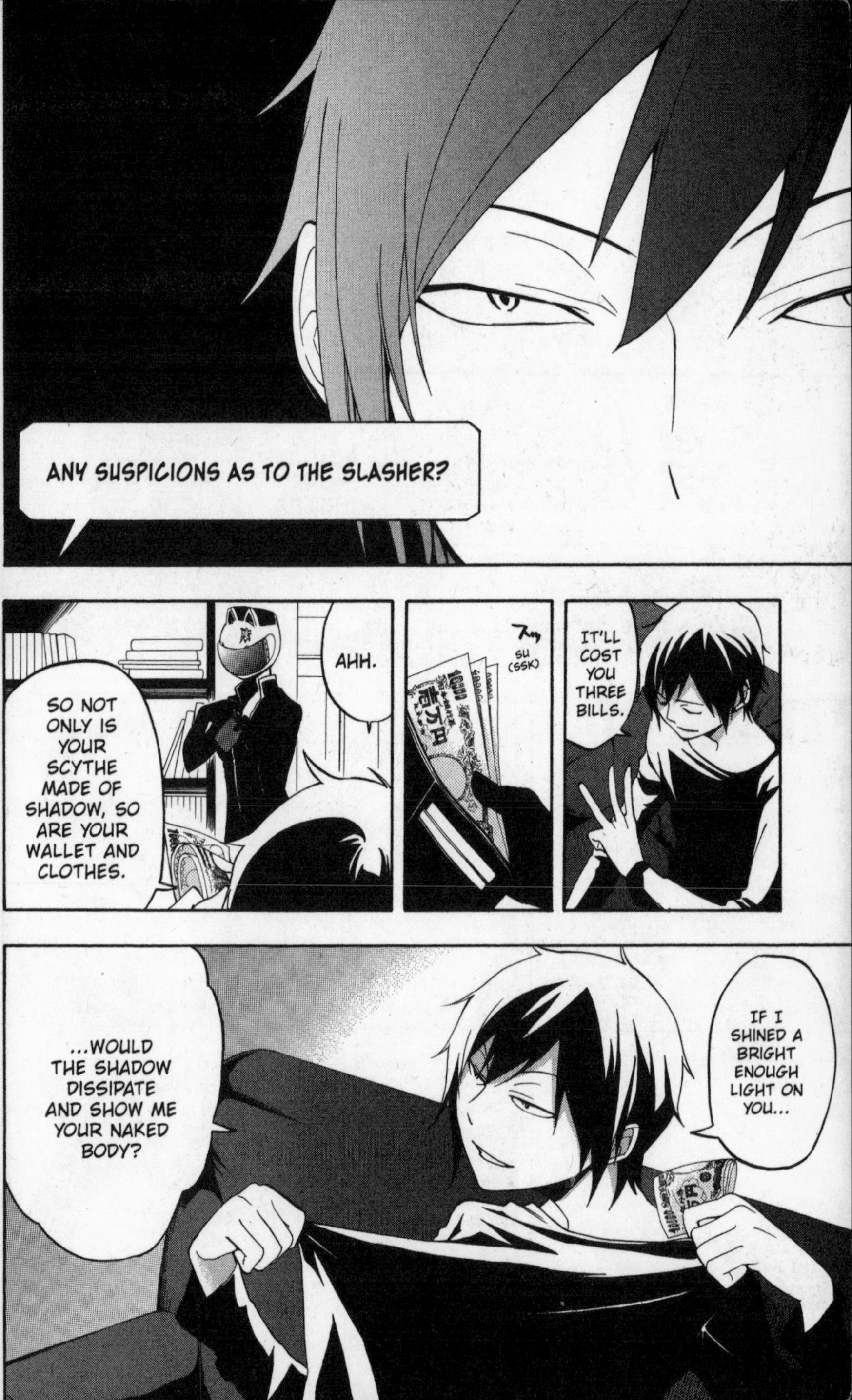
ANY SUSPICIONS AS TO THE SLASHER?
IT'LL COST YOU THREE BILLS.
スッ
SU (SSK)
AHH.
SO NOT ONLY IS YOUR SCYTHE MADE OF SHADOW, SO ARE YOUR WALLET AND CLOTHES.
IF I SHINED A BRIGHT ENOUGH LIGHT ON YOU...
...WOULD THE SHADOW DISSIPATE AND SHOW ME YOUR NAKED BODY?

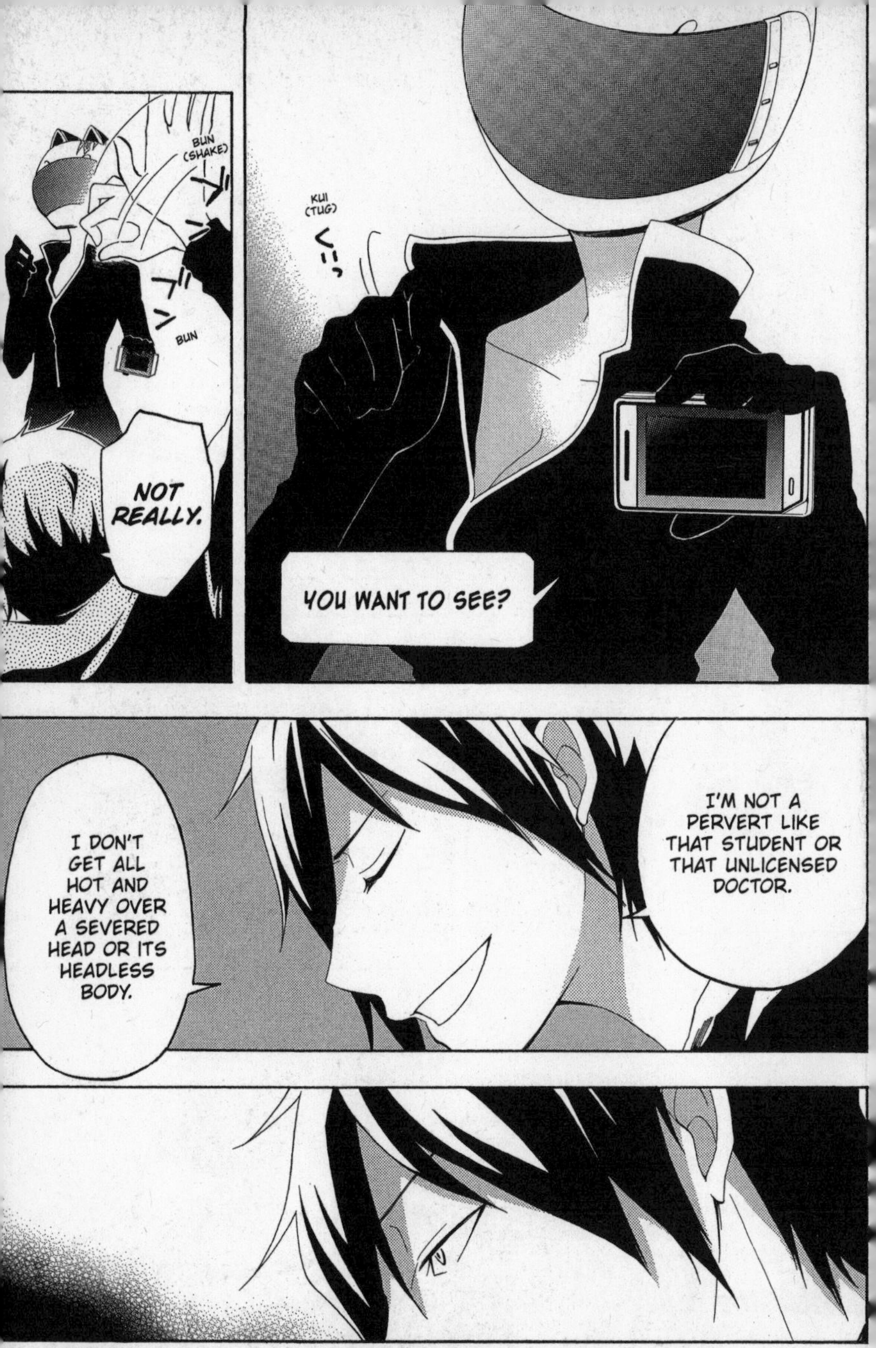
KUI (TUG)
YOU WANT TO SEE?
BUN (SHAKE)
BUN
NOT REALLY.
I'M NOT A PERVERT LIKE THAT STUDENT OR THAT UNLICENSED DOCTOR.
I DON'T GET ALL HOT AND HEAVY OVER A SEVERED HEAD OR ITS HEADLESS BODY.

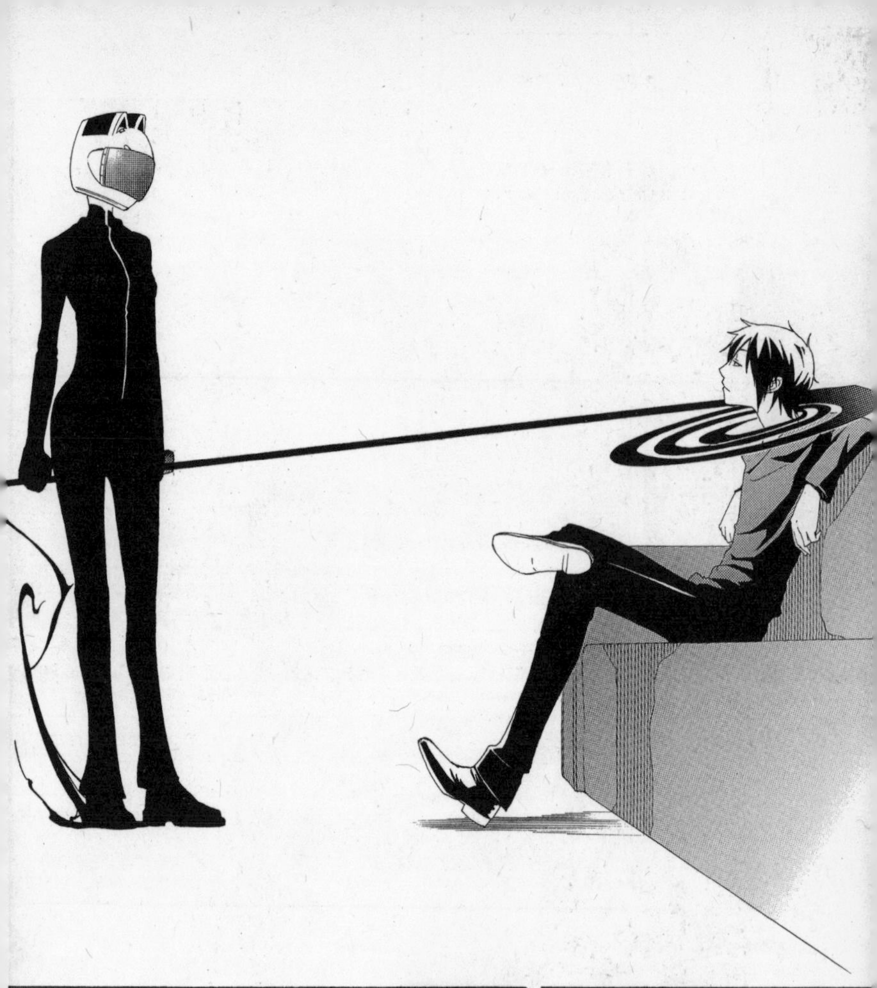

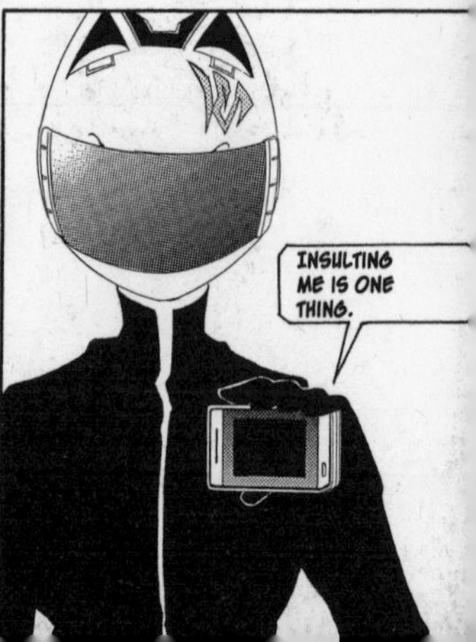
INSULTING ME IS ONE THING.

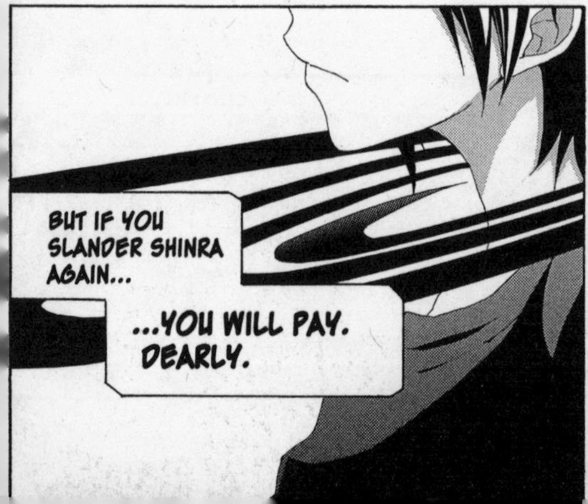
BUT IF YOU SLANDER SHINRA AGAIN...
...YOU WILL PAY. DEARLY.

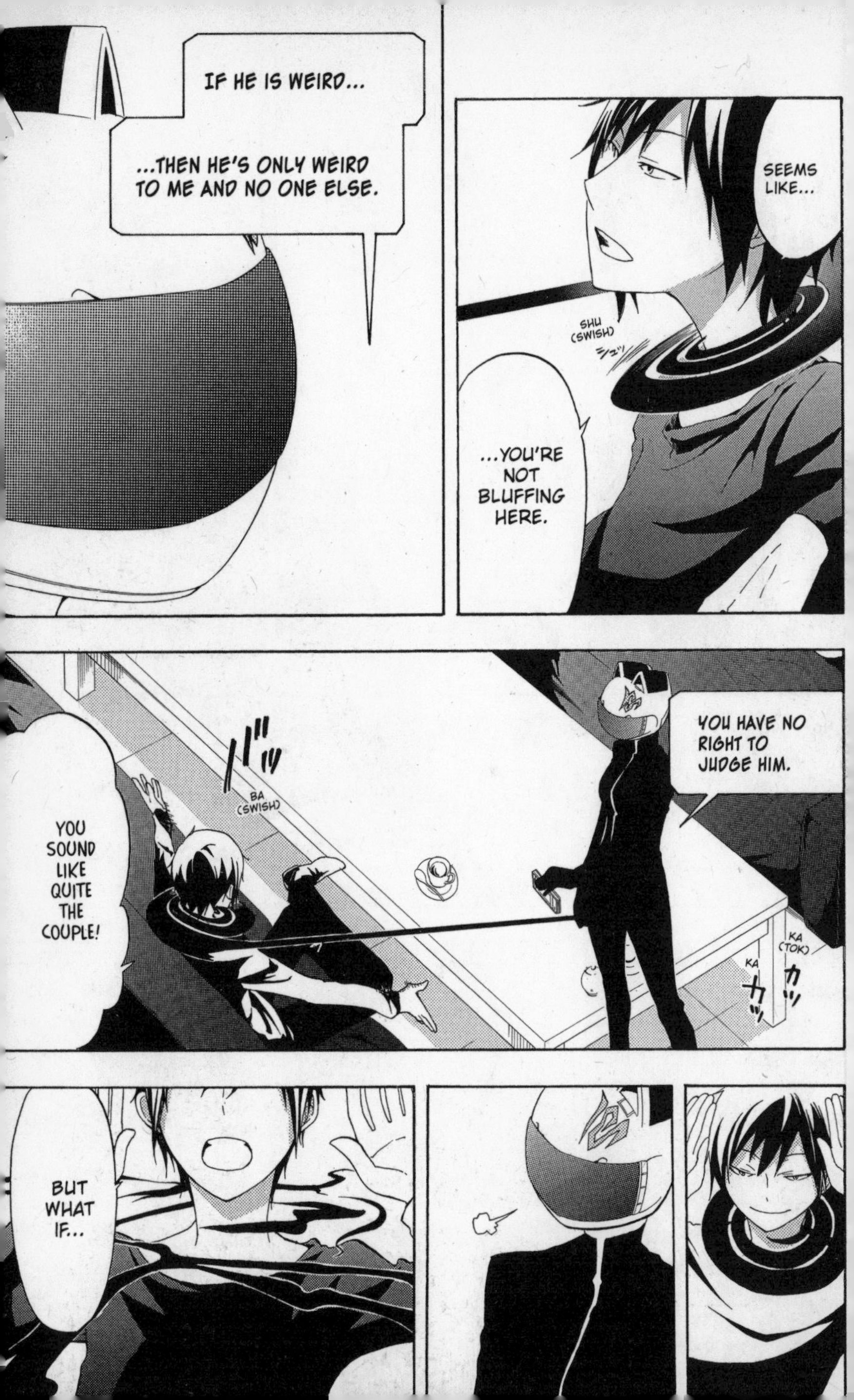
SEEMS LIKE...
SHU (SWISH)
...YOU'RE NOT BLUFFING HERE.
IF HE IS WEIRD...
...THEN HE'S ONLY WEIRD TO ME AND NO ONE ELSE.
YOU HAVE NO RIGHT TO JUDGE HIM.
KA (TOK)
KA
BA (SWISH)
YOU SOUND LIKE QUITE THE COUPLE!
BUT WHAT IF...

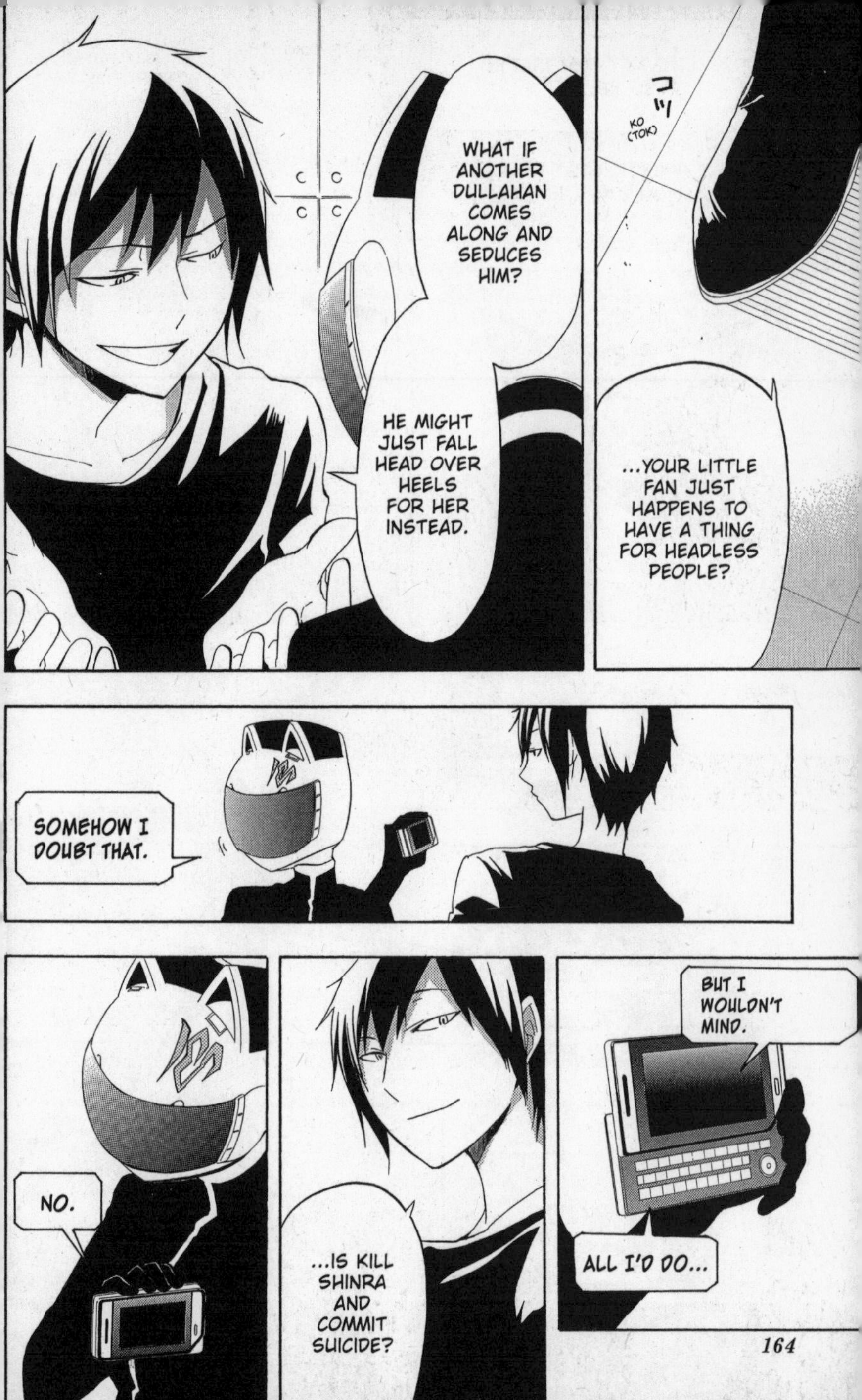
コッ
KO (TOK)
...YOUR LITTLE FAN JUST HAPPENS TO HAVE A THING FOR HEADLESS PEOPLE?
WHAT IF ANOTHER DULLAHAN COMES ALONG AND SEDUCES HIM?
HE MIGHT JUST FALL HEAD OVER HEELS FOR HER INSTEAD.
SOMEHOW I DOUBT THAT.
BUT I WOULDN'T MIND.
ALL I'D DO...
...IS KILL SHINRA AND COMMIT SUICIDE?
NO.

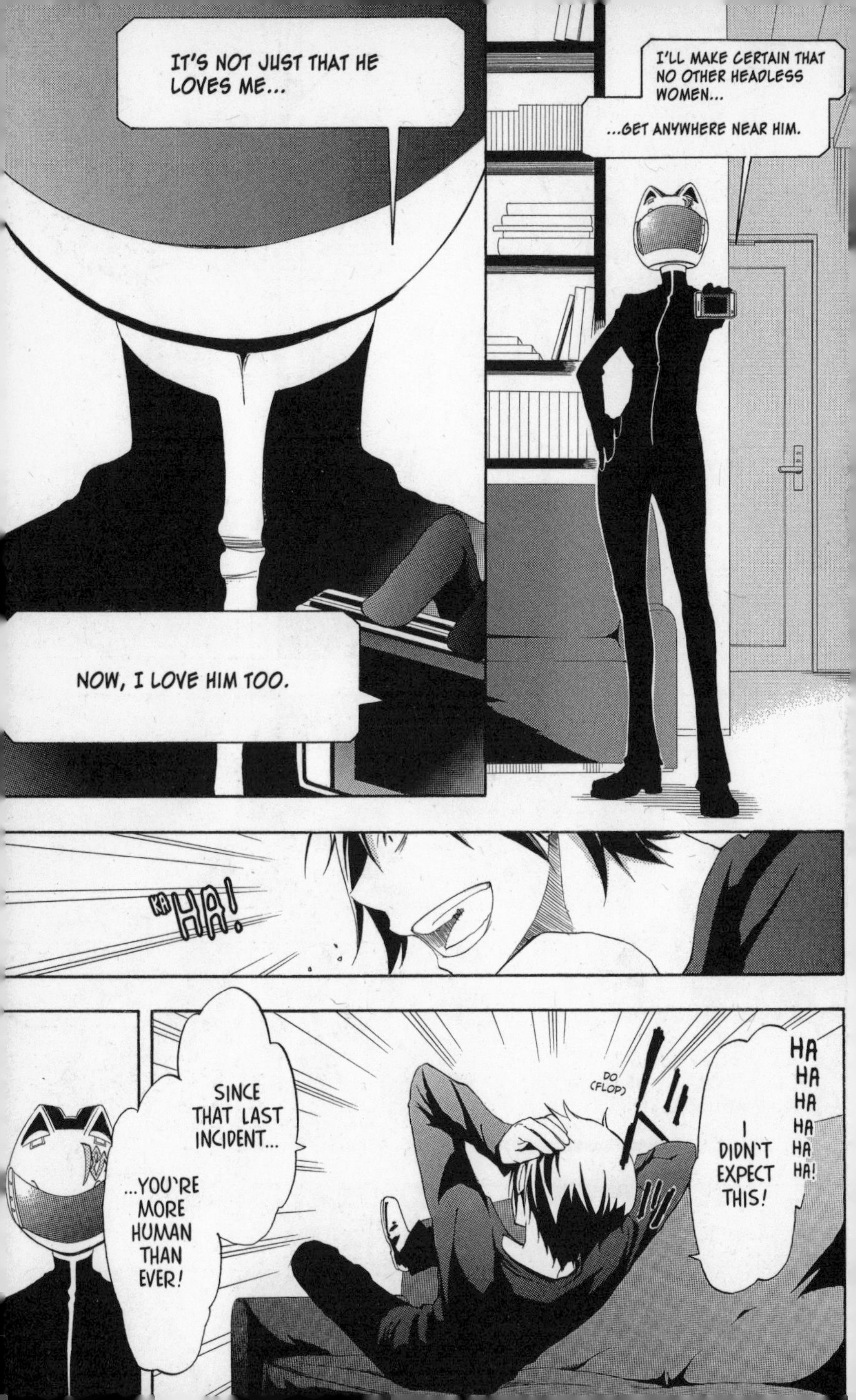
I'LL MAKE CERTAIN THAT NO OTHER HEADLESS WOMEN...
...GET ANYWHERE NEAR HIM.
IT'S NOT JUST THAT HE LOVES ME...
NOW, I LOVE HIM TOO.
KA HA!
HA HA HA HA HA HA!
I DIDN'T EXPECT THIS!
DO (FLOP)
SINCE THAT LAST INCIDENT...
...YOU'RE MORE HUMAN THAN EVER!

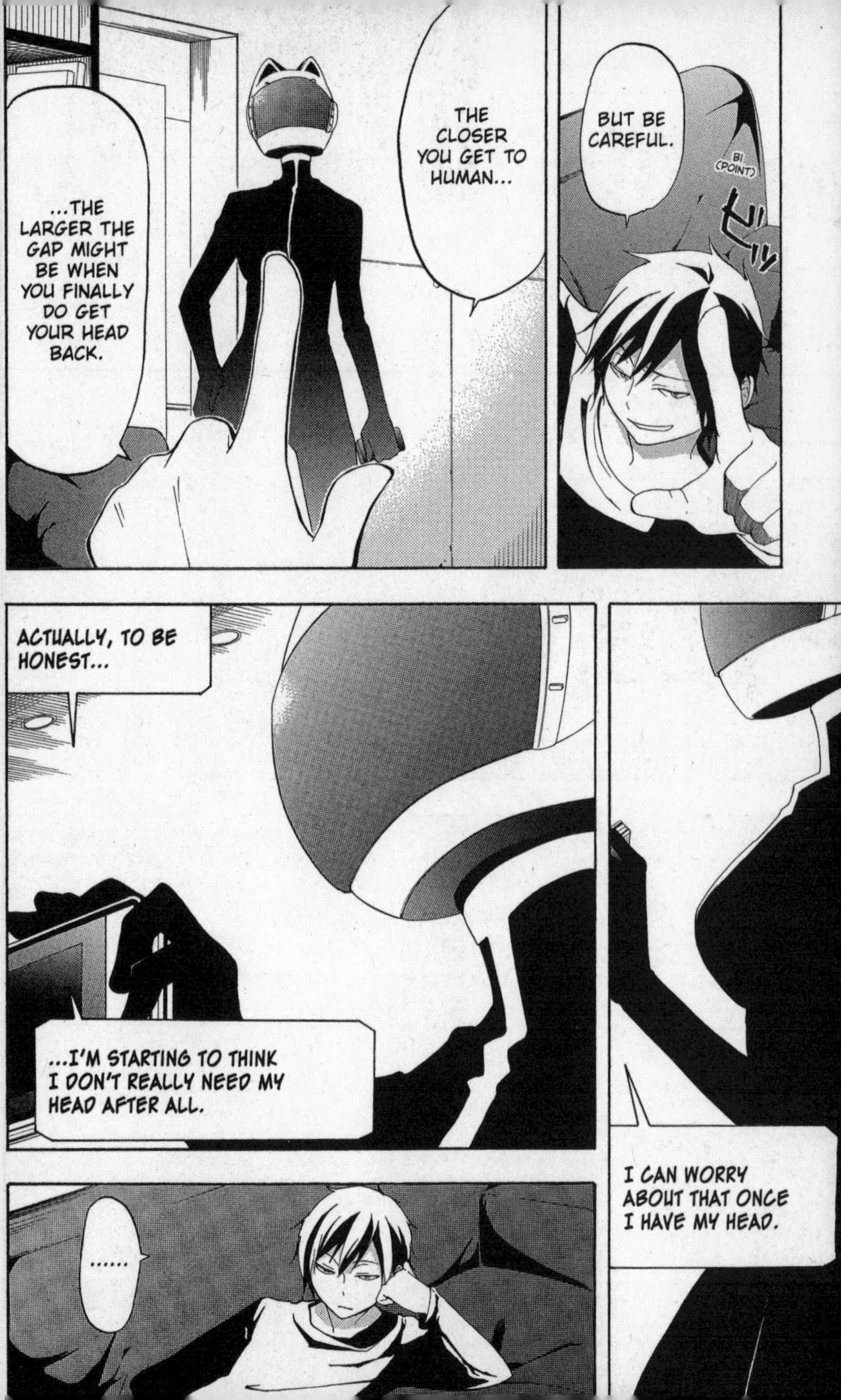
BUT BE CAREFUL.
BI (POINT)
ビッ
THE CLOSER YOU GET TO HUMAN...
...THE LARGER THE GAP MIGHT BE WHEN YOU FINALLY DO GET YOUR HEAD BACK.
I CAN WORRY ABOUT THAT ONCE I HAVE MY HEAD.
ACTUALLY, TO BE HONEST...
...I'M STARTING TO THINK I DON'T REALLY NEED MY HEAD AFTER ALL.
......

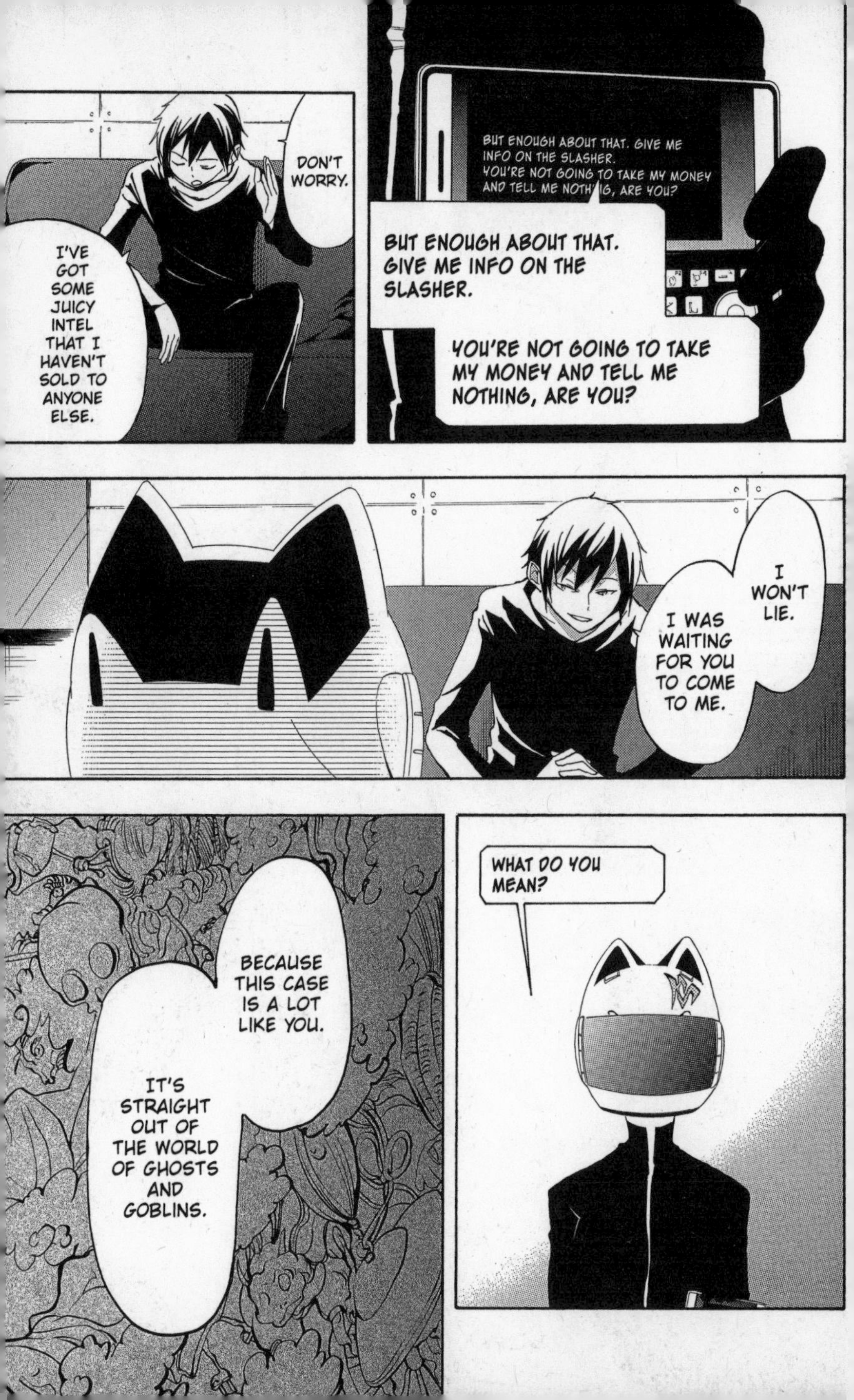
BUT ENOUGH ABOUT THAT. GIVE ME INFO ON THE SLASHER. YOU'RE NOT GOING TO TAKE MY MONEY AND TELL ME NOTH IG, ARE YOU?
BUT ENOUGH ABOUT THAT. GIVE ME INFO ON THE SLASHER.
YOU'RE NOT GOING TO TAKE MY MONEY AND TELL ME NOTHING, ARE YOU?
DON'T WORRY.
I'VE GOT SOME JUICY INTEL THAT I HAVEN'T SOLD TO ANYONE ELSE.
I WON'T LIE.
I WAS WAITING FOR YOU TO COME TO ME.
WHAT DO YOU MEAN?
BECAUSE THIS CASE IS A LOT LIKE YOU.
IT'S STRAIGHT OUT OF THE WORLD OF GHOSTS AND GOBLINS.

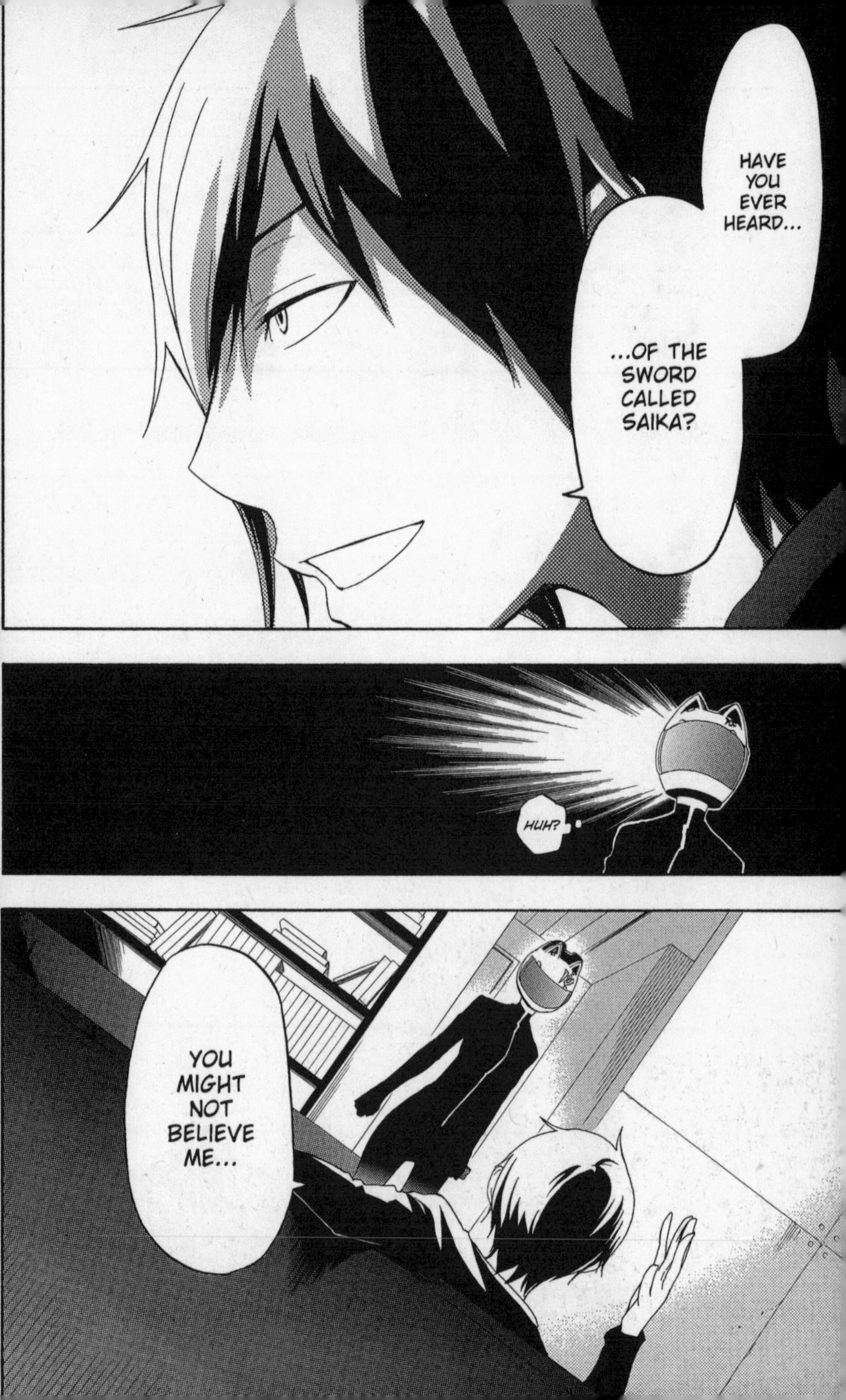
HAVE YOU EVER HEARD...
...OF THE SWORD CALLED SAIKA?
HUH?
YOU MIGHT NOT BELIEVE ME...

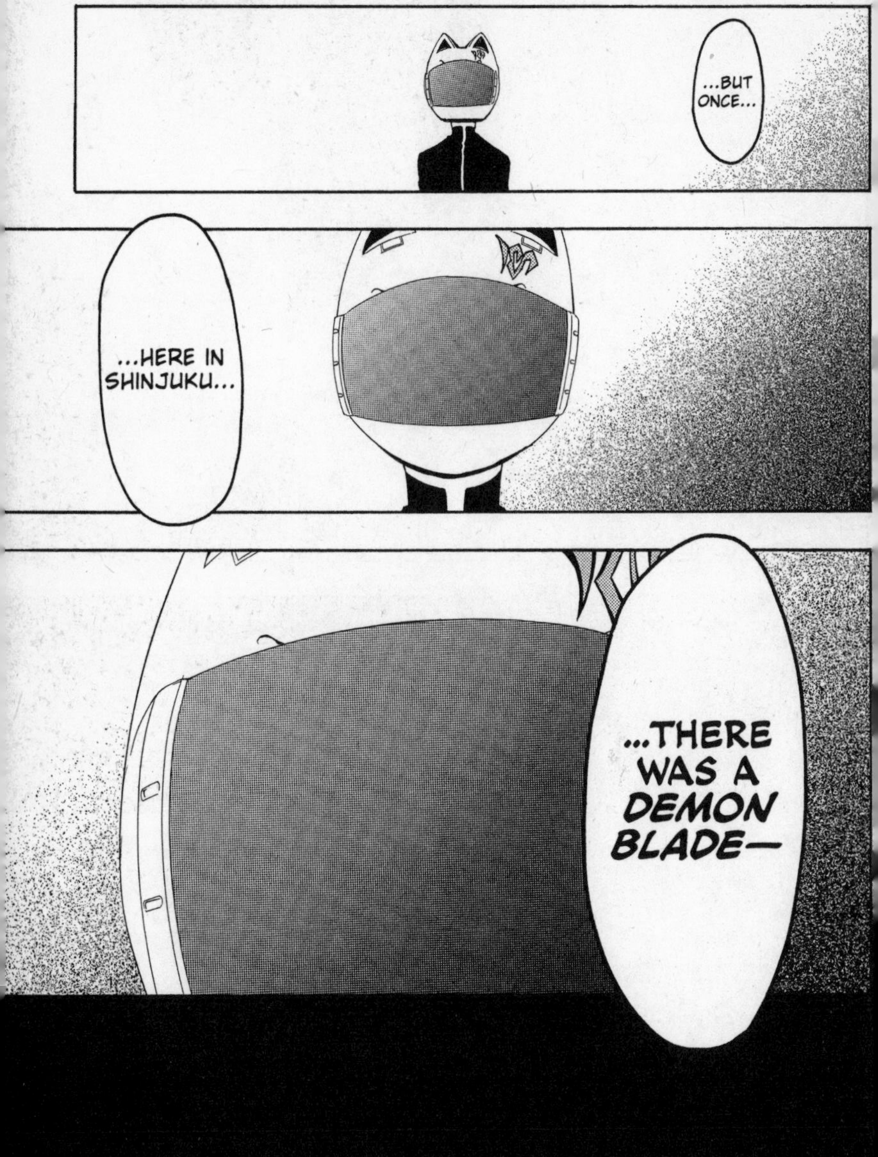
...BUT ONCE...
...HERE IN SHINJUKU...
...THERE WAS A DEMON BLADE—

—SAIKA HAS ENTERED THE CHAT—

Saika: I cut one person today.
       But one was enough.
       I don't want to spoil myself.

Saika: But I'll cut again tomorrow.
       The more people I love, the
       better.

Saika: The blade has grown full.

Saika: I'm looking for a person.

Saika: Shizuo Heiwajima.

Saika: The man I must love.

Saika: I know where Shizuo is.

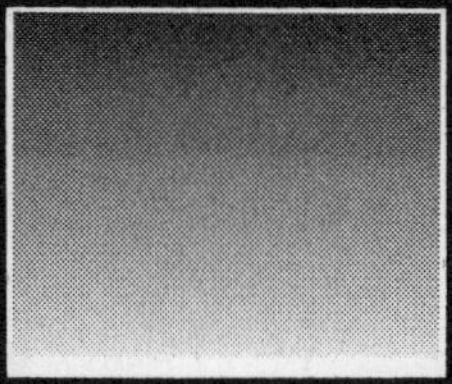

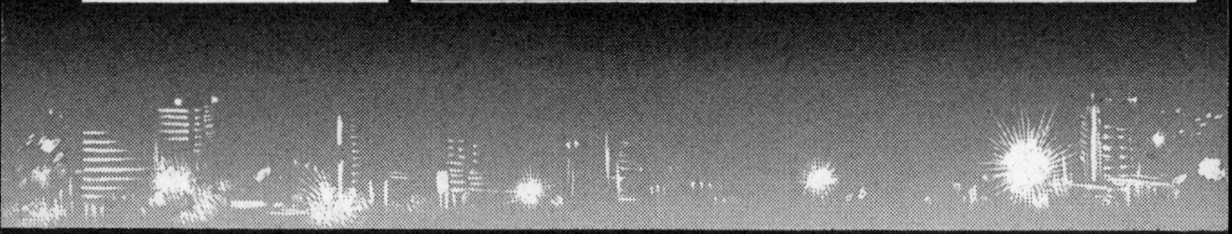

Saika: I want to know more about Shizuo.

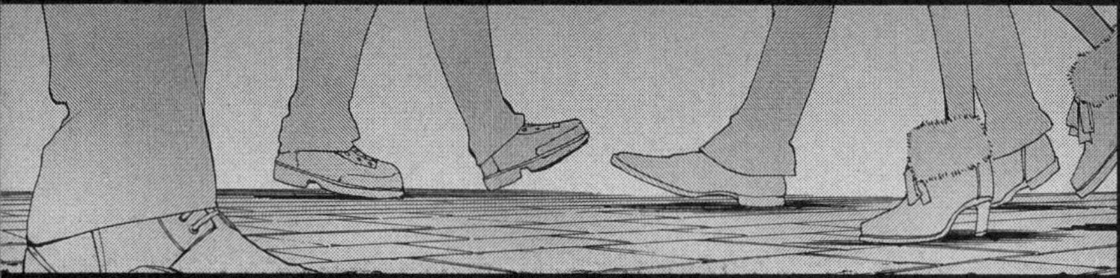

Saika: About the strongest man in this town.

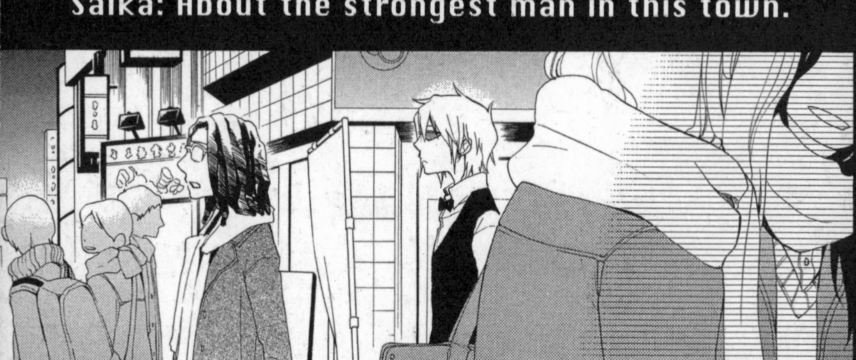

Saika: I'll cut someone again tomorrow.
Every day, until I meet Shizuo.

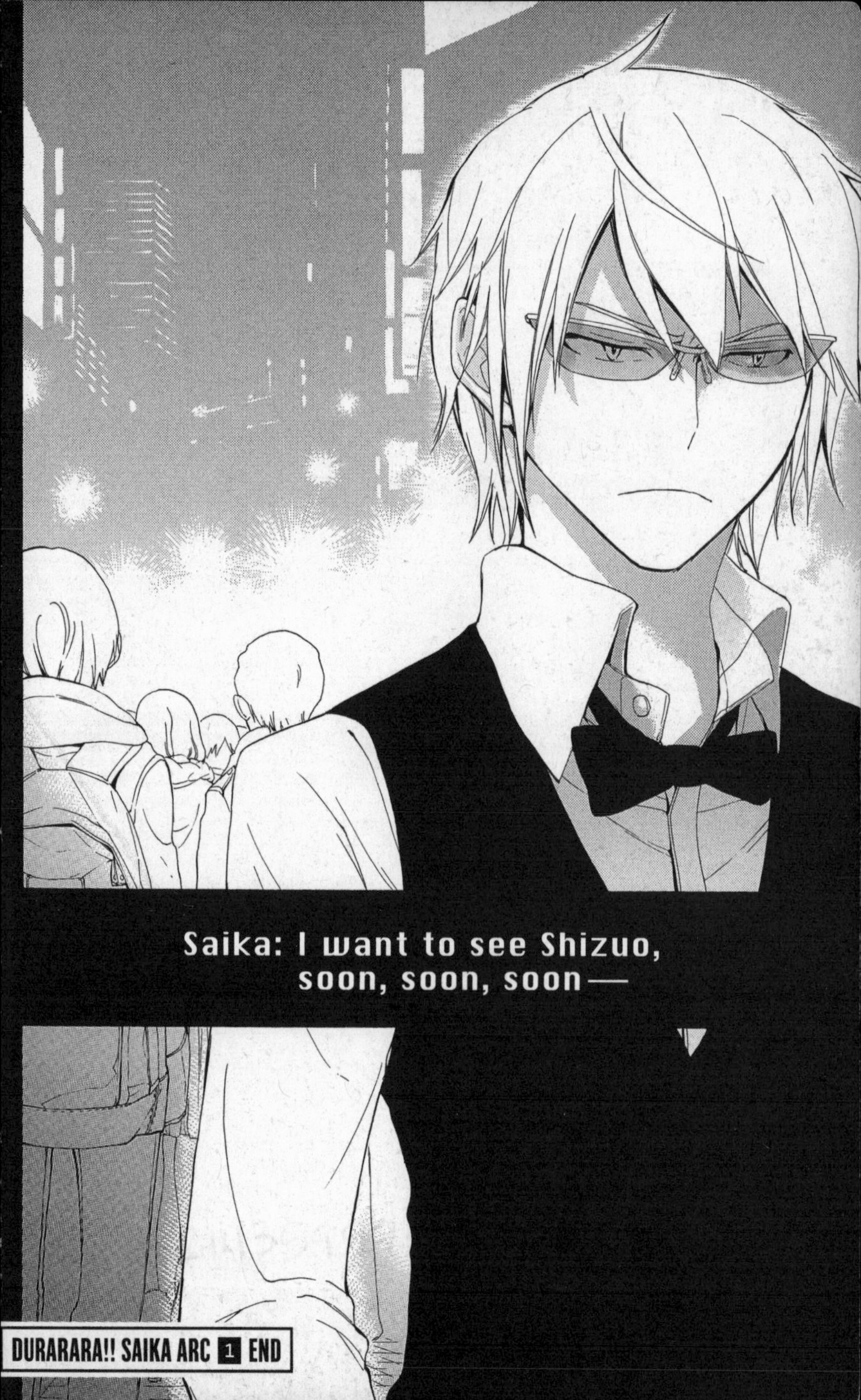
Saika: I want to see Shizuo, soon, soon, soon—
DURARARA!! SAIKA ARC 1 END

TRANSLATION NOTES

COMMON HONORIFICS
No honorific: Indicates familiarity or closeness; if used without permission or reason, addressing someone this way would constitute an insult.
-san: The Japanese equivalent of Mr./Mrs./Miss. If a situation calls for politeness, this is the fail-safe honorific.
-kun: Used most often when referring to boys, this indicates affection or familiarity. Occasionally used by older men among their peers, but it may also be used by anyone referring to a person of lower standing.
-chan: An affectionate honorific indicating familiarity used mostly in reference to girls; also used in reference to cute persons or animals of either gender.

Yen conversion: While exchange rates fluctuate daily, a convenient conversion estimation is about ¥100 to 1 USD.

PAGE 29
Khorosho: Russian for "very good." Despite their close geographic proximity, there's very little linguistic overlap between Russian and Japanese, and *khorosho* is probably the most popular Russian buzzword among the Japanese.

PAGE 72
"Peace" and "quiet": The characters used for the name Shizuo Heiwajima mean "Quiet Man, Peaceful Island."

PAGE 98
Kino, Shizu: Characters from the novel/anime/manga series *Kino's Journey*. The story revolves around Kino, a wanderer who travels with her talking motorcycle, Hermes, experiencing a wide variety of locales and towns on the way. Shizu is a fellow traveler who sometimes crosses paths with Kino. He rides a dune buggy with his companion, a talking dog named Riku.

Lone Wolf and Pup: A parody of the classic samurai manga, *Lone Wolf and Cub*.

PAGE 100
Inu x Boku SS: A manga/anime series about an apartment building housing human descendants of *youkai* (traditional Japanese monster/spirits) and their Secret Service (SS) bodyguards. Karuta Roromiya is an SS who gets possessed by a youkai and is forced to attack others. Soshi Miketsukami is another SS who is a reincarnation of the nine-tailed fox.

[redacted] Cast:

Mikado Ryuugamine

Masaomi Kida

Anri Sonohara

Namie Yagiri

Seiji Yagiri

Mika Harima

Izaya Orihara

Shizuo Heiwajima

Tom Tanaka

Simon Brezhnev

Walker Yumasaki

Erika Karisawa

Saburo Togusa

Kyouhei Kadota

Shinra Kishitani

Celty Sturluson

Takashi Nasujima

Shiki

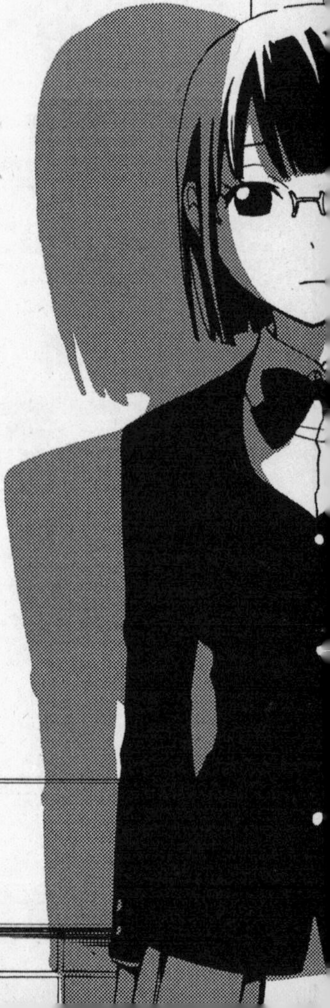

Staff:

Story: Ryohgo Narita

Character Design: Suzuhito Yasuda

Art: Akiyo Satorigi

Art Assistants:
Toka
Masako Shibata
Urata
Maiko Chiba
Fujimaru
Kazuki
Yuu
Satorigi's Family

Cover Design:
Masayuki Sato (Maniackers Design)

Editor:
Takeshi Kuma (Square Enix)

Supervision:
Atsushi Wada (ASCII Media Works)

Publisher:
Square Enix

Special Thanks:

Keiichi Shiguresawa
Kokoa Fujiwara
Dengeki Bunko
Ikebukuro Dollars

Hi, nice to see you again! I am Ryohgo Narita, the "creator" of this mixed-media project called *Durarara!!*

Finally, we have reached the first volume of the Saika Arc!

This is all thanks to Satorigi-san's work! She never fails to transform the text drafts that I send her into manga that is far beyond what I imagined!

She even takes care to portray the subtle details that I laid out in my original novels, and it's not rare that I notice a new side to the characters that I'd never picked up on before. In that sense, this manga isn't just a comic book adaptation, but another *Durarara!!* entirely—a rival to my books.

In fact, there are scenes depicting Anri's mental state and the atmosphere surrounding the Dollars where I begin to panic, thinking, "Oh no, I'm losing! My books are losing!" My rival? No, this manga is leaving me in the dust. This must be...the power of the great and mighty manga of Japan...But I can't afford to sit on my hands and get beaten. I've got to regroup and deliver a novel more powerful than ever before. Then, once Satorigi-san gets a chance to draw my powered-up scenes, I'll be...losing again? Wait...

But hey, I'm not ashamed to be losing!

Illustration: Suzuhito Yasuda

I really can't wait to see how the climax of the Saika Arc turns out.

I wrote some scenes where I arrogantly thought, "I'll do things you can't do in a novel," and it's the thought of how those will look in manga form that has me on the edge of my seat.

What form will the demon blade Saika take? At this point, I wouldn't be surprised if it's like Grelle's weapon from *Black Butler*— a death scythe that's a chain saw! Okay, I lied. I would be surprised.

Saika, the demon blade. The newest bizarre apparition to arrive in Ikebukuro after Celty.

What is it? What does it want? What will happen to Shizuo Heiwajima? If you haven't read the original novel, I hope these questions are racing through your mind with excitement!

And if you're not excited...then it's my novel's fault! Sorry!

And if you are excited, then it's probably because of Satorigi-san's artistic talent!

...Huh? Wait, am I losing again...?

Well, this losing battle is turned into entertainment only with the help of our editor Kuma-san and the editorial department of *GFantasy*. Thank you so much! Thank you!

Well, I hope you keep supporting Satorigi-san's manga *Durarara!!*

Ryohgo Narita

DU~~~~ ❶

RYOHGO NARITA
SUZUHITO YASUDA
AKIYO SATORIGI

Translation: Stephen Paul

Lettering: Lys Blakeslee

This book is a work of fiction. Names, characters, places, and incidents are the product of the author's imagination or are used fictitiously. Any resemblance to actual events, locales, or persons, living or dead, is coincidental.

DURARARA!! SAIKA-HEN Vol. 1
© 2012 Ryohgo Narita
© 2012 Akiyo Satorigi / SQUARE ENIX
Licensed by KADOKAWA CORPORATION ASCII MEDIA WORKS
First published in Japan in 2012 by SQUARE ENIX CO., LTD. English translation rights arranged with SQUARE ENIX CO., LTD. and Hachette Book Group through Tuttle-Mori Agency, Inc.

Translation © 2013 by SQUARE ENIX CO., LTD.

Yen Press
Hachette Book Group
237 Park Avenue, New York, NY 10017

www.HachetteBookGroup.com
www.YenPress.com

Yen Press is an imprint of Hachette Book Group, Inc. The Yen Press name and logo are trademarks of Hachette Book Group, Inc.

First Yen Press Edition: March 2013

ISBN: 978-0-316-24532-6

10 9 8 7 6 5 4 3 2

BVG

Printed in the United States of America